The
Translator's
Turn

Parallax:
Re-visions of Culture and Society

Stephen G. Nichols, Gerald Prince,
and Wendy Steiner, Series Editors

The Translator's Turn

Douglas Robinson

The Johns Hopkins University Press
Baltimore and London

© 1991 The Johns Hopkins University Press
All rights reserved
Printed in the United States of America

The Johns Hopkins University Press
701 West 40th Street
Baltimore, Maryland 21211
The Johns Hopkins Press Ltd., London

The paper used in this book meets the minimum requirements of
American National Standard for Information Sciences—Permanence
of Paper for Printed Library Materials, ANSI Z39.48–1984.

Library of Congress Cataloging-in-Publication Data
Robinson, Douglas.
    The translator's turn / Douglas Robinson.
        p.   cm. —(Parallax)
    Includes bibliographical references and index.
    ISBN 0-8018-4046-5 (h). —ISBN 0-8018-4047-3 (pbk.)
        1. Translating and interpreting. I. Title.   II. Series: Parallax
(Baltimore, Md.)
    P306.R63   1990
    418′.02—dc20   90-4629
                                                                        CIP

for K.B.,
one windy November day

Contents

Introduction

Translation theory, like most Western sciences of language and other human behavior, is traditionally an immaterial business: an ideal model of the finished product to be striven for by the translator; an ideal map or flow chart of procedures (to be) followed by the human translator and—ultimately—programmed into the computer. All in the head—cognitive, rational, logical, analytical—or in the working of hundreds of thousands of on-off switches.

"The second system of translation," Eugene A. Nida and Charles R. Taber wrote in 1969, summarizing in Chomskyan terms the mainstream Western theory of translation from Cicero and Horace through Augustine and Jerome and Luther to the present (the "first system," word-for-word translation, has mainly been a mere straw man for this mainstream approach that Nida and Taber are pleased to call the "second"), "consists of a more elaborate procedure comprising three stages: (1) analysis, in which the surface structure (*i.e.,* the message as given in language A) is analyzed in terms of (a) the grammatical relationships and (b) the meanings of the words and combinations of words, (2) transfer, in which the analyzed material is transferred in the mind of the translator from language A to language B, and (3) restructuring, in which the transferred material is restructured in order to make the final message fully acceptable in the receptor language" (33).[1]

Analysis: a mental operation bringing logical categories to bear on the complexity of a written text, facilitating the translator's cognitive processing of language by reducing it to an abstract systemic simplicity. *Transfer:* a second mental operation ("in the *mind* of the translator") involving the idealization or "transcendence" of syntactic and semantic difference in a realm where meaning is stable and universal and unitary. *Restructuring* (some theorists call it "synthesis"): a kind of mental architectural-restoration process by which a mind structure torn down in a foreign land is rebuilt in the translator's hometown.

In this book I want to offer an alternative paradigm for the study of translation—one that is not mentalist but explicitly and complexly physicalist. "Mind" is, in any case, as recent neurophysiologists have argued, only one rather specialized and (in the West) greatly overrated function of the body—or, to put that in more technical terms, the analytic selectivity of the cerebral cortex, which we are pleased to call "thought," "intelligence," "reasoning," "logic," and so on, is only one rather specialized function of the nervous system. The visceral processes of the limbic system, particularly the "emotional" (i.e., various motor and autonomic) responses that have been traced to the amygdala, constitute another function of the nervous system that has been systematically deprivileged in the mentalist, idealist, logicalist intellectual traditions of the West. Reason, as we are all taught, is mind, akin to spirit and thus to God, and therefore superior (occupies a higher level of the hierarchical creation) to emotion, which is body, akin to the flesh and its temptations and degradations and thus to Satan. Reason is the immortal in us. Emotion is part of our mortality.

The ideological history of this dualism is too long to go into here, and is in any event exceedingly familiar. To place the ideology of mind-and-body in its proper sphere one only has to draw up a short list of mentalist theorists: Plato, Aristotle, the New Testament, Paul, Aquinas, Descartes, Berkeley, Hume, Saussure, Chomsky. Our intuitive attachment to mentalist theories in the face of the neurophysiological research I pointed to a moment ago, like our intuitive attachment to the commonsensical notion that the sun "rises" in the east and "sets" in the west in the face of three-hundred-year-old astronomical research showing that the earth revolves around the sun, is the product of what I propose to call our "ideosomatic" programming, the collective values and belief systems inscribed in our autonomic system of "somatic" response. The "somatics" that I explore in Chapter 1 are in fact a humanistic, specifically a phenomenological way of talking about the autonomic system: I am concerned with the ways in which our body "signals" to us what we know and how we should act on it, through muscle memory and anxiety responses like constrictions of the chest or throat, clammy palms, tight shoulders, trembly legs, and so on. In everyday terms, we "know in our gut" what we have to do and say. We have a certain strong "feeling" about a situation or a person. A "bad" feeling makes us turn away or tense up for battle. A "good" feeling makes us relax and enter willingly into a situation. We are guided much more powerfully than our mentalist theories will let us recognize by those autonomic responses called "intuitions" or "gut reactions."

I do not propose to deal with the somatics of translation in the technical terms of neuroscience. I am not competent to do so, and am not sure my purpose would be entirely served by a dense thicket of technical terminology. I do think, however, that more work needs to be done on the neurology of translation—particularly work utilizing a model more complexly true to human realities than the mentalist/cybernetic one favored by some recent translation theorists—and hope that this passing attempt to connect my phenomenological "somatics" up with neuroscience here in the Introduction will suggest some directions that that work might take.

In the meantime, let my reference to neuroscience stand as a kind of truncated indication to scientifically-minded readers that I am not whistling in the dark—that this concern with the somatics of translation is not, say, some touchy-feely pop-psychological sixties thing, like the therapeutic value of a good backrub. I hope to show that, even apart from recent neurological research, the ideological (philosophical, intellectual) and social (interpersonal, practical) implications of a somatic approach to language are staggering. An open-minded look at the somatics of linguistic communication, and specifically of that cross-linguistic communication that we call translation, can unlock the stubborn cellblock doors that have imprisoned translation studies in the past.

It is instructive to note, for example, what has happened when translation theorists have insisted that translation is fundamentally a cognitive process governed systematically by abstract structures or normative rules: they have, almost by definition, situated themselves methodologically at an Archimedes' point above or beyond the complexity of translation practice and then convinced themselves that practical translation typically fails because it cannot lift itself up out of the muck and mire of specific cases. Translators traduce, in this view, because they translate intuitively. They translate now this way, now that, however feels right in each isolated situation, without organizing their intuitive decisions into a coherent system of norms—or else, worse, they intuitively organize their decisions into the *wrong* system of norms (word-for-word instead of sense-for-sense, say).

"We could help them!" these theorists cry. "We have considered the matter at a more comprehensive general level and could guide them to the right decision in *every* situation. And what a difference that would make! If translators would only follow our lead, translation would no longer be derogated as treason, distortion of the original, etc." It would be taken as seriously as, say, engineering, which stands in roughly the same relation to physics and the other natural sciences as translation stands (or should stand) to translation theory.

But in their attempts to abstract out of practice a systematic set of principles, rules, and procedures for translators to follow, these theorists typically—even perforce—alienate themselves from practice. Translation practice, after all, is the complex field theorists try to get *beyond,* the veil of appearances that they, latter-day Platonists, seek to pierce, in order to rise into the stable transcendental realm of system and structure. This leaves them uncomfortably open to the translator's charge that they do not know what they are talking about. One thinks of the parent's reaction to being told how to raise a child by an unmarried and childless child psychologist.

On the other side, consider what happens when translators believe that translation is fundamentally an intuitive process that is—and for best results must remain—ultimately mysterious. They leave themselves, by their very programmatic inarticulateness, uncomfortably open to the idealizing translation theorist's charge that they do not know what they are doing—and that in fact they are doing it all wrong. Intuitively they know that they are doing the best job they can; but intuitive certainty cracks easily under the onslaught of a carefully reasoned theoretical argument, and translators often feel obliged to apologize for their best work. It was intuitively right—but it did not obey the rules. Translators' prefaces are notoriously apologetic: "My humble efforts have produced but a fair approximation of my author's brilliance, and it is my sincerest hope that a later translator will be able to correct my deficiencies and better render this immortal work in English."

A somatics of translation will allow us to explore the feedback system between "mind" and "body," intellection and emotion, analysis and gut-level certainty, cerebral and visceral response. It seems undeniable that translation is largely an intuitive process. Good translators choose words and phrases by reference not to some abstract system of intellectualized rules, which most of us have never internalized in the first place, but rather to "messages" or impulses sent by the body: a given word or phrase *feels* right. Intuitively, not just for the translator but for all language users, sense is not cognition but sensation.

To be sure, we also think about language and organize our linguistic feelings or gut reactions intellectually—and in that "we" I include ordinary speakers as well as academically trained linguists. In this book I may occasionally place too polemical a stress on the somatics of language, to counteract the idealized mentalism of Western linguistics since Augustine; but my intention is not to stress somatics at the expense of "intellect" or "mind." My point is only that the Western insistence on deprivileging the body—intuition, emotion, somatic signals—in the study of linguistic communication has had a debilitating effect on our understanding of what happens when we speak. In the field of translation studies, the most obvious example of this effect is the widespread hostility between theorists and translators: caricaturing only slightly, we could say that, hostile toward practice, the translation theorist feels he or she cannot afford to feel; and, hostile toward theory, the translator thinks she or he cannot afford to think. The theorist thus cuts him- or herself off from the enlivening force of emotion, and the translator cuts her- or himself off from the organizing force of thought.

Translation theorists do feel, of course, and translators do think. But the tendencies I describe—the resistance of translation theory to feeling and the resistance of translation practice to thought—are very real problems. The best representatives of each group (I think of theorists like George Steiner and translators like Ezra Pound) do manage to overcome the problems by integrating feeling and thought, combining a richness of physical response with a toughness of intellect. But for the average translator or theorist, without ideological support for such integration—indeed, with powerful ideological support for *dis*integration, dissociation, hostility, conflict, rift—combining feeling and thought, practice and theory seems an impossible (and therefore perhaps even undesirable) dream.

This is, I suggest, the real underlying reason for the low status of both translation theory and translation practice: that they have been kept artificially apart; that a theoretical proximity to intuitive practice has been seen as (and often has been) debilitating for theory, and that a practical proximity to abstract intellectual theory has been seen as (and often has been) debilitating for practice. The translator's intuitive genius must not be hogtied by theory; the theorist's analytic systematicity must not be muddled by too much attention to practical detail. The translator who stands too close to theory produces lifeless mathematical travesties of translation; the theorist who stands too close to practice produces pathetically local and unanalyzed, unsystematic travesties of theory.

It seems to me that the only way to put an end to this situation is to insist, in both our theorizing and our translating, on an integration of warring opposites: feeling and thought, intuition and systematization. In my physicalist approach, this integration will take place under the aegis of body: specifically the nervous system, including both the systematizing selectivity of the cerebral cortex and the autonomic intensity of the amygdala. It would be possible to dualize these along traditional mind-body lines—to call the former "intellectual theorizing," say, and identify it as my vehicle or vessel, the latter "somatic response," and identify it as my theme or content, what Chapter 1 is "about." Or we could invoke pop-neurological terms and say that this is a "left brain" discussion of a "right brain" activity. The mind-body dualism is deeply ingrained in our ideosomatic response and dies hard. I would prefer to say, in line with current neurophysiological theories, that "thought" and "feeling" are almost never found in a pure state, ideally divorced from one another (in fact, when they are, the state can only be described as pathological), and that our "reasoning" is always going to be emotionally motivated and directed, just as our "feeling" will (almost) always be intellectually monitored and controlled. My "scholarly" style reflects this integration much less openly than I would have liked; the published text is a toned-down ("intellectualized") version of the book I first wrote and submitted. Even in a discursive climate that increasingly encourages the integration of reason and emotion, the professional and the personal, the objective and the subjective, university presses (their editors, copy editors, and hired readers) remain steeped in the ideosomatics of academic decorum, which favors a depersonalized and "deemotionalized" detachment.

Part 1 of this book is somewhat more general and historical; Part 2, somewhat more specific and taxonomical. Part 1 lays a theoretical and ideological foundation for the discussion of various translatorial hermeneutics or tools in Part 2. In Part 1 I am explicitly concerned with bodies in dialogue, with what happens somatically when we talk and translate in an interpersonal context. Since the "we" in that last sentence is historically problematic, I develop my argument in Part 1 diachronically, fleshing out a sense of the shifting ideosomatics of translation in the West. In Part 2 I shift to a consideration of how translators actually "turn" their texts and readers in a series of translation models (tropes and versions) that begin to hint at the astonishing complexity and variety of the translational field.

In Chapter 1, on the somatics of translation, I explore the ways in which somatic intuition guides the performance of the translator's task, and how the translator's physical or intuitive response to a text is not (only) uniquely his or her own but is conditioned by the culture. In Chapter 2, on the dialogics of translation, my focus is still on the body, but more broadly now, in a larger historical context. By looking closely at two dialogical engagements between theorists—Luther's with Augustine, in the "Sendbrief vom Dolmetchen," and Goethe's with Luther, in *West-Östlicher Divan*—I sketch a rough dialogical history of translation theory in terms of somatic resistance and challenge to cultural programming. These two theorists, I argue—Luther and Goethe—brought about paradigm shifts in Western translation theory by exploring the complexity of their own somatic responses to a predecessor; and by exploring the complexity of my own somatic response to both, at the end of that chapter, I hope to lay the groundwork for a third paradigm shift, to a theory of translation that I want to call, following Martin Buber, "dialogical."

In the last two chapters, on the tropics and ethics of translation, then, this dialogical model generates a variety of practical models for the translator's dialogical engagement with the source-language (SL) or original writer and text (tropics) and target-language (TL) receptor (ethics). Each chapter in turn, and the two taken together, trace the complexity of the "turn" the translator makes from the source language to the target language. Hence my title: *The Translator's Turn.*[2] In the tropics of translation, these "turns" are tropes (from the Greek for turn), active modeling patterns for the interpretive shaping first of the SL text, the "original," the text from which the translator translates, and then of the TL text, the translation, the text the translator creates. My argument here is that in hermeneutical dialogue with the SL author, the translator invariably turns the original, turns away from it into the TL; and that instead of pretending otherwise, instead of pretending that the translator constructs a stable one-to-one pattern of correspondence or equivalence between the SL and the TL text (which proves to be ultimately impossible), we should recognize and, contextually, encourage the translator's poetic creativity. Some tropes, which are useful in some but not all contexts, aim at equivalence: metonymy, the substitution of one part for another, is manifestly the trope behind sense-for-sense translation, where the actual SL and TL words are conceived as equivalent and interchangeable parts of a transcendental whole (the "meaning"). Metaphor, too, the impossible dream of total identity between two wholes, lies behind the messianic dream of romantic translation (Hölderlin, Goethe, Benjamin), in which perfect equivalence becomes a putative vehicle of salvation. But, seen tropically, equivalence is only a fiction for the shaping of a successful text—not an impossible ideal, failure to reach which means failure, period, but merely a practical tool whose usefulness is contextually contingent. And other tropes point us past fictions of equivalence, into the gray area usually dismissed as "free" translation or "imitation": synecdochic or propagandistic translation, hyperbolic or "enhancive" translation, metaleptic or archaizing/modernizing translation, and so on.

In the ethics of translation, the "turns" of my title are versions (from the Latin for turn), active modeling patterns for the shaping of purpose with respect to the TL receptor. Traditionally, translators (have been taught to) imagine their ethical task as one of introversion, self-effacement, becoming a window between SL text and TL receptor that the TL receptor will not even recognize as a window. No personality; no self-advertisement. This is another reason for the low status of translation, of course: an ethical conception appropriate to some translation contexts, for some TL receptor groups, is generalized to apply universally to translation. What happens when the translator conceives his or her ethical task differently—as conversion, for example, or subversion, or perversion, or inversion, or reversion? This sort of suggestion makes most translation theorists (and most translators) uneasy, but it is not exactly unheard-of, and anything that is heard-of might, in some cases, be productive. What about diversion? The translator as entertainer: why not? Or aversion: the translator as angry, disgusted parent, using the TL text to castigate the receptor for not having read the text in the original (Nabokov's translation of *Eugene Onegin,* for example).

My emphasis in these last two chapters on the variety of creative turns translators actually make with regard to both the SL text and the TL receptor is intended to imply that, in translation theory, it now *is* the translator's turn. It is no longer necessary for the theorist to assume that he or she can only be useful to translators by laying down the law—or, for that matter, to assume that there is no need to be useful to translators at all, that it is enough to spin out elaborate mathematical descriptions of translation in the abstract that have a certain notational beauty but are of no use to anybody. It is time to offer translators tools, not rules—and tools derived not from Christian theology and the dogmatic demands placed on Bible translating, as has largely been the case in Western translation theory, but from what translators actually do when they translate. In that sense, in fact, the translator's turn also becomes the theorist's turn: our turn to shrug off the role of secularized priests, and the exclusive priestly rules and restrictions we have thought it our task to deliver, and to mingle with the laity that we actually are. Our turn, in a word, to become ordinary humans like everyone else.

*   *   *

While writing this book I found James P. Carse's *Finite and Infinite Games* (1986) and found that, like Martin Buber, Mikhail Bakhtin, Ludwig Wittgenstein, and others, he was saying in brilliantly aphoristic ways what I wanted to say at greater length and in greater specificity (about translation). The result of my dialogue with Carse's book has been a kind of appropriation of his words, in all my epigraphs, in line with his own principle: "Spoken to me, your words become mine to do with as I please. As the genius of your words, you lose all authority over them" (68). Though in his rigorous dualization of finite and infinite games Carse sounds a lot like Buber (cf. the I-It and the I-You), in this insistence that we can never own our words, that our words are always caught up in dialogical exchange, he moves toward Bakhtin. "To speak, or act, or think originally is to erase the boundary of the self. It is to leave behind the territorial personality" (68). Reading this, I was sorely tempted to take him at his word (which, as he says, is no longer his, since I am the genius of what I hear him say), to play my own infinite game with his words, to "double-voice" them, as Bakhtin would say, to infuse them with the voice of my own active listening—to quote him freely, loosening up his dualisms, introducing my own sense of the internal power of ideology over all infinite games. But there is, of course, the very finite game of copyright law, so I backed down. The trace I have left of my dialogical engagement with Carse is that, when I use his words in an epigraph, I don't cite him by name, or by finitized "title"; I just cite him (in italics). Let this announcement stand as my forced participation in the finite game of copyright. In the text, let Carse's words blend dialogically with mine.

I worked out my ideas for this book in conversation with students and colleagues in the Department of Translation Studies at the University of Tampere, and their sharp comments and criticisms figure here and there in the book. Eugene Nida's response both to my plans for the book and to early drafts of it helped me to clarify some of my arguments, and his careful reading of the completed manuscript helped me to tone down some of my more extreme stylistic flights. Eric Halpern at the Johns Hopkins University Press supported my project from the start, and managed to find external evaluators whose advice was immensely helpful in revising the manuscript for publication: my thanks to Eric and to Dinda L. Gorlée and Paul J. Hopper. Carol Ehrlich exceeded the copy editor's task as conventionally defined in much the same way as I argue translators do: by engaging the words of the "original author" (me) dialogically and transforming them in the centrifugal spirit of that dialogue. In important ways this book (like every book) is collectively authored: as I became the genius of what I heard Bakhtin and Carse and others say, Carol became the genius of what she heard me say.

My dedication reflects a longstanding dialogue with some very quirky books and a long conversation one day in Andover, New Jersey, about Augustine and Luther and everything else under the sun. The quirkiness of this book has a lot to do with my encounter (not just that day) with a nonagenarian who somehow got under my skin. *Ad bellum amore commutandum.*

Part One

Dialogical Bodies

Chapter One

The Somatics of Translation

The paradox of infinite sexuality is that by regarding sexuality as an expression of the person and not the body, it becomes fully embodied play. It becomes a drama of touching.

The triumph of finite sexuality is to be liberated from play into the body. The essence of infinite sexuality is to be liberated into play with the body. In finite sexuality, I expect to relate to you as a body; in infinite sexuality I expect to relate to you in your body.

Infinite lovers conform to the sexual expectations of others in a way that does not expose something hidden, but unveils something in plain sight. In this exposure they emerge as the persons they are. They meet others with their limitations, and not within their limitations. In doing so they expect to be transformed—and are transformed.

The Somatics of Language

The meaning of a word, Augustine wrote in *On Christian Doctrine*, is a transcendental label identifying and unifying the fleeting physical (graphological or phonological) sign. It is the pure, stable "content" or "idea" that ties the accidents of fallen human enunciation to the divine Logos. As God is to his creation, as the undying spirit is to our mortal frame, so is meaning to the word. And because in the economy of spirit there is a congruence and convergence of spiritual things, because the meaning of a word is the Logos writ small, ultimately semiology recapitulates theology—ultimately, in fact, theology *is* semiology, as the surprising ligature between the semiotic argument and the dogmatic title of Augustine's book suggests. The implication is that, no matter how complex or diverse our speech is superficially, there is always a path that leads from signs through a series of carefully defined operations to originary unity. If this were not the case, we would have no access to God's truth; we would only have varying human approximations or interpretations of that truth.

This conception of language has, *mutatis mutandis,* constituted linguistic orthodoxy in the West ever since Augustine, up to and including our own century, when it was given its most influential modern form by the Swiss philologist Ferdinand de Saussure.[1] Meaning remains just as transcendental for Saussure as it was for Augustine, just as systematically abstracted out of the carnal messiness of actual speech into the realm of ideal or mental form; but as Jacques Derrida demonstrates at some length in *Of Grammatology,* part 1, Saussure effectively destabilizes linguistic transcendence by cutting signification loose from the Augustinian Logos. The meaning of a word for Saussure was purely arbitrary, derived through and defined by its systemic difference from some other word, not by its position in a semantic hierarchy topped by the Logos.[2] Then again, *something* holds the system together. It is not nomadic. *La langue,* the ideal system Saussure abstracts out of *la parole,* or speech, becomes the scientific-slash-existentialist survival of the medieval mind of God—the disowned son who remains the spit 'n' image of his father, and by the inertial ideological force of that image fathers a new science called linguistics. Due to the systematic forgetfulness that grounds our ideological conditioning, this new science no longer feels like the progeny of Augustine—indeed, most linguists trace the history of their discipline from Saussure as from Adam—but owing to the continuing operation of that conditioning, it feels right precisely because it is.

Despite a passing (but, while it lasted, immensely influential) fling with primitive Augustinian linguistics in the transformational-generative theories of Noam Chomsky in the fifties and sixties,[3] Saussure's structuralism has remained the canonical modernization of Augustine in twentieth-century linguistics—both in mainstream linguistics and, twisted, in the French poststructuralism of Jacques Lacan and Jacques Derrida and their followers.[4] But if Augustine and Saussure as ancient progenitor and modern father of Western linguistics have never actually been superseded, neither have they gone unchallenged; and since my argument in this book is specifically conceived as a translatological challenge (and potential successor) to Augustinian/Saussurean semiology, let me begin by taking a look at two previous challenges to the semiological tradition: those offered by William James and Ludwig Wittgenstein.

For James the pragmatist psychologist, in the famous "Stream of Thought" chapter of *The Principles of Psychology* (1890), the meaning of a word was nothing transcendental at all, neither an ideal object nor a differential slot in an abstract system, but the feeling we have when we say it or hear it: a "single pulse of subjectivity, a single psychosis, feeling, or state of mind" (1: 278)—"an altogether specific affection of the mind" (1: 253). "We ought to say a feeling of *and,*" James writes, "and a feeling of *if,* a feeling of *but,* and a feeling of *by,* quite as readily as we say a feeling of *blue* or a feeling of *cold*" (1: 245–46).

This has an immediate intuitive appeal. We do feel words, and most typically guide our choice of words when we speak (and our interpretation of words when others speak) emotionally, by recourse not to an abstract cognitive system of rules but to what *feels* right. We roll words around on our tongues, looking for the one that has just the right feel for what we want to say. We often have a gut-level sense that a word is wrong, off-base, inadequate, incorrect, or else perfect, exactly right for what we have in mind to say—and yet could not, if pressed, provide a dictionary definition for it, let alone analyze its semantic field. Words can evoke powerful memories in us, take us back in time to a moment when someone said those same words to us in just that tone. George Steiner reminds us in *After Babel* that "poets can even smell words" (293)—and, in fact, the only difference between a poet and an ordinary speaker of a language in this sense is that the poet has cultivated that ability and in the process has fashioned out of it a powerful interpretive and creative tool. We smell words, all of us, as well as see them; taste words as well as hear them. Because our culture discourages perception of language in terms of sensation, however, these somatic responses to words remain subconscious and therefore often dormant, unused, unacted-upon. We also feel words in the tactile sense—we can feel assaulted or bludgeoned by words. The old children's saw that "sticks and stones can break my bones but words can never hurt me" is flat-out wrong. What we mean by emotional violence is the physical hurt caused by words. Schizophrenogenic parents can drive their children insane with words; psychotherapists can cure with them.[5] Words can also caress, soothe, placate.

We can be bored by the first ten words a boring person says—our patience doesn't have to be tried by long speeches before our bodies respond with boredom signals. When we read novels and poems, we respond physically to them, fleshing them out with the sense-memories (sights, sounds, smells, etc.) and emotion-memories (amusement, romance, suspense, terror, etc.) of our own experience. When we read nonfiction we can often conjure up an image of the writer (even if we have never met the person, never seen him or her on television) talking the book, can hear the pauses, see the gestures, sense the body signals that indicate confidence, nervousness, defensiveness, and so on. When we do not feel the meaning of a word—a word we have never seen before, never heard before, that we cannot make out etymologically or analogically—it does not feel like a meaningful word at all. It feels like random marks or noise.[6]

This is a "somatic," or physicalist, approach to language, based on James's intuitive sense that to transcendentalize language, as the mainstream tradition of Western linguistics had done from Augustine to the present, was to dehumanize it. It was to remove language from the realm in which we actually *use* it—speak it, hear it, understand it—and thus not only to place it effectively beyond our reach but to turn it into a transcendental stick to beat us with. Saussure's *langue* and Chomsky's competence, the ideal systems of language that both linguists insisted must be the sole object of linguistic analyses, existed only in the mind of a rationalist god (and his scientistic priests) who chastised actual users of the language for their deviations from the ideal: the "messiness" of their *parole* or performance, their mistakes. To situate meaning in feeling, as James does, is to bring language back down to earth, into the realm of human subjectivity: precisely that realm consistently perceived as the root of all evil by scientistic thinkers from the early Middle Ages to the present. Where Saussure secularizes Augustine by destabilizing his system, James secularizes him by humanizing it, bringing it forcibly into the realm of the individual human subject.

Ludwig Wittgenstein was powerfully attracted to James's feeling-theory of meaning; he returned to it over and over again in the *Philosophical Investigations* and in preparatory works like the *Blue and Brown Books*. After all, the feeling-theory promised release from the stultifying abstractions of meaning theories to date, something that greatly interested Wittgenstein in his late period. But there was still something too systematic in James's theory to satisfy Wittgenstein, and his discussions of it in the *Investigations* are largely negative in tone:

Die Bedeutung ist nicht das Erlebnis beim Hören oder Aussprechen des Wortes, und der Sinn des Satzes nicht der Komplex dieser Erlebnisse.

The meaning of a word is not the experience one has in hearing or saying it, and the sense of a sentence is not a complex of such experiences. (181)

Bist du sicher, daß es *ein* Wenn-Gefühl gibt; nicht vielleicht mehrere? Hast du versucht, das Wort in sehr verschiedenartigen Zusammenhängen auszusprechen? Wenn es z.B. den Hauptton des Satzes trägt, und wenn ihn das nächste Wort trägt.

Denk dir, wir fänden einen Menschen, der uns, über seine Wort-Gefühle, sagt: für ihn hätte "wenn" und "aber" das *gleiche* Gefühl. Dürften wir ihm das nicht glauben? Es würde uns vielleicht befremden. "Er spielt gar nicht unser Spiel" möchte man sagen. Oder auch: "Das ist ein anderer Typus."

Würden wir von diesem nicht glauben, er verstehe die Worte "wenn" und "aber," so wie wir sie verstehen, wenn er sie so *verwendet,* wie wir?

Are you sure that there is a single if-feeling, and not perhaps several? Have you tried saying the word in a great variety of contexts? For example, when it bears the principal stress of the sentence, and when the word next to it does.

Suppose we found a man who, speaking of how words felt to him, told us that "if" and "but" felt the *same*: should we have the right to disbelieve him? We might think it strange. "He doesn't play our game at all," one would like to say. Or even: "This is a different type of man."

If he *used* the words "if" and "but" as we do, shouldn't we think he understood them as we do? (Anscombe's translations, 181–82)

Wittgenstein's critique might be construed as faulting James for simply inverting the medieval hierarchy whereby abstract objectivity is good and somatic subjectivity is bad. James deliberately occupies the despised lower rung on the scientistic hierarchy and, in a fiat characteristic of liberal humanism, proclaims the tables turned: the feeling human subject is now good, and all attempts to abstract out of subjective experience a transcendentalized object or objectified system are now pernicious. This is an inversion Wittgenstein himself practiced to great effect throughout the *Investigations,* but from his perspective James did not take it far enough, and so remained enslaved by the systematic terms of the old hierarchy. Is the feeling we have about a word always the same? Doesn't it vary contextually? What if someone else has a different feeling about a word? Must feeling-meanings be stable for communication to be possible?[7] Isn't this in fact simply a liberal restatement of the medieval/scientistic position, still locating meaning stably and systematically in the mind but replacing the transcendental conception of mind as universal reason with a physiological conception of mind as nervous system?[8]

Whatever his precise conceptualization of James's error (and much of the above is speculative), Wittgenstein seems here, in the unnumbered notes of section 6 at the back of the book, where he discusses James's theory in greatest detail, to have persuaded himself of the unworkability of James's theory: "Die Bedeutung ist *nicht* das Erlebnis beim Hören oder Aussprechen des Wortes." Period. Earlier in the *Investigations,* therefore, he offers in place of the feeling-theory what is probably the single most famous pronouncement in the book: "Die

Bedeutung eines Wortes ist sein Gebrauch in der Sprache"—"The meaning of a word is its use in the language" (§43). Its *use:* not its transcendental essence; not its arbitrary opposition to another word in a differential system; not a physiological but still stable and systematic state of mind; the way people actually use it. An action; something people *do.* Or, in J. L. Austin's famous formulation of a similar position around the same time, a "speech act": "to *say* something," as Austin put it, "is to *do* something" (12). Nothing so inchoate and incommunicable as an inner feeling; an external event. Nothing so stable as a meaning "attached" to a word, whether transcendentally or somatically; a once-off response to a specific situation.

This too has an immediate intuitive appeal. If I use a metaphor—for instance, "This tool is a gem"—there is no need to posit a primary and therefore normative dictionary meaning ("jewel," "precious stone") from which my use of the word "gem" can then be said to deviate. There is no need to set up any kind of hierarchy among primary ("normal") and secondary ("deviant") meanings or uses of words. There are only different uses, different ways of using words in different contexts.[9] All the endless (and therefore useless) arguments over semantic fields— defined hypostatically as the "properties" of words, like a farmer's fields surrounding his house—can be brought to a halt. Meanings arise out of, and invariably revolve around, contextual uses. Words do not "have" meanings in any objective sense, in the so-called null context, in abstract isolation from real speech-use situations. Neither the dictionary nor the thesaurus nor any other formalization of semantic fields holds sway over the volatility of actual speech use.

The notion of meaning as use is an important innovation in the Western study of language—so important, in fact, that Saussurean and Chomskyan linguists regularly feel compelled to address themselves to it, but so innovative that they just as regularly feel compelled to dismiss it.[10] In *Introduction to Theoretical Linguistics,* for example, John Lyons gets around the force of Wittgenstein's pronouncement by idealizing "use" into a transcendental system, or what Saussure calls *la langue:* there is *parole*-use, what people actually say, and there is *langue*-use, the system underlying use, and the only productive way to talk about meaning as use is in terms of the latter:

Normal communication rests upon the assumption that we all "understand" words in the same way; this assumption breaks down from time to time, but otherwise "understanding" is taken for granted. Whether we have or have not the same "concepts" in our "minds" when we are talking to one another is a question that cannot be answered otherwise than in terms of the "use" we make of words in utterances. It would probably be true, but rather pointless, to say that everyone "understands" a particular word in a slightly different way. Semantics is concerned with accounting for the degree of uniformity in the "use" of language which makes normal communication possible. (411)[11]

This implicitly defines semantics as a normative theory of meaning that sets the bounds of communicative "normalcy" and rules all problematic communication—all communication where we don't "understand" words in the same way—"abnormal" and therefore irrelevant to semantic analysis ("pointless" to talk about). This is clearly an idealizing move that places Lyons squarely in the mainstream of Augustinian/ Saussurean linguistic theory: dismiss communication problems as mere speech, mere *parole,* and retreat into the reassuring transcendental realm of *la langue.*

But Lyons raises an important issue that is not easily settled—certainly not by the mere stratagem of identifying his argumentative move as a transcendentalizing escape from it. Given the multiplicity of actual language use and the resulting variety and uncertainty of understanding, how do we account for the possibility of communication without the normative retreat into analytical stability that Lyons employs? How do we understand one another at all, if there is no transcendental level of understanding to retreat to such as mainstream Western linguists posit?

Wittgenstein himself worries this question throughout the *Investigations* and elsewhere, without offering any real solutions (it is, in any case, typically Wittgenstein's project to ask the questions, not to answer them). What is "use," and what does it mean to say that meaning is use (or that use is meaning)? Is the "use" of a word a "thing," an object, that is present in a given situation for identification and assimilation? Or is it our interpretive construct, a fiction by which we try to make sense of what the speaker is trying to do in and by saying what he or she said? If it is our construct, doesn't the act of construction just constitute another "use," which must be determined (or construed) in yet another interpretive act? And who are "we"? Can we assume that the listener will be a stable, predictable interpreter of speech? If the speaker understands his or her use of a word one way and his or her listener understands it another way (or does not understand it at all), what is the word's "meaning"? Does the word then have one meaning for the speaker and another (or no meaning at all) for the listener? Given the variability and unpredictability of understanding, how do we *ever* get someone else to understand us? What is the connection between a use and our understanding of it? If, as Wittgenstein says, we communicate with other people without access to their word-feelings (181), we just as surely lack access to their word-*use*. How you use a word is just as mysterious to me as how you feel about it. Both conceptions, James's and Wittgenstein's, objectify the speaker's intentional act; and if James places the object mainly inside, in the speaker's affective intention, and Wittgenstein places it mainly outside, in the speaker's verbal action, both objects must ultimately—precisely because they are objectified, projected as the subject's analytical other—elude the interpreter's grasp.

What is needed in order to move beyond both meaning-as-feeling and meaning-as-use is a theory of language that will account for the fact that meanings are almost always shared, are collective, but never perfectly or systematically so: for the fact that both misunderstanding and understanding are common. My proposal is a synthesis of the feeling-theory and the use-theory, according to which meaning and its interpretation are motivated and guided by feeling, or, more broadly, by body or somatic response; but that guidance is both contextually and personally variable (the flexibility and uniqueness of the individual speaking subject) and ideologically controlled (the shaping force of the speech community). In this conception ideological control is wielded, and collective meanings therefore shared, precisely through the mediation of the body—through the society's ideological (or "ideosomatic") programming of each individual's limbic system, seat of the emotions, habit, and rote memorization. We learn shared meanings by learning the proper (ideologically controlled) feelings that drive them; and we share them with other people through the empathetic power that bodies have over other bodies, emotional states over other emotional states. While this exceeds James's liberal humanist concern with individual subjectivity, it also provides a convincing rationale for his theory: we do have an if-feeling, an and-feeling, a not-feeling, and so on. Those feelings are collective, shared, "fixed," not transcendentally (by the mind of God), but socially, ideologically, by the socialization process.

As vastly successful as ideosomatic programming is, however, it never succeeds perfectly. It never (or hardly ever) generates ideological clones or robots (when it does, we consider the result pathological, and the only fail-safe way to achieve it is probably through a frontal lobotomy). This window of programming failure leaves open a space for both the (severely circumscribed but undeniable) "uniqueness" of the liberal subject and the necessity of defining meaning contextually, as "use," as however real people use language (speak it, interpret it) in real speech situations. Because we are shaped not only by social ideology but also by incidental experiences that happen to each of us separately, unpredictably, uncontrollably, idiosyncratically, there is also an "idiosomatic" aspect to language use—precisely the individual variability that Wittgenstein means when he asks whether someone might not claim to feel the same thing when he says "if" and "but." It is this idiosomatic aspect that generates misunderstandings, failures of communication, all the lapses and linguistic missteps that linguists derogate as "speech" or "performance" and rule beyond the analytical pale. It is also this idiosomatic aspect that drives linguistic change, that keeps language always vital, alive, restlessly shifting ground.

I began this discussion with James and Wittgenstein, but the true starting point for my challenge to Augustinian/Saussurean semiology, the impetus that sent me back to James and Wittgenstein, is Kenneth Burke's work on language in terms of the negative and the body. For example, in "A Dramatistic View of the Origins of Language," his long essay on the role played by the "dramatistic No" ("Thou shalt not") in the development of language, Burke quotes a passage from Fritz Mauthner's *Wörterbuch der Philosophie* on the origin of the negative from "a wholly physiological voicing of disgust and refusal, an abrupt expulsion of breath through the nostrils," and comments:

Dramatistically, we should not derive the linguistic negative from physical repugnance. But we should note how, once such a negative has taken form, it can on many occasions so affect the body that the violating of moralistic proscriptions may produce acute bodily distress and revulsion. Dramatistically, we watch always for ways in which bodily attitudes can affect the development of linguistic expression. (423n)

Angus Fletcher elaborates:

Burke holds that, in action, the negative involves a more than intellectual issue: The command mobilizes or immobilizes our motives, our feelings. Hence psyche and soma are reconnected. Body as well as mind assents to, or rejects, the command. From childhood on, man keeps rediscovering that his own body is not someone else's body, that his "body image" needs defining, that his body has endlessly to say Yes and No to an outside, impinging world. (159)[12]

Psyche and soma are indeed reconnected, as Fletcher says; but they are reconnected (methodologically, in an ideological tradition that has denied the connection) specifically under the sign of collective norms, which Burke exemplifies through "moralistic proscriptions." The parent shouts "No!" and in the child's bodily imagination the sound

[nou]—as yet devoid of cognitive content—is complexly engulfed in both the parent's angry or cold or shocked or fearful (or whatever) tones, gestures, and expressions and the child's own feeling of inward shrinking or shriveling that they precipitate. The child learning to imitate that [nou] verbally will participate in the imitation with his or her entire body, shaking his or her head vigorously No! while reaching for the forbidden object, or bursting into tears and hurling him- or herself down on the floor as if forcibly removed from the object. Gradually, then, approach to a forbidden object begins to trigger a bodily warning signal, a somatic response that says (in body language): *Anger! Burning anger!* Or, *Cold, no love, no warmth, shrink away. Hurt arm* (where the parent jerks the child away), *hurt bottom* (where the spank lands), and so on. The child's body has been programmed to steer him or her away from actions the parents consider dangerous or wrong.

And, of course, what parents thus pass on to their children is no private language, no accidental, haphazard, purely situational or reactive set of somatic responses, but collective norms: somatically inscribed ideology. Actions that the infant's parents consider wrong are "wrong" because they *feel* wrong to the parents—because the proscriptions that they inscribe on their child's body were once inscribed on theirs. The dramatistic no is pronounced not only when the child reaches for a hot stove but also when she reaches for her genitals. The former seems a more naturalistic proscription, based on science, cause and effect, the undeniable fact that if you touch a hot stove you will burn your hand, while the latter is more clearly moralistic, social, ideological; but in fact, before screaming "No!" at the child reaching toward a hot burner, the parent does not take time to review his or her scientific knowledge, and does not need to. Like the fear of moral deviation, the fear of hot stoves is programmed into his or her somatic response, and the "No!" just bursts out, impelled not by reason but by sheer ideosomatic terror.

And we never lose this—the somatic charge, the power of bodily inscriptions. Growing up is partly a process of developing psychic defenses against those inscriptions, but the process is never entirely successful, and there are moments when the adult feels all the primitive body magic of the infantile "no" or, say, "mama" or "dada," which are cathected with an overwhelming (for the infant) complex of need and anxiety and warmth and laughter and rage and fear. The shouted word "No!" will often return adults instantaneously to early childhood: they will feel in their bodies the irrational fear they felt when they were children and their parents were angry at them; they will freeze in horror, their hearts pounding, and so on. The maternal mama/mommy/ mom/mother verbal complex continues to wield its ideological weaponry (the denied impulse to idealization, emotional manipulation, martyrdom, etc.) over the adult, with socially derived variations for sons and daughters. The paternal dada/daddy/dad/father complex likewise, with its weapons (the denied impulse to hierarchization, emotional withdrawal, tyranny, etc.) traced approvingly by Freud in the theory of the Oedipus complex and therapeutically, cathartically, transoedipally, by the women's and men's movements and anti-Freudians like Gilles Deleuze and Felix Guattari.[13]

We develop consciousness, intelligence, and analytical thought in large part as an ideosomatic protection against just this emotional regression, just this vulnerability to the emotional charge of words used in early childhood. The limbic system has the power to paralyze the analytical cerebral cortex, to freeze thought, and that can be both dangerous (when a terrified shout of "Look out!" has the effect of paralyzing you, rendering you unable to move out of the way of an oncoming car) and profoundly disturbing (when a call from your mother makes you feel six years old again and ready to burst with hurt frustration). We do not want to regress. We do not want to feel as vulnerable as we did then. We do not want to find ourselves as much at the mercy of other people as we were at the mercy of our parents. But even the best protection we can devise is flimsy before the emotional power of words. Even the most manly man, one who associates manliness with robotic intelligence (a "mind like a steel trap") and claims he has no feelings, can be hurt to the quick by a well-chosen word. Indeed, since both his infantile vulnerability to an emotionally suffocating mother and his defensive rationality are ideologically prescribed and ideosomatically inscribed, a man's strength and weakness, vulnerability and invulnerability, are mutually defining, part of an ideological loop or vicious circle that is actuated ideosomatically as the double bind.

Our bodies often react to language use that seems different, deviant, somehow "wrong," with anxiety signals: there is a twinge in the chest, or a slight constriction of the throat. Most people do not know the rules that would allow them to define the triggering usage as "wrong" in any systematic, grammatical sense. But it *feels* wrong. It clashes with the body conditioning that they have for that usage or that context, with the ideosomatics of syntax, semantics, stylistics. "Bad grammar" feels wrong. Foreign words feel wrong. Other dialects feel wrong. Pretentious speech feels wrong. An American affecting a British accent sounds wrong. Bad acting on television grates on our ears like sandpaper. When members of our family make even the slightest change in their speech—begin to swear slightly more or less, pick up new words all of a sudden, begin to use a new jargon (from a new job, say), slip back into the dialect they spoke when they were children—we detect the difference immediately, and it feels wrong. "Don't talk that way, it sounds stupid." Actually, it doesn't sound stupid; it just *feels wrong*.

Officious, authoritarian interference with another person's speech behavior on the order of "Don't talk that way, it sounds stupid" is obviously a protective reaction—a defense against the anxiety signals that the body is producing. We do not want to feel that fist in our chest or that stranglehold on our throat. So we muster up the authority to make our somatic sense of rightness sound like a universal—precisely the ideological strategy used on us in childhood by our parents, teachers, and bossy peers. We reify somatics as system, and so transmit ideology. We appeal to logic: "more better" is tautological. We appeal to mathematics: "ain't none" is a double negative, which (in multiplication, anyway) makes a positive. We appeal to grammar: in the grammar book I used in school, or in Freshman English, the correct form was such-and-such. We appeal to the authority of a teacher: Mrs. Johnson in my high school English class always said that people who talked that way would never amount to anything.

In this way we protect ourselves not only against our somatic response—the anxiety—but also against the recognition that it *is* a somatic response. If we are simply enforcing a general rule that all right-thinking people obey, we aren't vulnerable; we don't harbor a traitor in our own body; we have nothing to fear.

As I have been saying, a large part of the somatics of our personal language use is not originally personal, but collective: it is conditioned, with greater or lesser success, into all members of a society. This somatic conditioning constitutes an embodied web of prescriptions and proscriptions often called "conventions." It is this conventional or ideological conditioning that enables us to communicate despite the ever-present possibility of misunderstanding—and despite the lack of anything so fail-safe as a transcendental linguistic system to which all language users have access. It is due to that conditioning that, when someone says "Look at the cat," we automatically seek out a visual impression of a furry feline creature. We do not close our eyes, and we do not look at a dog. We do have shared linguistic norms—but they are neither cognitive nor transcendental; they are somatic and situational. (I will return to the conditioning process later in the chapter.)

On the other hand, conventional or ideological conditioning is always only partly successful. No matter how efficient and rigorous our conditioning, there are always body responses that are purely idiosyncratic, that arise from our specific experiences—experiences that *we* have had, nobody else. Everyone, for example, has slightly different experiences with cats. Not only will the "meaning" of the word cat be orange for some, black and white for others, silky for some, scraggly for others; cat will be a positive, cuddly, furry thing for some (they may even hear the purring) and a negative, stiff-backed, scratching thing for others (they may even hear the hissing). For the latter, it will seem quite natural to hear a woman described as "catty"; for the former, it will seem quite odd.

These personal associations sometimes become habitualized, assimilated into the somatic structure of response, and thus in the "naturalness" or "automaticness" of the response they trigger become almost indistinguishable from ideologically programmed response. Others are more unusual, more individuated, and can be consciously linked with a specific event or occasion. The effect of our ideological programming is to blanket over these latter, to tuck powerfully idiosyncratic associations into the flaps and folds of programmed somatic response, and to assimilate less powerful associations to a habitualized collective knowing.[14]

This is also why native speakers of a language can argue forever over the connotations of a word (in a poem, say): each has personal associations that awaken idiosomatic responses, and each has been programmed to objectify (reify, externalize) somatic response as textual property. Each responds to the poem slightly differently, and each wants to believe that his or her response is the true or correct one.

The Idiosomatics of Translation

I mentioned earlier that a word that awakens in us no somatic response will feel unreal, "spiritual": for example, fancy-looking words that the desperate student looks up in the thesaurus and sticks in a paper, words that are sheer transcendental objects, symbolic images with a systemic locus (the thesaurus) but no ideosomatic reality. This is roughly how foreign languages feel to us as well, until we begin to learn them. "'This means nothing,' asserts the exasperated child in front of his Latin reader or the beginner at Berlitz" (297), in George Steiner's example. I cannot feel it, so it has no meaning.

Foreign languages begin to take on reality, not through cognitive understanding—though that must certainly follow—but through our somatic responses to them. And, of course, one of the surest ways to obstruct the learning of a foreign language is to teach it (usually an idealized standard form of it) through inert grammatical rules and vocabulary lists, all in isolation from real-use situations. Language taught like this is disembodied *langue,* not richly somatic *parole.* "Classroom" German or French *feels* abstract, lifeless, both to the second-language speaker who speaks it and to the native listener who hears it. As a result, even if the speaker makes him- or herself understood, the native listener will feel uncomfortable in the conversation. The foreigner will sound like a cleverly programmed robot. The words will feel like cardboard in the speaker's mouth: no life, no feeling. Beginning actors have the same problem: "Say it again," says the acting instructor, "but this time with *feeling!*"

To speak a foreign language well you have to feel the words. Ideally, you should feel what the native speaker feels, but that ideal is impossible, since every native speaker will feel the words in a slightly different way. The idiosomatics of words are never universal. But then, pragmatically speaking, universality is not important. The main thing is to feel *something.* If what you feel is radically different from what native speakers feel—if, to put it technically, your second-language syntax and semantics are guided by first-language somatics—your speech will sound somewhat ludicrous, but at least it will not sound mechanical or dead. Somatically charged interference from your native language is better than "spiritualized" syntactic and semantic correctness.

And, in fact, one of the obvious ways of "physicalizing" foreign speech when you are first learning it is by assimilating the unfamiliar foreign words to words that already have a physical meaning for you: beginning American students of German giggling over "Fahrt" or "damit," for example. To the native speaker of German this sounds silly, but in fact it is crucial for the beginning foreign-language student to do this: the words have to start *feeling* real. Sometimes language learning remains at this stage, with an individual word here or there being "translated" into the listener's native tongue, adopted or adapted with a meaning derived from physical response. The classic example of this was the "translation" of *hoc est corpus* ("This is the body [of our Lord Jesus Christ]") from the medieval Latin Mass as "hocus pocus," a magically charged nonsense phrase that awoke in the hearer gut-level fear.

Part of learning a language well is watching what native speakers' bodies do when they speak it: how they move their mouths, how they gesture and shift their weight, how they stumble over words, where and how they pause, how they use stress for emphasis—in general, how they stage their speech. But even that will not be enough if it is done mechanically, if you simply observe native speakers' bodies and mimic them. You have to do more than watch; you have to intuit, sense what their bodies are doing inside, sense how they *feel* when they speak. It is, of course, possible to ask: "How do you feel about a person when you say *Ich kenne ihn?* What is the difference between the way you feel when you say that and when you say *Ich weiss ihn?*" But native speakers are not always able to articulate these things. (Try to do it yourself sometime with your native language.) So you have to sensitize yourself to bodily signals, to project yourself imaginatively into the other person's body. In a sense, the foreign-language learner has to be at once a playwright, a director, and an actor, in the foreign language: he or she must generate out of fleeting impressions living, breathing images of native speakers inside his or her own body, create them as vehicles for identification—and then become them, grow into them, body them forth.

Obviously, something like this imaginative, identificatory self-projection into the body of a native speaker is a primary requirement for the good translator as well. If you do not feel the body of the SL text, you will have little chance of generating a physically tangible or emotionally alive TL text. The TL text you create will read like computer-generated prose: no life, no feeling.

In fact, it might even be argued that self-projection into the body of a native speaker is a more crucial requirement for the good translator than a comprehensive cognitive understanding of the SL (if one could only have one or the other). In *Cathay*, Ezra Pound exceeded the limitations of Ernest Fenollosa's crib (which was itself based on a Japanese translation) by just such a somatic projection. This is what my body says it must mean; therefore, that is what it does mean.[15] The Armenian-American poet Diane derHovanessian, who (having no Armenian herself) worked with an Armenian scholar to produce her translations of Armenian poetry, told me that she once fought for hours with her collaborator over a certain word, which he told her was flat-out wrong, but which she *felt* was right. On a visit to Armenia, she met the original poet and asked him about it; he told her that the word in question not only exactly captured what he had meant but was better than the word he himself had used, and he wished, he said, that he had thought to use the Armenian equivalent of her translation when he first wrote the poem.

Nor is this in any way unusual in good translation.[16] Translation succeeds best not when the translator has obeyed every cognitive rule—

performed a painstaking textual analysis and planned his or her restructuring out carefully in advance—but when he or she is most sensitive to the feel of both the SL and the TL words. To the extent that it makes sense to talk of translational equivalence at all, in fact, it is a matter not so much of minds—analytical correspondences—as it is of bodies, of feel. Equivalence between an SL and a TL word or phrase is always primarily somatic: the two phrasings feel the same.

And I would guess that this comes as no surprise to anybody. Everybody knows it, everybody is aware of the somatic grounds of translation equivalence—especially translators, but even translation theorists. The only reason translation theorists do not like to link equivalence explicitly with somatic response is that response is always partly idiosomatic: what feels equivalent to one person may well feel completely off-base to another. Somatic response is too unpredictable to be "adequately" theorized, that is, rigorously and universally systematized.[17]

There seems to be an unwritten rule among translation theorists, in fact, that for theory somatic response is the kiss of death. The only person who would dare talk about equivalence in terms of feeling, intuition, body response, is a translator; and among translators, probably only a literary translator; and among literary translators, only a maverick poet with a reputation for erratic brilliance.[18] A theorist who talked that way would surely reveal his or her ignorance, his or her inadequate powers of intellection, abstraction, generalization, systematization. Theorists are supposed to be scientists, and scientists do not play around with real bodies. If they have to do with bodies at all, they must be what Paul calls "spiritual bodies," safely removed to an idealized realm of forms.

Here as elsewhere, the notable exception is George Steiner:

Words have their "edge," their angularities, their concavities and force of tectonic suggestion. These features operate at a level deeper, less definable than that of either sound or semantics. They can, in a multilingual matrix, extend across and between languages. When we learn a new language, it may be that these modes of evocative congruence are the most helpful. Often, as we shall see, great translation moves by touch, finding the matching shape, the corresponding rugosity even before it looks for counterpart of meaning [though in great translation, I would say, "rugosity" and meaning are the same thing]. It was probably the mellifluous convexity of *quamvre* (cf. German *Qualm*) followed by the literal sharpness—acoustic as well, of course—of *bibistis,* and reinforced by *aquam,* itself a less "liquid" word than *quamvre,* which set off Pound's traverse in the *Homage to Sextus Propertius:* "what water has mellowed your whistles?" Poets can even smell words. (292–93)

But even Steiner, as he moves into the workshop chapter of his book (chapter 5, "The Hermeneutic Motion"), begins to forget the idiosomatic grounding of equivalence. To be sure, his practical criticism of the translations he discusses is based firmly on his own somatic response, and he hints throughout at the principle of idiosomatic equivalence: "Where language is fully used *meaning is content beyond paraphrase*. This is to say that where even the most thorough paraphrase stops, meaning begins uniquely" (375). This implies that meaning is somatic content; it is what the language user feels as meaning. But (driven by his ideosomatic programming) Steiner soon forgets the instability of somatic meaning, soon forgets that his response is *idiosomatic*, and begins to treat his feelings about translations as objective truth. Here he is, for instance, on Francis Steegmuller's French translation of "The Owl and the Pussycat": "But *ménage* is irremediably domestic; *la plage* banishes the magic of Shakespearean reminiscence in 'on the edge of the sand'; and *au clair de la lune,* no doubt because of the children's song, is oddly flatter than 'the light of the moon.' Transfiguration slips suddenly into diminution" (406). Or, in terms of Steiner's own reading, the feel of readerly dissatisfaction slips suddenly into the fact of translatorly failure.[19]

I find *After Babel* a monumental achievement, the most impressive and comprehensive philosophical study of translation ever published. (Louis Kelly's *True Interpreter* competes for the title in the history of translation theory.) But Steiner too, it seems to me, contributes to the philosophical vagueness he seeks at some length to clear up. I am tempted to quote him out of context, so that he seems to be referring to my own claims regarding the idiosomatic grounding of equivalence when he writes, "Only in this way, I think, can we assign substantive meaning to the key notion of 'fidelity.' Fidelity is not literalism or any technical device for rendering 'spirit'" (302). Exactly, I want to go on: it is a technical device for rendering not spirit but "body." Body, somatic response, is the "substance" Steiner looks for in meaning. But Steiner is not talking about somatics, here, despite all his suggestive hints in that direction; he is talking about a mysterious ideal of "reciprocity" or "equalization," the notion that the ideal translation is one that gives back to the original as much as it took from it:

The whole formulation [of fidelity], as we have found it over and over again in discussions of translation, is hopelessly vague. The translator, the exegetist, the reader is *faithful* to his text, makes his response responsible, only when he endeavours to restore the balance of forces, of integral presence, which his appropriative comprehension has disrupted. Fidelity is ethical, but also, in the full sense, economic. By virtue of tact, and tact intensified is moral vision, the translator-interpreter creates a condition of significant exchange. The arrows of meaning, of cultural, psychological benefaction, move both ways. There is, ideally, exchange without loss. In this respect, translation can be pictured as a negation of entropy; order is preserved at both ends of the cycle, source and receptor. (302)

I must confess that I cannot make the connection, here, between Steiner's lofty ideal and real translation. In what sense does the translator "disrupt" the SL text? What disruptive effect can translation have on a *text*? And how can a translator "restore" to a text what he or she has "taken" from it? What possible "exchange" can there be—with or without "loss"—between two texts?

If Steiner's theory of disruption and reciprocity is to have any reference to reality at all, it seems to me that he must be talking not about texts but about our somatic responses to them. The disruptive effect of a translation is not on the original, but on the receptor's response to the original: having read an appropriative translation, the receptor may come to feel differently about the original. It may begin to feel like a different sort of text. Steiner writes of Paul Celan's magnificent German version of Jules Supervielle's "Chanson": "After this it is almost impossible to go back to Supervielle; translation of this order being, in one sense, the cruellest of homages" (405). "Almost impossible to go back"—for the *reader* to go back, that is. Celan is disrupting the reader's appreciation of Supervielle, not Supervielle himself—not the SL text.

And in any case, "almost impossible to go back" is Steiner's feeling about the disruptive effect. At the level of his own somatic response, I would guess him to be saying: "It is hard for *me* to go back, and when I do, I do not feel the same about Supervielle any more. I would rather read Celan." Other readers might feel differently: some might not even like Celan's rendering. It is possible. Steiner has a native feel for German, French, and the English in which he is recording his impressions, and he is an extraordinarily sensitive reader of texts; but sensitivity does not make his readings universal. Another reader, one who feels differently, even if that difference were shown to stem from "insensitivity" (and how would you show that? how could that sort of thing be proved?), is still entitled to his or her own response. A bilingual reader who, having read Celan, still preferred Supervielle would have experienced no disruptive effect at all; there would thus be nothing to restore.

No reciprocity would be necessary, or for that matter even conceivable. No one would even think to demand it.

And what about the French reader of Supervielle who has no German? What is the effect of Celan's translation on his or her somatic response? The answer is obvious: none. Such a reader might, of course, hear of a German translation that supposedly surpasses the original; and if the reader is emotionally attached to Supervielle (if, say, Supervielle came from this reader's hometown and has come to embody a nostalgic pride in his or her native region, or has come to evoke both an anxiety about the deadening effect of his or her childhood and a childhood daydream of promise and possibility: if Supervielle made it, I can too), then perhaps the mere rumor of a German translation that surpasses the original might be somatically disruptive. Then all the defensiveness of national and regional pride would be aroused—a German, eater of wurst, surpassing a Frenchman, citoyen du monde? Jamais! But clearly, Celan cannot be held accountable for a response of this sort; certainly there is nothing he could have done as translator to avert it. In any case, the rumor is itself no objective fact, no universal truth; it is based on someone's somatic response to the two poems. Celan may himself feel that his translation, so far from surpassing the original, so far from appropriating its reputation or integrity, falls far short of it. We have no reason to assume that Celan would necessarily agree with Steiner's appraisal. He might be flattered and might agree out of a combination of courtesy and writerly pride; but underneath he might still feel like a fraud for accepting flattery that feels so patently untrue.

The point that I am trying to make is that all talk of "equivalence," "fidelity," or even "reciprocity" in the abstract is, and must remain, philosophically vague because the reality underlying it is a constantly shifting and therefore ultimately unsystematizable human response. Or rather, a series of human responses. Translation theorists, like their colleagues in the other so-called human sciences, like to talk about texts, intertextualities, structures of correspondence, and the like—all hypostatized abstractions. But the reality of translation and all human communication is *people*. A person writes the SL text, charging the SL words with all the force of his or her idiosomatic experience. A second person reads the SL text, recharging the SL words with all the force of his or her own idiosomatic experience—an experience that, owing to our ideosomatic conditioning, will probably overlap in significant ways with that of the author, but never exactly. A third person (or the same person in a third capacity) reads the SL text with an ear to translating it into a TL and charges the transfer with the force of his or her idio-somatic experience: *feels* the SL and works to dredge up out of his or her TL storehouse words that feel the same, words that seem charged with something like the same force. Since the somatic charge of the words we use is something of a mystery to us (we are often surprised at the vehemence of our speech when we thought we were calm, or at the disgust our words embody toward a person we thought we loved), our own transfer may begin, after the fact, to feel somehow faithless or unequivalent—*that* is not what I was trying to convey! A mediocre translator will quickly repair that sort of accident, restore the TL text to a more lifeless equivalence—an idealized dictionary equivalence, say. A good translator, on the other hand, will leave him- or herself open to this sort of unexpected swerve, will explore it, in order to learn more about his or her somatic response, in order the better to tap it, draw on it, bring it to verbal expression. And, finally, a fourth person (or one of the earlier people in a fourth capacity) reads the TL text and charges the TL words with all the idiosomatic force of his or her experience.

And note that at no point in this series of responses, at least outside the schools and the theory books, can any one act of somatic (re)charg-ing be brought into ideal conformity with all the others. In fact, it is difficult enough to bring an act of somatic charging into conformity with itself—to know, for example, just what one is feeling and why, to feel "consistently" or "coherently," to charge a reading or writing of a text with a unified vision. A mediocre translator, again, will strive for logical consistency by suppressing somatic confusion; a great translator will not shrink from somatic confusion, somatic inconsistency, will not retreat into protective intellection, but will boldly flesh out the contra-dictory and conflicting body of his or her response with the overriding conviction that, if it all came from the guts, it is all of a piece.

Now, a common objection to this theory of the idiosomatics of translation, typically lodged by my linguist colleagues, is that it is pat-ently predicated on the translation of literature and has little or no ap-plicability to "ordinary" translation, such as the translation of weather reports. I think it important to deal with this objection here. It is true that translation theorists tend to frame their conceptions of translation either linguistically, resting methodologically and ideologically on the mainstream tradition of Augustinian/Saussurean semiology, or herme-neutically, resting methodologically and ideologically on the romantic tradition of Goethe, Schleiermacher, and Wilhelm von Humboldt.[20] And, depending on which approach you prefer, it is true that you will tend to construe the field of translation either around texts that you consider "ordinary" and therefore theoretically interesting (and methodologically manageable) like weather reports and business letters, or around texts that you consider "complex" and therefore theoretically interesting (and methodologically challenging) like lyric poems.

If you take the former approach, you will tend to privilege ritualized texts that lend themselves to systematic formalizations and to deprivilege texts that defy such formalizations as "special" or "parasitical"; if you take the latter, you will tend to privilege gnomic or vatic texts that engage all the knottiest problems of human expression and to deprivilege texts that have been reduced by long, ritualized use to mechanical formulas. And since I do take the latter approach, because I am more interested in complex texts than in formulaic ones, it will probably make no difference how many other types of translation I discuss besides literary—and the list includes technical and scholarly translation, simultaneous and consecutive interpretation, simultaneous signing (speech into sign language), TV subtitling, advertising translation, Bible translation, classroom translation, and the translation of weather reports—this book will probably be described as a theory of literary translation.

But let me try nonetheless, in the face of what is almost an inevitability, to dispel the notion that I am *only* interested in the translation of literature, by taking a look at the exemplary case for the former approach, weather reports. It is true that weather reports are so formulaic that they lend themselves both to systematic linguistic formalization and to machine translation; and if the conclusions linguists traditionally draw from that fact are true, this very formulaic nature should exclude somatic response. The translation of weather reports should be purely cognitive, purely logical, purely systematic—purely, in other words, something an asomatic machine could perform.

There is an interesting article by Benoît Thouin in Veronica Lawson's essay collection *Practical Experience of Machine Translation* that bears out this expectation, up to a point. Thouin writes about the METEO system developed by the University of Montreal's Automatic Translation Research Team for the Canadian Meteorological Center, under the auspices of the Translation Bureau of the Canadian government's Secretary of State Department, back in the late seventies. The system has had great success, partly because weather reports *do* lend themselves to machine translation (MT), partly because Canada is a large, bilingual country with a heavy demand for English-French and French-English weather report translations. But there are several obstacles to the traditional linguistic conclusions. The first, and in some sense most trivial, is that not even the METEO system can process all meteorological texts: not even weather reports are formulaic enough to be reliably decoded by a computer without human assistance.[21]

But this is, as I say, a trivial obstacle, since, as Thouin points out (though he does not actually recommend it, for reasons related to job satisfaction), it is always possible to impose stricter rules on the writers of weather reports and thus to eliminate nondecodable texts—in other words, to extend the restrictions imposed on translation by an asomatic machine to the humans involved as well, by simple institutional fiat. Thou shalt not write so the computer cannot understand thee.

A more interesting and theoretically complex obstacle to traditional linguistic formalization arises toward the end of Thouin's article, when he comes to the "human" side of things:

> The fastidious nature of the texts put off translators to the extent that few of them would remain more than six months with the Meteorological Sub-section. . . . Now, all the translators except one in this unit have been there at least two or three years and all are happy in their working environment. . . . The existence of the system has allowed the French translation service for the weather bulletins to be extended across Canada without any increase in staff. In any case, personnel were quite hard to find—given how little interest translators showed in this kind of repetitive work. The new working framework created by this system contributed to improving the working lives of the translators, which represents a sure gain even though it is difficult to measure. (43–44)

It is significant, I think, that the form of translation that most interests linguistic translation theorists, because it is amenable to their brand of formalistic analysis, interests translators so little that it is considered a "sure gain even though it is difficult to measure" when humans can be replaced by machines. Perhaps linguists too could one day be replaced by machines? Is this implicit in the Augustinian idealization of cognitive system over feeling? In any case, the point I want to make is that the lack of interest that the Canadian translators showed in their work was itself a somatic response: boredom generated by repetitive work. The Meteorological Sub-section could not keep human translators on the payroll for longer than six months precisely because the translators' *bodies* rejected the work. Ritualized, formulaic language is too close to the Augustinian/Saussurean ideal to nourish humans' emotional needs for variety and challenge. It thus becomes both economically and emotionally feasible to fulfill the Augustinian robotic ideal up to a point—let computers decode those purely formulaic texts that they are capable of decoding—and let humans handle the "deviant" texts that both require and nourish feeling.[22] The humans maintain some degree of interest in their work, and so stay on the job, saving the government the trouble and expense of training new translators every six months; and the computers do the work of many humans more quickly and efficiently and reliably, saving the government even more expense in hiring translators and checking and correcting their work.

The considerations of automation, cost-effectiveness, and linguistic formalization are ideologically congruent, of course: they are the technological, economic, and scientific applications of the Augustinian systemic ideal (in the specific historical form assigned it by commodity capitalism, of course), abstracting out of a complex human reality a transcendental (cybernetic, mathematical, analytical) system that is privileged over the human reality it at once unifies and displaces.

But note what is excluded from view in this formulation: the patent fact that the ideosomatic programming of bourgeois society has not yet successfully rooted out of human individuals their somatic aversion to boredom, their need for variety and challenge, for life-enhancing affect. The successful human products of Western bourgeois ideosomatic programming would constitute a dehumanized proletariat that strikingly resembled the METEO computers: so completely inured to (or, ideally, relieved of) somatic response as to be able to process repetitive texts, without contentment or disgruntlement or *any* kind of affect, till the cows come home. This has not happened in translation or any other industry.

And in any case, the formulaic ease with which a human translator performs a repetitive task is the function not of cognitive control but of somatic programming. The human translator of weather reports or other ritualized texts does not master the task by reducing it to an abstract system, with rigidly hierarchized rules, but rather by programming his or her body to do the work without thinking about it—and this is precisely what makes it so boring. When you address yourself to yet another text in the formulaic mode all your work revolves around—weather report, technical document, business letter, and so on—you do not have to engage your mind; you just sit down at the keyboard and start banging away. Your fingers do the work; and your fingers are the instruments not of your cerebral cortex (that might even make it slightly interesting) but of your limbic system. Your body knows what to do. Somatic equivalence is formulaically programmed in.

But not immutably. This formulaic or programmatic quality of a given act of translation is not a feature or property of a text; it is a by-product of your repeated exposure to a text. You produce it; and to the extent that you have any control at all over your body (and I am not suggesting that this control is a self-evident or simple matter), you can stop producing it or start producing something different.

Not only that: other kinds of repeated exposure to a text can have the opposite effect, an effect not of numbing sameness (petrifaction) but of bewildering difference (erosion or disruption). While we are examining the kind of lowly, despised forms of translation that usually get ignored in discussions of literary translation (like Steiner's) and emphasized in discussions of machine translation, let us look at an example from classroom translation—the absolute lowest of the low, to many minds. For six years in the late seventies and early eighties I taught translation from Finnish to English at the University of Jyväskylä in Finland—or rather, technically speaking, I didn't teach translation, I used translation to teach grammar. Since I was fluent in Finnish and spoke more Finnish than English in my day-to-day life, Finnish syntax had a habit of interfering with my English: my body (somatic response) was attuned to both languages, and sometimes, when I was not paying strict attention, literal translations from Finnish would creep into my English. (Literal translations from English creeping into my Finnish was no news; that is standard in all language learning.) This made me particularly susceptible to the "errors" I was supposed to be correcting on translation exams. I would mark the first five or ten papers that rendered "Hän asui 50 km Helsingistä pohjoiseen" as "He lived 50 km north from Helsinki" wrong; then, as the next ten bombarded my (already Finnicized) somatic response with the same preposition ("from"), I would begin to wonder, hearing (as it were) the introjected voices of my students saying, "Here we are in Finland, you're the outsider, you're the interloper, we should know what's right, believe us, notice that we're all in agreement here, we're right and you're wrong, admit it." Could I really be right and all forty students wrong? As the bombardment continued, as I reached the thirtieth and then the fortieth paper, the translation that I had begun by feeling "incorrect" now seemed like the only "natural" one. "North from Helsinki"—of course! How else could you say it? What alternatives were there? I was then ready to go back and accept all the "froms" I had marked wrong. My body had been brought around, persuaded, literally "swayed." This is a problem faced by everyone who lives abroad: broken forms of your native language caused by interference from the local language seem to overwhelm your own somatic response; once you learn the local language (once it penetrates to your somatic experience, begins to feel real), the effect is only intensified.

This example pushes us, in one sense, in the exact opposite direction from the translation of weather reports: where the repetitive predictability of meteorological translating made machine translation feasible, the dizzying variability of my response to my students' grammar translation seems to point to the impossibility of *all* translation. But in terms of idiosomatic response, the examples tend in the same direction. The key is context. In a context of deadening sameness, the translator's body will gradually be programmed to respond in a mechanically predictable way, which will seem to justify the idealized Augustinian notion that machine translation might be universally possible, might replace all human translation. In a context of dynamic flux or conflict, however, where the translator's body is simultaneously and continuously being bombarded by conflicting impulses, tugs and pulls in two directions at once, it will gradually be deprogrammed, confused, opened up to the kind of vulnerability to complexity that we usually call muddledness.

On the other hand, we are never doomed to either mechanical boredom or dynamic muddledness. The translation teacher who feels confused can fight back with a dictionary and grammar book, fighting confusion with the authoritarian tools of the trade. My authority lies not in my native competence (since that is under assault) but in these books. Thou shalt not question *our* word. Or, with a bit more courage, the translation teacher can begin to sort out somatic responses, explore the complexity, tap its richness for better teaching. Similarly, the meteorological translator who feels bored can begin to vary his or her translations, experiment with variety, staying at first within the bounds of acceptability—referring to groundhogs or bunions, livening up his or her discourse with sportswriter-type verbal creativity—then carefully pushing past those bounds, testing the water. This means risking his or her job, of course; but then, surrendering to the boredom means risking his or her sanity, and one has to set one's priorities in this sort of thing. You change little things: you melodramatize the weather, deck a 30 percent chance of rain in the trappings of Elizabethan tragedy or Aristophanic comedy; you personify meteorological events, portraying the sunny sky as pining away for a rain cloud (as you are for an interesting translation task). Take this road to its end and you wind up with actionable offenses like false hurricane warnings, of course; and the translator who starts down that road is probably ready to quit the weather bureau and find some other line of work. But it is arguably better to quit after six months of subversive delight than after six months of mind- and body-numbing boredom: better a life-enhancing rehumanization of one's work, however contrary to the ideals of good craftsmanship, than a destructive compliance with ideosomatic dehumanization.

By the same token, even literary translation, which is usually thought of as the most exciting and challenging form of all translation, can fall into tedious routine. Contracted by a publisher to translate, for example, the complete works of a contemporary German best-selling novelist, the translator might find the first novel difficult; the second still full of surprises, but surprises rendered pleasant by their vague familiarity; the third easy; and the fourth routine—and there are seven more to go. This happens all the time. Not all literature is Sappho.

Likewise conference interpretation, which in some contexts might rival literary translation in its excitement and challenge. Certainly simultaneous interpretation has the element of surprise or unpredictability that is apparently essential for translational challenge. In Glemet's vivid description of the simultaneous interpreter's work, "As you are following the speaker you start a sentence. But as you start a sentence you are taking a step in the dark, you are mortgaging your grammatical future; the original sentence may suddenly be turned in such a way that your translation of its end cannot easily be reconciled with your translation of its start" (cited in Gerver, 168). Anyone who has given a talk or taught a class when hung over or ill will recognize the very slim thread that binds the coherence of a spoken text: nervousness before a hostile or skeptical audience can reduce a speaker's syntax to gibberish; a memorized speech may come out garbled, with crucial parts of speech or sound patterns missing or scrambled. The simultaneous interpreter gambles that the SL text will make sense—and, more than gambling, has a commitment to an SL text that makes sense, in fact to *making* sense of even a garbled text. But bodies often conspire against such commitment. The interpreter may have a good feeling about one speaker, may feel that he or she is eminently predictable; the speaker hardly has to open his or her mouth before the interpreter is off, confidently translating with a minimal ear-voice span, five or six words behind. Another speaker is different; this one looks erratic, and even before he or she begins to speak the interpreter knows there is going to be trouble. The speaker twists his or her neck in a peculiar way, suggesting some mental disturbance; words come out in a sudden flood of almost incoherent verbiage, which then stops while the speaker digs ferociously at an ear, giving the interpreter time to catch up, of course, but along with the time a case of the heebie-jeebies. The easiest speaker to follow may also be the most boring, so that the interpreter finds it hard to stay alert; a dense, erratic speaker may be so full of fire that he or she motivates the interpreter to a razor-sharp concentration.

But simultaneous interpretation too can become routinized, ritualized, and thus characteristically numbing or boring. This is especially true in ritualized speech situations like academic conferences or the United Nations, where institutionalized formulas impose on all speakers certain role expectations that tend to flatten somatic response. Be serious; be judicious; speak instrumentally, as the depersonalized vehicle of objective fact (at academic conferences) or your government (at the UN). Use ritualized phrases; don't charge your speech with idiosomatic experience. Don't let anyone see that you are personally excited, upset, or bored by the things you feel called upon to say. This ritualistic assumption of a mechanical, robotic speech role does not preclude somatic response; it just flattens it, narrows it, controls it. Depending on the interpreter's tolerance for boredom, it may have the effect of ritualizing the interpreter's response as well, so that the interpreter becomes as much a speech robot as the SL speaker. Or it may have the opposite effect: it may generate frustrated, pent-up, rebellious anger, warped and twisted signs of repressed life, which the interpreter may at first suppress, then begin to let out, allow into verbal expression—until he or she quits or is fired.

The Ideosomatics of Translation

The robotization of somatic response, generated as it is out of a fear of feeling and a need to muster up cognitive resources against the dreaded encroachments of feeling, feeds the Western myth of the purely cognitive nature of language. Language users use language by reference to a transcendental system of linguistic rules and structures. Translators make translations out of conceptual analyses, transfers, and restructurings. *Feeling plays no part in translation.* Stress that. Remember that. Drum it into your head. Feeling plays no part in translation. If it does, there is something wrong, something fishy: you are not *translating,* then, you are creating, projecting, emoting. Only weak, muddled, intuitive translators feel when they translate and translate out of their feeling. The result is always a mishmash. Good translators obey the cognitive rules, follow the analytical procedures, do what *we* say they should do, not what *they* feel is right. A good translation is always an intellectual construct, something like a good theory—something, in fact, that feels (no! I don't feel: *is*) profoundly reassuring, profoundly unthreatening. Feeling plays no part in translation.

This verges on caricature, I know; I am making it sound as if analytical translation theory is purely an idiosomatic invention, a defensive maneuver somatically charged with insecure people's need to protect themselves against their own somatic responses. It is not that—or rather, it is not only that. I do believe that intellectual sneers at and dismissals of feeling and the body come out of the sneerers' profound insecurity about feeling and the body and constitute an attempt to suppress what they fear; but neither the sneers nor the insecurity is purely individual. There is, as I have been suggesting, a long and illustrious ideological history behind them. We—especially we men, but women too—have been ideologically conditioned to fear feeling and the body and to protect ourselves against them by building out of consciousness a kind of intellectual barricade. In that sense we might say that analytical translation theory is not merely an id*i*osomatic but also an id*e*osomatic invention: an invention whose somatic motivation derives as much from collective ideology (ideo-) as from individual experience (idio-).

We are, after all, permeated with the values of our society. Collective values saturate our every cell. We are good citizens; we obey the laws; we are kind to animals, children, and the weak of mind; we try not to be racist, sexist, or classist; we try to respect other people's religious views, no matter how ridiculous they seem (when we ridicule them, we certainly do not do it to their face). We know it is *right* to act this way. We are not sure how we know it is right, but for as long as we can remember, everybody we respect has insisted on it, and their words have always felt like a continuing confirmation of what our bodies already knew: this is right, that is wrong. Do this, don't do that.

This inner sense of right and wrong is often called "conscience," as if it were an intellectual activity, somehow related to formal science. Theologians like to call it the Holy Spirit, the work not of our own spirit but of God's all-permeating spirit in us. But my exploration of the way a toddler learns the meaning of the word "No!" may point us in a different direction: our inner sense of right and wrong is not spirit, but body. It is a bodily impulse that is drummed into us at an extremely early age. The very fact that it usually operates within us without our conscious awareness suggests its somatic nature. Our bodies know how to act, even when "we" (the conscious, intellectualized part of us that we like to think of as the "real" us) dither. Our bodies make us sick when we mistakenly think we have plenty of strength left: this we know.

It is called psychosomatic illness. But that is not all. Our bodies produce guilt signals when we honestly (rationally) believe we were not to blame. Our bodies surprise us with compassion signals when we think we want to rejoice that an enemy is down. The somatic power of "conscience," or of ideological conditioning, remains strong even when we think we have reasoned it away, intellectually dispelled it from our psychic makeup. The body is not so easily dismissed.

Ethnologists call this process of bringing collective values into the individual and the individual into the collective values "enculturation"; the only people it does not apply to are people raised in the woods by wolves. Anyone raised in society has been enculturated by that society. Enculturation is the means by which culture reproduces itself: an enculturated person will work throughout his or her life to enculturate others, to bring peers, children, grandchildren, students, and so on, into the same set of cultural values—precisely because it *feels right* to do so, because the ideosomatic anxiety generated by other people's socially deviant behavior can only be (temporarily) relieved by bringing that behavior into conformity with your ideosomatic ideal. The anxiety you felt when your own childhood behavior deviated from your parents' and teachers' ideosomatic expectations survives into adulthood, particularly into parenthood, and you pass it on to your children—and they to theirs.

Because this process begins at birth, it is misleading to think of enculturation as something tacked on to our fundamental personalities. The period in which personality is formed through experience of the world is precisely the period in which adults and peers work to enculturate the individual into those collective values. So far from being added on to personality, in fact, collective values for many people *are* personality: they define themselves in terms of an enculturated ideal, so that a man may think of himself as being basically intellectual, thrusting, aggressive, unemotional, and so on. That is his entire personality; there is nothing else there; it is *him*—despite the patent fact that this "personality" conforms exactly to our culture's masculine ideal. He feels this enculturated ideal as his truest self. Collective values, or what some political philosophers call "ideology" or "hegemony," are programmed into the deepest core of our somatic response to the world, so that, even when we most slavishly enact some collective ideal, it feels like we are being completely ourselves.[23]

This kind of talk, I realize, makes many people feel uneasy. "Are you saying I'm *not* myself?" I am not saying that; I am saying that what we think of as "ourselves" is a complex mixture of idiosomatic and ideosomatic experience—our individual experience is a combination of truly individual or private or personal experiences and the collective experience that was programmed into us at an early age. (Since we experience being programmed, that is part of our individual experience too.)

One of the reasons for the uneasiness that this talk of ideological conditioning or enculturation provokes, in fact, is that in the West, in the last three or four centuries, a central tenet in our ideosomatic programming has been the liberal belief in the autonomy and the uniqueness of the individual. Each individual is his "own" self; he "owns" himself like an industrialist owning a factory. He is boss. (As we will see in a minute, the "he" is exactly right here.)

On the other hand, despite the lip service we pay to the liberal ideology of individual autonomy (self-possession) and uniqueness, we know, at least at some level, that it is not true. We talk, for example, about "types" of people, which would not be possible if everyone were truly unique. Our bodies are programmed to make us feel guilty about typecasting people (after all, everyone is unique), and we try hard not to do it; but somehow we keep right on doing it. And in any case there are striking similarities among people: men generally seem to share certain common features, as do women, working-class people, middle-class people, the upper crust, and so on. We see similarities among all two-year-olds (the "terrible twos"). We see similarities among all members of a racial or ethnic minority. No matter how we fight the impulse to typecast, the evidence is *there*, right in front of our eyes: whether because we have been programmed to see it (and to suppress all evidence to the contrary), or because the people we are observing have been programmed to display it—or both.[24]

We also sense that our motivations are not always as clear and coherent and articulate as they would be if we were truly autonomous. There seem to be mysterious forces inside us, prompting us to do things we do not really want to do: acting out of duty or responsibility when we want to be selfish, or acting selfishly when we want to be responsible; saying nasty things just when we had told ourselves to bite our lip; losing our temper with no inner warning, no personal sense that we were being pushed to the breaking point. Matthew Arnold noted in *Culture and Anarchy* that in the West we have traditionally offered two answers to this question of our undesirable impulses: in one, which he called "Hebraic," the problem is sin, a perversion of our will to do right, and the only corrective is a system of restraints that keeps us from doing wrong (punishes us for wrongdoing). This mode is found throughout the Bible—cf. Paul to the Romans (7:19): "For the good that I would I do not; but the evil which I would not, that I do"—and, for that matter, in much paternalistic legislation still today. It is also found in translation theory, whenever the theorist conceives his or her task as one of preventing translators from surrendering to their "natural" impulses.

In the other answer, which Arnold called "Hellenic," the problem is ignorance, a lack of sufficient information regarding the right course or the right implementation of that course, and the obvious corrective is education. This has been the liberal answer to human shortcomings, starting in the Middle Ages in the universities, burgeoning in the Renaissance, and picking up speed in the Enlightenment and under romanticism—and it is the explanation that is largely offered today (thus the popularity of self-help books and seminars). The emphasis on education also runs through contemporary translation theory, where one ruling idea seems to be that all the information the translator needs to translate well is available, if he or she only knew where to look and were subtly nudged in the right direction. Self-help books for translators are now being published in increasing numbers, and the various translator organizations (FIT, ATA) organize seminars and conferences for their members with much the same idea in mind: to educate the ignorant.

But note that both of these answers are essentially authoritarian. They assume that the solution to undesirable impulses is better control, and they differ only in their channeling of that control: the Hebraic controller would impose external constraints, while the Hellenic controller would encourage the internalization of constraint. Note also that neither of them really works: "rules are made to be broken," we tell ourselves when faced with external constraint, "just so long as you don't get caught"; "nobody's perfect," we tell ourselves when faced with internal constraint, "and I did try." No matter how we educate ourselves to act better, be better people, when push comes to shove we slip right back into our old selves. No matter how men educate themselves not to make sexist remarks, for example, the first time they tell a dirty joke they give themselves right away. Civilization is skin-deep. Liberalism is a Band-Aid on a great festering sore.

Or, in other words, on the body—on the complex body of somatic response. Thinking through the idealizing lens of Western spiritualism, it is easy to see the body as a great festering sore, something to suffer, to fear, to suppress. If you cannot heal the sore, at least cover it up. Put it in chains, say the impatient Hebrews; dress it up with education, say the liberal Greeks. Whatever you do, *don't let it loose.* Keep it under control. Hide it away.

But I want to offer another solution: instead of controlling the body, explore it. Instead of hiding it away, dive down into it and bring what you find to consciousness. Explore the somatic complexity of real translation. Do not assume that the translator's "natural" impulses will be wrong and that education or regulation is therefore in order; learn to feel what you do when you translate. The chances are that your body has a fairly good idea of what kind of translation is appropriate in given circumstances; by ignoring your body, by allowing translation theorists and teachers to direct your attention away from your own somatic sense of appropriateness into the abstract realm of rules and structures, you are alienating yourself from the best tool you have.

Certainly, somatic self-exploration is not easy. The simmering kettle that I call somatic programming contains an exceedingly complex stew. In the terms that I have been using, it is next to impossible to distinguish idiosomatic from ideosomatic experience.[25] We are programmed, as I said before, not to notice our somatic responses at all—to "forget" we ever had any, and if we do notice them, to downplay or flat-out dismiss their significance. This is the first seal: *There is no somatic response, and if there is, it means nothing.*

Then, if we do come to realize that somatic response may indeed be significant, we are programmed to think of it as entirely idiosyncratic, idiosomatic, "unique." If I find that my body reacts with signals of disgust around blacks, say, or with signals of contempt around women, that is just me: I can develop some theory of psychological trauma, perhaps, that will explain why I react in this particular way to blacks or women. If I find that my belief in my own rigorous masculine intellect is backed up by a powerful somatic reaction against the threat posed by feeling, that is just me: I felt smothered by my mother's emotional demands and raised these barriers to protect myself. This is the second seal: *All somatic response is idiosomatic, unique to each individual, produced by specific psychic traumas or other experiences in that individual's life.*

Next, I can begin to recognize uncanny similarities between my supposedly idiosomatic response and the somatic responses of others. Other men feel the same way about themselves and about women as I do: the fear of feeling, fear of emotional smothering by the mother, fear of father's coldness, the need to protect against these fears with a forbidding intellectual chill. Why? Why should all these men have undergone essentially the same experiences as I did? Could mothers and

fathers be somehow uniformly programmed by society to act the way
they do? Could they be programmed to program their sons and daughters in uniform ways? Other whites feel the same way about blacks and
other minorities as I do. Other members of the professional middle
class share my class envy of the rich and my uneasy contempt for workers. Could this all be programmed too? As we begin to explore these
uniformities throughout a society, we begin to uncover the workings
of ideology. This is liberating, at least at first: we begin to realize that
we are not alone in feeling the way we do, that everybody has been
programmed in some way, that nobody escapes it, and if someone else
seems to be better off than I am—Prince Charles, for example, or
whoever happens to be featured in today's tabloid—chances are that he
is just as imprisoned internally by the society's ideosomatic programming as I am. But the knowledge that everyone else is imprisoned too
is only liberating for a while; ultimately it leads to bitter frustration or,
if you learn to accept your lot, to fatalism. That is the third seal: *Ideosomatic programming is the rock bottom of personality; there is no escape; we
are all robots programmed by society to perform a variety of tasks without true
freedom of will or thought anywhere.*

But finally, when we have reached what we are supposed to think is
rock bottom, we feel a squishiness underfoot, a softness in the floor,
and find we can thrust our foot straight through to—what? Something
else. Reaching the bottom of his ideosomatic programming, the unemotional intellectual man discovers his feelings, reaches through the
shame that kept him from exploring them, and realizes that the world
does not fall apart when he expresses them, gives in to them, allows
himself to be swept up by them. Reaching the bottom of her ideosomatic programming, the submissive emotional woman discovers her
toughness, her competence, reaches through the fears that kept her
from exploring them, and despite signs that the world is falling apart
(hostility from husband and male co-workers), she persists and begins
to discover her self-esteem. Once this threshold has been crossed, once
we have smashed through the rotten floor of our ideosomatic programming to the truly idiosomatic impulses we have been suppressing for
so long, the only seals are in other people's behavior: they want us to
keep acting in the old safe ways, to keep confirming the rightness of
their own seals. The only thing to do, then, is to find ways of expanding
those fragmentary idiosomatic responses without bringing society's
ideosomatic wrath down upon us.[26]

Note that I am using "idiosomatic" in a double sense: (1) the personal body response that we discover when we begin to pay attention

to our bodies (when we break the first seal), which later (when we break the second seal) begins to look like a programmed and therefore *im*personal ideosomatic response; and (2) the truly individual-specific body response that we begin to discover when we plumb the depths of our programming (break the third seal). The two senses of the word come together in the realization, after the third seal is broken, that what makes all body response idiosyncratic is the systematically forgotten working of unprogrammed response: that the body response we discover when we begin to pay attention is a mixture of ideosomatic programming and unprogrammed (idiosomatic) experience. No matter how effective or how thorough our programming has been, we never become robots, we never lose the creative instability of idiosomatic response.

I have structured Part 1 of this book (the somatics and the dialogics) to work down through the three seals, starting at the top. Thus, my first insight into translation, which appeared earlier in this chapter—having broken the first seal—was that equivalence is always idiosomatically grounded. Once we recognize the importance of body response to translation, we understand that any given individual's response to a text—as writer or reader, or as translator-as-reader-and-writer, responding to SL or TL text—will be personal, unique, based on his or her idiosomatic experience. To the extent that we can speak of equivalence at all (as I said earlier in the chapter), it is no systematizable structure of correspondence between two texts in the abstract but an idiosomatic response.

Breaking the second seal, however, takes us past that first formulation—my concern in the rest of this chapter. Once we recognize the importance of ideological conditioning to body response, we understand that any given individual's response to a text will be collectively controlled and conformed by the society's dominant ideology. This suggests that there may be something that all Western translators have in common when they seek or pronounce on the "equivalence" between two texts. And this in turn suggests that translation theorists who take "equivalence" or "fidelity" to be a rule-governed structure are not entirely wrong—are not simply protecting themselves against the threatening complexity of their own somatic responses. To the extent that the ideological rules governing equivalence are programmed into us by our culture, a "structure" of equivalence does exist.

The error in traditional thinking about translation equivalence lies elsewhere. In fact, it is twofold: it consists in the belief (a) that the structure of equivalence is natural and universal, and (b) that it is therefore inevitable and immutable. The first part of this belief, that our conception of translation equivalence is natural and universal, is part of the working of ideology: as political philosophers like Antonio Gramsci remind us, one of the things we are ideologically conditioned to believe in is the "naturalness," the unconditional or universal status, of our beliefs. It is obvious to everyone what true equivalence is. It does not need to be examined; it can be assumed, or at most simply explicated. My sense of what equivalence "is" (in the abstract, "objectively") is not mine alone; it is shared by all human beings. After all, are humans so different? Can they disagree substantially with me?

A belief in the universality of one's belief tends to include a sense of its inevitability and immutability as well; but that latter sense, significantly enough, can survive even the kind of ideological self-analysis that exposes the historical contingency of a specific ideological program. That survival is made possible by what I have dubbed the "third seal": it may be true, one line of resistance might proceed, that our beliefs in a certain kind of translation equivalence are ideologically programmed into us. But as a program those beliefs are still inevitable and immutable. We are the products of our programming. We are robots. It does not matter who programmed us, and how; we can do nothing to change our own psychosomatic constitution.

I want to argue, here, against both errors: against the naturalness and universality of traditional Western thought about translation, and against its inevitability and immutability. The first is my concern in the rest of this chapter; by exploring the ideosomatic programming that artificially (culturally) unifies Western translation theory, I want to show that what seems intuitively right, natural, the way things are, is ideologically created and enforced and ideosomatically inherited, not transcendentally encoded. The second will be my concern in Chapter 2: by exploring the gaps and cracks in our ideosomatic programming, I want to make a gut-level (idiosomatically persuasive) case for the possibility and desirability of personal and political change.

First, then, in the remainder of this chapter, a brief look at the ideosomatic programming that controls our thought about translation. But not in the abstract. Ideosomatic programming is not just an abstraction: it comes to us as feeling, as somatic response. Our bodies tell us when we are doing what feels right and when we are doing what feels wrong. Beyond that, ideologies were not born in some state of abstract completeness—they are not, and never were, abstract structures or systems that just "happen" to be dominant in society. Ideologies are born out of what people do. They are born out of human interactions, the need for some people (a class, a race, a sex, a group of some sort) to wield power over others, to protect their own interests, and the willingness (forced or persuaded) of some other groups to go along with all that. To the extent that they have any coherence, the group that propagates them tends to look to a single "father" or "formulator" of ideology, an ideologue whose formulation has the function of unifying diverse factions within the ruling group and thus of consolidating their authority for as long as that central formulation goes unchallenged.

For the dominant or mainstream ideology of translation, as of culture in general, we can isolate three great ideologues: Plato, Paul, and Augustine. Augustine in particular (with significant Aristotelian revisions by Thomas Aquinas in the thirteenth century) formulated the medieval synthesis of Plato and Paul that lasted for a thousand years— or rather (since it is still with us today) went unchallenged for a thousand years. Luther's Protestant challenge to Augustine's hegemony and Goethe's romantic challenge to Luther's hegemony proved significant transformative events in the later history of that synthesis, and a discussion of their key texts on translation will take up most of Chapter 2; but for now I want to look (mainly) at the Augustinian ideosomatics of translation, as fleshed out in the *Confessions* and *On Christian Doctrine,* and as characterized by the principles of dualism, instrumentalism, and perfectionism.

Dualism

We are, of course, programmed to dualize everything and to align ourselves emotionally with one side of the dualism, everything and everybody that is unlike us with the other. Then, to cover our tracks, we are programmed to reconceive this emotional alignment in moral terms: our side is "good," the other side "bad." There is to be no concern for gray areas between the two sides of the dualism; all middles are to be rigorously excluded, or rather shunted over to the "bad" side. This is a Greek (Platonic) idea that is picked up by Paul in his formulation of Christian theology and inherited by Augustine as a kind of cultural given.

Inherited—but not slavishly passed on. What Augustine brought to Platonic/Pauline dualism was a stronger emphasis on the blessedness of the spirit and the cursedness of the body than either Jesus or Paul ever imagined. Mind and body, spirit and flesh were important dualisms for those New Testament figures, too; but compared with Augustine, both of them (Jesus especially) seem relatively secure in their bodies, relatively willing to allow people their physical frames, relatively flexible in their understanding of mind/body relations. Jesus said that if your eye betrays you, gouge it out; but he also ate and drank, flew into purple passions at moneychangers and his disciples, stole donkeys, and generally broke the rules whenever he felt like it. He was God's son, after all, the Word made *flesh*. If in fact he was what he said he was, he had no human insecurity about appearances to turn him into a fanatic for principles; and even if he was not, he seems to have been possessed of a powerful enough vision that he let the vision, not strict dualistic rules, guide him. Paul advocated celibacy but said that it was better to marry than to burn—he recognized that perfect spirituality is impossible in the flesh and was flexible enough to bend on the very human matter of sexual desire. Also, for Paul, it is not what goes into the body, but what comes out: thus, there is no point in ritualizing certain eating habits, in protecting the body against contamination, since the problem is not the body and its contamination but what one does with one's body.

But Augustine makes it quite clear in his *Confessions* that he came to the mind/body, spirit/flesh dualism out of a very different background.[27] As an adolescent boy, his body seems programmed for sex—not just biologically, the way everyone's body is, but ideosomatically. Not just programmed for sex, in other words; programmed to seek all satisfaction from sex, to subordinate all desire to physical pleasure. (Or almost all: he was also ambitious.) In our own day consumer capitalism programs us this way, blatantly exploiting sexual desire, intensifying and redirecting it from real people to commodified fantasy images that make us buy consumer products. We are bombarded with pornographic images from early childhood, and the images program us (males especially, but not exclusively) ideosomatically to escalate the *image* of sexual satisfaction to a white-hot fantasy pitch that makes the real satisfactions of sex seem blah by comparison. In our desperation to make reality live up to controlled fantasy expectations, we buy and buy—and the economy prospers.[28] Augustine did not have that, but he evidently had some ideosomatic equivalent (his parents were libertines, for example, who encouraged his sexual adventures and only cautioned him against getting mixed up with married women), since it is obvious that he was extremely susceptible to fantasy images of ultimate satisfaction through sex. Here he is at sixteen, a fourth-century Alexander Portnoy:

Et quid erat, quod me delectabat, nisi amare et amari? sed non tenebatur modus ab animo usque ad animum, quatenus est luminosus limes amicitiae, sed exhalabantur nebulae de limosa concupiscentia carnis et scatebra pubertatis, et obnubilabant atque obfuscabant cor meum, ut non discerneretur serenitas dilectionis a caligine libidinis. utrumque in confuso aestuabat et rapiebat inbecillam aetatem per abrupta cupiditatum atque mersabat gurgite flagitiorum. invaluerat super me ira tua, et nesciebam. obsurdueram stridore catenae mortalitatis meae, poena superbiae animae meae, et ibam longius a te, et sinebas, et iactabar et effundebar et diffluebam et ebulliebam per fornicationes meas, et tacebas. o tardum gaudium meum! tacebas tunc, et ego ibam porro longe a te in plura et plura sterilia semina dolorum superba deiectione et inquieta lassitudine. (2.2)

I cared for nothing but to love and be loved. But my love went beyond the affection of one mind for another [or rather, never reached that "pure" mental state], beyond the arc of the bright beam of friendship. Bodily desire, like a morass, and adolescent sex welling up within me exuded mists which clouded over and obscured my heart, so that I could not distinguish the clear light of true love from the murk of lust. Love and lust together seethed within me. In my tender youth they swept me away over the precipice of my body's appetites and plunged me in the whirlpool of sin. More and more I angered you, unawares. For I had been deafened by the clank of my chains, the fetters of the death which was my due to punish the pride in my soul. I strayed still farther from you and you did not restrain me. I was tossed and spilled, floundering in the broiling sea of my fornication, and you said no word. How long it was before I learned that you were my true joy! You were silent then, and I went on my way, farther and farther from you, proud in my distress and restless in fatigue, sowing more and more seeds whose only crop was grief. (Pine-Coffin's translation, 43–44)[29]

"Excesserunt caput meum vepres libidinum," he says in the next chapter, "et nulla erat eradicans manus" (2.3)—"The brambles of lust grew high over my head, and there was no one to root them out" (45). His father, in fact—his earthly father, an important distinction for Augustine—even rejoices in those brambles, brags about them, drunk, to Augustine's mother. Later, as he writes the book, after his conversion to Christianity, he realizes that his heavenly father had already begun to build his temple in his mother, and it is his mother (or God working through his mother) who eventually leads him away from bodily lust into spiritual truth. In some sense this is a progression down through the three seals: recognizing his lust (first seal); recognizing that it is not just him, that other people are similarly afflicted (second seal); and discovering that he is not stuck with it, he is not powerless before it, he can be liberated from it, and in his conversion in the garden *is* liberated from it (third seal). This is the "eradication" or "rooting out" he talks about: pulling up his programmed somatic response by the roots.[30]

And it is a tremendously important process. We too (modern men like me) need to root out the publicity images of sex programmed into us by capitalist pornography—not "men's magazines" specifically, but all patriarchal advertising, especially the sexy tire ads and car commercials (and so on) that work on us much more powerfully because less consciously than men's magazines. But notice the error that Augustine makes, and that, through Augustine's vast cultural influence, we go on making too. He says his sex mania is the *body's* fault: that it is biological programming, not ideological programming. If it is biology, of course, then we are either stuck, as Freud said we are, at the third seal (no escape from programming), or else, if we want to break through that seal, we need a force from outside biology—God, for instance—a spirit to overthrow the tyranny of the body. We also need an extensive system of political restraints on all those sinners who have not yet let God overthrow their bodies and dedicated themselves to pure spirit. This is the route taken by Augustine, as also by his fundamentalist followers in our day.

Significantly enough, it is also the route taken, in reverse, by contemporary pornographers, who make the very Augustinian assumption that any attack on pornography is an attack on the body, on sex. Hugh Hefner and Company like to play up the agreement between feminists and fundamentalists in their opposition to pornography, saying that they are all anti-sex, anti-body; but feminists and fundamentalists oppose pornography for very different reasons. For feminists, it is not a biological question at all, nothing that can be reduced to the "body" in general, or to sex. It is ideology, or what I have been calling ideosomatic programming, and the answer to that is neither God nor political restraints (although I know some feminists are fighting for the latter as well), but consciousness raising, or what I have called working down through the three seals.[31] The idea then becomes that it is really only possible to enjoy sex when you shake off the programming that makes you compare real sex with the fantasy images that we have been filled with, images of perfect satisfaction that we will never attain (see the section on perfectionism, below). In some sense, in fact, it is pornography that is anti-sex: it tries to replace our real sexual dialogues or interactions (real people, real feelings) with idealized images, usually to sell a product, from *Playboy* to Pontiacs.[32]

Like contemporary fundamentalists, then, Augustine mistook the ideosomatic programming that made him a slave of his "lust" for the natural workings of his body, and condemned all carnality. This is one of the pitfalls of idiosomatic liberation: you liberate yourself from ideosomatic programming, and your liberator becomes your new jailer. To free yourself from a pornographic ideosomatic that makes you see inert sexual objects (satisfaction machines) when you look at women, you put your body in chains (Augustine called it "mortification"). Augustine's liberators from his libertine programming, of course, were Plato and Paul—a fact of immense importance for Western culture. If the Manichees or the Gnostics or some other group had managed to liberate him, and he had put his rhetorical and political talents to work on their behalf, Western civilization might look very different today. That it was the dualizing, idealizing, totalizing Plato and his Jewish follower Paul, with his theology of vicarious sacrifice, who freed Augustine from his programmed somatic response to women meant that the culprit had to be defined as strictly and exclusively *physical,* carnal, bodily—which in fact contributed to the formation of our modern version of the first seal, the insignificance or irrelevance of the body, of somatic response. And liberation had to be conceived in strictly and exclusively idealized, spiritualized, totalized terms: no halfway solutions, no "little of this, little of that," no mediated mind-body answers to the problem. All mind, no body. All faith, no sex. All God, no humans.

The key transitional passage from Augustine's objectification of women as satisfaction machines to his swearing off all sex in the celibacy of the priesthood, therefore, is where Continence (an idealized or desexualized woman) comes to him in a vision:

Sed iam tepidissime hoc dicebat. aperiebatur enim ab ea parte, qua intenderam faciem et quo transire trepidabam, casta dignitas continentiae, serena et non dissolute hilaris, honeste blandiens, ut venirem neque dubitarem, et extendens ad me suscipiendum et amplectendum ias manus, plenas gregibus bonorum exemplorum. ibi tot pueri et puellae, ibi iuventus multa, et omnis aetas, et graves viduae et virgines anus, et in omnibus ipsa continentia, nequaquam sterilis, sed fecunda mater filiorum, gaudiorum de marito te, domine. et inridebat me inrisione hortatoria, quasi diceret: "tu non poteris, quod isti, quod istae? an vero isti et istae in se ipsis possunt ac non in domino deo suo? dominus deus eorum me dedit eis. quic in te stas et non in te stas? proice te in eum, noli metuere; non se subtrahet, ut cadas: proice te securus, excipiet et sanabit te." et erubescebam nimis, quia illarum nugarum murmura adhuc audiebam, et cunctabundus pendebam. et rursus illa, quasi diceret: "obsurdesce adversus inmunda illa membra tua, ut mortificentur. narrant tibi delectationes, sed non sicut lex domini dei tui." (8.11)

But by now the voice of habit was very faint. I had turned my eyes elsewhere, and while I stood trembling at the barrier, on the other side I could see the chaste beauty of Continence in all her serene, unsullied joy, as she modestly beckoned me to cross over and to hesitate no more. She stretched out loving hands to welcome and embrace me, holding up a host of good examples to my sight. With her were countless boys and girls, great numbers of the young and people of all ages, staid widows and women still virgins in old age. And in their midst was Continence herself, not barren but a fruitful mother of children, of joys born to you, O Lord, her Spouse. She smiled at me to give me courage, as though she were saying, "Can you not do what these men and women do? Do you think they find the strength to do it in themselves and not in the Lord their God? It was the Lord their God who gave me to them. Why do you try to stand in your own strength and fail? Cast yourself upon God and have no fear. He will not shrink away and let you fall. Cast yourself upon him without fear, for he will welcome you and cure you of your ills." I was overcome with shame, because I was still listening to the futile mutterings of my lower self and I was still hanging in suspense. And again Continence seemed to say, "Close your ears to the unclean whispers of your body, so that it may be mortified. It tells you of things that delight you, but not such things as the law of the Lord your God has to tell." (176)

Delight versus God's law—this is a dualism that would trouble Luther a thousand years later. The voice of bodily delight must be *completely* silenced, so that the voice of God's law might speak unhindered. Chastity, continence, celibacy: herein lies holiness. The mortification of the body. The only fruitfulness is a spiritual fruitfulness: the offspring are not real children but "joys born of you, O Lord, her Spouse." Augustine next hears some children playing some game, repeating over and over, "Tolle lege" (8.12), "Take it and read" (178), so he picks up his Bible, opens it at random, and his eyes light on a passage from Romans denying the body (13:13–14). Now he is flooded by God's spirit, and he "turns"—is converted. "statim quippe eum fine huiusce sententiae, quasi luce securitatis infusa cordi meo, omnes dubitationis tenebrae diffugerunt" (8.12)—"For in an instant, as I came to the end of the sentence, it was as though the light of confidence flooded into my heart and all the darkness of doubt was dispelled" (178).

His next step, once his friend Alypius has converted by the same method, is to go in and tell his mother (now sainted, on the analogy of Jesus and Mary, by a church grateful to her son) what had happened. The progression is clear: from mistresses, through a vision of Continence (as idealized woman), to mother. In his section on the *Confessions* in *The Rhetoric of Religion* (a treatment that I have relied on throughout), Kenneth Burke shows how Augustine's rhetoric of eternity, an "inhering" or "clinging" ("inhaere") to "everlasting plenty" ("ubertatis indeficientis," 9.10) is implicitly a clinging to the breast ("uber"), a breast that never runs dry, is never withdrawn from the hungry infant. His mother was his first glimpse of eternity, in the form of a breast—which is to say, he conceives of eternity by idealizing his infantile experience of complete satisfaction at the breast and deidealizing the dissatisfactions of "bodily" life that began, presumably, with his weaning, and that included his fruitless attempts in adolescence and early manhood to regain that lost ubertatis by clinging to the breasts of his female peers. So, understandably, when he converts, the first thing he does is to go in and tell her of it; and, again understandably, when she dies in book 9 he uses that event to bring his narrative to a close: the death of his mother allows him to spiritualize her, to see her in transcendental terms, to idealize her in terms not of mortality (body) but of God's eternity (spirit). The four remaining books are theology—which is to say, his attempt to transform his transcended (spiritualized) mother into an ideological program for the mother church.

This in a nutshell is Augustine's confessional progress from body to spirit: from an evil, fallen carnality that impinges upon him too insistently for his peace of mind, to its opposite, spiritual celibacy, conceived as complete salvation from the dissatisfactions of carnal life. Either-or: flesh or spirit. No mixture between the two. No gray areas. Any passion that seems to point to God (his love for his mother, for example) must be separated from the body, must be seen as strictly spiritual. The corporeality of Jesus as the Word made flesh must be explained in a spiritual sense: one understands without being told, one's body knows, ideosomatically, that one is not supposed to imagine Jesus having, say, erections (or the celibate Augustine, for that matter, having wet dreams). This fierce separation of spirit from body, motivated by Augustine's own adolescent susceptibility (to put it mildly) to the demands of the flesh, becomes one of the cornerstones of the medieval church—and, through the cultural heritage left us by that church, one of the cornerstones of our ideosomatic response still today.

Or is that true? Am I making just a bit too much of Augustine's relevance to the late twentieth century? Hasn't Augustine been dead fifteen hundred-odd years? His body has, certainly; but what has been called his "spirit," and what I prefer to call his ideological body, the ideosomatic programming built on the phenomenal success of his conversion and confession, is with us still today. Even as Christianity has begun (over the past two or three centuries) to lose its intellectual or theoretical credibility as a systematic explanation of the universe, Augustine's mind/body, spirit/flesh dualism has retained all its original force in our ideosomatic response. Some of the reasons are obvious. Science, Christianity's ideological successor, has only recently begun to question the mind/body dualism. And even then we resist scientific formulations that seem to us counterintuitive: the notion some neurophysiologists have proposed that there is no such thing as mind, for example; that mind is only one name we like to give to the working of the body (mind as a function of the synapses). The deepest strata of our ideosomatic programming have not changed: our fear of the body, our fear of emotional vulnerability, our fear of losing control, our fear of anything that would leave the adult in the fearful position of childhood dependency—all this remains unchanged from the Augustinian church. (My own example in the first part of this chapter is instructive: having learned to recognize my own conditioned fear of the body, I do an about-face and begin defending the body against the mind. The same dualism, only now in reverse.)

Probably the best evidence of the survival of this dualistic medieval ideology in our day is in our still very Augustinian conception of men and women. Men are still linked with mind or spirit (and are therefore privileged), women with body (and are therefore deprivileged). In *The Resisting Reader,* Judith Fetterley bitterly attacks the patriarchal ideology according to which "the only good woman is a dead woman" (in the American novel, specifically, but generally also, she claims, in patriarchal society). But in one sense this is just a demystification of the idealization by which Augustine "transcended" the death of his mother. Since bodies for Augustine were purely evil and real women (Eve's daughters) were purely carnal, the only good woman in his patriarchal ideology is an *ideal* woman, which is to say a purely spiritual woman (Continentia). And the best way to idealize or spiritualize a woman is after her death. The same thing applies to men, for Augustine, except that men in his Platonic system are more closely allied to intellect and spirit and therefore can take on ideal spiritual qualities in this life (insofar as they have dedicated their lives to God and sworn off sex). It is rhetorically useful for a radical feminist like Fetterley to attack men for their supposed desire to see all women dead. But from a masculist point of view all that is really involved is men's ideosomatically programmed fear of their own bodies, which have a nasty habit of making them feel vulnerable and childlike, and their attempts to idealize everything that seems to protect them from their bodies (especially from an awareness of their bodies) and to deidealize everything that leaves them feeling vulnerable. Women—carnal, emotional creatures that remind men too much of their mommies—become the instruments of these attempts. (This is not to deflect feminist charges; it is only to put them in a different perspective, the perspective of masculine psychology.)

Minds and bodies. Men and women. And then: meanings and words. Augustine himself made the connection between the mind/body dualism and language clear all through his writing. As a word-man himself, an ex-teacher of rhetoric who after his conversion put his considerable rhetorical skills to work for God, Augustine was fascinated by the parallels between minds and bodies on the one hand and meanings and words on the other. One of the key events in his conversion was the teaching of Ambrose on Paul's principle from 2 Corinthians, that "the letter killeth, but the spirit giveth life": the letter, the body, is no good, so throw it out; the spirit, the meaning, or a spiritualized (allegorically interpreted) meaning is good (6.4). And at several points in the *Confessions* (especially in book 11) he specifically equates God's Word with the "meaning" of a sentence that is only clear in the listener's mind after the sentence has been completed. But the full doctrinal force of Augustine's equations between language and minds/bodies is really only clear in *De doctrina Christiana,* in passages like this:

Quomodo venit, nisi quod *verbum caro factum est et habitavit in nobis?* Sicuti cum loquimur, ut id, quod animo gerimus, in audientis animum per aures carneas inlabatur, *fit sonus* verbum quod corde gestamus, et locutio vocatur, nec tamen in eundem sonum cogitatio nostra convertitur, sed apud se manens integra, formam vocis qua se insinuet auribus, sine aliqua labe suae mutationis adsumit: ita verbum dei non commutatum caro tamen factum est, ut habitaret in nobis. (1.13)

How did He come except that "the Word was made flesh, and dwelt among us"? It is as when we speak. In order that what we are thinking may reach the mind of the listener through the fleshly ears, that which we have in mind is expressed in words and is called speech. But our thought is not transformed into sounds; it remains entire in itself and assumes the form of words by means of which it may reach the ears without suffering any deterioration in itself. In the same way the Word of God was made flesh without change that He might dwell among us. (Robertson's translation, 14)

Thought ("cogitatio") is to spoken words ("locutio") as the spiritual Word of God is to the carnal body of Christ: as what is permanent is to its temporary vehicle or container. This is one of the central statements of Western ideology concerning words and meanings, bodies and spirits/souls/minds. But we do not experience ideology in the form of statements like this; we experience it in our own ideosomatic impulses, responses, needs, motivations: an example is our inclination to agree with Augustine, at least allegorically, on some level, even if we discard his specific theological formulations. It *feels right* to think of meaning as something that assumes the form of words without actually becoming subject to the flux and change of physical speech—as something permanent, stable, unchanging. It *feels right* to think of words as labels that can be peeled off a meaning and replaced with no change in the meaning. This is the ideosomatic "rightness" behind Saussure's insistence that we study not *la parole,* actual speech, that unpleasantly physical, and therefore chaotic and fallen, phenomenon, but *la langue,* the "spiritual" or idealized system that supposedly undergirds our speech. It is the rightness that Saussure feels in propounding it and the rightness that tens of thousands of linguists have felt in following it. Of course: what else can we do but ignore the "body" of speech?[33] And it is the ideosomatic rightness that motivates most mainstream translation theory in the West: translate sense for sense, not word for word. Peel off the SL verbal label and replace it with a TL verbal label. Anything that can be expressed in one language can be expressed without loss of meaning in any other. Meaning is stable and universal. We are all humans, aren't we? We can't be *that* different, surely?

This works with men and women, too. Men are creatures of many thoughts (deep meanings) but few words. Women talk too much—and think too little. Nowadays there is a good deal of talk about men's inability to express their feelings—the old ideosomatic ideal has become a handicap. But it remains an ideosomatic ideal. If two thousand years of cultural programming have taught you to keep things in, you are not going to open up the floodgates the instant some blabbermouth woman says you ought to. All of a sudden everybody is supposed to be a woman! That is what it feels like. Note also Augustine's mixed feelings about language: the word master, the brilliant rhetorician, one of the most influential writers of all time, despised his own facility with words because God's Word was above or beyond all speech. I *should* be more self-contained! I shouldn't blab all this stuff about my childhood to God and everybody. Keep it in! Save it up! "et quid diximus, deus meus, vita mea, dulcedo mea sancta, aut quid dicit aliquis, cum de te dicit? et vae tacentibus de te, quoniam loquaces muti suut" (1.4)—"You are my God, my Life, my holy Delight, but is this enough to say of you? Can any man [not woman] say enough when he speaks of you? Yet woe betide those who are silent about you! For even those who are most gifted with speech [me, for instance] cannot find words to describe you" (23).

In Augustine's Platonic/Pauline synthesis, the mind/body, meaning/ word, and men/women dualisms take other forms, too—*all* forms, in fact, since for his theology to be "universal" and therefore spiritually "true" everything has to be reduced to the same two terms, which ultimately coalesce as God and Satan. One that he inherited directly from Plato was ideal/real, as skeptics prefer to phrase it, or real/apparent, as believers would have it. This dualism trains us to doubt the evidence of our senses (our bodies): what lies immediately before us, underneath our noses, what feels real, is sheer appearance, sheer unanalyzed matter. What is "real," really real, lies somewhere "beyond," in what Plato called the Realm of Forms, or what Paul and Augustine called the Word of God, and can only be retrieved by the power of mind to sift through complexity to simplicity, through flux to stability, through chaotic impressions to system. What is visible, tangible, "sensible," is less real and less valuable than what is invisible and therefore only thinkable, conceivable, analyzable. What can be felt is less real and valuable than what can be thought. Emotional sensation is inchoate and therefore unreal; rational thought is clearly articulated, structured, stabilized, and therefore real. Women's domestic world seems unreal; men's intellectual world seems real. Translation rules are more real and more valuable than individual translator decisions. Structures of equivalence are more real and more valuable than translator- and situation-specific, idiosomatically grounded "feelings" of equivalence.

The split between what is ideal and what is real (between what is invisible and what is visible, and so on) also suggests or generates a distinction I wrestled with in my Introduction: the one between theory and practice. Translation practice is "unreal," or possesses only a secondary reality as a confused veil or mask for the simple and stable clarity of systematic translation theory; that simplicity, that stability, that clarity, that system is to be obtained, as Melville's Ahab said of the "unreasoning thing" behind the whale, only by striking through the mask. But theory and practice is a modern phrasing. For Augustine and his ecclesiastical successors down to the thirteenth or fourteenth centuries, it was a distinction between God's law and fallen worldly life— which in turn required a distinction between the clergy and the laity, between the men who had most thoroughly internalized God's law (as we see Augustine doing in his *Confessions*) and were therefore best qualified to oversee its proper operation in the fallen world, and the men and women and children who were supposed to internalize the principles the clergy taught, or at the very least conform to them externally. (Note that the lay public may have been biologically men or women, boys or girls, but in the medieval hierarchy they were all idealized as women [God's bride], children [God's children], or sheep [the pastor's flock].)

As Alexander Murray shows in *Reason and Society in the Middle Ages,* this ecclesiastical hierarchy flowed gradually into its most influential modern form in the High Middle Ages (thirteenth and fourteenth centuries), in the rise of a secular intelligentsia. This group propagated reason instead of faith and drew a sharp distinction between their own urban sophistication and the uncritical beliefs of the *rustici,* the rustics, or country bumpkins, who never questioned anything.[34] This gives us the opposition between the philosopher or the scientist or the expert or the consultant on the one hand and pragmatic, practical, common-sensical know-how on the other. Intellectuals and the masses. Translation theorists and translators.

This hierarchy is reenacted in our gender expectations. Men, we assume, "naturally" intellectual and ill at ease in the alien (feminine) world of feelings and intuitions, gravitate toward translation theory; if they translate, they like to rise above "mere" translation by generalizing from practice to universal rule, or participate in projects aimed at the development of a working machine translator. Women, on the other hand, "naturally" emotional and unequipped to operate in the alien (masculine) world of ideas and analyses, gravitate toward translation (the majority of translators in the West, including interpreters and those cross-lingual secretaries known as business translators, appear to be women). When a woman decides to become a theorist, she must prove herself by being at least as logical, analytical, and systematic as her male peers. There is no question of somatic response; that would be sneered at as "feminine" translation theory—that is, no theory at all.

What this hierarchized dualism's medieval background shows is that, as a specifically Christian (Augustinian, medieval) dualism, it is not just a neutral or pluralistic distinction between groups (you do your thing, I'll do mine). It is *morally* charged. It entails a morally charged distinction between the theorist (the person able to strike through the mask of appearances and grasp the stable reality beyond) and the practitioner (the uncritical slave of mundane perception who takes appearances to be realities). It is easy to miss this, however, since one of the things the onward march of humanism has meant is a trickling down of self-respect to ever lower and lower levels of the medieval hierarchy, so that mechanics and factory workers and women and foreigners and alcoholics and the insane (et cetera) all want a share of the self-esteem that was once the prerogative only of the ruling class.

Liberal ideology has tried to charge that shift with the moral values of pluralism—equality, different but equal, every man, woman, child, animal, whale, seal, and tree for him-, her-, or itself (you may have money and power and a penis, but I have my self-respect too)—but it doesn't really work that way. As an excluded group raises its consciousness and begins to develop self-respect and to demand the respect of others, it typically tries to reverse the reigning moral and political hierarchy, to seize power from the oppressors and become the new oppressors, or, barring that (since it is usually a pretty difficult task), at least to imagine themselves as morally superior to their oppressors ("good" as opposed to their "evil"). Workers are better than owners (Marx). Women are better than men (radical feminists). Translators are better than translation theorists (my students). Labor, emotion, and practice are better than capital, reason, and theory. Given the difficulty of usurping power from the oppressors, all this usually means is opposition, setting up a counterhierarchy or countermorality—hostile relations, in other words, defended on each side by a hierarchical ideology that privileges *us* and deprivileges *them*. Thus the situation I described in the Introduction—the situation I am trying to talk our way out of in this book.

Instrumentalism

One of the key principles of Platonic/Pauline/Augustinian hierarchized dualism is that everybody (except God, who is at the top) is an instrument of the level above and an instrumentalizer of the level below. Laymen are instruments of the clergy, and the clergy are instruments of God. Laymen instrumentalize laywomen. Women instrumentalize children. Boys instrumentalize girls. Girls instrumentalize dolls. Given any two levels in the hierarchy, the higher level is the "good" side of the dualism that wields the lower, or "evil," side of the dualism as its instrument.

Augustine as the Bishop of Hippo and founding father of medieval Christianity is up there at the top of the human scale and can beg God to instrumentalize him directly: "Sed nunc in anima mea clamet deus meus, et veritas tua dicat mihi: non est ita, non est ita" (*Confessiones* 1.13.)—"But now, my God, let your voice ring in my soul and let your truth proclaim to me that it is wrong to think this" (34). "Exaudi, domine, deprecationem meam, ne deficiat anima mea sub disciplina tua" (1.15.)—"Grant my prayer, O Lord, and do not allow my soul to wilt under the discipline which you prescribe" (35). As the Middle Ages grow old, this direct instrumentalizing dialogue between God and man (not woman yet) slips down to lower and lower rungs on the hierarchy, until even a lowly monk like Saint Francis can pray, "Lord, make me an instrument of thy will." And then the bourgeois intellectuals who in the sixteenth and seventeenth centuries gradually shift ground from Aristotelian philosophy to empirical science can split off some abstract attribute of Augustine's God, like truth (for the metaphysician), or justice (for the judge), goodness (for the ethical philosopher), beauty (for the aesthetician), fact (for the scientist), history (for Marx), and so on, and beg that they be instrumentalized by *it*. The abstraction becomes a sovereign power in its own right: a force that wields the secular thinker as a tool in its own propagation. The thinker does not ride on the abstraction to the satisfaction of his (still not her) own propagandistic program, out of inner emotional motivations; the thinker subordinates his will to the abstraction's use.

As conceptions of God are secularized and demystified, of course—removed from the awesome aura of mystical possession that we associate with gods—this idealized image becomes harder to maintain. The thinker's own emotional motivations become more and more transparent, which is why, for example, scientists (especially physical scientists up until the mid-twentieth century, when quantum physics became widely accepted, and social and linguistic scientists in our day) become increasingly obsessed with the research methodology and technology that protect their reputation for objectivity.

One constant in this development is the Logos, or Logic, a stable structure of meaning that we are all taught to seek out and subordinate ourselves to. Because the writers of the Bible subordinated their words to the Word of God—the Logos, which was no uttered word but sheer meaning—we can speak of the Bible itself as God's Word. Strictly speaking, it is not that, since God's Word is single and pure and unified and so on, but it is instrumentally subordinated to God's Word, and therefore the next best thing. Translators, too—first Bible translators, later all translators—are expected to subordinate their words and their wills to the deified "meaning" of the original text as well. It is in this sense that we can speak of a Bible translation too as "God's Word." It is not God's Word, strictly speaking; in fact it stands at two human removes from God's Word, since first the human writer and then the translator has had to interpret it in fallen human language. But if the translator allows him- or herself to be instrumentally subordinated to God's Word, a Bible translation too can be the next best thing. The works of Eugene A. Nida, translation consultant to the American Bible

Society and himself a confessing Christian, bristle with this assumption; we expect that. But the same assumption is everywhere present in contemporary translation theory: that the translator has a responsibility to the original writer, that the translator is not to usurp the authority of the original writer, that the translator is a TL instrument of the SL writer, and so on. At some deep ideosomatic level, Bible translation even today remains the model for all Western thought about translation.

Augustine again provides the paradigmatic formulation. In *De doctrina Christiana,* for example, he charts a seven-step progression to wisdom that I believe is the procedure that ideosomatically still underlies all translation (I quote Augustine and Robertson's translation, then paraphrase for translation):

1. Ante omnia igitur opus est dei timore converti ad cognoscendam eius voluntatem, quid nobis appetendum fugiendumque praecipiat. (2.7.9)

Before all it is necessary that we must be turned by the fear of God toward a recognition of His will, so that we may know what He commands that we desire and what He commands that we avoid. (38)

Translators must first be turned by the fear of critical censure toward an awareness of the SL writer's intention—what he or she wants them to convey, what not to convey, to the TL receptor.

2. Deinde mitescere opus est pietate neque contradicere divinae scripturae sive intellectae, si aliqua vitia nostra percutit, sive non intellectae, quasi nos melius sapere meliusque praecipere possimus. (2.7.9)

Then it is necessary that we become meek through piety so that we do not contradict Divine Scripture, either when it is understood and is seen to attack some of our vices, or when it is not understood and we feel as though we are wiser than it is and better able to give percepts. (38)

Translators must become meek through a sense of their professional responsibility so that they do not contradict the original writer's intention, no matter how personally attacked or affronted they may feel.

3. Post istos duos gradus timoris atque pietatis ad tertium venitur scientiae gradum. . . . Necesse est ergo, ut primo sequisque in scripturis inveniat amore huius saeculi, hoc est, temporalium rerum, implicatum, longe seiunctum esse a tanto amore dei et tanto amore proximi, quantum scriptura ipsa praescribit. Tum vero ille timor, quo cogitat de iudicio dei, et illa pietas, qua non potest nisi credere et cedere auctoritati sanctorum librorum, cogit eum se ipsum lugere. (2.7.10)

After these two steps of fear and piety the third step of knowledge confronts us. . . . Then it follows that the student first will discover in the Scriptures that he has been enmeshed in the love of this world, or of temporal things, a love far remote from the kind of love of God and of our neighbor which Scripture itself prescribes. Then, indeed, that fear which arises from the thought of God's judgment, and that piety which can do nothing except believe in and accede to the authority of the sacred books, will force him to lament his own situation. (39)

Translators must gain knowledge of the SL text, study its vocabulary, do a textual analysis, study the author's life and times, and so on. This will teach them their own inadequacy in comparison to the SL author, their enmeshedness in the here and now of their own TL situation, their enormous limitations as translators of this particular text. Having learned to fear criticism and submitted to what cultural authorities call their responsibility, they will now learn to lament their own situation.

4. Quo affectu impetrat sedulis precibus consolationem divini adiutorii, ne desperatione frangatur, et esse incipit in quarto gradu, hoc est fortitudinis, quo esuritur et sititur iustitia. (2.7.10)

This attitude causes him to ask with constant prayers for the consolation of divine assistance lest he fall into despair, and he thus enters the fourth step of fortitude, in which he hungers and thirsts for justice. (39)

Lest instrumentalized translators, wracked with the sense of their own inadequacy that they have been taught to cultivate, fall into despair and stop translating, they must cling to an institutionally generated fortitude that says, "No matter if it can't be done perfectly; the translator is always a traducer; do your best. No one can fault you for that." Deep in their hearts they long for a time when translation will either succeed perfectly or be unnecessary (rescission of the curse of Babel).

5. Quam ubi aspexerit, quantum potest, in longinqua radiantem, suique aspectus infirmitate sustinere se illam lucem non posse persenserit; in quinto gradu, hoc est in consilio misericordiae, purgat animam tumultuantem quodammodo atque obstrepentem sibi de appetitu inferiorum conceptis sordibus. Hic vero se in dilectione proximi naviter exercet in eaque perficitur. (2.7.11)

When, in so far as he is able, he has seen this Trinity glowing in the distance, and has discovered that because of his weakness he cannot sustain the sight of that light, he purges his mind, which is rising up and protesting in the appetite for inferior things, of its contaminations, so that he comes to the fifth step, the counsel of mercy. Here he eagerly exercises the love of his neighbor and perfects himself in it. (39–40)

Translators too, aware of their own lamentable inability to grasp or contain the brilliance of the SL text, are expected to purge their minds (not to mention their bodies, which are unmentionable) of all personal contaminations, idiosomatic experiences, the desire to draw on the inner resources that feel so important, and all protest against the injustice of ideosomatic programming. If nothing else, they should think of the TL reader, who deserves an accurate reproduction of the SL writer's intentions.

6. Et spe iam plenus atque integer viribus, cum pervenerit usque ad inimici dilectionem, ascendit in sextum gradum, ubi iam ipsum oculum purgat, quo videri deus potest, quantum potest ab eis, qui huic saeculo moriuntur, quantum possunt. (2.7.11)

And now, filled with hope and fortified in strength, when he arrives at the love of his enemy he ascends to the sixth step, where he cleanses that eye through which God may be seen, in so far as He can be seen by those who die to the world as much as they are able. (40)

The translator, too, is programmed to cleanse that interlingual eye through which meaning may be seen, and to become (or generate in the TL) a transparent window to the original text—insofar as this is possible for translators who die to their own personal experience as much as they are able.

7. Erit ergo iste sanctus tam simplici corde atque mundato, ut neque hominibus placendi studio detorqueatur a vero nec respectu devitandorum quorumlibet incommodorum suorum, quae adversantur huic vitae. Talis filius ascendit ad sapientam, quae ultima et septima est. (2.7.11)

Therefore this holy one will be of such simple and clean heart that he will not turn away from the Truth either in a desire to please men or for the sake of avoiding any kind of adversities to himself which arise in this life. Such a son ascends to wisdom, which is the seventh and last step, where he enjoys peace and tranquillity. (40)[35]

Perfectionism

That is the consolation: peace and tranquillity, the rewards for doing as your body tells you to do, not struggling against the ideosomatic current. And the result, textually speaking, is perfect translation:

Et latinis quibuslibet emendandis graeci adhibeantur, in quibus Septuaginta interpretum, quod ad vetus testamentum attinet, excellit auctoritas; qui iam per omnes peritiores ecclesias tanta praesentia sancti spiritus interpretati esse dicuntur, ut os unum tot hominum fuerit. Qui si, ut fertur, multique non indigni fide praedicant, singuli cellis etiam singulis separati cum interpretati essent, nihil in alicuius eorum codice inventum est, quod non iisdem verbis eodemque verborum ordine inveniretur in ceteris. Quis huic auctoritati conferre aliquid nedum praeferre audeat? Si autem contulerunt, ut una omnium communi tractatu iudicioque vox fieret, ne sic quidem quemquam unum hominem qualibet peritia ad emendandum tot seniorum doctorumque consensum aspirare oportet aut decet. Quamobrem etiamsi aliquid aliter in hebraeis exemplaribus invenitur, quam isti posuerunt, cedendum esse arbitror divinae dispensationi, quae per eos facta est. (2.15.22)

And in emending Latin translations, Greek translations are to be consulted, of which the Septuagint carries most authority in so far as the Old Testament is concerned. In all the more learned churches it is now said that this translation was so inspired by the Holy Spirit that many men spoke as if with the mouth of one. It is said and attested by many of not unworthy faith that, although the translators were separated in various cells while they worked, nothing was to be found in any version that was not found in the same words and with the same order of words in all of the others. Who would compare any other authority with this, or, much less, prefer another? But even if they conferred and arrived at a single opinion on the basis of common judgment and consent, it is not right or proper for any man, no matter how learned, to seek to emend the consensus of so many older and more learned men. Therefore, even though something is found in Hebrew versions different from what they have set down, I think we should cede to the divine dispensation by which they worked. (49)[36]

Inspiration by the Holy Spirit makes it possible to reach beyond the words of the original text to God's true meaning, God's Logos, and to translate it so perfectly that the translation supersedes the original. This is the great ideal of all mainstream (ideosomatically controlled) Western translation. The translator's perfect submission to instrumentalism, through the seven steps of fear, piety, knowledge, fortitude, mercy, cleansing the eye, and wisdom, makes possible the perfect transmission of SL meaning. Or of Meaning itself, meaning with a capital *M*, transcendental meaning, God's Word—conveying that meaning better than the corrupt (because humanly inscribed and transmitted) SL text. The perfectionist ideal of Western (Christian) translation is to extract the meaning from one verbal expression and to fit it with another and *better*—a perfect vehicle, one that embodies the true meaning imperfectly fleshed out by the SL text. In Augustine's praise for the Septuagint, there is a good deal of underlying insecurity and anxiety with regard to the Hebrew original, which (partly because he was ignorant of Hebrew) he instructed Jerome *not* to use for the Vulgate; but the idea itself rests on the Pauline doctrine of the resurrection of the body, which Augustine refers to repeatedly in the *Confessions* (all through book 7 and in 10.31) by way of proving that God cannot be a body:

35 Ἀλλὰ ἐρεῖ τις, Πῶς ἐγείρονται οἱ νεκροί; ποίῳ δὲ σώματι ἔρχονται; 36 ἄφρων, σὺ ὃ σπείρεις οὐ ζῳοποιεῖται ἐὰν μὴ ἀποθάνῃ· 37 καὶ ὃ σπείρεις, οὐ τὸ σῶμα τὸ γενησόμενον σπείρεις ἀλλὰ γυμνὸν κόκκον εἰ τύχοι σίτου ἤ τινος τῶν λοιπῶν· 38 ὁ δὲ θεὸς δίδωσιν αὐτῷ σῶμα καθὼς ἠθέλησεν, καὶ ἑκάστῳ τῶν σπερμάτων ἴδιον σῶμα. 39 οὐ πᾶσα σὰρξ ἡ αὐτὴ σάρξ, ἀλλὰ ἄλλη μὲν ἀνθρώπων, ἄλλη δὲ σὰρξ κτηνῶν, ἄλλη δὲ σὰρξ πτηνῶν, ἄλλη δὲ ἰχθύων. 40 καὶ σώματα ἐπουράνια, καὶ σώματα ἐπίγεια· ἀλλὰ ἑτέρα μὲν ἡ τῶν ἐπουρανίων δόξα, ἑτέρα δὲ ἡ τῶν ἐπιγείων. 41 ἄλλη δόξα ἡλίου, καὶ ἄλλη δόξα σελήνης, καὶ ἄλλη δόξα ἀστέρων· ἀστὴρ γὰρ ἀστέρος διαφέρει ἐν δόξῃ.

42 Οὕτως καὶ ἡ ἀνάστασις τῶν νεκρῶν. σπείρεται ἐν φθορᾷ, ἐγείρεται ἐν ἀφθαρσίᾳ· 43 σπείρεται ἐν ἀτιμίᾳ, ἐγείρεται ἐν δόξῃ· σπείρεται ἐν ἀσθενείᾳ, ἐγείρεται ἐν δυνάμει· 44 σπείρεται σῶμα ψυχικόν, ἐγείρεται σῶμα πνευματικόν. εἰ ἔστιν σῶμα ψυχικόν, ἔστιν καὶ πνευματικόν. 45 οὕτωθ καὶ γέγραπται, **ἐγένετο ὁ πρῶτοθ ἄνθρωπος** ᾽αδὰμ **εἰς ψυχὴν ζῶσαν·** ὁ ἔσχατοθ ᾽αδὰμ εἰθ πνεῦμα ζῳοποιοῦν. 46 ἀλλ᾽ οὐ πρῶτον τὸ πνευματικὸν ἀλλὰ τὸ ψυχικόν, ἔπειτα τὸ πνευματικόν. 47 ὁ πρῶτοθ ἄνθρωπος ἐκ γῆς χοϊκός, ὁ δεύτερος ἄνθρωπος ἐξ οὐρανοῦ. 48 οἷος ὁ χοϊκός, τοιοῦτοι καὶ οἱ χοϊκοί, καὶ οἷος ὁ ἐπουράνιος, τοιοῦτοι καὶ οἱ ἐπουράνιοι· 49 καὶ καθὼς ἐφορέσαμεν τὴν εἰκόνα τοῦ χοϊκοῦ, φορέσομεν καὶ τὴν εἰκόνα τοῦ ἐπουρανίου.

50 Τοῦτο δέ φημι, ἀδελφοί, ὅτι σὰρξ καὶ αἷμα βασιλείαν θεοῦ κληρονομῆσαι οὐ δύναται, οὐδὲ ἡ φθορὰ τὴν ἀφθαρσίαν κληρονομεῖ. 51 ἰδοὺ μυστήριον ὑμῖν λέγω· πάντες οὐ κοιμηθησόμεθα, πάντες δὲ ἀλλαγησόμεθα, 52 ἐν ἀτόμῳ, ἐν ῥιπῇ ὀφθαλμοῦ, ἐν τῇ ἐσχάτῃ σάλπιγγι· σαλπίσει γάρ, καὶ οἱ νεκροὶ ἐγερθήσονται ἄφθαρτοι, καὶ ἡμεῖς ἀλλαγησόμεθα.

(1 Cor 15:35–52)

35. Now someone will ask: "How do the dead live again? What kind of body do they have?" Listen, silly, when you plant something, it won't come up unless it dies. And what you plant is not the new stalk but just a plain seed of, say, wheat or some other plant. Then God gives to it the form that he thinks best, and to each kind of seed its own particular form. . . . And that's the way it is with the afterlife. Something perishable is planted, and it comes up imperishable. Something weak is planted, and it comes up powerful. A vessel of the mind is planted, and a vessel of the spirit comes up. There's a Scripture which says, "The first man Adam became a rational being." The last Adam (Christ) became a life-creating spirit. Note that the spiritual does not precede the rational, but vice versa. The first man sprang from earth, a lump of clay. The second man sprang from the spiritual realm. Just as the descendants of the lump of clay are themselves lumps of clay, so the descendants of the Immortal One are them-

selves immortal. And as the lump of clay gave form to us, even so shall the Immortal One give form to us.

50. I'm saying simply this, brothers: Skin and bones just aren't able to get into God's realm of spirit, nor can that which is subject to decay take part in that which is immortal. Listen, I'll let you in on a secret: Not all of us will die, but all of us will be changed. It'll happen in a flash, like the batting of an eye, at the last bugle call. (Jordan's translation, 72)

This begins to sound like the romantics, whose translation theories I look at in the next chapter: the translator writes the perfect translation, and in a flash all is changed. The imperishable essence, or meaning, of the perishable SL text is extracted and fitted with a perfect "soma pneumatikon," or "spiritual" body, a new vessel for the SL "mind," or meaning, a TL text that is ideally suited to its payload—purified, perfected, made to last forever. No more dusty old translations, worse than the original; instead, a heavenly translation, infinitely better than the original, made by the Holy Spirit, made redemptive by the Spirit. And the bugle sounds, and we are changed.

The problem with all this is that perfectionism idealizes translation out of the realm of the possible. Not only translation, of course: all action aimed at satisfaction. Anything less than perfect satisfaction cannot satisfy at all, because it is not perfect. Augustine says in his *Confessions:*

Sed inter flagitia et facinora et tam multas iniquitates sunt peccata proficientium, quae a bene iudicantibus et vituperantur ex regula perfectionis, et laudantur spe frugis sicut herba segetis. (3.9)

Among these vices and crimes and all the endless ways in which men do wrong there are also the sins of those who follow the right path but go astray. By the rule of perfection these lapses are condemned, if we judge them aright, but the sinners may yet be praised, for they give promise of better fruit to come, like the young shoots which later bear the ears of corn. (66–67)

Paraphrased, this could be seen as the definitive statement of translation perfectionism in the West: "Among these slips and inadequacies and all the endless ways in which translators err there are also the failings of those who strive toward sense-for-sense equivalence but go astray. By the rule of perfection these lapses are condemned, if we judge them aright, but the translators may yet be praised, for they give promise of better fruit to come, like the young shoots which later bear the ears of corn." Better fruit—but never the best. They may be praised, on a relative human scale, for their proximity to the perfectionist ideal; but they will never attain perfection, and anything less than perfection is, if judged aright, to be condemned.

This ideology of perfection both proceeds from and activates the fourth step in Augustine's seven-step progression to wisdom, the controlled dialectic between despair and fortitude. We are programmed not only to dualize experience into good (our side) and bad (their side) and to align ourselves with an idealized force representing good that wields us as its tool or instrument, we are also programmed to believe that oneness with that force—and therefore perfect knowledge of the good, perfect subordination to the good, perfect instrumentality—is impossible on this earth. We are programmed, in other words, to submit our desires to inaccessible images of promise, and thus to frustration.

Thus the impossibility also of ever translating perfectly. The original is a goal that we will never reach. It possesses a perfection of phrasing and diction that we will never attain. *Traduttore,* therefore, is always *traditore.* The translator always traduces. Translation must be defined in terms of inevitable failure. But we must keep trying: we are programmed not only to experience our task as inherently impossible but to conceal that very programmed experience from ourselves, to hide it behind the ever-alluring image of a successful translation—precisely that which, by the terms of our ideosomatic programming, we feel we will never achieve. Institutional, gut-wrenching fortitude. Keep hoping for what you can never have; keep conceiving what you hope for in terms of never having.

Chapter 3 of Kenneth Burke's *Rhetoric of Religion,* on the first three chapters of Genesis (his reworking of the last four chapters of Augustine's *Confessions*), is the best discussion I know of Christian perfectionism. As in his treatment of Augustine, Burke's method here is "logological": "words about God," or theology, are taken as having their secular counterparts in "words about the Word," or logology (Burke's coinage), so that, say, the Logos, or rationally creative divine word, becomes Logic, a principle of order taken to be immanent in all reality. Burke's logology works best, in fact, if you think of it somatically: the logological connection between Logos and Logic is that, despite our ostensible secularity, we feel about Logic much as our medieval forebears felt about the Logos. The word's theological image is progressively secularized (from personal Orderer to impersonal order), but secularization does not overcome our ideosomatic response, our religious awe at order; somatic response unifies, and permits us to trace, the range of images a word takes.

Here is the relevant passage from Burke's discussion of perfectionism:

Logologically, the "fall" and the "redemption" are but parts of the same cycle, with each implying the other. The order can be reversed, for the terms in which we conceive of redemption can help shape the terms in which we conceive of the guilt that is to be redeemed. In this sense, it is "prior" to the guilt which it is thought to follow (quite as the quality of a "cure" can qualify our idea of the "disease" for which it is thought to be the cure—or as a mode of "wish-fulfillment" can paradoxically serve to reinforce the intensity of the wishes). But narratively, they stand at opposite ends of a long development, that makes one "Book" of the two Testaments taken together.

Thus, whereas narratively the Lord God's thou-shalt-not preceded the serpent's tempting of Eve, by appealing to the imagination, in mixing imagery of food with imagery of rule ("and ye shall be as *Elohim*"), and whereas the tempting preceded the fall, logologically the thou-shalt-not is itself implicitly a condition of temptation, since the negative contains the principle of its own annihilation. For insofar as a thou-shalt-not, which is intrinsic to Order verbally guided, introduces the principle of negativity, here technically is the inducement to round out the symmetry by carrying the same principle of negativity one step farther, and negating the negation. That is the only kind of "self-corrective" the negative as such has.

This principle of yes and no, so essential to the personal, verbal, "doctrinal" "sense of right and wrong," is potentially a problem from the very start. And when you add to it the "No trespassing" signs of empire, that both stimulate desires and demand their repression, you see why we hold that guilt is intrinsic to the idea of a Covenant. (218–19)

There it is, the logic of perfection: "the 'No trespassing' signs of empire, that both stimulate desires and demand their repression." The property that the translator is traditionally forbidden to trespass on is the creativity of the SL author, conceived (logologically) as an analogue of the creativity of God's Logos. Thou shalt not aspire to be God— look what happened at Babel: our languages were scattered and translation became necessary. Because translation, the need for which was generated by sinful aspirations to deity at Babel, itself repeats those aspirations—by seeking to overcome language barriers, by seeking at its most presumptuous to supplant the original text—it is always sinful, always an attempted trespassing on holy ground. To paraphrase Burke, in mainstream Western theories of translation *traditore* is intrinsic to the idea of *traduttore*.[37] Translation is by definition a betrayal or traduction of the original. Translation always distorts, always fails in its presumptuous attempt to become original, as the builders at Babel failed in their presumptuous attempt to become gods.

What this account lacks, of course, is the finger of the gods, the Elohim, thrust into history specifically to prevent the builders at Babel from becoming gods. In the logological cycle we have internalized, the tower had to fail, and translation has to fail, as if by sheer mechanical inevitability; but the Bible gives us the originary act of intervention from without, reminding us that failure was not inevitable (built into the system) but desired. The gods did not want the tower to succeed; they felt threatened by it and wanted it stopped. And, cleverly, in order to make sure that this intervention would work once and for all (to save themselves the bother of coming down and stopping the building of towers every few weeks for all eternity), the gods scattered human languages: they built into our speech (into the ideosomatics of language) the logological cycle that convinces us of the impossibility of building a tower to heaven or a bridge to the original SL text.[38] It is all right to keep trying, just so long as we keep trying in ways that will not work or keep defining our successes in terms of failure. We can build skyscrapers; it is all right to do that, since we have been conditioned to know that skyscrapers do not actually scrape the sky, and that in any case scraping the sky would not make us gods. We can translate; it is all right to do that too, since we have been conditioned to know that translations do not really "capture" the meaning of the SL text. They pose no threat to the integrity of the original, which is fundamentally inaccessible. But we must rest easy in that compromise; to rummage around in the ideology motivating it is to stir up old taboos, to feel in our bodies the old danger signals: No! You are going too far! Turn back before it is too late! Be sensible! Be reasonable! That way lies the abyss!

Perfectionist programming also lies behind the mainstream arguments against "translationese"—against letting the translation sound like a translation (this is specifically a bourgeois tradition that I explore in the next chapter, but it is about time to start moving in that direction anyway). Only bad translations sound like translations. Usually this happens accidentally, through the translator's weak somatic feel for the TL; but even when it happens intentionally, or perhaps especially when it happens intentionally, as in Nabokov's *Eugene Onegin*, it is deplored by mainstream translation theorists. Good translations sound like the (or an) original. They have the same effect on the TL receptor as the SL text had on the SL receptor. It is not possible to have *exactly* the same effect on the TL receptor, of course, and people like Eugene

Nida willingly admit this; but you have to come as close as possible. Almost but not quite. Strive for the impossible. To succeed would in fact be presumptuous: it would raise to the level of divine revelation the scratchings of a mere mortal translator. You must fail, therefore. But just barely. The closer you come without actually succeeding, without actually supplanting the original in the TL receptor's mind, the better your translation. The inescapable failure of the translator to achieve precisely the same effect protects the SL text against usurpation; and the near-successful achievement of that effect ties the TL receptor too to the perfectionist ideology that binds the translator's fortitude and despair.

Psychologically, of course, the effect on the receptor of making a translation not sound like a translation is to generate an illusion of immediacy, of no verbal and interpretational mediation between the receptor and the sense of the original. In Bible translation this means a shading out or glossing over of the translator's mediatory act between the SL writers' words and the TL receptor, and ultimately of all verbal mediation between God and mankind: the original disappears too. Thus the implicit belief of many devout readers of *The Living Bible* or *Today's English Version* that (as we saw a minute ago) they are not reading a Bible translation, but the Bible—or even that they are reading God's Word. This is the instrumentalist illusion. The perfectionist illusion arises out of the necessary failure of instrumentalist ideals. It *feels* like God's Word; it *must* be God's Word; but why does it hang just out of my reach? Why does it resist my complete understanding? Why do these words take me just so far and no farther? There must be some perfect understanding that I could grasp if only . . . well, what? The "sophisticated" Bible reader begins to suspect that the problem may be in the translation: if only I had a better translation, I could understand God's Word perfectly, embrace it, clasp it to my heart. So the cry goes out for a new translation, better, closer to the original, a better vehicle for the original's effect. Then the new translation appears and the same thing happens with it: almost but not quite.

Of course, as long as we are made to think that the problem is with the translation, our attention is drawn away from the ideosomatic programming that blocks success. We keep trying to come closer and closer to the original, but we miss the way that the ideosomatics of "coming closer"—of perfectionism—programs us for failure. It feels right to set the SL text up as an unattainable goal. It feels right to settle for coming close as the next best thing to hitting the mark, which we know we can never do.

The psychological (subjective, phenomenological, hermeneutical—somatic) effect of this perfectionist programming can perhaps best be illustrated through the character of Jesus in the New Testament. The Bible translator's perfectionist ideal is to make Jesus feel immediate, familiar, like your best friend or next-door neighbor, a contemporary white middle-class American male (or whatever is the TL receptor's ideosomatic ideal), but also, simultaneously, different, distant, alien, a man of his time, a man of God, the Son of God, someone more than human, someone perfect and therefore almost inconceivable. He feels familiar: he speaks our language just as we speak it, without liturgical adornment, without all the solemnities of ecclesiastical tradition, in flat prose like any other ordinary person. The translation, remember, is not to sound like a translation. Therefore, we can know him; he is accessible to us; he can be our friend. But he also feels unfamiliar: he wanders through a fantasy landscape (it may once have been real, but now it is just as much a part of our cultural fantasy as the king who had three daughters) full of fantasy props like Pharisees and Sadducees, lepers and high priests, the Sea of Galilee and the temple full of moneychangers, and he talks to us of an even more alien fantasy landscape that he calls the kingdom of heaven, a place or state where everything is perfect, where we will find perfect satisfaction of desire, where the nagging feeling of "almost but not quite" will be dissolved and we will have exactly what we want.

Paradoxically, his talk of the perfect satisfaction of our desires alienates him from us: we clasp him to our hearts, but somehow he slips through our fingers. The kingdom of heaven feels real only as a negative ideal—as everything we cannot have here and now. It is like a magic ingredient that we add to our desires to make them seem impossible—to escalate them, in fact, into impossibility. Without Jesus and his talk of the kingdom of heaven, we might be content to wish for things we could have, like a job we mostly enjoy and a spouse we mostly get along with and children that are mostly a delight. But no: he has to entice us with talk of perfect contentment, the perfect conformity of reality to our desires. Not an okay marriage: a perfect marriage. Not good friends that we sometimes have misunderstandings with: the perfect friend, Jesus Christ. The man whom we can almost know but not quite. The man who fills our hearts with impossible desires. The man who keeps us on edge: soon, very soon, in the lifetime of some now living, it will all happen, I *will* be your perfect friend, I *will* make all my promises come true, I *will* satisfy all your deepest desires—just keep waiting, just a little longer.

The unfulfillment or frustration of desire in the present points, of course, as Augustine made clear ("give promise of better fruit to come"), to the future, which is precisely the ideological function of unfulfillment in Christian theology: to harness our present experience of frustration by tying it ideosomatically to a future expectation, the hope that Jesus will return to establish the millennium on earth, banish Satan to hell, judge the quick and the dead, and so on. In order to round up all the loose ends of frustrated desire that the potential or current believer may have lying around and tie them all firmly to specifically *Christian* expectations for the future, Christian theology works to channel desire in the right direction, to generate a controlled image of fulfillment that will herd frustration into the proper holding pen.

Most translation theorists do not follow Jesus out onto this limb: they settle, more timidly, for cautious fortitude, for compromise, for coming somewhat close in a full recognition of their own mortal fallibility. The romantics from Goethe and Schleiermacher to Benjamin and Steiner took this eschatological hope to (but never quite past) its *eschaton:* what is not translatable today may be translatable tomorrow; the satisfaction of ultimate desire, ultimate oneness, may not be achieved in this translation, but it may be in the next one. It is just around the corner. It always is. It must be. If it is not, everything we do is pointless. Some postromantic translation theorists—Jacques Derrida, for instance—do in fact take this option, that translation is pointless, that it is impossible. Again, commonsensical translation theorists deplore this extremism (why take it so far?), but in fact it is only a working out of the implicit assumption behind their own theory and practice: the perfectionism ideosomatically built into all mainstream Western thinking about translation. Commonsensical theorists like Nida and Newmark back away from the eschatological extreme toward which their own assumptions "naturally" (ideosomatically) lead, because they cannot take the conflicting pressures of despair and fortitude out on that edge; radical romantic theorists like Benjamin and Derrida risk everything out on that edge and shake their heads at the faint-hearted who stayed behind; but nobody can break free, nobody can shake off the ideosomatic programming that makes frustration seem inevitable. Timid and brave alike remain convinced that they are doomed to frustration. It is inescapable.

Well, it is not. There is an escape. I have been stressing the masterful web of perfectionist appeal and inevitable frustration in which Christian ideology has wrapped translation in order to counsel not despair but hope: it is possible to break out. It is possible to break the third seal, to find the rotten spots in the floor of Western ideology and crash through to new experience, to deprogrammed idiosomatic experience. It is possible to translate without a subliminal sense of necessary failure. That is what this book, especially Part 2, is about: how to translate with a subliminal sense of success, or at the very least of the possibility and likelihood of success.

Before we can explore that possibility and that likelihood in any detail, however, we need to trace the breaking of the third seal, the move from ideosomatically controlled dualism, instrumentalism, and perfectionism to an open-ended idiosomatic dialogue. That is my subject in Chapter 2.

Chapter Two

The Dialogics of Translation

To speak, or act, or think originally is to erase the boundary of the self. It is to leave behind the territorial personality. A genius does not have a mind full of thoughts but is the thinker of thoughts, and is the center of a field of vision. It is a field of vision, however, that is recognized as a field of vision only when we see that it includes within itself the original centers of other fields of vision.

This does not mean that I can see what you see. On the contrary, it is because I cannot see what you see that I can see at all. *The discovery that you are the unrepeatable center of your own vision is simultaneous with the discovery that I am the center of my own.*

Paradigm Shifts in Translation Theory

In his influential book *The Structure of Scientific Revolutions,* Thomas S. Kuhn offers a historical model of scientific progress in terms of what he calls "paradigm shifts." All too often idealized as an accumulative process of adding new knowledge to old knowledge, the history of science is, in fact, according to Kuhn, a continuing dialectic of paradigm construction ("revolutionary science") and proof/disproof ("normal science"). In the historical scenario or myth that he constructs, an old scientific theory or explanation (paradigm) begins to fail, begins to generate more and more questions that it cannot answer, and thus also generates more and more gaps in scientific knowledge. In response to this situation, revolutionary scientists begin to offer new theories, theories based not on experiment but on the need to explain the discrepancies generated by the old paradigm. When one seems to cover the right territory, normal scientists flock to it with great enthusiasm and begin the process of testing it (proving it right) experimentally. This process continues until the new paradigm begins, like its predecessor, to generate new gaps and discrepancies, and a new paradigm shift becomes necessary. And so on: on and on. This is all there is. No progress; just a series of paradigm shifts.

Now, Kuhn quite rightly denies the direct applicability of his remarks on the history of science to the history of the humanities: there is no "objecthood" in the humanities, no alienness, no way we can get far enough outside our own humanity (the way we can get outside a rock) to objectify it convincingly, and thus no body of hard scientific observation to falsify paradigmatic explanations. This means that there is no convincing way to prove the inadequacy of a humanistic paradigm. But my discussion of somatics suggests that there may be another means of applying Kuhn's ideas to humanistic research. A humanistic paradigm may not be provable or disprovable, the way a scientific paradigm is, but it can *feel* wrong, alien to idiosomatic experience. The revolutionary thinker who breaks through the three seals I spoke of in Chapter 1 may begin to feel the alienness of ideosomatic explanations to idiosomatic experience—may begin to discover that unprogrammed idiosomatic experience falsifies paradigmatic programming, and may then begin working to expand his or her own experience into a new paradigm. This would suggest that in the humanities, the only path to a paradigm shift lies through somatic response, down through the three seals, through the block against feeling, the block against generalizing, and the block against escaping robotic ideology, into a powerfully felt new experience.[1]

How would one go about engineering a paradigm shift in translation theory? We might look for an answer in the history of translation theory, where at least two such shifts have already been successfully brought off.[2] I think specifically of the changes that Luther and the other Reformers brought to medieval thinking about translation, and then of the changes that Goethe and the other romantics brought to orthodox Catholic and Protestant thinking about translation. By exploring these two shifts, I hope to make a case for a third, adumbrated by Martin Buber in "Zu einer neuen Verdeutschung der Schrift": a shift to a theoretical paradigm that I want to call, following Buber and his most illustrious follower, Mikhail Bakhtin, "dialogical."

One way that we might explore the earlier paradigm shifts is thematically, in terms of the central ideological and methodological stances assumed in each paradigm. In the Augustinian paradigm, for example, there was the complex of dualism, instrumentalism, and perfectionism that I outlined in Chapter 1, combined with a scholarly or scientific point of view that sought to understand things as they are, objectively, in their totality.[3] In the Middle Ages, this meant placing them in the stable hierarchy of Christian theology that Lovejoy called the Great Chain of Being. Augustine tended to reason circularly, assuming what he pretended to be proving, while Aquinas, steeped in Aristotle, reasoned by deduction; but both worked to construct a stable hierarchical model for all being. The specific formulations of this model have varied greatly in the centuries since Aquinas, but the dedication to stable, hierarchical, logical, systematic, objective description remains strong in all scientific approaches to translation today.

The Lutheran paradigm contains the same dualism, instrumentalism, and perfectionism instituted by Augustine, but the old dedication to descriptive stability is now cast aside. The determinedly neutral semiotics of Augustine and Aquinas, according to which all language exists for the transmission of information, is more and more overtly subordinated to the politics of conversion. Scientists in the Augustinian/Thomistic tradition sneer at the unscientific nature of this approach; but proselytizers in the Lutheran tradition rightly point out the blindness of science to power and persuasion, to value, to human dignity and self-worth, the human realities of day-to-day life. In translation theory, the Lutheran paradigm stresses the importance of translating into the everyday language of all men and women, everywhere in the world, not just of a small scholarly (Latin- or jargon-speaking) elite, and seeks to control the everyday language of ordinary people through education in the mechanics and the ideology of reading and writing.

Here we get the first signs that the TL reader should not be aware that he or she is reading a translation: it is the Bible, the Holy Scriptures, God's Word, not an artificial verbal construct at some remove from the original. The instrumentality of the translator thus becomes a tool in the process of conversion. The fragmentation of ecclesiastical authority, too—the breakdown of the church's monopoly on truth, the Protestant insistence on dehierarchizing the institution in order to bring about an immediate contact between the believer and God, the proliferation of denominational splinter groups—meant the necessity of internalizing authority, so that the Bible reader would ideosomatically know how to read "correctly." That is, the relation between the believer and God was increasingly to be mediated not externally, by the ecclesiastical hierarchy, but internally, by ideosomatic programming.

In the romantic paradigm instituted by Goethe and others (Herder, Schleiermacher, etc.), then, the Lutheran concern with the politics of conversion is intensified into a concern with the poetics of direct messianic salvation. The ideology of dualism, instrumentalism, and perfectionism carries over, but now in a new context. The "evil" or "sin" generated by dualistic thinking is now no longer Satan or the Roman Catholic church but all institutions, all ecclesiastical and scientific ideology that teaches men and women to be worms; the "good" is the spark of imagination (what I have been calling unprogrammed idiosomatic experience) inside even the most internally oppressed (ideosomatically programmed) of humans; and all dualisms are enlivened, dynamized, through the restless motion of dialectic. The translator remains a tool, but no longer of stable truth (as for Augustine) or of conversion (as for Luther); rather, of the imagination that the romantics imagine to be the messianic savior, the liberator from internal oppression. This entails a belief in the imaginative power of words not to *record* or *transmit,* but to *create,* specifically to re-create, to demolish the deadening institutional barriers to freedom and restore us to primeval paradise. The tool in this process is (at least superficially) word-for-word, or "interlinear," translation—long despised in mainstream (Augustinian and Lutheran) translation theories, which always followed Cicero and Horace in stressing sense-for-sense translation. Actually, the romantic ideal is word-for-word *and* sense-for-sense: the Augustinian display of determined fortitude in submerging despair over the impossibility of ever knowing or translating God's (or the SL writer's) total meaning is here intensified into a powerful (although still always frustrated) messianic hope. Translation soon becomes an all-or-nothing affair, either total meaning, total understanding, total liberation from oppression, or total failure, total untranslatability.

Another way of exploring these paradigms would be to name names:

—Augustine, Aquinas, Roger Bacon, Du Bellay, Pope, Dryden, Campbell, Tytler, Arnold, Bally, Vinay and Darbelnet, Jakobson, Levý, Jumpelt, de Beaugrande, Wilss, Catford, House, Newmark, and so on. (The Augustinian paradigm remains dominant.)

—Luther, Wycliffe, Erasmus (these last two preceding Luther, of course, having been organized retroactively by his aggressive bluster into precursors), and all subsequent Protestant Bible translators up to Nida. Also people like Matthew Arnold, who secularized Protestant concerns with conversion into moralistic culture worship.

—Herder, Goethe, Novalis, Hölderlin, Schleiermacher, von Humboldt, Benjamin, Heidegger, Steiner, Derrida. (Here we might just say the German tradition, as it is anthologized by Hans Störig and, in English—and more comprehensively—by André Lefevere.)

The lists are, needless to say, nothing like complete.

Both approaches, however, thematizing and name-naming, are static. Both suggest a mail-sorting room with slots for various themes and names; or a set of operating system diskettes that successive theorists have used to format their theoretical computers. No sense of human contact; no sense of somatic engagement among theorists. I want to take a different tack, therefore—one closer to the somatic dynamics of change that I sketched in Chapter 1 in terms of the three seals. Specifically, it is a hermeneutical and dialogical approach in which an idiosomatic understanding of translation is dynamically generated out of the pioneering theorist's dual dialogical engagement with his or her predecessor(s), on the one hand, and his or her reader/successor(s), on the other. Because the pioneering theorists (Luther, Goethe, Buber) that I will be talking about are historical figures, however, the primary "pioneering theorist" to engage predecessors and successors dialogically will have to be me: I have constructed the dialogues that I will be describing out of my own idiosomatic understanding of these other men whom I take to be my predecessors. The dialogist can make no claims to objectivity. Dialogue can never pin the past down to the mat of descriptive accuracy. It is my word against yours, or his, or hers, whoever else is participating in this dialogue. All I can do is try to convince you that I am right—or at least interesting, worth listening to.

Martin Luther

Martin Luther was an Augustinian monk; his idiosomatic response to medieval thought was specifically a reaction against the ideology formulated by Augustine and institutionally maintained in his order (and many others) for a thousand years. We (or, all right, I) can imagine it, hermeneutically, dialogically (out of my somatic engagement with Luther's writings), as a feeling of entrapment, imprisonment, unpleasant restriction. Doctrinal restriction, cognitive restriction, certainly; but also, deeper than that, ideosomatic restriction, restriction felt in the body as a fettering of freedom. And then the theological arguments against celibacy, for example, arising out of a rethinking—or rather refeeling—of the desire to marry: I can feel, deep down, Luther says, that there is nothing wrong with my desire for a woman; I know in my body that everything we have been told and taught to believe about concupiscence is wrong; it is an institutional lie, a weight around our necks that must be cast off. Et cetera. Luther begins to feel differently, to work down through the ideosomatic programming that kept the Middle Ages more or less in line and to discover idiosomatic responses that demand expression, demand institutional recognition.

The "Sendbrief vom Dolmetchen" of 1530 is a revealing document in this sense. Luther sets out to answer a criticism or question sent him by a certain Herr N., who has been hard put to defend Luther's Bible against the carping of the papists. Specifically, Luther has rendered Jerome's Vulgate "Arbitrámur hóminem iustificári ex fíde absque opéribus" (Rom. 3:28) as "Wir halten, daß der Mensch gerecht werde ohne des Gesetzes Werke allein durch den Glauben," and the papists feel that by introducing "allein" into a sentence that did not have "sola" in the original Luther has mistranslated (15). This argument is easily answered with a sense-for-sense theory of translation, of course, which Luther argues for throughout, citing Jerome's letter to Pammachius (a document similar in every way to Luther's "Sendbrief") as his authoritative predecessor: the "allein" is implicit in the meaning of the original.

It is interesting, however, that Luther does not seem to feel that the argument can easily be answered. In fact, he gets himself exceedingly worked up about it. He has obviously been hit on a sore spot, and he reacts with hurt fury: "Wenn euer Papist sich viel Beschwer machen will mit dem Wort 'sola-allein,' so sagt ihm flugs also: Doktor Martinus Luther will's so haben und spricht: Papist und Esel sind ein Ding" (18). Or, in the kind of English that my own idiosomatic response generates to being hit on a sore spot: "If that dumbass papist of yours won't get off your back about this 'sola-alone' business, tell him that Doctor Martin Luther *wants* it that way, and if he doesn't like it, he can shove it."

Why this touchiness? In his book on Thomas Aquinas, G. K. Chesterton says it was because Luther was a bully.[4] But people are not born bullies; there is usually a good somatic reason when they start to throw their weight around. What was bothering Luther?

My guess is that for Luther the "sola-alone" business is not a simple question of translation principles. The question that Paul is addressing is how people are "justified" (KSV) or "put right" (TEV)—an extremely sensitive somatic issue. How can we feel right? How can we feel good about ourselves? Through the Law? By obeying the commandments of the Fathers? By knuckling under to an oppressive institution? By surrendering to ideosomatic programming? Maybe so, if we can stifle our idiosomatic response effectively enough. But the slightest inkling that we feel bad in the first place *because* of the Law, because of the institution's attempts to control us, because of its attempts to bring us into line with its legalistic principles, conform us to its idealized image of obedience—the slightest inkling of all this will make us shudder at the very suggestion that we might be put right by submitting to the institution. There has to be some other source of justification or of revenge[5]—some other channel by which we can get back at our institutional oppressors and come to feel good about ourselves under the present state of oppression. There has to be something beyond the third seal that says there is *nothing* beyond ideosomatic programming (you are a robot, you are completely under the institution's control).

That "something beyond," that elusive wisp of unprogrammed idiosomatic response, for Paul was faith, *pistis, fides,* something that the ecclesiastical institution (the Roman Catholic church, for Luther specifically the Augustinian order) had attempted to swallow up in the authoritarian rhetoric of stable hierarchical system but that Luther experienced somatically as believing, Glauben. Believing in what? Well, in God, of course, but not necessarily the rational Platonic God of Augustine—believing, rather, in some force of liberation from institutional authority, a force to be felt and lived now and named later, if at all. Believing is a somatic experience: it is a feeling of certainty, a feeling that things are not hopeless, that revenge, justification, liberation, are possible. And, at least at first, as Luther must have experienced it, believing is a very private experience: a groping past ideosomatic experiences of petrifaction to a lonely, living hope at the core of one's being, and a gradual expanding of that hope into an articulable, therefore sharable, experience. Thus, I suggest, the complex somatic importance of "sola-alone": at his Augustinian monastery, Luther is alone in his feeling of imprisonment, and alone also in his budding feeling that there may be something else, some source of hope, some channel of liberation, which he learns from Paul to call believing. I draw here on Erik Erikson's brilliant psychohistory of Luther:

He was alone now; alone against his temperament, which his father had predicted would refuse submission to celibacy; and alone against his wrath, which his father had shown was indomitable in the Loders [Luthers]. Incredible as it seems, at this late date [in his early twenties] Martin was thrown back into the infantile struggle, not only over his obedience toward, but also over his identification with, his father. This regression and this personalization of his conflicts cost him that belief in the monastic way and in his superiors which during the first year had been of such "godly" support. He was alone in the monastery, too, and soon showed it in a behavior that became increasingly un-understandable even to those who believed in him. *To be justified* became his stumbling block as a believer, his obsession as a neurotic sufferer, and his preoccupation as a theologian. (145)

As he receives political support for his aloneness, as his aloneness explodes into a massive religious movement, it becomes gradually something more, something greater, elevated, almost deified: his aloneness in the monastery, the aloneness of his idiosomatic believing in the overcrowded prison of his ideosomatic being, becomes the world's only hope, the acorn that grows into a great oak. Dr. Martin Luther wants it that way—or rather, something inside Dr. Martin Luther wants it that way, the idiosomatic aloneness at the center of his being wants it that way, and that aloneness is greater than all of us: it is God. It is the liberating force that he found when he broke the third seal, when he burst down through the prison floor and found his redeemer, down where it had been isolated from him, locked away in solitary confinement, so that he would never escape.[6]

Thus also Luther's protests about not forcing anyone to read his Bible:

Zum andern könnt Ihr sagen, daß ich das Neue Testament verdeutscht habe nach meinem besten Vermögen und auf's gewißenhafteste; habe damit niemand gezwungen, daß er's lese, sondern es frei gelaßen, und allein zu Dienst getan denen, die es nicht besser machen können. Es ist niemand verboten, ein bessers zu machen. Wer's nicht lesen will, der laß es liegen; ich bitte und lobe niemand drum. Es ist mein Testament und mein Dolmetschung und soll mein bleiben und sein. (15–16)

Second, you can tell them that I've put the New Testament into German conscientiously and to the best of my ability; never forced anybody to read the thing, but left it up to them, and I did it all to help those who couldn't do it better themselves. Nothing's stopping anybody from making a better one. Whoever doesn't want to read it can leave it lay; I'm not going to beg or praise anybody for it. It's my Testament and my translation and nobody can take it away from me.

There is that "allein" again: alone for the service of others. There's nothing in it for me; I just expanded that idiosomatic core of aloneness that I found in myself into a Testament for anybody and everybody to read. It's mine, but it's also everybody's. It's my *testament;* nobody can take it away from me. I found it inside me, all alone—but yes, a testament is for other people: I will it to you; you may inherit my aloneness, since I did it alone for you.

The subtle emotional blackmail of "und allein zu Dienst getan denen, die es nicht besser machen können" begins to suggest just how powerful a paradigmatic shift Luther achieved in Christian theology, and through Christian theology in translation theory as well. For Augustine, the sinner should read and believe the Bible because it is *true:* it is a true system that stabilizes the chaos of everyday life, it is founded on the rock of the Logos (or, by Aquinas's day, of logic). For Luther, the sinner should read and believe the Bible because *I did it all for you:* I can't force you, I don't have the paternal authority of an Augustine, all snug and smug in his circular theological system, institutionalized as the great father of all order, but I can bring emotional pressure to bear on you, I can manipulate you into reading it by appealing to the great sacrifices I made to bring the Bible to you. I am tempted to say that if Augustine assumed the traditional father's role, aloof in his authoritarian appeal to truth, Luther assumed the traditional mother's role, frantic in his sense of the powerlessness that threw him back on indirect manipulation to get his way. Look at all I've done for you, and how do you thank me? Kick me in the teeth.[7]

The subliminal message here is that I am like you; we are both powerless, both oppressed by the father. You and I, mother and child: we should stick together. Show me that you are on my side by doing what I want you to do; show me that you love me by appreciating my sacrifices. We do not speak Latin, the language of power; we speak German, the vernacular, the language of the oppressed. We must stick together.

Denn man muß nicht die Buchstaben in der lateinischen Sprache fragen, wie man soll Deutsch reden, wie diese Esel tun, sondern man muß die Mutter im Hause, die Kinder auf der Gassen, den gemeinen Mann auf dem Markt drum fragen, und denselbigen auf das Maul sehen, wie sie reden und darnach dolmetschen; da verstehen sie es denn und merken, daß man deutsch mit ihnen redet. (21)

Only an idiot would go ask the letters of the Latin alphabet how to speak German, the way these dumbasses do. You've got to go out and ask the mother in her house, the children in the street, the ordinary man at the market. Watch their mouths move when they talk, and translate that way. Then they'll understand you and realize that you're speaking *German* to them.[8]

They will also forget, of course, that the words were ever written in another language; they will forget that this is a translation from the Latin, which in turn was a translation from the Greek, which in turn was partly a translation from the Hebrew and partly a narration of events that originally happened in Aramaic. Then they will never notice the alienness of this text, this "testament"—it will be a bond, in ordinary German, between mother and child, between Luther and his flock, between the Protestant peddler and the prospective buyer. It will seem natural to them to buy his wares: after all, isn't he one of us? Doesn't he speak our language? Isn't that sign enough that he can be trusted?

Thus is achieved what Nietzsche termed *the internalization of mastery:* what was once brought about by edict, by force, by paternal command and enforcement (this is the truth, and if you don't believe it I'll wallop you), is now to be brought about by stealth, by indirection, by the maternal manipulation of trust and familiarity and loyalty and affection. Woo them over to your side. Be their friend; urge them, in the name of friendship, to accept the gift of your love, your faith, your ideology. Teach them *how* to be your friends: by agreeing with you; by seeing things your way; by understanding your point of view and appreciating your sacrifices. Never threaten them with physical punishment if they stray; only show them that you are very, very disappointed in them, very sad. Punish them with emotional withdrawal, not with the whip. Reward them with smiles and encouragement. Be their friend: believe that you truly are their friend and that everything you do is for their own good. You're helping them get into heaven! Isn't that something? Isn't that what a friend *ought* to do?

Luther says to the Augustinians: You're oppressors; you're oppressive fathers, always on my back, locking me in, but I've gone beyond the reach of your institutional laws. I've found an out, an aloneness of believing, and now that I've successfully expanded that aloneness into a testament, I'm free of you—I don't need you, you hear? I'm free! (Thus is idiosomatic response freed from its ideosomatic shackles—or almost freed. Luther's defensive name-calling suggests that he still feels trapped by Augustine.)

Then he turns around and says to his readers: Look, I made this, it's my testament, I made it out of my aloneness, it's mine alone; but you know what they say, what's mine is yours, *if* you're my friend, if you'll be a friend to me, if you'll listen to me, appreciate me, do what you know I want you to do before I have to say it. (Thus is idiosomatic response forged into new ideosomatic shackles. So the world turns.)

Note, however, what I have done here. While I was talking about Luther's idiosomatic reaction to Augustine, I *was* (hermeneutically speaking) Luther. I projected myself somatically into his words, and through his words into his *in-der-Welt-sein*. I probably caricatured him a little, coming out of my own anger at authority in the American sixties (the Establishment) and seventies (conservative colleagues), but essentially I was on his side. When I shifted to talking about his dialogical relations with reader/successors, I began to lose contact with his somatic response; I began to react to him *as* a reader/successor, specifically as a Protestant reader/successor who has been reading Luther's successor Nietzsche's *Genealogy of Morals*. From Luther's point of view, his dialogue with reader/successors was one of equality, of children growing up together and supplanting the oppressive father. From my (increasingly belated and Nietzschean) point of view, that image of equality contained an element of deception; it was an attempt to conceal the power move that Luther wanted to make on his readers. I *feel* the power move, in other words; I feel the restrictions that Protestantism has placed on me. I am aware of Lutheran ideosomatic programming—something Luther himself could not have known about, but I certainly feel it, four hundred years later, and I project it somatically into him. I feel him beginning to do to his readers what Lutheranism has done to me; I look for evidence in his words that he was already heading in the direction that I somatically associate with Lutheranism. He thought of himself as a child rising up with other children against the fathers; I think of him as a mother pretending solidarity with her children in order to consolidate her rebellion against her husband. "Allein zu Dienst getan denen, die es nicht besser machen können"—that is my cue.

Part of this, of course, is my rebellion against mainstream Western translation theory, which Luther played almost as important a role in shaping as Augustine did. I feel all "descriptive" (Augustinian) and "encouraging" (Lutheran) talk of commonsense-for-sense norms in translation studies as a restriction, a handicapping, a clapping of glasses on the clear-visioned and of weights on the athletic, as in Kurt Vonnegut's story "Harrison Bergeron." This feeling is not, I realize, entirely or strictly idiosomatic; it is ideosomatically shaped by romanticism, by the Emersonian currents in American culture, which I learned to articulate and consolidate later, in college, reading Goethe, Blake, Whitman, Nietzsche, and still later, teaching translation, reading George Steiner, Walter Benjamin, Ezra Pound. My shift from Luther to Goethe in the hermeneutical argument of this chapter is not, therefore, a historically innocent move for me: Goethe helped to condition my deidealizing response to Luther.

Goethe and Luther

In his well-known remarks on the three types of translation in the notes to *West-Östlicher Divan* (1819), Goethe begins by praising Luther for his leveling approach to translation, but in terms that (my own romantically conditioned response tells me) reveal Goethe's profound mistrust of such an approach:

Es gibt dreierlei Arten Übersetzungen. Die erste macht uns in unserm eigenen Sinne mit dem Auslande bekannt; eine schlichtprosaische is hierzu die beste. Denn indem die Prosa alle Eigentümlichkeiten einer jeden Dichtkunst völlig aufhebt und selbst den poetischen Enthusiasmus auf eine allgemeine Waßerebene niederzieht, so leistet sie für den Anfang den grössten Dienst, weil sie uns mit dem fremden Vortrefflichen mitten in unserer nationalen Häuslichkeit, in unserem gemeinen Leben überrascht und, ohne daß wir wissen, wie uns geschieht, eine höhere Stimmung verleihend, wahrhaft erbaut. Eine solche Wirkung wird Luthers Bibelübersetzung jederzeit hervorbringen. (Störig, 35)[9]

There are three kinds of translation. The first acquaints us with foreign countries on our own terms; here a simple prose translation is best. For since prose totally cancels all peculiarities of any kind of poetic art, and since prose itself pulls poetic enthusiasm down to a common water level, it renders the greatest service in the beginning by surprising us with foreign excellence in the midst of our national homeliness, our everyday existence; before we realize what is happening, it ennobles our mood and so truly edifies us. Luther's Bible translation will produce this kind of effect at any time. (Lefevere's translation, slightly modified, 35)

Listen to his choice of words: "indem die Prosa alle Eigentümlichkeiten einer jeden Dichtkunst völlig aufhebt und selbst den poetischen Enthusiasmus auf eine allgemeine Waßerebene niederzieht . . ." Pulling poetic enthusiasm down to a common water level: it sounds like drowning a rat. It is not a matter of working at a certain level; Goethe sees it (feels it [or I feel him feeling it]) as a suppressing of nobler instincts, a leveling, a refusal to let poetry lift her head out of the water. "Aufhebt," of course, is Hegel: the implication here is that you can push poetry down all you want, but eventually she is going to spring back up, twice as powerful, in a new synthesis (which is, of course, where Goethe is headed).

In a less well-known remark on translation in *Dichtung und Wahrheit* (1811–31), Goethe praises Luther again, suggesting that Luther did religion a greater service by translating plainly, for the common people, than he could have through stricter faithfulness to the form of the original. But notice, again, how he puts it:

[Luther] hat die Religion mehr gefördert, als wenn er die Eigentümlichkeiten des Originals im einzelnen hätte nachbilden wollen. Vergebens hat man nachher sich mit dem Buche Hiob, den Psalmen und andern Gesängen bemüht, sie uns in ihrer poetischen Form genießbar zu machen. Für die Menge, auf die gewirkt werden soll, bleibt eine schlichte Übertragung immer die beste. Jene kritischen Übersetzungen, die mit dem Original wetteifern, dienen eigentlich nur zur Unterhaltung der Gelehrten untereinander. (34–35)

[Luther] helped religion more than if he had aspired to re-create the idiosyncrasies of that original down to the smallest detail. Later translators have tried in vain to make us enjoy the book of Job, the Psalms, and other canticles in their poetic form. For the masses, on whom the Bible is supposed to make an impression, a simple translation is always best. Critical translations that vie with the original really only give the learned something amusing to talk about. (Lefevere's translation, slightly modified, 39)

For the masses, on whom the Bible is supposed to make an impression: the sneer here is unmistakable. Or the shudder, the body's reaction to the prospect of being in a position to *be* impressed by Luther's testament—or rather (since Goethe doesn't mind being impressed so long as he can do it on his own terms) of not being in a position *not* to be impressed by it. A shudder, disguised as a sneer, which is in turn disguised as simple neutrality, Augustinian aloofness, objectivity. Hide the shudders, hide the sneers: they betray Goethe's vulnerability to being impressed, to the emotional pressure that Luther-as-mother can still bring to bear on him. Or, perhaps, if emotion is allowed to enter into it, transform the shudder and the sneer into a good-natured amusement—untroubled, unthreatened, unworried by Luther, comfortable in a calm superiority. His argument for a "schlichte Übertragung" in the *Dichtung und Wahrheit* passage, for example, so far from ringing with the conviction that Louis Kelly finds in it (49), seems to me to tinkle precisely, deliberately, with the light ironic amusement of the learned. Earlier in the passage, in fact, Goethe recommends unpretentious prose translation for the schools, so that boys can bring their natural irreverence to bear on the classics: "durch eine Art von parodistischen Mutwillen des tiefen Gehalt des edelsten Werks zerstören" (34)—"to destroy through a kind of parodistic mischief the profound content of the noblest works." He will leave to educators the practical details of turning this into a strict pedagogical program (zu Gebote), he says; they have demonstrated their proficiency in that field. Am I wrong to hear ironic amusement in this? I can imagine Goethe seeing some good in his proposal, in the chipping away of the petrifying culture worship that encases living works in stone—but only as a beginning, only as a heuristic toward a more dynamic understanding. Not, certainly, as an end in itself. And never, heaven forbid, in a pedagogical program entrusted to educators.

Luther reacts against the paternal command of Augustine (at least in my somatic reconstruction) as the child-become-mother; Goethe, I suggest, reacts against the maternal command of Luther (and Katharina Goethe's pietism) as the child-become-father. More specifically: Goethe as child reacts to Luther as mother by becoming the self-engendered father who smiles indulgently (paternalistically) at the mother-as-child. Each of them felt his illustrious predecessor as a constriction, a limiting or leveling impulse that inhibited freedom and life lived at its fullest. But Luther, always embarrassingly straightforward ("schlicht"), bodies forth his defensiveness: he calls the papists dumbasses but treats them like oppressive fathers. Goethe, more "civilized," better trained in the art of protective dissembling, cloaks his chafing against the father of the German language in a carefully controlled superiority, an Olympian irony: he praises Luther for his service to religion (to the masses on which a Bible translation is supposed to make an impression) but treats him like a child, a schoolboy.

The dialogical somatics that I am eliciting in these engagements between Luther and Augustine, Goethe and Luther, are not, I realize, strictly interpersonal (interidiosomatic). Part of it, certainly, is the ideosomatics of social class: although both Luther and Goethe were middle-class boys who made good (Luther the doctor of divinity and professor of theology, Goethe the lawyer, the minister of state, the peer), Luther came of reasonably well-to-do but low peasant stock, while the young Goethe with his private tutor could only be called, by modern standards, upper middle class. Luther also seems to have been less socially adaptable than Goethe; where Goethe, the upstart peer, quickly and slickly assumed the protective covering of his new rank, Luther always stubbornly clung to the rough ways of his peasant origin. Add to class the effect of period: Goethe was born three centuries after Luther. The middle class had come a long way in that time: it had gained self-respect and a new social power, and along with increased status had gained a heightened awareness of both the techniques and the anxieties associated with upward mobility. Luther's boorish, bullying manner is part sheer fifteenth-century peasantry (an inability to adapt), but partly also an unwillingness to surrender to the uncertainties of social pretense (a refusal to adapt). Goethe both could and did adapt and seems to have suffered the somatic consequences: the trip to Italy and the shift from *Sturm und Drang* to a determinedly serene neoclassicism arose partly, I believe, out of dissatisfaction at the gap he felt between his high social status and his somewhat lower self-image, a gap that must have generated in him a nagging suspicion of fraudulence. Certainly his falling stock at Weimar when he returned from Italy points in this direction: perhaps he was no longer quite so willing to play the game, be the peer, be the great romantic author of *Werther*.

Such social and political considerations are unquestionably important in a discussion of these two influential men. But neither man (indeed, no one) is entirely the product of social and political forces, and cannot therefore be entirely explained through social and political indicators. (That would be to remain at the third seal, the block against escaping ideosomatic programming.) Luther and Goethe come down to us in the history books and translation theory (and other) anthologies at least partly because they were able to break through the floor of ideosomatic programming, break through the wall of *re*pression into new *ex*pression: were able, in Luther's terms, to transform the idiosomatic aloneness of believing into a testament.

Not only were Luther's response to Augustine and Goethe's response to Luther in part idiosomatic, arising out of personal experience; my response to both, including my construction of a social and political framework for the explanation of their tonal differences, is in part idiosomatic as well, arising out of my own personal experience. It is significant for this discussion, for example, that my father was raised a Missouri Synod Lutheran and my mother was raised a Baptist. She rebelled against the Baptists, associating the legalism of her church with her own legalistic mother; but it is significant that she channeled her rebellion specifically toward the denomination (changed denominations, in fact, several times) and not against Protestantism or Christianity as a whole. It is significant that I lived in Finland, a Lutheran country, for fourteen years, and wrote this book while teaching in a Translation Studies department there; that my wife is the daughter of a Lutheran minister, who died in 1976, and that until our removal in 1989 to Mississippi she worked for the local parish; that lately she has begun to rage against the sterile authoritarianism of the Lutheran clergy that she once idealized in terms of her father. It is significant that I rebelled against Christianity and Protestantism when I was sixteen but have never been able to dismiss it calmly, that I have raged at it or clung to it or hovered nervously at the fringes of it for most of my adult life. All this is somatically significant in the construction of an image, however "objective" (and I don't really claim to be that), of the past.

The Entrepreneurial Translator

Goethe's antithesis to Lutheran translation, the next rung on the dialectical ladder he is climbing, is something he calls parodistic, but in a different sense from the parodistic mischief he encourages in schoolboys:

> Eine zweite Epoche folgt hierauf, wo man sich in die Zustände des Auslandes zwar zu versetzen, aber eigentlich nur fremden Sinn sich anzueignen und mit eignem Sinne wieder darzustellen bemüht ist. Solche Zeit möchte ich im reinsten Wortverstand die parodistische nennen. (Störig, 36)

> A second epoch follows in which [the translator] really only tries to appropriate foreign content and to reproduce it in his own sense, even though he tries to transport himself into foreign conditions. I would like to call this epoch "parodistic," in the purest sense of that word. (Lefevere's translation, slightly modified, 36)

Goethe's first shift comes in the third word: where "schlichtprosaische Übersetzung" was a "kind" of translation, parodistic translation is an "epoch." We have shifted, here, out of static dualism into a dialectical dynamic in time. More specifically, we have shifted out of the mind/body dualism conceived, in the Augustinian formulation I discussed in Chapter 1, as a Platonic hierarchy giving stable form to the entire created universe, and thus out of mainstream divisions of translation into sense-for-sense (mind = good), word-for-word (body = bad), and "free" translation (everything else, everything that hardly deserves the name of translation at all)—out of all that, into a dialectical succession of translation models conceived as progress toward an ideal.

Luther did not question the mind/body dualism of sense-for-sense versus word-for-word translation; like Augustine, like Jerome, like Aquinas, he took it for granted that there was only one correct way to translate, sense-for-sense, and that anyone who accused him of mistranslating (introducing "allein" into a verse that Jerome had translated without "sola," for example) was quite simply on the wrong side of the theoretical fence. Like Hegel, like a whole generation of progressivists, Goethe challenged the static deadness of medieval dualism by charging it with the power to bring us ever closer to perfection. Every move from one side of an opposition to the other meant progress. It was emphatically not, as it had been for Augustine and Luther, a move from truth to error or vice versa; truth for the romantics and their idealist counterparts in philosophy was not stable, not static, not an objective property or a dead husk of creation discernible by systematically rational observation, but rather emerging, dynamic, organic, a living process discernible by a revelatory series of intensifying pendulum swings.

Goethe's conceptual shift from "Art" to "Epoche" is driven, in fact (I feel), by a somatic shift from rigidity to fluidity—one that is strikingly congruent, somatically speaking, with Luther's shift from legalism to believing. If truth is situated in a stable legalistic system, Luther realized, it is dead, a petrified body of hierarchical distinctions that deadens everything it touches. If it is found in the act of believing, in a dynamic idiosomatic response from beneath the iron floor of stable abstract system, it is alive, a living organism that enlivens everyone who dedicates him- or herself to its emergence. Goethe agrees, but adds: if truth is situated in a stably *dualized* system, as it remained (by default, through a failure to confront the issue) for Luther as for Augustine, it is indeed dead, a petrified body of static distinctions that deadens everything it touches. More, the emergence of life may be somatic—what Luther called believing the romantics called imagination, but logologically it is the same idiosomatic spark—but the mere charismatic assertion of idiosomatic experience against ideologically petrified system is not enough. It is not enough to *oppose* system; you have to *contaminate system with life*. You have to inject frozen dualism with time, delta t, change over time, progress. If truth is found dynamically emerging from an ongoing dialectical process, Goethe says, *then* it is alive, *then* it is a living organism that enlivens everyone who dedicates him- or herself to its emergence.

In other words, Goethe begins to sense that charismatic self-assertion alone (allein) is not a particularly effective weapon against inert system. It is not enough to sneer with Luther, "Papist und Esel sind ein Ding." It is not enough to hurl your idiosomatic response against the impassive edifice of ideology. Ideology only feels impassive, in fact, because it is a defensive intellectualization and self-repressing denial of ideosomatics, that deep-down right feeling that seems to guide our behavior like underwater rails—seems indeed to be a biological imperative, the inexorable voice of universal human nature. An attack of the magnitude of Luther's, with its broad political base not only in the chafing of the German Electors but in the emergent middle class, can of course bring about much change; but ideosomatic programming ensures that change will only go so deep, no deeper. Augustine can still say, with his infuriating paternal calm, "All right, so you got Bible translators to translate for the masses, so what? What they're translating is still my system." Their differences notwithstanding, Augustine and Luther still collaborated on the mainstream theory of translation in the

West: translate sense-for-sense, and let the sense you translate be approved by the institutional authorities, whether they be external judges or internalized (ideosomatic) norms.

The stable dualistic system of medieval Christianity was fundamentally conservative, protective. It was dedicated to the conservation of ecclesiastical power and institutionally approved values through the rigorous exclusion of otherness: the body and its emotions and pleasures, women, illogical thought processes, Arabs, heresy—the list goes on and on, with a kind of dreamlike familiarity, since we still carry with us the ideosomatic traces of these beliefs, and put them into practice when we least suspect it (the repressed sexism, racism, xenophobia, etc. of the contemporary white liberal male is perhaps the most prominent example). It was this kind of protective exclusionism that Goethe and his contemporaries were fighting against with their notions of progressive dialectic: take an exclusionary stance like Augustine's (or Luther's) and introduce into it its opposite; once the two have mixed, blended, merged, and generated out of their mixture a new exclusionary stance, introduce into that *its* opposite, and so on. Confuse all clarity with alterity; relax all rigor with otherness. Never let a stance harden into a system.

And in fact, six years before the *Divan,* in *Zum brüderlichen Andenken Wielands* (1813), Goethe had opposed to Luther's "familiarizing" approach precisely alterity, otherness:

Es gibt zwei Übersetzungsmaximen: die eine verlangt, daß der Autor einer fremden Nation zu uns herüber gebracht werde, dergestalt, daß wir ihn als den Unsrigen ansehen können; die andere hingegen macht an uns die Forderung, daß wir uns zu dem Fremden hinüber begeben und uns in seine Zustände, seine Sprachweise, seine Eigenheiten finden sollen. (35)

There are two maxims in translation: one requires that the author of a foreign nation be brought across to us in such a way that we can look on him as ours; the other requires that we should go across to what is foreign and adapt ourselves to its conditions, its use of language, its properties. (Lefevere's translation, slightly modified, 39)

Here we have a good, strong antithesis: ours versus theirs; bringing to us versus going to them; domesticating the strange versus estranging the domestic. And in fact this still seems essentially to be what Goethe is getting at in the *Divan* when he speaks of an epoch in which "man sich in die Zustände des Auslandes zwar zu versetzen . . . bemüht ist." The problem is that it is hard to imagine what this would mean in practice. Certainly a language learner can move abroad and allow him-

or herself to be redomesticated into a foreign culture—to acclimate, to adjust, to reprogram him- or herself with foreign ideosomatics. But how do you translate that without "bringing it back"? How does the translator, as translator, estrange the domestic? Strict literalism is usually cited as an estrangement of the domestic, but any kind of TL rendering, no matter how eccentric, remains a bringing back, a domestication of the SL.

Goethe seems to realize this in the *West-Östlicher Divan* passage: his original antithesis is only a theoretical hypothesis, required by the dialectic but not found in reality. So he tries something else, something along the same lines but fundamentally different. Just what, he doesn't seem to be quite sure, which is what makes his remarks seem to George Steiner so "gnomic" (259). (They are not gnomic; they just are not clearly enough worked out.) Goethe says that in his second "epoch" the translator tries to transport him- or herself into the foreign situation but is unable to do it: "aber eigentlich nur fremden Sinn sich anzueignen und mit eignem Sinne wieder darzustellen bemüht ist." What is the difference between this and Luther? We still have "eigner Sinn." The only real difference between Goethe's first "kind" and second "epoch" of translation seems to be that the first familiarizes us with the foreign land in *our* own sense (submission to the TL reader's speech habits); the second appropriates and represents the foreign situation in the *translator's* own sense (personal expression). It all comes down to a question of the translator's populist identification or elitist nonidentification with his or her readership—a difference that looks to me more graded than antithetical.

One way of getting at the real antithesis Goethe was trying to articulate is by looking at the rhetoric of the passage. "Aber eigentlich nur fremden Sinn sich anzueignen und mit eignem Sinne wieder darzustellen bemüht ist": rhetorically speaking, notice how lonely that "fremder Sinn" looks among the "eigens" in that phrase. Eigentlich eignet man seinen eignen Sinn an—zwar kein fremdes. Eig(n)en is "own," in the fullest sense of that word: one's own, which one owns. Eigentum is property in the legal (real estate) sense of the word, Eigentümlichkeit in the psychological or ontological sense. In his discussion of the first kind of translation, Goethe has "eigenem Sinne" and "Eigentümlichkeit"; in his discussion of the second epoch of translation he has "eigentlich," "anzueignen," "eignem Sinne," "seinem eignen Grund und Boden," "eigentümlichen Verstands- und Geschmackssinn," and "zueignete." The eigens proliferate. (Significantly, in his discussion of the third epoch, they are gone.) One might even say that, judging from

Goethe's rhetoric, the SL's ownership of its own sense amounts to a kind of obstinacy (Eigensinn): try as they might to escape the rigidifying effect of exclusionary property, ownership, appropriation, the translators of the first two kinds or epochs of translation are brought forcibly back to their "proper" place, their "proper" role and function as servants of their SL proprietor.

Clearly, Goethe's rhetorical retreat in his second epoch from the alterity of "fremder Sinn" into the ownness of "aneignen" and "eigner Sinn" rehearses the history of capitalism. Or rather, since the "property" and "ownership" I am talking about are psychological rather than economic, perhaps it is the history not of capitalism but of Lockean liberalism (the two go hand in hand), which begins in the seventeenth century to generate the individualistic psychology that we think of as "natural" today. Locke stressed the autonomy of the individual; his psychology was essentially an internalization of private ownership, or a restructuring of the psyche on the analogy of private ownership. Man (not woman) owns himself like an industrialist owning a factory. Everyone is his own man (every*one* being implicitly male: every female is her man's woman, one of his possessions). The properties of my personality are *my* properties, mine alone; I am unique. You must respect my uniqueness or I will punch you in the nose.

In one sense, this is a clear antithesis to Augustine: not us, but me; not God, God's truth, God's Church, but me. In another sense, it is an intensification of Augustine: the good side of every dualism is still aligned emotionally with me, the individual, and is still exclusive. I am good, a few of my friends may be good (though not quite as good as I am), and everybody else is bad, so I had better protect my uniqueness (my property). But is it an antithesis to Luther? Luther said "me" too:

Ich kann Psalmen und Propheten auslegen; das können sie nicht. Ich kann dolmetschen; das können sie nicht. Ich kann beten; das können sie nicht. . . . Ich verstehe ihre eigene Dialektika und Philosophia besser, denn sie selbst allesamt. (18)

I can interpret the psalms and the prophets, and you can't. I can translate, and you can't. I can pray, and you can't. I understand your own dialectics and philosophy better than you do yourselves.

Luther was just as defensively exclusive with his dualizing as any of the papists he attacked. But Luther went from *my* sense to *our* sense: from the aloneness of my believing to the testament I pass on to you, in your tongue, which thus becomes ours. He moved from self-assertion to self-denial for the common good, and that move has remained fundamental to mainstream translation theory right up to our time. The translators that Goethe seems to be pointing to go from *that other* sense to *my* sense: from the alienness of a foreign tongue to an import marketed under the translator's own imprint. They move from self-denial (openness to penetration from the outside) to self-assertion—a move that remains antithetical to mainstream translation theory into our time.

A truly capitalist or liberal—Lockean, "entrepreneurial"—conception of translation, such as Goethe seems to be imagining in his second epoch, will stoutly resist all ideosomatic pressure toward self-denial and self-effacement and move toward appropriation, annexing the SL writer's property as the translator's own. Free the translator from the tyranny of the SL writer *and* the TL reader! Every translator, after all, is his own man, isn't he? Why should he put up with wage slavery? Why shouldn't he go into business for himself? Nobody ever got rich working for somebody else. Let's fight for a general recognition of translators as original artists! Royalties for translators! Away with this talk of self-sacrifice; away with all the subtle emotional pressures brought to bear on the translator to conform (and to conform the TL reader) to institutionally approved ideals. The translator as an "instrument," a "tool" of the SL text, or of God, or of the ecclesiastical or political institution? Rubbish! Don't let those guys push you around. Translate the way *you* want to, not the way you think the SL writer or TL reader would want you to. Be a man! Be unique! Exert your autonomy! Be different! Stand out from the crowd!

This, I believe, and not the eigner Sinn/fremder Sinn opposition, is the antithesis Goethe was really looking for: self-assertion rather than self-denial; autonomy rather than instrumentality. He doesn't say so straight out, but certainly his description of the French points strongly in this direction:

Der Franzose, wie er sich fremde Worte mundrecht macht, verfährt auch so mit den Gefühlen, Gedanken, ja den Gegenständen, er fordert durchaus für jede fremde Frucht ein Surrogat, das auf seinem eignen Grund und Boden gewachsen ist. (Störig, 36)

Just as the Frenchman adapts foreign words to his pronunciation, just so does he treat feelings, thoughts, even objects: for every foreign fruit he demands a counterfeit grown on his own soil. (Lefevere's translation, slightly modified, 36)

It is always an exchange, imported goods exchanged for locally grown (the opposition that Goethe highlights), the real thing for the "real thing," a surrogate or counterfeit marketed as real (the capitalist technique of transferring our affections from objects and people to publicity images), but also, finally, public for private control of the market. (I return to this in Chapter 4, under "Conversion and Advertising.") *I* decide what I'm going to take in exchange for what; *I* decide how I'm going to market what I've got for sale. Nobody tells *me* what to exchange for what and how. If I decide to translate the Bible so as to demonstrate my own uniqueness and autonomy as an individual, that's my business; nobody has any right to interfere with what I do. Laissez faire! Hands off! If I want to market my translation as a "new and improved" Bible, and think I can get people to buy it, that's my business too—stay out of it! Get government out of business! Get translation theory out of translation! Deregulate!

Now it may seem strange, in a culture so imbued with the capitalist ideology of private enterprise and ownership and with the liberal ideology of the uniqueness and autonomy of the individual, that translation should still so widely (and so unconsciously, so ideosomatically) be thought of in terms of idealized instrumentality. Why should the principle of laissez faire run rampant in every other area of Western thought, but not in translation theory?

The answer surely lies in the submerged survival in capitalist society of the old exclusionary dualisms of medieval thought: good and evil traditionally translate as power and powerlessness. The equivalents of Augustine's God and Satan in contemporary society are male and female, owner and worker, autonomous man and subhuman service robot—and, of course, original writer and translator. Only original writers own their own words; only they have the power and therefore the right to exert private control over the textual market. Translators are women, workers, service robots who do the bidding of the writer/owners: they are tools in the entrepreneur's mastery of the market.

This is, of course, the old instrumentalist ideal in a new social guise; it makes little difference for the translator's self-conception whether we say that he or she is the instrument of ecclesiastical authority (as for Augustine), of internalized dogmas (as for Luther), or of the writer as capitalist proprietor. What distinguishes Goethe's second epoch of translation from the first is not, in other words, that it begins to be contaminated by capitalist imagery, but rather that here, for the first time, the translator claims for him- or herself the role of the owner, the entrepreneur, the proprietor of meanings and words. The old stable dualism remains intact; there is no challenge to dualistic thinking here. Owners and workers, men and women, are still strictly separated. But now the translator insists that he or she be thought of as an owner, as a white-collar worker, as a man, no matter what his or her actual sex or social origins. Thus, the translator as self-made man rising from poverty and powerlessness to a position of authority, a position of control over his or her own text.[10]

Because the validity and the stability of the underlying dualism are not challenged in this epoch, however, its proponents and practitioners have remained isolated cases in the history of Western translation, mavericks like Ezra Pound. They are "exceptions"—and, as we all know, in the Augustinian tradition of dualistic stability, which insistently and exclusively elevates rules over the complexity of life, the exception always (by definition) proves the rule. It must: otherwise it could not be explained (away). Otherwise, it might become the wrench that sabotages the entire works. How do you explain the Catullus of Celia and Louis Zukofsky, who is *their* Catullus, not his own? You cannot: he is a freak, an aberration, a sport, which you either ignore (as most translation theorists do) or cite in passing as an oddity.[11]

You may have noticed that I feel a certain sympathy toward these self-assertive entrepreneurial translators, the Wielands and the Zukofskys and the Pounds of translation history. The argument that translators should receive book royalties is one I have often made myself. I both write ("originally," "creatively") and translate, and see no reason why I should have to change out of my white-collar shirt and into my blue-collar shirt when I pick up somebody else's text. You may also have noticed that my insistence on the existence of "genuine idiosomatic insight"—the possibility of breaking through the third seal to unprogrammed bits and pieces of personal experience and expanding them into an integrated and increasingly autonomous new personality—itself remains heavily in debt to Lockean liberalism. I want to insist on some tiny hidden guarantee of individuality, of uniqueness, maybe even of autonomy.

Well, that is how I was raised. I am a product of the middle class. And nobody escapes his or her ideosomatic past; in fact, because it can never be escaped, it is never exactly past. It is always there, always in the somatic present. And if the argument of this paragraph seems to contradict that of the preceding one, that contradiction lies at the heart of my own (barely) controlled waffling or dialectic.

On the one hand, we can never escape our ideosomatic past, because we carry it with us in our bodies. On the other hand, we *can* escape our ideosomatic past, by discovering idiosomatic enclaves that we have been programmed to ignore and expanding them into new somatic power centers, new internal movers and shakers, new grounds for action. We can oppose, challenge, relativize, downplay, peripheralize our ideosomatic programming; but we can never supplant or excrete it. We can never become entirely our own men.[12] But we can recover more of our own selves than the ideosomatic programmers would allow.

Romantic Redemption

Something like this mixed (dialectical) conclusion motivates Goethe's third epoch as well:

Weil man aber weder im Vollkommenen noch Unvollkommenen lange verharren kann, sondern eine Umwandlung nach der andern immerhin erfolgen muss, so erlebten wir den dritten Zeitraum, welcher der höchste und letzte zu nennen ist, derjenige nämlich, wo man die Übersetzung dem Original identisch machen möchte, so dass eins nicht anstatt des andern, sondern an der Stelle des andern gelten solle. . . . Eine Übersetzung, die sich mit dem Original zu identifizieren strebt, nähert sich zuletzt der Interlinearversion und erleichtert höchlich das Verständnis des Originals; hiedurch werden wir an den Grundtext hinangeführt, ja getrieben, und so ist denn zuletzt der ganze Zirkel abgeschlossen, in welchem sich die Annäherung des Fremden und Einheimischen, des Bekannten und Unbekannten bewegt. (Beutler, 296, 298)

Since it is impossible to linger too long either in the perfect or in the imperfect, and one change must of necessity follow another, we experienced the third epoch, which is to be called the highest and the last, namely the one in which the aim is to make the original identical with the translation, so that one would not be instead of the other, but in its place. . . . A translation which attempts to identify itself with the original in the end comes close to an interlinear version and greatly enhances our understanding of the original; this in turn leads us, compels us as it were, toward the source text, and so the circle is closed at last. Inside it the coming together of the foreign and the native, the unknown approximation and the known, keep moving toward each other. (Lefevere's translation, slightly modified, 36–37)

This is not the ultimate source of the romantic insistence on translating word-for-word *and* sense-for-sense, that is, perfectly, identically; its source may be in Kabbalism, where absolute cosmic correspondence, translating sense-for-sense, word-for-word, even letter-for-letter, was essential, or more than essential, crucial (anything less meant doom and destruction). But it is probably the most influential statement of that insistence, until George Steiner reformulated it in our time in terms of the hermeneutics of restitution. Important things are at stake in this notion, so important as to override (for the romantics and their heirs, at any rate) all practical, commonsensical objections regarding its impossibility. So what if it is impossible? *It has to be done!* It is not something we would sort of like to try to do; it is a messianic imperative, a question of life or death for all humanity. The translator is the romantic savior, charged with the task of undoing the damage done at Babel. God, or the evil demiurge the Gnostics said was responsible for the horrible things that the Elohim did to mankind in the early centuries of creation, was afraid of us—afraid of our restlessness, our rebelliousness, our willingness to risk death in the Garden of Eden by eating of the Tree of Life (and not dying!) and by eating of the Tree of the Knowledge of Good and Evil (and becoming as one of the gods), our willingness to challenge the gods' primacy and inaccessibility by building a tower into the heavens—and so he or it or they imposed the law on us, imposed exile, confusion, the scattering of tongues, did everything possible to thwart us, stymie us, keep us down. Well, we were once gods, the romantics believed, and we will become gods again, as soon as the romantic poet/translator/savior has undone the verbal magic that traps us in impotence, that blinds our eyes to the present reality of paradise (if we could but see it!). Here is Walter Benjamin's version of this hope:

Bei den einzelnen, den unergänzten Sprachen nämlich ist ihr Gemeintes niemals in relativer Selbstständigkeit anzutreffen, wie bei den einzelnen Wörten oder Sätzen, sondern vielmehr in stetem Wandel begriffen, bis es aus der Harmonie all jener Arten des Meinens als die reine Sprache herauszutreten vermag. So lange bleibt es in den Sprachen verborgen. Wenn aber diese derart bis ans messianische Ende ihrer Geschichte wachsen, so ist es die Übersetzung, welche am ewigen Fortleben der Werke und am unendlichen Aufleben der Sprachen sich entzündet, immer von neuem die Probe auf jenes heilige Wachstum der Sprachen zu machen: wie weit ihr Verborgenes von der Offenbarung entfernt sei, wie gegenwärtig es im Wissen um diese Entfernung werden mag. (161–62)

In the individual, unsupplemented languages, meaning is never found in relative independence, as in individual words or sentences; rather, it is in a constant state of flux—until it is able to emerge as pure language from the harmony of all the various modes of intention. Until then, it remains hidden in the languages. If, however, these languages continue to grow in this manner until the messianic end of their history, it is translation which catches fire on the eternal life of the works and the perpetual renewal of language. Translation keeps putting the hallowed growth of language to the test: how far removed is their hidden meaning from revelation, how close can it be brought by the knowledge of this remoteness? (Zohn's translation, slightly modified, 74–75)

The "heilige Wachstum der Sprachen . . . bis ans messianische Ende ihrer Geschichte": this is a quasidivine teleology, a progress toward revelation in which translation acts as both spur and control, at once testing the readiness of language for revelation and shaping its growth toward it. The failure of a given translation is a sign that the languages in question are not yet ripe for revelation—but also, Benjamin implies, an index of the distance yet to be traveled and thus a vehicle of the "knowledge of remoteness" that may narrow the distance. A successful translation, on the other hand, is always a redemptive agent whose effect is to transform flux into growth, chaos into harmony, multiplicity into unity.

All this is implicit in Goethe, with his talk of the restlessness of all stability, the constant flowing of things into their opposites and of these new mixtures into *their* opposites, higher and higher, until they reach the "highest and last" stage of all, paradise, perfection, what Hegel called *Absolute Geist*. SL and TL too are opposites and flow into each other in every act of translation (as Benjamin says explicitly), now leaning toward the SL (der fremde Sinn), now toward the TL (unser eigner Sinn), but every swing of the pendulum brings the two closer together until they merge in perfect identity.

The built-in dilemma of this romantic dialectic, the insistence that every synthesis becomes a new thesis, the next step in the upward movement, does doom romantic translation to eternal failure, or "impossibility," as the commonsensical carpers insist. Goethe too, although he says that perfect identity between SL and TL is the "highest and last" epoch of all translation, begins his paragraph with a reminder that "man aber weder in Vollkommenen noch Unvollkommenen lange verharren kann": every "highest and last" epoch we reach proves unstable, unable to hold the center; nothing can long persist in either perfection or imperfection but must keep straining upward. But the romantics, clinging more intensely than any orthodox Christian ever did to the dialectic of desire and unfulfillment, hope and disappointment, despair and fortitude, go right on insisting on the urgency of perfect translation despite its impossibility.

As the capitalist translator in Goethe's second epoch intensified Luther's assertive and manipulative self-sacrifice into autonomous self-assertion, then, the messianic translator in his third epoch intensifies Luther's proselytizing instrumentalism into universal self-salvation.

Away with this timid concern for converting the heathen, one by one; let the translator tap the world's resources for instantaneous redemption! Paul said we would be transformed in the blink of an eye; why wait? Let's do it now! Let the translator do it for us, or show us how it is done, so we can follow suit. In this conception, as its dialectical synthesis of Protestant self-denial and capitalist self-assertion already suggests, the translator is both nothing, a tool, a mere instrument of world redemption, and everything, the redeemer, a re-creative artist whose dialectical ability to bring SL and TL, East and West, day and night, into juxtaposition and then once and for all *join* them will save us all from death. Mainstream instrumentalism is synthesized with liberal autonomy in a new ("higher") instrumentalism that asserts the translator's creative activity precisely in his or her utter surrender to the spirit of world self-redemption.

Of the three definitive features of mainstream Western thought about translation, then—dualism, instrumentalism, and perfectionism—the romantics enlivened the first by stretching dualities out over time (dynamizing them as dialectic), complicated the second by incorporating into it the radical self-assertion of the liberal entrepreneur, and intensified the third by raising the stakes to all-or-nothing. They enlivened, complicated, and intensified, in other words—but did not fundamentally change anything.

So what? you say. What does it matter what the romantics did or didn't do? But it does matter. One result of the romantics' failure to see their way clear to fundamental changes in the dualizing, instrumentalizing, and perfectionizing mainstream of Western translation theory is that, among contemporary heirs of the romantics, we are presented with a choice between, say, the massively erudite and rather heavy-handed philosophizing of George Steiner and the light, playful dephilosophizing of Jacques Derrida. The one offers us an impressive scholarly complication of the issues that ultimately, despite its author's best efforts, leads nowhere; the other a delightfully baroque complication of the issues that insists with that forced grim smile of Camus's Sisyphus that nothing can ever lead anywhere. Steiner, in his exfoliation of Goethe and Benjamin, keeps trying, hoping against hope that something can be made of all this; Derrida, in his deconstruction of Benjamin (in "Des Tours de Babel"), knows there is no hope, and traces on the margins of Benjamin's text the hopelessness that he (and we) knew all along lay at its core.

But is that all there is? Must we choose among the Augustinian coolness of the "science" of translation, so blind to power and persuasion, value and human worth; the Lutheran pressures of Protestant Bible translation, so blind to its own power and persuasion; the capitalist assertiveness of maverick translators, defensively blind to anything but their own autonomy and uniqueness; and the hopeless intensity of romantic messianism, which in its dedication to all or nothing in an nonideal world inescapably proliferates nothing? Among scientists of translation, must we choose between the humanistically inclined work of a Juliane House (who is also indebted to the German romantics), say, and the hardcore science of machine translation? Among romantic hermeneuticists, must we choose between George Steiner and Jacques Derrida? Is that it?

No. My dialogical engagement with only two major translation theorists, Luther and Goethe (with side excursions into Steiner and others), has inevitably simplified the field. I still believe that the result of my simplification is not merely a figment of my imagination but something like the mainstream of Western translation theory—that, in other words, I have been *tracing* a simplification, not merely perpetrating one. But since the simplification I have been tracing is one ideosomatically engraved on my body, I have no way of knowing whether the simplification is the culture's or mine alone. Certainly my students' conception of translation tends to be simpler still, largely restricted to Eugene Nida's mixing of Augustinian science with Lutheran propaganda; and the "culture's" conception of translation as I find it in casual pronouncements on the subject by parents, friends, and journalists tends to be ultrasimple.[13] But the ideosomatically programmed "mainstream," whether it takes the form I have sketched or not, is not all there is. In the folds and around the fringes of the ideosomatic mainstream there are rich idiosomatic possibilities by the hundred, possibilities buried in the passing remarks and ad hoc theories of sensitive marginal translators and theorists and eminently salvageable for our use.

Martin Buber

One marginalized idiosomatic possibility might be the dialogism of Martin Buber. Buber will not take us very far in the direction I want to go; even at his most dialogical, he clings to a Jewish/romantic mysticism that places him firmly in the camp of Goethe and Company. But a hundred years had passed since the *West-Östlicher Divan* when Buber and Franz Rosenzweig began their new German translation of the Hebrew Scriptures—a quarter of a century more when it was finished and Buber wrote his preface, "Zu einer neuen Verdeutschung der Schrift"

(1954)—and in the interval, time did its usual work on romanticism. It is old hat now—still there, still alive at some cultural level, but debased and discredited (the myth of the seedy poet's genius)—and Buber finds himself driven to conflicting rhetorical extremes in his attempt to keep it alive: down-to-earth pragmatism charged with high mystical hopes; hard-hitting commonsensical polemic laced with purple mystic ether. God still speaks to us, if we would but listen; but—and here is the first trace of a new idiosomatic possibility—he speaks to us through our bodies, dialogically. Mystical paradise lies not at the end of a dialectical process, as it did for the High romantics; it lies in the ongoingness of dialogue, *between* extremes, not beyond them. Nor is it a paradise of *Absolute Geist*, as it was for Hegel; it lurks among the flaps and flanges of our imperfection, the rough edges of our day-to-day living.

Here, for example, is Buber's comment on Goethe's first kind of translation, which he attacks more polemically than Goethe ever did:

Auch die bedeutendsten Übersetzungen der Schrift, die uns erhalten sind, die griechische der Siebzig, die lateinische des Hieronymus, die deutsche Martin Luthers, gehen nicht wesenhaft darauf aus, den ursprünglichen Charakter des Buches in Wortwahl, Satzbau und rhythmischer Gliederung zu erhalten; von ihrer Absicht getragen, einer aktuellen Gemeinschaft, der jüdischen Diaspora des hellenismus, der frühchristlichen Ökumene, dem Glaubensvolk der Reformation, eine zuverlässige Stiftungsurkunde zu übermitteln, ziehen sie den "Inhalt" des Textes in die andre Sprache herüber, auf die Eigentümlichkeiten der Elemente, der Struktur, der Dynamik zwar nicht etwa von vornherein Verzicht leistend, wohl aber sie da unschwer aufgebend, wo die spröde "Form" die Weitergabe des Inhalts behindern zu wollen scheint. Als ob eine echte Botschaft, ein echter Spruch, ein echter Gesang ein von seinem Wie ohne Schaden ablösbares Was enthielte, als ob der Geist der Rede anderswo als in seiner sprachlichen Leibesgestalt aufzuspüren und anders als durch deren zugleich treue und unbefangene Nachbildung den Zeiten und Räumen zuzutragen wäre, als ob eine auf Kosten der ursprünglichen Leiblichkeit gewonnene Gemeinverständlichkeit nicht notwendigerweise eine Mißverständlichkeit wäre oder doch werden müßte! Gewiß standen die großen Übersetzer in der begeisterten Einsicht, daß das Wort Gottes allen Zeiten und Räumen gelte; aber sie verkannten, daß durch solche Einsicht das Gewicht des "Von wo aus," des Dort und Damals in all seiner volkhaften, personhaften, körperhaften Bedingtheit nicht gemindert, sondern erhöht wird. Vollzogene Offenbarung ist immer Menschenleib und Menschenstimme, und das heißt immer: *dieser* Leib und *diese* Stimme im Geheimnis ihrer Einmaligkeit. (351–52)

Even the most significant surviving translations of Scripture, the Greek of the Seventy, the Latin of Jerome, the German of Martin Luther, aim not to preserve the original character of the book in diction, sentence structure, and rhythmical arrangement, but rather to convey a reliable founding deed to a specific community—the Jewish Diaspora for the Greeks, the early Christian Church, the believers in the Reformation—by pulling the "content" of the text over into the other language. Not that they systematically renounce the elemental, structural, dynamic properties of the original; but they do rather facilely abandon those properties wherever reluctant "form" seems to want to hinder the transfer of the content. As if an authentic missive, an authentic saying, an authentic song could ever be reduced to a detachable What and its How sloughed off without suffering damage; as if talk's spirit could ever be tracked down anywhere but in its linguistic body, and time and place ever be at once truly and openmindedly reproduced except through that body; as if common understanding gained at the expense of original corporeality would not, or indeed must not, necessarily become misunderstanding! To be sure, the great translators worked on the inspired understanding that God's word is true in all times and all places; but they wrongly believed that this understanding would not diminish but would rather enhance local point of view, the Then and There in all its cultural/personal/bodily thinghood. Consummate revelation is always human flesh and human voice, and I mean always: *this* flesh and *this* voice in the mystery of its onceness.

This is very close to Goethe's call for perfect identity with the original. And indeed, a few lines down Buber finds himself back at the old chestnut of mainstream Western translation theory, in its intensified romantic form:

Dies erkennen, heißt dem Übersetzer eine grundsätzlich unerfüllbare Aufgabe zuweisen; denn das Besondere is eben das Besondere und kann nicht "wiedergegeben" werden, die Sinnlichkeiten der Sprachen sind verschieden, ihre Vorstellungen und ihre Weisen sie auszuspinnen, ihre Innervationen und ihre Bewegungen, ihre Leidenschaften und ihre Musik. *Grundsätzlich* kann denn auch Botschaft, in ihrer schicksalhaften Verschweißung von Sinn und Laut, nicht übertragen werden; sie kann es nur praktisch: annähernd—wie nah zu kommen es einem jeweils von den Grenzen der Sprache, in die er überträgt, verstattet wird. (352)

To recognize this is to present the translator with a fundamentally impossible task; for the particular is particular and cannot be "transferred," the significances of languages are different, their imaginations and ways of spinning them out, their innervations and emotions, their passions and music. *Fundamentally,* in their fatal commingling of sense and sound, missives are untranslatable; they can only be translated in practice, approximately—one comes as close as the boundaries of the language into which one is translating permit.

Here we are, then, back where we started: at an infinite approach to an impossible goal. Fundamental despair and practical fortitude. Translation as Zeno's arrow that never hits the tree. Never mind that we all know it does hit the tree, sometimes (sometimes it shoots on past, or falls short, but sometimes it even hits the bull's-eye, and it never hovers just shy of the tree). In the idealized fantasy world that Zeno and Buber (like most translation theorists) posit, it is impossible to hit it, ever; and our experience that it does (we *see* it plunk right into the tree! with our own eyes!) must somehow be explained away as an unfortunate illusion.

But Buber's own insistence on "Einmaligkeit," onceness, once-offness, points a way out of this fantasy world that Buber himself does not see—does not want to see, perhaps, since even in his most radical dialogism he retains a loyalty to a transcendentalized image of the original text. If "consummate revelation is always human flesh and human voice," and that always means "*this* flesh and *this* voice in the mystery of its onceness," then nothing is ever untranslatable, even "fundamentally." Who cares if, in some transcendental perspective, the passions of languages are "different"? In the onceness of my dialogical engagement with them, my passions—my somatic responses—may be complex, but I will certainly not find any impassable chasms in them. They will not be different in kind. Buber's insistence (neatly reversing the path that Augustine followed from Manicheanism to Platonic Christianity) on lodging spirit firmly in body, which I have highlighted in my translation, is specifically an attempt to block "spiritualizing" interpretations that suppress body, transcendentalizing interpretations that seek a disembodied universality at the expense of felt thingy onceness. And in that sense, Buber's insistence that "das Besondere ist eben das Besondere und kann nicht 'wiedergegeben' werden, die Sinnlichkeiten der Sprachen sind verschieden," and so on, is specifically a spiritualizing or transcendentalizing account of the situation in which translators find themselves. Only from a spiritualized (fantasized) Archimedes' point outside onceness and embodied thinghood is it possible to discern and describe differences in this stable, systematic manner. Only from what Buber derogates as a "religious" (read Platonic/Pauline/Augustinian) standpoint is it possible to talk of stable "boundaries" between languages and of what they will or will not "permit." In the terms of Buber's earlier book, *Ich und Du,* in fact, the stabilized object-world of "die Sinnlichkeiten der Sprachen sind verschieden" and of "die Grenzen der Sprache" comes from Buber's speaking the Ich-Es, the I-It:

Das Ich des Grundworts Ich-Es, das Ich also, dem nicht ein Du gegenüber leibt, sondern das von einer Vielheit von "Inhalten" umstanden ist, hat nur

Vergangenheit, keine Gegenwart. Mit andern Wort: insofern der Mensch sich an den Dingen genügen läßt, die er erfährt und gebraucht, lebt er in der Vergangenheit, und sein Augenblick ist ohne Präsenz. Er hat nichts als Gegenstände; Gegenstände aber bestehen im Gewesensein.

Gegenwart ist nicht das Flüchtige und Vorübergleitende, sondern das Gegenwartende und Gegenwährende. (19–20)

The I of the basic word I-It, the I that is not bodily confronted by a You but surrounded by a multitude of "contents," has only a past and no present. In other words: insofar as a human being makes do with the things that he experiences and uses, he lives in the past, and his moment has no presence. He has nothing but objects; but objects consist in having been.

Presence is not what is evanescent and passes but what confronts us, waiting and enduring. (Kaufmann's translation, 63–64)

Gegenwart, the bodily presence of the You that "waits against" us when we speak the basic word I-You, in translation is the translator's engagement with the SL text, and through the text with the SL author-as-You; then it is the translator's confrontation with the TL reader-as-You. Once. Every translation dialogue occurs that once; there is no repetition, since every dialogue is present for the moment that it *is* present, and it never comes again. (On the next reading, even by the same person, the dialogue is a different one.) Any attempt to stabilize these confrontations into a pattern evokes the I-It, which hardens all presence into pastness. In the confrontational presence of the I-You, the translator feels both languages, responds to them somatically, senses their passions and "innervations" all at once, and swirls them around, rubs them up against each other to see which two might at any given moment—any present moment of engagement—go together. In the dialogical I-You, there are no rigid differences between the significations of languages, no boundaries between languages, no besonderes this and besonderes that. Those differences arise out of the slipping into the security of pastness that Buber calls I-It. Only in the dead object-world of the I-It is translation impossible.

Now, Buber might reply that in the I-You the I responds fully to the You, with the fullness of the I-You, and that a response that in any way distorts the message or the missive of the You is not dialogical at all, not I-You relational at all, but purely personal, subjective, experiential, and therefore fundamentally I-It. The I objectifies the You as It by bringing it into itself. Certainly, this seems to be the implicit assumption behind Buber's argument in "Zu einer neuen Verdeutschung der Schrift": the translator is not to distort the original Botschaft! But exactly the same argument could be used against him. If the I is expected to subordinate its will to the You, to subsume itself in the transcendental meaning of the You, you don't have any dialogue then either. The I has become the You's transcendentalized It. The translator is God's instrument. "Beziehung ist Gegenseitigkeit," Buber says in *Ich und Du*. "Mein Du wirkt an mir, wie ich an ihm wirke. Unsre Schüler bilden uns, unsre Werke bauen uns auf" (23). "Relation is reciprocity. My You acts on me as I act on it. Our students teach us, our works form us" (Kaufmann's translation, 67)—and our translators shape us, our readers shape us. Any SL writer who submits to translation as an I-You dialogue with the translator inevitably submits to being shaped by the dialogue, shaped by the relation. The translator who submits to publication as an I-You dialogue with the TL reader also submits to being shaped by the dialogue. Translation as an I-You dialogue in the confrontational present—as *"dieser* Leib und *diese* Stimme im Geheimnis ihrer Einmaligkeit"—must, in Buber's own terms, involve mutual shaping. It cannot be artificially stabilized in favor of either the SL (as for Buber) or the TL (as for Luther). It must be left open to an immediacy of relation. And in that immediacy, translation is always possible.

Revealingly, when Buber evokes the two "worlds" of the I-It and the I-You, he sounds very much as if he were describing Augustinian/Lutheran translation theory (I-It) and the quiddity of day-to-day translation practice (I-You):

Die Welt ist dem Menschen zwiefältig nach seiner zwiefältigen Haltung.

Er nimmt das Sein um sich herum wahr, Dinge schlechthin und Wesen als Dinge, er nimmt das Geschehen um sich herum wahr, Vorgänge schlechthin und Handlungen als Vorgänge, Dinge aus Eigenschaften, Vorgänge aus Momenten bestehend, Dinge ins Raumnetz, Vorgänge ins Zeitnetz eingetragen, Dinge und Vorgänge von andern Dingen und Vorgängen eingegrenzt, an ihnen meßbar, mit ihnen vergleichbar, geordnete Welt, abgetrennte Welt. Diese Welt ist einigermaßen zuverlässig, sie hat Dichte und Dauer, ihre Gliederung läßt sich überschauen, man kann sie immer wieder hervorholen, man repetiert sie mit geschloßnen Augen und prüft mit geöffneten nach; sie steht ja da, deiner Haut anliegend, wenn dus annimmst, in deiner Seele eingekauert, wenn dus so vorsiehst, sie ist ja dein Gegenstand, sie bleibt es nach deinem Gefallen, und bleibt dir urfremd, außer und in dir. Du nimmst sie wahr, nimmst sie dir zur "Wahrheit," sie läßt sich von dir nehmen, aber sie gibt sich dir nicht. Nur über sie kannst du dich mit andern "verständigen," sie ist, ob sie auch sich jedem anders anbildet, bereit, euch gemeinsam Gegenstand zu sein, aber du kannst andern nicht in ihr begegnen. Du kannst ohne sie nicht im Leben beharren, ihre Zuverlässigkeit erhält dich, aber stürbest du in sie hinein, so wärst du im Nichts begraben.

Oder der Mensch begegnet dem Sein und Werden als seinem Gegenüber, immer nur *einer* Wesenheit und jedem Ding nur als Wesenheit; was da ist, erschließt sich ihm im Geschehen, und was da geschieht, widerfährt ihm als Sein; nichts andres ist gegenwärtig als dies eine, aber dies eine welthaft; Maß und Vergleich sind entwichen; es liegt an dir, wieviel des Unermeßlichen dir zur Wirklichkeit wird. Die Begegnungen ordnen sich nicht zur Welt, aber jede ist dir ein Zeichen der Weltordnung. Sie sind untereinander nicht verbunden, aber jede verbürgt dir deine Verbundenheit mit der Welt. Die Welt, die dir so erscheint, ist unzuverlässig, denn sie erscheint dir stets neu, und du darfst sie nicht beim Wort nehmen; sie ist undicht, denn alles durchdringt in ihr alles; dauerlos, denn sie kommt auch ungerufen und entschwindet auch festgehalten; sie ist unübersehbar: willst du sie übersehbar machen, verlierst du sie. Sie kommt, und kommt dich hervorholen; erreicht sie dich nicht, begegnet sie dir nicht, so entschwindet sie; aber sie kommt wieder, verwandelt. Sie steht nicht außer dir, sie rührt an deinen Grund, and sagst du "Seele meiner Seele," hast du nicht zuviel gesagt; aber hüte dich, sie in deine Seele versetzen zu wollen— da vernichtest du sie. Sie ist deine Gegenwart, du hast nur Gegenwart, indem du sie hast; und du kannst sie dir zum Gegenstand machen, sie zu erfahren und zu gebrauchen, du mußt es immer wieder tun, und hast nun keine Gegenwart mehr. Zwischen dir und ihn ist Gegenseitigkeit des Gebens; du sagst Du zu ihn und gibst dich ihr, sie sagt Du zu dir und gibt sich dir. Über sie kannst du dich mit andern nicht verständigen, du bist einsam mit ihr; aber sie lehrt dich andern begegnen und ihrer Begegnung standhalten; und sie führt dich, durch die Huld ihrer Ankünfte und durch die Wehmut ihrer Abschiede, zu dem Du hin, in dem die Linien der Beziehungen, die parallelen, sich schneiden. Sie hilft dir nicht, dich im Leben zu erhalten, hilft dir nur, die Ewigkeit zu ahnen. (39–42)

The world is twofold for man in accordance with his twofold attitude.

He perceives the being that surrounds him, plain things and beings as things; he perceives what happens around him, plain processes and actions as processes, things that consist of qualities and processes that consist of moments, things recorded in terms of spatial coordinates and processes recorded in terms of temporal coordinates, things and processes that are bounded by other things and compared with those others—an ordered world, a detached world. This world is somewhat reliable; it has density and duration; its articulation can be surveyed; one can get it out again and again; one recounts it with one's eyes closed and then checks with one's eyes open. There it stands—right next to your skin if you think of it that way, or nestled in your soul if you prefer that: it is your object and remains that, according to your pleasure—and remains primally alien both outside and inside you. You perceive it and take it for your "truth"; it permits itself to be taken by you, but it does not give itself to you. It is only *about* it that you can come to an understanding with others; although it takes a somewhat different form for everybody, it is prepared to be a common object for you; but you cannot encounter others in it. Without it you cannot remain alive; its reliability preserves you; but if you were to die into it, then you would be buried in nothingness.

Or man encounters being and becoming as what confronts him—always only *one* being and every thing only as a being. What is there reveals itself to him in the occurrence, and what occurs there happens to him as being. Nothing else is present but this one, but this one cosmically. Measure and comparison have fled. It is up to you how much of the immeasurable becomes reality for you. The encounters do not order themselves to become a world, but each is for you a sign of the world order. They have no association with each other, but every one guarantees your association with the world. The world that appears to you in this way is unreliable, for it appears always new to you, and you cannot take it by its word. It lacks density, for everything in it permeates everything else. It lacks duration, for it comes even when not called and vanishes even when you cling to it. It cannot be surveyed: if you try to make it surveyable, you lose it. It comes—comes to fetch you—and if it does not reach you or encounter you it vanishes, but it comes again, transformed. It does not stand outside you, it touches your ground; and if you say "soul of my soul" you have not said too much. But beware of trying to transpose it into your soul—that way you destroy it. It is your present; you have a present only insofar as you have it; and you can make it into an object for you and experience and use it— you must do that again and again—and then you have no present any more. Between you and it there is a reciprocity of giving: you say You to it and give yourself to it; it says you to you and gives itself to you. You cannot come to an understanding *about* it with others; you are lonely with it; but it teaches you to encounter others and to stand your ground in such encounters; and through the grace of its advents and the melancholy of its departures it leads you to that you in which the lines of relation, though parallel, intersect. It does not help you to survive; it only helps you to have intimations of eternity. (Kaufmann's translation, 82–84)

Fine. What I begin to wonder as I read this, though, is whether it is just a bit too "reliable." Obviously, Buber is dualizing human activity in terms of two objects, two objectified worlds: translation theory and translation practice, as I said above. Science and art. Intellection and intuition. We cannot live entirely in the I-You (practice/art/intuition), but neither can we live without it. To live entirely in the I-It (theory/ science/intellection) is not to live at all—to be dead—but without it we could never talk about anything, never share anything, never see the relationships between events or people. Everything would be a swirl of confrontational presence. The solution is clear: it is the traditional one. Live in the I-It at the university, in the I-You at home (at odd moments, anyway). Live in the I-It when you do translation theory, in the I-You when you translate. Maintain the reliable, objectified, I-It dichotomy between them, keep it stable; but order your life into separate moments, moments of reliable pastness and moments of enlivening presence.

This seems to me pernicious. By so rigidly dualizing his two worlds—by seeing no relation or reciprocity between them, no I-You between the I-It and the I-You—Buber only perpetuates the old rift between theory and practice, science and art. His dialogical conception of the I-You points to a new conception of translation that is (potentially) immensely fruitful; but if the I-You is so fragile that the slightest self-consciousness, the vaguest memory, can destroy it and shunt us back into the I-It, it is useless.[14] What we need is a conception of relation and dialogue that commingles not only sound and sense, and not only self and other, but also theory and practice. We need ways to theorize practice that will not destroy the confrontational presence of the I-You but will enhance it, heighten it, improve it; and we need ways to practicalize theory that will not banish all thought in a blooming mystical confusion but will ground it, give body to it, carnalize it. We need ways not only of living *"this* flesh and *this* voice in the mystery of its onceness," but of talking about it as well, ways of theorizing practice that will affirm and celebrate its onceness and its mystery—that will never forget that *I* speak, *I* feel the SL and TL in this particular way; and that for this flesh and this voice (mine) in this particular context, that particular way of feeling is the only right one.

In the rest of this chapter I want to sketch out some methods for doing just that—just sketch, by way of a prolegomenon to Part 2, where I will be concerned with the practical/theoretical details of dialogical confrontation with the SL text/writer (tropics) and TL receptor (ethics). The three definitive characteristics of mainstream translation ideology in the West that I outlined in Chapter 1, dualism, instrumentalism, and perfectionism, will serve me as framework. Specifically, I want to consider first how we might begin to bridge the gap between dualized extremes not by extending them dialectically, over time, but by blending them dialogically, in what Mikhail Bakhtin calls the internal dialogism, or heteroglossia, of speech. Then I want to look at our mutual implication or instrumentalization through dialogue, the way speech makes us instruments of the interchange, but active instruments that shape the very process that shapes us. Bakhtin will be helpful here too, but I find the most powerful counter to Augustinian instrumentalism in the "primal scene of instruction" charted out by Harold Bloom, and Bloom will (much modified, brought willy-nilly into my dialogical conception of intertextuality) serve as my theoretical guide in Chapter 3. Finally, I want to suggest some ways in which we might begin to relax the ideosomatically programmed perfectionism that keeps us desiring what we can never have, pining for the impossible. Here, and in Part 2, I choose Kenneth Burke as my guide, his logological discussion of Christian theology from *The Rhetoric of Religion* here and in Chapter 4 and his dramatistic of motivation from *A Grammar of Motives* in Chapter 3.

Dialogue contra Dualism

The dualism that Bakhtin seeks to undo in his theory of internal dialogism, or heteroglossia, is that between self and other, subject and object. The problem with Saussurean linguistics, as Bakhtin sees it, is not only that it is predicated on the Platonic dualism of the visible and the invisible, body and mind, speech (*parole*) and system (*langue*). That is an obvious problem, and one that many Saussurean linguists (especially pragmatists and sociolinguists) have addressed. Never mind, either, that the Platonic preference for the invisible over the visible always subtly (ideosomatically) tends to discredit real speech; Saussure himself, in the *Cours de linguistique général*, does point the way to a serious study of speech, and with a little work linguists could redress the balance until speech and system were almost on a par with each other.

No, for Bakhtin these are important questions, but not the key. The key, which has been ignored by all of Saussure's Western critics, is the submerged bourgeois ideology that plants in Saussure's head (body), as in the heads and bodies of all of his Western supporters and detractors, the notion that language has no ideology—that, like all idealized objects of bourgeois science, it is "value-free"; that it is not charged with the ideologically controlled values of the culture. Bakhtin insists that language is saturated with ideology—specifically, with the voices of everyone who has spoken it, with the heteroglossia, or many-voicedness, of the babble of actual speech. This takes the form, for Bakhtin, of "internal dialogism," which is to say, in my terms, somatically stored dialogue, the interchange or interaction (Beziehung or Gegenseitigkeit, in Buber's terms) of actual speech internalized in the form of somatically felt voices. "Подлинная среда высказывания," Bahktin says, "в которой оно живёт и формируется,—диалогизованное разноречие, безымянное и социальное как язык, но конкретное, содержательно-наполненное и акцентуированное как индивидуальное высказывание"(86)—"The authentic environment of an utterance, the environment in which it lives and takes shape, is dialogized heteroglossia, anonymous and social as language, but simultaneously concrete, filled with specific content and accented as an individual utterance" (Emerson and Holquist's translation, 272).

Ведь всякое конкретное слово (высказывание) находит тот предмет, на который оно направлено, всегда, так сказать, уже оговоренным, оспоренным, оцененным, окутанным затемняющею его дымкою или, напротив, светом уже сказанных чужих слов о нём. Он опутан и пронизан общими мыслями, точками зрения, чужими оценками, акцентами. Направленное на свой предмет слово входит в эту диалогически взволнованную и напряжённую среду чужих слов, оценок и акцентов, вплетается в их сложные взаимоотношения, сливается с одними, отталкивается от других, пересекается с третьими; и всё это может существенно формировать слово, отлагаться во всех его смысловых пластах, осложнять его экспрессию, влиять на весь стилистический облик.

Живое высказывание, осмысленно возникшее в определённый исторический момент в социально определённой среде, не может не задеть тысячи живых диалогических нитей, сотканных социально-идеологическим сознанием вокруг данного предмета высказывания, не может не стать активным участником социального диалога. Оно и возникает из него, из этого диалога, как его продолжение, как реплика, а не откуда-то со стороны подходит к предмету. (89–90)

Indeed, any concrete discourse (utterance) finds the object at which it was directed already as it were overlain with qualifications, open to dispute, charged with value, already enveloped in an obscuring mist—or, on the contrary, by the "light" of alien words that have already been spoken about it. It is entangled, shot through with shared thoughts, points of view, alien value judgments and accents. The word, directed toward its object, enters a dialogically agitated and tension-filled environment of alien words, value judgments and accents, weaves in and out of complex interrelationships, merges with some, recoils from others, intersects with yet a third group: and all this may crucially shape discourse, may leave a trace in all its semantic layers, may complicate its expression and influence its entire stylistic profile.

The living utterance, having taken meaning and shape at a particular historical moment in a socially specific environment, cannot fail to brush up against thousands of living dialogic threads, woven by socio-ideological consciousness around the given object of an utterance; it cannot fail to become an active participant in social dialogue. After all, the utterance arises out of this dialogue as a continuation of it and as a rejoinder to it—it does not approach the object from the sidelines. (Emerson and Holquist's translation, 276–77)

This has important consequences for the study of language. It means that the I-You, which Buber idealizes as an almost impossible, mystically life-giving relation, is always already built into language. It means that by learning a language we learn relation, interrelatedness. It means that to learn a word is to bring the speaker of that word into your body, in the form of a somatic response to that person as You, and to respond is to give yourself back to the You, donate your I to your interlocutor in the form of a word that provokes a dialogized somatic response. It means that, as we *live* language, in what Buber calls the I-You, there simply is no self-other dualism. We sense that small children live language this way, and know that sometimes, when we "forget ourselves," forget the bourgeois conditioning that teaches us to maintain a strong sense of separate self, or "ego," we adults live it that way too. Bakhtin doesn't quite avoid the temptations of self/other dualization; like Buber, he too speaks of boundaries, of "borderlines"; but notice, in this next passage, how he quickly shifts from the stale idea of mediated dualism to a sense that "self," or "ownness," as one side of the dualism is no given but precisely the product of an ideologically controlled (capitalist) act of (self-)appropriation:

В сущности, язык как живая социально-идеологическая конкретность, как разноречивое мнение, лежит для индивидуального сознания на границах своего и чужого. Слово языка—получужое слово. Оно станет "своим," когда говорящий населит его своею интенцией, своим акцентом, овладеет словом, приобщит его к своей смысловой и экспрессивной устремлённости. До этого момента присвоения слово не в нейтральном и безличном языке (ведь не из словаря же берётся слово говорящим!), а в чужих устах, в чужих контекстах, на службе у чужих интенций: отсюда его приходится брать и делать своим. И не все слова для всякого одинаково легко поддаются этому присвоению, этому захвату в собственность: многие упорно сопротивляются, другие так и остаются чужими, звучат по-чужому в устах присвоившего их говорящего, не могут ассимилироваться в его контексте и выпадают из него; они как бы сами, помимо воли говорящего, заключают себя в кавычки. Язык—это не нейтральня среда, которая легко и свободно переходит в интенциональную собственность говорящего,—он населён и перенаселён чужими интенциями. Овладение им, подчинение его своим, интенциям и акцентам—процесс трудный и сложный. (106–7)

As a living, socio-ideological, somatic thing, as heteroglot opinion, language, for the individual consciousness, lies on the borderline between oneself and the other. The word in language is half someone else's. It becomes "one's own" only when the speaker populates it with his own intention, his own accent, when he appropriates the word, adapting it to his own semantic and expressive intention. Prior to this moment of appropriation, the word does not exist in a neutral and impersonal language (it is not, after all, out of a dictionary that the speaker gets his words!), but rather it exists in other people's mouths, in other people's somatized contexts, serving other people's intentions: it is from there that one must take the word, and make it one's own. And not all words for just anyone submit equally easily to this appropriation, to this seizure and transformation into private property: many words stubbornly resist, others remain alien, sound foreign in the mouth of the one who appropriated them and who now speaks them; they cannot be assimilated into his context and fall out of it; it is as if they put themselves in quotation marks against the will of the speaker. Language is not a neutral medium that passes freely and easily into the private property of the speaker's intentions; it is populated—overpopulated—with the intentions of others. Expropriating it, forcing it to submit to one's own intentions and accents, is a difficult and complicated process. (Emerson and Holquist's translation, slightly modified, 293–94)

And, I would add, it is never an entirely successful process, in the idealized sense posited by dualizing linguists: no one's language is ever entirely other, entirely public property, the property of a transcendentalized system, say, like the one that Saussure imagined; but neither is it ever entirely one's own, entirely private property, pure idiolect. Even the most aggressively appropriative speaker must find his or her words entangled with the words of others—or rather, *every* word he or she speaks is also always someone else's word, many other people's word. There is no verbal purity—no purity of systemic otherness, and no purity of unique ownness, either. We are caught up in ideosomatic dialogue, heteroglot dialogue, with every word we speak.

As if to illustrate this dialogical interflowing, in that last quotation I inflected or "double-voiced" Emerson and Holquist's translation of Bakhtin with my own theory of the somatic grounding of language: in the first line Emerson and Holquist had "concrete," not "somatic," and I added "somatized" later. In the idealized ethos of liberal translation theory, according to which everyone owns his or her own words, this constitutes bad translation: it is *my* theory of language that conceptualizes the materiality of language as somatic response, not Bakhtin's; I should allow Emerson and Holquist to keep them distinct, with the word "concrete." But "concrete" sounds to me like cracked sidewalks, so hard and unbending that shifts in the ground crack it, nothing at all like the living somaticity I take Bakhtin to be referring to. It seems to me, in other words, that my reading of Bakhtin's theory as translated by Emerson and Holquist is a dialogized somatic response specifically to a dialogized Bakhtinian word that already contains the somaticity I feel in it. Bakhtin *meant* me to say "somatic" instead of "concrete"—or rather, "somatic" was implicit in the dialogue that we pursue. In the idealized terms of liberal theory, this sounds like casuistry; but it is precisely congruent with Bakhtin's theory (as I read it, as Bakhtin and Emerson and Holquist and I dialogically construct it, or as I construct it out of my dialogical engagement with those three, in the mystery of that engagement's onceness). It is as James Carse says:

> Since being your own genius is dramatic, it has all the paradox of infinite play: You can have what you have only by releasing it to others. The sounds of the words you speak may lie on your own lips, but if you do not relinquish them entirely to a listener they never become words, and you say nothing at all. The words die with the sound. Spoken to me, your words become mine to do with as I please. As the genius of your words, you lose all authority over them. So too with thoughts. However you consider them your own, you cannot think the thoughts themselves, but only what they are *about*. You cannot think thoughts any more than you can act actions. If you do not truly speak the words that reside entirely in their own sound, neither can you think that which remains thought or can be translated back into thought. In thinking you cast thoughts beyond themselves, surrendering them to that which they cannot be. (67–68)

This is one implication that Bakhtin's theory obviously has for translation (theory): since words do not really belong to anyone, since they aren't "property" that can be allotted or stolen or trespassed upon, but float freely in the dialogical public domain, there can be no pure or perfect or ideal distinctions between texts, and thus no pure or perfect or ideal correspondences between them either. (You have to have a difference before you can have a correspondence.) There is no way of establishing the objective "equivalence" between texts, or between receptor responses to texts. Artificial boundaries can be set up and jealously maintained, but dialogized words flow back and forth across any such boundaries and render them thus politically and historically contingent. The boundaries between texts or responses that translation theorists have taken to be impregnable barriers to successful translation do not exist as stable objects or obstacles in the real world; they are anxious fictions imposed on the field by the ideosomatic imaginations of people afraid of the instability of flux. The reality of any text lies in the once-off dialogized response of a real person—a response that, because it is once-off, will always defy stable characterization or classification, but that also, because it is (ideosomatically) dialogized, partakes in the collective imagination of the language community and thus permits tentative or contingent generalization. This dialectical tension between once-off individuality and generalizable collectivity will inform my classification of tropes and versions in Part 2.

Another (and related) implication of Bakhtin's theory for translation studies might be that in the translator's body, somatically charged words of two or more languages are always multiply entangled. The boundaries between languages that Buber imagined as impregnable barriers to successful translation are likewise anxious fictions maintained socially and politically—not real walls. After fourteen years of living in Finland, eighteen years of speaking Finnish, my Finnish is so much a part of my somatic/linguistic understanding of myself and my world that it often invades my English speech, in the form of literal translations of words and phrases, actual Finnish words, and language switches (with my wife, who does the same) between English and Finnish. Somatically, inside my body, English and Finnish are not really separated from each other; there is no boundary, no territorial border between them, no sign saying "No trespassing." They conflow freely. In different moods, or different speech contexts, I have varying access to English and Finnish words; sometimes I feel that I cannot say a thing in English and have to use Finnish; other times I feel that my Finnish would be useless for what I have to say. But there are no patterns that I can see. It is entirely situational. George Steiner describes a similar merging of languages in his own "mind" (I would say body), in the opening pages of his third chapter; but unlike Steiner, who was raised trilingual, I first heard Finnish when I was sixteen. Sheer dialogical exposure to Finnish, not some mystical process of bilingual language acquisition, did this to me, swirled Finnish and English around inside my body in an unindividuated mass.

As Bakhtin says, this happens all the time in our native tongues: we store all the dialects we have ever heard, all the class accents, race inflections, expressions of anger and love and anxiety and all the emotions in all their situational variety, everything we have heard in one language, in an unindividuated mass; why not in two or more languages? What is Bakhtin's heteroglossia or polyphonia but an internalized (somatized) Babel? What is the translator but a person who has, in one way or another, been somatically polyphonized, and then has trained him- or herself in the art of Maxwell's Demon, sorting mixed molecules into two jars, hot and cold? What is the bad translator but someone who either lacks that somatic polyphonia—does not feel both languages with an inner heteroglot richness—or surrenders to it entirely, fails to sort out the interjostling words and phrases into separate languages? [15]

The translator, then, or the translator's body, is the ground on which the artificially dualized languages—SL and TL—meet, conflow, commingle. In the act of what we might call "pretranslation," the translator's somatic gearing up to a translation task, SL and TL are indistinguishable. They both inhabit the translator's body in a great swirling confusion. The act of translation, then, involves the unidirectionalizing of the bilingual confluence, a channeling of internal heteroglossia into a current from one (SL) to the other (TL). At first, when the translator begins reading (or when the interpreter first begins hearing) the SL text, there is an intuitive damming up of somatic response into a more or less artificially constructed SL "lake" or "reservoir"; then the translator opens up the floodgates, which were only momentarily closed (by an act of univocalizing will) anyway and lets SL words direct somatic response into a more or less artificially constructed TL "lake."

The Finnish brain scientist Matti Bergström suggests another way of imagining this process: in his model, words (syntactic structures, etc.) are generated by the cerebral cortex but are carried out into the world by what he calls "clouds of possibility," chaotic masses of interpretive multiplicity generated by the brainstem. Without these clouds of possibility, language would be univocal, homophonous, monoglot—pre-Babelian, in fact, unscattered, in the stable logical unity fantasized by cortically idealizing linguists. The clouds, which Bakhtin would identify as the stuff of heteroglossia, allow not only for multiplicity of interpretation and linguistic variation in time and space but also for the richness of emotional association and connotation that characterizes our response to (use of) language. Without the clouds of possibility, language would be like the electronic transfer of data: neutral, logical, mechanical.

Using Bergström's model, then, it becomes possible to reconceive translation in fruitful postdualistic ways. When utterer and interpreter come from different speech communities (speak different languages natively), communication between them is hindered by the divergence of syntactic and semantic structures, the bare cortical bones of language; but even then it is facilitated by clouds of possibility, which would include gestures and facial expressions, tone and pitch, various colors and textures of speech, and a certain somatic empathy that allows us to "sense" another person's somatic "directedness" preverbally. Since both expression and interpretation are borne on these clouds, chances are doubly good that communication will be possible despite a total *cogni-*

tive language barrier—that one or the other interlocutor will be able to actualize the possibilities surrounding each utterance. The experience of catching the drift of an utterance in a language you don't know a word of, based on contextual and paralinguistic features, is common; absolute certainty and clarity of understanding in similar circumstances is not unheard-of. And of course the more we learn of a foreign language—the more attempts we make to communicate in it, the more encounters we have with native speakers of that language—the more possibilities we become able to actualize and generate in the clouds that surround each utterance, and the easier communication becomes.

Bergström insists that the potential content of these clouds of possibility is universally human—variations on human emotions and motivations, for example, are not limitless—but that this potentiality is always shaped by each individual's own experience. Bakhtin would say that the clouds are internally dialogized in and by specific speech communities, in specific speech situations; I would say that they are both ideo- and idiosomatic. As a result, even though communication across language barriers is always possible, it is always radically problematic (as is, in fact, all communication, since it is across the language barriers erected by uncollectivized idiosomatic experience: even with people we have known all our lives, we cannot be sure we will be understood).[16] The translator's task, in this scenario, is clearly to generate what we might call mediatory clouds of possibility, clouds in which the dialogized communicative (expressive and interpretive) possibilities of two or more speech communities blend and swirl together. Out of these mediatory clouds, expanded and enriched by the translator's somatic response to both the SL and the TL (and specifically to both the SL utterer's and the TL interpreter's linguistic capabilities, to the clouds swirling into the translator's hermeneutic mediation from two directions in this particular dialogue), the translator then generates a focused and channeled TL text, which filters both interpretation of the SL utterer's cloud and anticipation of the TL interpreter's cloud through the totality of the translator's somatic experience.

Lest this swirling and filtering and channeling be thought (or felt) excessively chaotic or mystical and experienced as threatening by the logically minded, let me note that distinctions can certainly be made. The selectivity of the cerebral cortex is always at our disposal, and we can, if we choose, draw up simplified mentalist maps of the process (analysis, transfer, and restructuring) or mark off a discrete analytical territory for each actor (writer, translator, and reader) or lay down quantitative and qualitative standards for the mix of SL and TL (sense-for-sense, word-for-word, etc.). But it should be understood that these distinctions are neither neurologically nor experientially primary: they are secondary cortical fictions imposed after the fact on a complex experience. To overcome the ideosomatic power of dualistic thinking, we must retreat or regress to a level of experience that precedes and underlies dualistic ideologies—not an easy task, certainly, but not an impossible one either.

Dialogue contra Instrumentalism

Liberation from instrumentalism in the gender clashes of marriage and other male-female relationships has been one central project of the women's movement, and over the past few years it has increasingly become the central project of a new men's movement as well.[17] Women, as feminists have been persuasively arguing, are instrumentalized by men under conditions of patriarchy and must liberate themselves from that instrumentalization if they are to live full lives. Men too, as masculists are beginning to argue, are instrumentalized by patriarchal ideology—made into role-robots for the use of power and cut off from the vitalizing force of emotion, somatic response—and must liberate themselves from that instrumentalization if *they* are to live full lives.

As far as I can tell, no one has even considered the necessity, much less the possibility, of working for liberation from the same instrumentalist conditioning in the writer-translator relationship. After all, this relationship is "natural." It is an integral part of translation, just as, until the early and mid-sixties, the wife's unthinking submission to her husband was an integral part of marriage. In fact, one of the things I mean by "the translator's turn" in my title is translators' liberation, on the analogy of women's and men's liberation.

In Chapter 1 I showed how Augustine's seven-step path to wisdom in *On Christian Doctrine* might be read as the ideosomatic pattern for the translator's instrumentalization. In order to liberate instrumentalized translators, we must somehow reverse that process, chart the individual's path back from Augustine's severely circumscribed "wisdom" as ideal submission to God's will to a more active, self-determining state. In this, the six-phase "primal scene of instruction" that Harold Bloom charts for the strong poet in *The Map of Misreading* may be useful:

1. "Election-love, the Hebrew *'ahabah*, is . . . love unconditioned in its giving, but wholly conditioned to passivity in its receiving. Behind

any Scene of Writing, at the start of every intertextual encounter, there is this unequal initial love, where necessarily the giving famishes the receiver. The receiver is set on fire, and yet the fire belongs to the giver" (51).

2. "Covenant-love or *chesed,*" whose "root means 'eagerness' or 'sharpness'" but also "embraces that kind of 'keenness' that moves from 'ardent zeal' to 'jealousy,' 'envy,' and 'ambition,' and so Covenant-love is uneasily allied to a competitive element. We can deduce, for the purposes of hypothesizing a poetic Primal Scene of Instruction, that the antithetical element in *chesed* leads to the ephebe's [young poet's] first accommodation with the precursor as compared with the absolute assimilation of Election-love. This first accommodation might be called the initial *persona* that the young poet adopts, in the archaic, ritual sense in which the *persona* was the mask representing the *daimonic* or tribal father" (53–54).

3. "The rise of an individual inspiration or Muse-principle, a further accommodation of poetic origins to fresh poetic aims. Here the Old Testament *ruach* for 'spirit' or 'power of God's breath' can be a precise shorthand" (54).

4. "The bringing forth of an individual *davhar,* a word [of] one's own that is also one's act and one's veritable presence" (54).

5. "The deep sense in which the new poem or poetry is a total interpretation or *lidrosh* of the poem or poetry of origin" (54).

6. "Revisionism proper, where origins are re-created, or at least a re-creation is attempted" (54).

The relevance of Bloom's six-stage primal scene to a discussion of translation should be obvious. In the first phase, we find the translator in that state of idealized passivity with regard to a deified SL author that all mainstream translation theory prescribes (compare the idealized passivity of the wife with regard to her husband prescribed by patriarchal gender ideology). The receiver—the translator—is set on fire, Bloom says, but the fire belongs to the giver, the SL writer. The translator is imagined as an infant with no fire of his or her own, nothing to bring to the scene of election-love; the translator *is elected, is loved:* passively chosen, passively used. What Bloom calls election-love is the instrumentalist ideal of Western translation.

You see my strategy: if idealized instrumentality is the translator's infancy, as my modification of Bloom's myth suggests that it might be, then the translator must learn to grow out of it. As Bloom himself says, "Since the Primal Scenes are fantasy traumas, they testify to the power of the imagination over fact, and indeed give an astonishing preference to imagination over observation" (48). The thing about fact, and the "scientific" observation that generates fact, is that it is—or is supposed to be—neutral, divorced from power and persuasion, from value and worth, and therefore strictly conservative. The way things are is the way things are, and I am not to desire change (that would be subjective bias). To "observe" the "fact" that most translators are passive instruments (and I am not even sure that it is a fact) is to gloss over the steady ideological pressures that have been brought to bear to keep translators in that state of infancy. It is to ignore (and to encourage others to ignore) the ways in which passive instrumentality (election-love) is an uneasily maintained ideological ideal, not a neutral fact, and the ways in which all talk of neutral facts serves only to maintain the ideal. What I am trying to do in setting up a Bloomian primal scene of translator instruction is not, therefore, to describe, in some neutral scientific way, the actual path that translators take to their craft, or even to prescribe, in a normative authoritarian way, the path that translators *should* take to their craft. Maybe some translators have followed that path. Maybe I have, or maybe I am so taken by Bloom's primal scene of instruction that it only seems as if I have. In any case, my modification of Bloom's primal scene is not primarily descriptive and should not stand or fall through "accuracy." It is a polemical device, designed only to open up new perspectives onto an ideologically frozen field.

In the second stage, which Bloom evokes in terms of a trying on of masks representing the tribal father, we see the translator injecting into his or her submission to the father (or the SL writer) something of his or her own—not quite visibly yet, not arrogantly or appropriatively; rather, as Bloom says, accommodatively, but still creatively. The SL writer says: Be me. Subsume your will into mine. So the translator does, but with expanding consciousness of the effect that subsumption has on his or her emerging sense of self. The surrender of initiative to the SL writer is no longer utter and unconscious; it is self-conscious, and therefore subtly undermined. Ezra Pound provides an excellent example of this approach in his remarks on his early translations: "I began this search for the real in a book called *Personae*, casting off, as it were, complete masks of the self in each poem. I continued in a long series of translations, which were but more elaborate masks" (cited in Wright 130). "Casting off," here, belongs to a later stage; what the translator in the second stage of covenant-love seeks to do is to make the masks, to accommodate him- or herself to the SL writer by creating personae of that writer, and thus also of the self that he or she is supposed to be accommodating to the writer, in the form of translations. Each translation is a way of saying, "Who am I going to be today?"—the "today" relativizing instrumentality, situating it in time and space, and thus raising the possibility that someday I will be myself, or some other self than the one I am told to be.

Bloom associates his third stage with *ruach,* or spirit; my explorations of the somatics of translation in Chapter 1 suggest that it might be useful to think of it as *soma,* or body, an ideosomatic word that feels persuasive because it has been internalized. The translator is now no longer under the direct sway of the SL writer's authority, is no longer the overt instrument of the SL writer's intention; but when the translator looks inside for a personal response, some unknown "force" takes over and guides him or her back to instrumentality. And it feels like his or her own desire! I *want* to be the instrument of the SL writer: I choose instrumentality!

In the fourth stage, the translator does break through ideosomatic programming to a "word of his or her own," as Bloom says, a word conceived not as *logos,* which in Greek was always a static representation of the object, but as *davhar,* which, as Bloom says, in Hebrew "involves the notion of driving forward something that initially is held-back. This is the word as a moral act, a true word that is at once an object or thing and a deed or act" (*Map* 42). The *logos,* we might say, is a frozen mental picture; *davhar* is a living somatic response.

Bakhtin gets at something like Bloom's third and fourth stages in his distinction between "authoritative discourse" and "internally persuasive discourse." The former, he says, has to do with inertia and calcification, the latter with independence and "one's own word." This is, roughly speaking, instrumentalizing ideosomatic (third-stage) and liberating idiosomatic (fourth-stage) response but does not, I think, get at anything like the full complexity of the issue. Here is Bakhtin:

В отличие от внешне авторитарного слова слово внутренне убедительное в процессе его утверждающего усвоения тесно сплетается со "своим словом". В обиходе нашего сознания внутренне убедительное слово—полусвое, получужое. Творческая продуктивность его заключается именно в том, что оно пробуждает самостоятельную мысль и самостоятельное новое слово, что оно изнутри организовывает массы наших слов, а не остаётся в обособленном и неподвижном состоянии. Оно не столько интерпретируется нами, сколько свободно развивается дальше, применяется к новому материалу, к новым обстоятельствам, взаимоосвещается с новыми контекстами. Более того, оно вступает в напряжённое взаимодействие и

борьбу с другими внутренне убедительными словами. Наше ид-
еалогическое становление и есть такая напряжённая борьба в нас за
господство различных словесно-идеологических точек зрения, подх-
одов, направлений, оценок. Смысловая структура внутренне
убедительного слова не завершена, открыта, в каждом новом
диалогизующем его контексте оно способно раскрывать все новые
смысловые возможности. (158)

Internally persuasive discourse—as opposed to one that is externally authoritative—is, as it is affirmed through assimilation, tightly interwoven with "one's
own word." In the everyday rounds of our consciousness, the internally persuasive word is half-ours and half-someone else's. Its creativity and productive-
ness consist precisely in the fact that such a word awakens new and independent
words, that it organizes masses of our words from within, and does not remain
in an isolated and static condition. It is not so much interpreted by us as it is
further, that is, freely, developed, applied to new material, new conditions; it
enters into interanimating relationships with new contexts. More than that, it
enters into an intense interaction, a *struggle* with other internally persuasive
discourses. Our ideological development is just such an intense struggle within
us for hegemony among various available verbal and ideological points of view,
approaches, directions and values. The semantic structure of an internally persuasive discourse is *not finite,* it is *open;* in each of the new contexts that dia-
logize it, this discourse is able to reveal ever newer *ways to mean.* (Emerson and
Holquist's translation, 345–46)

The problem with this is that we are ideosomatically conditioned to
think of *all* our words in just this way: that is precisely the idea behind
liberalism, to stress the rich variety or pluralism ("it enters into an intense interaction, a *struggle* with other internally persuasive discourses") of inner voices, all persuasive, all enticing, and all more or
less of equal value. This ideosomatic image of inner freedom to choose
obscures the operation of an authoritative (or authoritarian) discourse.
The translator, for example, may think him- or herself free to choose
between a plurality of translation methods: between dynamic and functional equivalence, say, and within the field of functional equivalence
among the functions of conveying information, expressing emotion,
and rhetorically persuading. Isn't that freedom? In a manner of speaking, it is; it is the freedom to choose among a variety of cells in the
prison of sense-for-sense translation. Condition a translator to believe
that translation *is* sense-for-sense translation, that there simply is nothing else, that anything else would not be translation, and the various
choices available within that severely circumscribed field begin to look
like "internally persuasive discourses." (I will come back to this at the
end of Chapter 4, under "Diversion.")

So it is not enough to dualize instrumentalizing authoritarian words and liberating internally persuasive words, as Bakhtin does. Once it has been internalized, an instrumentalizing authoritarian word *is* internally persuasive. The authoritarian word of liberalism, rendered internally persuasive by ideosomatic programming, feels like liberation.

Bakhtin's discussion of internally persuasive discourse really only works in the sense that he wants it to (and in the sense that Bloom wants his discussion of *davhar* to work) once what I have called the third seal has been broken. Only then are the "various available verbal and ideological points of view, approaches, directions and values" that we find ourselves choosing among "not finite"; only when the finitizing power of ideosomatic programming has been eased off, relaxed, side-tracked, relativized, can the "semantic structure of an internally persuasive discourse" be called "open." What then opens, in fact, is what first seems like a void, a great hollowness, a cavernous empty hall with no light and no objectification; only gradually do objects begin to appear, fragments of objects, scattered like three or four pieces of string in the empty ruins of a great medieval cathedral, and seeming at first only to add to the emptiness, to intensify it by their very insignificance. They are, in fact, the first glimmers of what Bakhtin calls "ever newer *ways to mean*." They are bits and pieces of idiosomatic experience—experience that, come to think of it, now that we have been letting Bakhtin educate us about the internal dialogism of all verbal experience, is not in fact strictly idiosyncratic, but dialogized. What makes it seem idio- (personal, individual, uncontaminated by otherness) is its marginality vis-à-vis the central ideostructure. It too always brings dialogical experience of otherness with it, other people, other voices, other ideas; but the people and voices and ideas that it brings are ones we were programmed to ignore, to "forget," to repress.

The fifth stage for Bloom is *lidrosh*, or "total interpretation," and it is tempting to say that for the translator it is the TL text as total interpretation. But there is no such thing as total interpretation. That would imply some sort of logical accounting, a drawing up of logical ledgers that would indicate that each point in the SL text has indeed been properly accounted for. What Bloom seems to me to be moving toward is a *fullness of somatic response:* the translator's willingness, for example, to tolerate all manner of contradictions and inconsistencies in a translation that feels full or total, feels complete precisely because it incorporates the translator's somatic vision of the text. "Do I contradict myself?" Walt Whitman asks in his lidroshic "Song of Myself." "Very well, then, I contradict myself. I am large, I contain multitudes."

The sixth stage, "revisionism proper," is for Bloom the strong poem as act, and so, here, the strong translation as act, the act of translation as a dialogical engagement with both the SL writer and the TL receptor—my subject in Part 2.

The implication of this discussion for the translator, as for any other artist—or, for that matter, human being—who longs to be free of instrumentalism, is that "intuition" (somatic understanding) must be progressively trained, through something like this "primal scene of instruction," to true internal persuasiveness. The translator who pursues that desire to be rid of instrumentalist impulses soon begins to move past the blind routines of election-love into new, unfamiliar areas, areas that feel fraught with risk. The translation as TL persona for the SL writer; the translation as reproduction of SL intention, but controlled by the translator, by the ideosomatic voice in the translator's head; the translation as idiosomatic act; the translation as a somatic fullness, a bodying forth of the completeness of the translator's somatic response. The translator grows from infancy into maturity: grows up.

Needless to say, the translator who begins to question the hegemony of translational instrumentalism will inevitably come up against the (programmed) question: What right do I have to do this to the SL writer? Who am I to go changing things, deciding that I know better? Self-liberation always entails self-discovery: who *am* I? Am I the service robot that I have been trained to think I am—the "instrument" of an "original" writer's "intention"? Is that me? Is that all of me? Is that the me I want to be? Is that all the me I want to be?

The question about our right to make changes in the SL author's work is one that I will deal with in some detail in Chapter 3. For now, let me note only that our fear that the SL author would not like us to take liberties with his or her text is based on an ideologically idealized image of the SL author that has more to do with keeping translators in line than with representing reality. In real-life author-translator dialogues, things are considerably more complex, more varied, and more amenable to the translator's growth ("instruction") as a writer and as a human being. Most of my translation work has been with scholarly and technical and other special texts, all of which tend to be written by people who do not think of themselves as writers. Since I do think of myself as a writer, and as a good one, I have an immediate advantage over most of the people whose texts I translate—and most of them, after they have seen my first translation of their work, recognize that too. With the best writers in the lot, I feel no need to touch up their work, no need to add my contribution to their textual project; the somatic flow from SL to TL is sheer pleasure. When I work with a less competent writer, we both know that my contribution is essential to the success of the finished product, and we either have a standing agreement that I will turn their sloppy, awkward Finnish into good, strong English, or they say to me over the phone, when they ask me whether I can take on a translation, "Can you do it the way you did before? Fix it up?" One professor of physical education was giving a paper at an international conference, and the Finnish paper I got read like a bad student essay; the man had done the research but did not have a clue how to write it up. It was my first translation for him, so when he came to pick it up I told him I had rearranged some things, clarified his argument here and there, tightened it up, and so on. He nodded and said, "Yes, you don't notice where your writing falls down until you have it translated." This seemed like a cavalier attitude to me—I could not imagine entrusting the editing of my work to a translator—but it reflected his awareness of his limitations as a writer and his gratitude for the organizational work a translator can do. I do magazine summaries for the Finnish Institute of Export; after the first couple of translation jobs based on bad summaries that had obviously taken someone at the institute a good deal of time and effort to write up, I asked that they send me the actual articles, with the passages marked that they wanted to go in the summary. That way I could do the summary myself in the very act of doing the translation and could include extra material from other parts of each article to improve transitions. This saved the institute time and money, and they were only too happy to pay me more for the translations.

All this is by way of illustrating that the image we have been given of the SL author sitting in wrathful judgment upon the humble translator who dares change the intended meaning of the SL text even slightly is often largely false. In fact, it is derived from medieval images of a wrathful God, SL author of the Bible, and carried over by instrumentalist translation theory into our own more secular day. I will try to give some sense of the wide range of potential SL author images we can construct for our translation work in Chapter 3; it should be enough for now (and it seems incredible to me that it should even be necessary) to say that SL authors are not gods, and that we as translators are not the gods' humble servants. Translators engage in dialogue with SL authors—also with TL readers, as we will see in Chapter 4. And the dialogical richness of real life (once we have left institutional idealizations behind) allows for all kinds of relationships, including some where the SL author feels inferior to the translator and a good many where author and translator feel like equals, collaborators.

Some dialogues, to be sure, are manipulative and instrumentalizing—with the boss, say, whose letters have to be translated exactly as he says, or you will be fired. Other dialogues are shot through with unilateral awe secularized from medieval responses to God: translations of classics written, we think, by giants, superhuman beings whose stature we can never hope to approach. Challenging raw instrumentalist authority in the former case may cost you your job; but as you begin the process of self-discovery and -liberation, you may start to wonder whether the job is worth it to you. Challenging institutionalized authority in the latter case may make your translation unpublishable, or an editor may require you to make substantial revisions, but if you keep at it you will eventually find yourself with very much the same kind of verbal authority as the awesome classical SL author him- or herself. What, after all, is a great artist but someone who has undergone the liberating process that I have been discussing? Some artists make it farther down that road than others; but nobody becomes an artist, or even a fully alive human being, by timidly clinging to the submissive role prescribed for his or her social activity.

Dialogue contra Perfectionism

It may seem that I am harping on the medieval underpinnings of contemporary translation theory; but I come to the field from literary theory, where the normative moralizing so typical of translation theory was largely eradicated in the thirties and forties by the New Critics— those nowadays much-disparaged pioneers who by the fifties and sixties had taught a whole generation of teachers how to teach (and not to teach) literature—and the medieval authoritarianism of translation theory hits me especially hard. I was taught by New Critical high school and college teachers how to read and not to read literature, and one thing I learned *not* to do was to set up explicitly authoritarian systems of rules and norms controlling morally "right" and "wrong" ways to write or read novels and poems. Thus, translation theory as it has been practiced for nearly two millennia and is still practiced by most people today—here is what you must do if you want to be considered a translator—breaks all the rules of my early training in literature.

In fact, what authoritarian rules and norms were laid down by the New Critics were specifically designed to protect the reader from the

continuing cultural force of medieval instrumentalism and perfectionism. The famous essays of the fifties by Wimsatt and Beardsley, "The
Intentional Fallacy" and "The Affective Fallacy," went to deplorable
extremes, it seems to us now, to deny the relevance of *all* authorial
control over the reader and of *all* affective or somatic reader response
to the writer (I have been committing both, especially the affective fallacy, unrepentantly throughout this book). But it was all an attempt to
free readers from the ideosomatically programmed instrumentalism
that said readers *must* humbly submit themselves to authorial intention
and that writers *must* take care to affect their readers in morally acceptable ways. Texts for the New Critics were just texts—what a liberating
discovery! They were not the inaccessibly luminous repositories of genius (secular Bibles) that the late romantic nineteenth century had
made them out to be; they were just texts, things to study. And studying them was relatively easy, not the awestruck bowing before the great
that, say, biographical approaches to literature had been, and that had
maintained the Christian dialectic of desire and frustration, despair and
fortitude, in a secular context. All that you had to do was to find patterns of irony, paradox, tension, in them. Simple! Anyone could do it.
Just take a class at college from a New Critic. Anyone!

In the two decades since the late sixties, we have seen a flurry of
theoretical activity designed to outgrow the New Critics. Phenomenology, existentialism, structuralism, deconstruction, reader response,
Marxism, feminism—the list goes on and on. Literary critics and theorists have taken the liberating work done by the New Critics as given
and have begun to complicate it, question it, move off in liberating new
directions from it. Phenomenologists and reader-response theorists
stress the importance (indeed, the inescapability) of subjectivity. De-
constructionists uncover the disabling contradictions built into the
Western metaphysical tradition, which our implicit assumptions about
texts had been based on without our knowledge. Marxists and feminists
uncover the capitalist and patriarchal ideologies that govern our
thought about writing and reading.

And then, in translation theory, we still get Augustine "modernized"
as Matthew Arnold.[18]

After this theoretical build-up, it may seem perverse to say that the
solution to translational perfectionism is detheorization, but detheorization is precisely what most of the interesting literary theories seem to
me to be about. Dismantling the theoretical/theological frameworks of
Western culture. Exposing them, drawing our attention to them (since
we are ideosomatically programmed not to see them, to take them for

granted, to consider them "natural"), and then setting them aside. One of the hot debates in the pages of *Critical Inquiry* in recent years had to do with the "consequences" of theory: it was started by two theorists who said that theory was completely inconsequential.[19] This seemed to me extreme, but I sympathized entirely with the impulse behind it: let's learn to detheorize life! Let's slip out of our muscle-bound theorizing and learn to *live*. Not uncritically; not in a flat rejection of thought, understanding, intelligence; but not a priori, either, not in an idealized subordination of all praxis to a comprehensive and covertly dogmatic theoretical system. Let's use theory if we have to, but only against theory, only to dismantle the old restrictive theories and to free ourselves to engage people and ideas situationally.

The best way to combat translational perfectionism, for example, is to imagine ourselves in a real translational situation, a translation dialogue, and ask what makes it work, what enables the translation to succeed in the total speech situation. For example, one day in Finland I was standing in the post office waiting to pick up a package, and beside me a customs official was trying to tell the girl in front of me in line to open her package, to show him what was in it. In broken Finnish she said that she did not speak Finnish, and he seemed to be at a communicative loss, so I "translated" for her: I picked up a pair of scissors on the counter and handed them to her. It was a successful translation: she understood me and started to open her package. It certainly was not a "perfect" translation in the traditional sense because I did not use words. But it worked. As it turned out, she was an American exchange student and I could have used English, but with just her broken Finnish to go on I had no way of knowing what language to try on her; handing her the scissors was the fastest and most effective way to translate the customs official's request.

Isn't this all we need? Dialogically speaking, the key is not perfection but success: *what works*. What works not in the abstract, not in general, not in the null context—this is no anarchistic carte blanche, no "anything goes"—but precisely in context, in the specific situation in which a translation is needed or offered. The basic dialogue of translation is a transaction involving three people, two speaking two different languages, the third speaking both; and all that really needs to happen for the act of translation to succeed is for both of the monolingual speakers to come out of the transaction more or less satisfied. I am talking about real life here, in all its situational variety, not an ideal model, so I admit that it may not work in every situation, that someone will say, "Look at that summit meeting, the interpreters did their job successfully but both participants went away unsatisfied." If this were an ideal model, we could argue over the precise meaning of "satisfaction" that we would allow: satisfaction with the outcome versus satisfaction with the nature of the transaction ("understanding"), for example. But it is not. "Satisfaction" is just a rough description of the feeling of success held by any one of the participants in the dialogue.[20] This means, of course, that one person may think that the translation was a success, and another may think that it was a failure: when you leave the ideal world of theory for the pragmatic world of real situations, you have to proceed without perfect guarantees, or even criteria, of success.

Let me stress once more what I am *not* saying. I am not saying that we must learn to proceed blindly or stupidly. The assumption that to proceed without perfect criteria of success is to proceed blindly comes, in fact, from our dualist/perfectionist programming. If you lack a perfect, unified theory, you have blind, stupid practice. By detheorizing translational perfectionism I am not ruling out critical thought; I am just trying to free specific situations from the tyranny of petrified critical thought, of institutionalized theory. In ordinary speech we do say, "I've got a theory about what's wrong with that car," which usually means that we have an idea of how it might be fixed, a more or less articulate hunch or guess by which to guide our actions, our attempts to locate and solve the problem. A theory of this sort is based on past experience, but it remains flexible and open to new experience and is in any case strictly situational: we check out the problem, test theories, see what works. Vocational schools try to teach mechanics the proper procedure for every conceivable mechanical failure, just as translator schools try to teach translators the proper procedure for every conceivable translation problem. But every good mechanic, like every good translator, knows better than to follow rules like that. You figure things out ("theorize") by the seat of your pants and make up solutions as you go along. The slavishly rule-obeying mechanic fixes minor problems by replacing whole units; vocational schools and auto shops agree that this is the best way to do things, and since it stands to reason that they know best, the slavish mechanic does as they say. The flexible, inventive mechanic takes the unit apart, finds the real problem, and fixes it with nuts and wire and rubber bushings lying around the garage. In the process, he or she entertains and discards a whole series of theories— no question of working blind here—and finally proves one theory right by putting it to the test.

Just detheorizing perfectionist translation does not liberate us from perfectionism, of course, any more than articulating the patriarchal ideology that instrumentalizes women liberates them from their inner feeling of instrumentalization. A change of mind, as the popular wisdom has it, must be accompanied by a change of heart—a somatic shift. We have to learn to feel differently about translation success, by working down through what I called the three seals. But then the ideosomatics of perfection affect us differently, and often less powerfully, than do the ideosomatics of either duality or instrumentality. There is also more variety in the ideosomatic hold that perfectionism has on people than in either dualism or instrumentalism. Those hit hardest by perfectionism are those who are most threatened emotionally by complexity and best able to construct perfectionist fictions to combat their insecurity— which is to say, the kind of people who tend to become theorists in the first place. Most translators are more immune to the disease; while they may feel threatened emotionally by complexity, practically minded translators tend to lack the theorist's ability to construct perfectionist systems, and so have to learn to live with compromise. In them the ideosomatics of perfection mainly generates guilt: they go ahead and do the translation, often very well, and then feel guilty about not having done it better, perhaps apologizing for their failure in a preface. The liberation that a dialogical theory of translation would bring them is liberation from guilt: reassurance that pragmatic success is enough, that they do not have to achieve the impossible.

Many theorists are also relatively immune to perfectionism: for instance, the descriptive theorists who are drawn to theory not because they are threatened by complexity but because they enjoy intellection. Perfectionism is built into the very foundation of scientific inquiry, so as long as they go along with established academic practices they will be expected to strive toward perfection (a *complete* theoretical description of their field); but if their main academic motivation is delight rather than emotional self-protection, this will not do much damage to them. They will be able to take it or leave it.

The people most deeply stricken by perfectionism are the normative theorists: the ones who fervently believe, and fervently strive to get other people to believe, that there is only one right way to translate, and that if they do not devote their lives to the propagation and elaboration of that way, something terrible is going to happen. There must be norms! There must be rules! There must be guidelines! Translators must not be abandoned by theorists, left to muddle through translation after translation without a ray of light to illuminate their path. Translators desperately need our help! It would be irresponsible to cast them adrift, turn our backs, turn a deaf ear to their pathetic (often scarcely audible) cries for assistance! Translators languish for want of clear arbitrations on pressing issues like whether (and when) one is allowed to improve a badly written SL text: there *has* to be a standardized rule on things like this! We cannot have translators just doing whatever *they* think right!

Fortunately, perfectionist theorists usually have little direct power over translators in their day-to-day practice. Translation tends to be an activity performed by one person at a time, all alone or, if in the company of others, pretty much beyond their direct control. I say "fortunately," but for perfectionist theorists this state of affairs is, of course, anything but fortunate. It is precisely why they feel it so important to drum their perfectionism into future translators in schools of translation and interpretation, in "practical" guides to the translator's task, and in the statements of principle drawn up by professional translator organizations. A perfectionist will sometimes find his or her way into a position of power over translators' actual work, as an editor at a publishing house, say, or as the boss who tells his cross-lingual secretary precisely how he wants his letters translated; but such a person tends not to be a perfectionist *theorist,* and so usually fails to articulate this perfectionism in any very effective way.

And in fact the power of perfectionist theorists to make their students and readers feel guilty about their best efforts is at worst not really very great. It can be fairly intense for the duration of the book or the course (which is why students of translation, beaten down by constant harping on their errors, tend to be so demoralized), but books and courses come to an end at last, and the reader or the student can go out into the real world and begin to shed perfectionist norms and guilt like last year's skin. Bits and pieces of it do stick, of course; whenever translators talk about their work, they drift uneasily back into the only rhetoric that they are familiar with, which tends to be perfectionist. But perfectionist rhetoric has little effect on the way most competent translators translate. Theory is theory; practice is practice. The one does not have much to do with the other.

Nor need it. I firmly believe that the competent translator does not need theory—certainly does not need dualist, instrumentalist, and perfectionist theory, and finally does not need any kind of theory at all. The competent translator knows how to be flexible enough to adapt his or her translation skills and methods to each individual translation task. As I said before, this flexibility will involve the formulation of working theories as tentative and disposable tools; but the competent translator does not need someone else to theorize on his or her behalf.

So why am I writing this book? For two reasons, one mainly tied to Part 1, the other mainly tied to Part 2. The first is that I want to give competent translators theoretical tools with which to defend their best work against the carping of perfectionist critics, and to help translators who feel susceptible to perfectionist guilt fight back. I hope that I have shown in these first two chapters that there are good arguments to be made against dualism, instrumentalism, and perfectionism; but maybe it takes a theorist to formulate them powerfully enough to have an effect.

The second is that, freed from the perfectionist drive to reduce all translation to a single correct approach, translators may want to expand their horizons, and I want to provide a few glimpses of the incredible diversity out there. You really do not have to translate every text you get sense-for-sense; and if you decide not to translate sense-for-sense, translating word-for-word is not your only alternative. What else is there? Practically grounded translators are well aware of the diversity within the field they work in; but most translators only work in a few fields, and they may want to be exposed to possibilities beyond their experience. That will be my business in the rest of this book: to start opening what Blake called the doors of perception; to let diversity in.

Part Two

Dialogical Turns

Chapter Three

The Tropics of Translation

If the rules of a finite game are unique to that game it is evident that the rules may not change in the course of play—*else a different game is being played.*

It is on this point that we find the most critical distinction between finite and infinite play. The rules of an infinite game must change in the course of play. *The rules are changed when the players of an infinite game agree that the play is imperiled by a finite outcome—that is, by the victory of some players and the defeat of others.*

The rules of an infinite game are changed to prevent anyone from winning the game and to bring as many persons as possible into the play.

If the rules of a finite game are the contractual terms by which the players can agree who has won, the rules of an infinite game are the contractual terms by which the players agree to continue playing.

The Dramatics of Translation

Poised here at the turning point of my argument, the point at which I turn from the background of dialogical bodies to the foreground of dialogical turnings (tropes and versions), I think it may be useful to step back from dialogics for a moment and look at dramatics, or what Kenneth Burke calls dramatism—dialogics in a larger context, in the context not only of who says what to whom, but also, as the journalists say, where, when, why, and how. In his *Grammar of Motives,* Burke suggests that all motives (our reasons for doing things) can be discussed dramatistically in terms of five key terms based on the journalistic five *W*'s: act, scene, agent, agency, and purpose. Burke's idea is to understand human behavior not as machine (as the empirical social scientists do) but as drama, and specifically as a drama that is constantly shifting, constantly changing perspective, so that one person's act is another person's scene, and I as agent (or actor) am another person's agency (or instrument). I can see myself as agent, agency, or scene, depending on my perspective. I can think of myself as agent when I am in fact acting as agency—especially when I have been programmed to think of my agency or instrumentality as agenthood (autonomous subjecthood).

Here, for example, is Burke from "Terministic Screens," on the difference between his (and my) dramatistic/dialogical/dialectical approach and what he calls a "scientistic" and I have been calling an Augustinian or "mainstream Western" approach:

The two approaches, the "scientistic" and the "dramatistic" (language as definition, and language as act) are by no means mutually exclusive. Since both approaches have their proper uses, the distinction is not being introduced invidiously. But though at this moment of beginning, the overlap is considerable, later the two roads diverge considerably, and direct our attention to quite different kinds of observation. The quickest way to indicate the differences of direction might be by this formula: The "scientistic" approach builds the edifice of language with primary stress upon a proposition such as "It *is*, or it *is not*." The "dramatistic" approach puts the primary stress upon such hortatory expressions as "thou *shalt*, or thou *shalt not*." And at the other extreme the distinction becomes quite obvious, since the scientistic approach culminates in the kinds of speculation we associate with symbolic logic, while the dramatistic culminates in the kinds of speculation that find their handiest material in stories, plays, poems, the rhetoric of oratory and advertising, mythologies, theologies, and philosophies after the classic model.

The dramatistic view of language, in terms of "symbolic action," is exercised about the necessarily *suasive* nature of even the most unemotional scientific nomenclatures. And we shall proceed along those lines, thus:

Even if any given terminology is a *reflection* of reality, by its very nature as a terminology it must be a *selection* of reality; and to this extent it must function also as a *deflection* of reality. (44–45)

The implication is that, from a dramatistic point of view, there is a "Thou shalt not" buried in even the most apparently neutral or scientistic "It is not": the translation theorist who defines translation in terms of sense-for-sense rendering, for example, and states as a self-evident descriptive fact that literal and "free" renderings *are not translation* is implicitly saying, *Thou shalt not render literally or freely.*

My colleague at the University of Tampere, Justa Holz-Mänttäri, has offered what is perhaps the most comprehensive (and increasingly influential) overview of translation in terms of key terms—roughly the same as Burke's, but borrowed from the medieval scholastic Mathieu de Vendôme—in her *Translatorisches Handeln,* on translatorial activity, translation as doing, or, in Burkean terms, translation as drama.[1] By directing attention away from the linguistic conception of translation as abstract correspondence between texts to what *happens* in translation, Holz-Mänttäri has opened a potentially dramatistic alternative to translation conceived as applied linguistics.

But only potentially. My reservation about her work is that she still tends to conceive the drama or doing of translation in logical and analytical terms—a shift that Burke's dramatistic pentad is susceptible to, too. Burke's *Grammar* is a kind of quirky structuralism, and Holz-Mänttäri's *Translatorisches Handeln* is a kind of social semiotic: this is who does what in what circumstances using what tools for what purpose, each category (or *W*) connectable with others but never really permeable by others. Who can never become a How, in her formulation. Why can never be built into How, and Why and How can never be built into Who.

They can in Burke, however. Especially in his second chapter in part 1 of the *Grammar,* "Antinomies of Definition," he points the way past tidy structuralist classification into the heady swirl of dialectical perspectivizing. He worries, for instance, about the paradox or pun buried in the phrase "the motivation of an act":

We may discern a dramatistic pun, involving a merger of active and passive in the expression, "the motivation of an act." Strictly speaking, the act of an agent would be the movement not of one *moved* but of a *mover* (a mover of the self or of something else by the self) [this is especially true in liberal ideologies of the autonomous subject]. For an act is by definition active, whereas to be moved (or motivated) is by definition passive. Thus, if we quizzically scrutinize the expression, "the motivating of an act," we note that it implicitly contains the paradox of substance. Grammatically, if a construction is active, it is not passive; and if it is passive, it is not active. But to consider an *act* in terms of its *grounds* is to consider it in terms of what it is not, namely, in terms of motives that, in acting upon the active, would make it a passive. We could state the paradox another way by saying that the concept of activation implies a kind of passive-behind-the-passive; for an agent who is "motivated by his passions" would be "moved by his being-movedness," or "acted upon by his state of being acted upon." (40)

In other words, act is inextricably wrapped up with scene. The "substance" of an act or of the agent performing it seems to us like the "real thing," the essence or defining quality of the act or person, but as Burke points out earlier in the chapter, the paradox of substance is that it is always something that (as its etymology reveals) "stands beneath," supports from below, "grounds" the act or its human performer. "Substance" is the "scene" of an act that is somehow built into the "essence" of the agent. No agent acts autonomously; all acts, dramatistically viewed, are motivated, and motivations are not only scenes (substantial "grounds" for our actions) but agents that turn us as human agents into agencies.

Something like this complication and dialectical interpenetration of dramatistic terms is what I tried to work toward in Part 1. I would say that somatic response is precisely what Burke is talking about when he discusses the paradox of substance, and that the "paradox" he sets up as an irresolvable logical conundrum is in fact resolvable in terms of ideosomatic programming and unprogrammed idiosomatic experience.[2] Our ideosomatic programming is the internalized authoritarian agent (what Freud called the *Ideal-Ich,* or superego) that wields us as its tools or agencies; but it is also the internalized liberal scene (the ideosomatic conditions under which we work) that encourages us to (and controls the way we) imagine ourselves as agents. Part of that scenic control is the belief that the scene in which we translate is *not* ideosomatic programming, which is to be studiously ignored (repressed), but the specific situation in which we find ourselves, the context in which someone wants a certain text translated for someone. Similarly, that ideosomatic agent/scene conditions us to choose certain translation models as agencies and to ignore or deplore others (translate sense-for-sense, not word-for-word), and to superimpose a single, unified, overriding purpose on all specific, situational purposes (all translations, no matter who will use them how, must be windows between SL meaning and TL reception).

As I conceive the mainstream Western drama of translation, or the drama of translation-idealization, then, it is (has been) controlled from start to finish by the ideosomatic scene as agent. It prompts us (translators), as its agencies, to conceive ourselves as autonomous agents operating in a social setting or scene, using various tools or agencies for various purposes. It prompts us, in other words, to conceive the drama of translation in roughly the way that Holz-Mänttäri describes it. It controls the way we dramatize our work as translators, teaching us to idealize this, ignore that. Focus on this, until it seems like all there is and all there ever could be; relegate that to the periphery, until it no longer seems to exist. (Most of what Holz-Mänttäri describes, in fact, has long been relegated to the periphery in theory; only in unarticulated practice has her description corresponded to the ideosomatic ideal.) Focus on texts and on formal equivalences; let the dramatic interactions of translator with bosses, translation commissioners, writers, speakers, receptors, billpayers, tax offices, union leaders, and so on, fall into the periphery. That is the idealization behind linguistic theories of translation, which Holz-Mänttäri has struggled to overcome. But her theory still allows (and tacitly encourages) translators to relegate, say, the ideosomatic drama of translation to the periphery. What is the translator to do if presented with a text that grossly offends his or her sensibilities—a neo-Nazi text, for example? Be a window to it, our ideosomatic programming tells us: simple. Don't even ask. Just translate it. And when you hear that inner ideosomatic voice say, "Just translate it," understand "translate" to entail perfect submission to the SL meaning. Don't even notice that there might be other possibilities. If you notice that there are other possibilities, resign yourself to what you *know* is right: say with a sigh, "Too bad I'm a translator and have to translate this; otherwise I'd make it obvious to my reader just how pernicious this stuff is." Making that sort of response obvious to the TL reader is not translation. Repeat: *It is not translation*. It is propaganda. Rule it out of court. The original writer has the right to be propagandistic (though we all know that it is not very nice), but the translator does not.

That is one side of Burke's "paradox": all acts are motivated by substance as agent, grounded by substance as scene. Our acts are not our own. The other side is that we can, by working our way down what I have called the three seals, progressively make our acts more and more our own. "The motivation of an act," after all, only undermines our agent status when we understand or feel motivation to be a mysterious agent arising out of our somatic substance, a programmed programming force that controls our action from within. The effect of exploring our motivations, coming to understand them, making friends with them, is to cross or bridge the gap between agent and somatic motivation, to feel agent as a larger force, part conscious or "psychological," part somatic or "substantial," psychosomatic in fact, an integrated being in which "mind" and "body" (mentalized body and emotionalized body) may disagree, may remain in conflict, but not in ideally *divorced* conflict: not as two distinct agents, each trying to deny the other's activity. This is my idea behind tropes and versions. Having (I hope) made a case for this integration of mind and body in Part 1, I now want to explore some of the ways translators can *act,* out of increasingly idiosomatic responses to ideosomatic programming, to create—successful TL texts, perhaps, first of all, but ultimately, and more importantly, to create themselves as (more) fully alive human beings.

Burke suggests focusing in on ratios of two terms: scene-act, for example, which might highlight the interrelations of the "doing" or action of translation and, perhaps, its social and psychological setting (there could be many other scenes); or scene-agent, which might highlight the interrelations of the various physical, interpersonal, or psychological scenes of translation and translational agents either as people (the various relevant people involved in commissioning, doing, and receiving a translation) or as forces, "such as 'drives,' 'instincts,' 'states of mind,' . . . [or] nation, group, the Freudian 'super-ego,' Rousseau's '*volonté générale*,' the Fichtean 'generalized I'" (*Grammar* 20). Burke himself shows a marked preference for these two particular ratios and the three terms they foreground, but he says that the five terms together will generate a total of ten ratios, and that in any case as he conceives them ratios are "principles of determination" (15) or "principles of selectivity rather than . . . thoroughly causal relationships" (18). That is, they are ways of focusing an inquiry, not ways of tying it down to strict logical operations.[3]

My discussion of somatics, for example, was based on a scene-agent ratio: the intermingling of the autonomous individual (agent) with social control (scene), or the individual as the scene of intermingling agents, of collective and personal experience. The interpenetrability of these terms—the way agent can contain scene, the way scene can act as agent, the way internalized agents can conflict and conflow—illustrates the potential complexity of a Burkean ratio. Or rather, it illustrates the complexity of reality if you are willing to look hard enough. My discussion of dialogics shifted ground, from a scene-agent to an act-agent ratio: the follower-agent's separation (act) of idiosomatic experience from the ideosomatically petrified (scenicized) traces of the precursor-agent's innovation, and the resulting engineering of a paradigm shift (act) in translation theory—both in the historical past and in the desired future of this text.

Note that parenthetical "scenicized": neither of these ratios *excludes* the other three terms. The foregrounding of two terms does not make the background disappear. That is why I wanted to stop for a moment here at the beginning of Part 2 and flesh out Burke's dramatism: even when I do not explicitly consider certain terms, I have only backgrounded them; I am not ignoring them. Purpose, for example, at the broadest level of generalization, is what I call throughout this book therapeutic or transformative, personal and political change; agency is translation and/or translation theory as equipment for living. We would live better and make the world a better place to live: purpose. And I see no reason not to put every act, every translation and every translation theory, every class taught, every book written or read, to work toward the attainment of those goals: agency. It is sentimental to talk this way, I know; academics are supposed to be disinterested, which in practice (since we can never conform to the robot-ideal of perfect value-free neutrality) means either uninterested or cynical. I am neither. I believe in this, and I will do it no matter what you think. If I do it well enough, I might get you to believe in it too.

Here in Part 2 I want to shift ground again, and foreground agent and agency, the translator and his or her hermeneutical tools: tropes here, versions in Chapter 4. The various somatic and situational scenes and acts of Part 1 will hover in the background, of course, and jostle their way into the foreground whenever there is a danger of their being forgotten. Purpose at a somewhat lower level of generality (and sentimentality) will be engaged at each step as well: the translator who decides or wants or in a specific dramatic situation feels compelled or called upon to do an unassuming translation of an unassuming text, for example, may call on a metonymical agency: tropical purpose as SL text-oriented intent. The translator who thinks his or her receptor needs to resee things he or she once knew, on the other hand, might use a reversionary agency: ethical purpose as TL receptor-oriented intent. The act in each case is translation as a dialogical interaction, between translator and SL writer in Chapter 3, and between translator and TL receptor in Chapter 4. Scene is not only that dialogue in its multifarious forms and social contexts but Harold Bloom's primal scene of instruction, in its sixth phase of revisionism proper.

Six Master Tropes

In the dominant logical tradition of Western thought it is, perhaps, only to be expected that translation theory should set up static ideals of structural equivalence for translation quality or success: two texts, SL and TL, are placed side by side or superimposed like transparencies (the "feel" of the language used fading away like a dream, leaving only the bare bones of lexical, syntactic, and semantic structure), then checked for correspondences. And where structural correspondence is king, it is, again, only to be expected that the translator be conceived as a mechanical device for the achievement of equivalence—a human being, to be sure, but one who must not draw on the full creative range of his or her humanity, must not access emotional predilections or associations, indeed must access only the most carefully controlled and circumscribed sort of *linguistic* experience, exposure to the logical system underlying everyday speech.

If logic has reigned among intellectuals (philosophers, theologians, scientists), however, it has never entirely succeeded in displacing another tradition among poets, mystics, and ordinary storytellers: I mean the rich and resonant tradition of rhetoric, which has always preferred soft methods to hard, flexible to rigid. Logicians since Aristotle have tried to tame rhetoric, either by conceiving it as one "function" of linguistic communication, as I noted a moment ago, or by reducing it to a stable set of topoi or commonplaces that are to be used in certain prescribed ways in certain prescribed situations. But in the strong sense preserved by poets and persuaders, rhetoric has always been a shifting, unformalizable channel for *bending* language, twisting it to serve specific situational needs.

If the basic logical tool is structure, the basic rhetorical tool is the trope, the figure of speech that (in its Greek etymology) *turns* language in new directions. If structures are stable, tropes are volatile. If logic prefers predictability, rhetoric prefers mutability.

The definitive image for translation in the mainstream logical theory of the West is the bridge, the structure that will enable the monolingual reader to cross over from SL to TL reliably, safely, confidently, and above all duplicably, as in the perfect scientific experiment, with no surprises. In all of the major European languages, the words for translation tend to point etymologically to this sort of crossing: it is a carrying over in Latin and English, a leading over in the Romance languages, and a setting over in the Germanic languages.

And there would be nothing wrong with this, certainly, if it were possible to make the crossing reliably, safely, duplicably—if a bridge really could be built from the SL to the TL. The problem is that "language" only lends itself to this sort of stable civil engineering solution in the abstract, in the transcendental realms favored by linguistic Platonists. In the real world, language is too multiple, too shifting, too *human* to sit still long enough for a bridge to be built—to be completed, even, much less to last for centuries (or even to make the crossing duplicable *once*). The translational bridge is above all an ideal structure which translators as engineers strive hopelessly to actualize, in the perfectionist double-bind between despair and fortitude.

If we imagine translation rhetorically, as a troping, many of the knottiest problems of logical translation theory—those focused on the need to attain translational equivalence—drop away. The uneasy truth for logical theorists of translation is that equivalence between two texts has never been precisely definable or measurable, which makes the assessment of translation quality, in Juliane House's book title, problematic at best. There is no way to know when or whether equivalence has been attained. And in any case, as I stressed in Chapter 1, in the theological tradition of the West the striving for equivalence necessarily falls short. Equivalence between two texts is a structural ideal, and to attain an ideal would by definition be to transcend our nonideal, fallen world, and thus, at least mythically, to redeem it—the hope of the romantics. Barring that apocalyptic hope, as most commonsensical translation theorists do, means barring the very possibility of translation equivalence.

But this is only a problem if we insist on defining translation success in terms of a structural ideal. Admittedly, in the ideosomatics of the Western Platonic/Christian/scientific tradition, it is easier to talk about relinquishing structural ideals for success than actually to do it—and it is hard enough just to talk about it. It feels right to define translation in terms of attaining equivalence between texts—so right, in fact, that it is difficult to imagine how else it might be defined. I realize, in other words, just how counterintuitive my claims must be. There has developed, however, especially in the bourgeois era, an increasingly influential tradition that has replaced the criterial structures of medieval thought with *people*—and we, the twentieth-century bourgeoisie, are the cultural and intellectual heirs of that tradition.

In a people-centered theory of translation, for example, we would study translation in terms not of structural equivalence but of *what translators and readers do*—how people interact in the many different activities surrounding translation. How translators act as social beings: as employees of a translation agency or other firm, as freelancers hired by clients, as users of libraries and other research resources, as professionals recognized (or unrecognized) for their work in society. This is the focus of Justa Holz-Mänttäri's work. How translators act as hermeneutical beings: as interpreters of the SL text in and through the TL text. This will be my primary focus here. The translator acting may *strive* for equivalence—but that striving is only one of many goals of his or her activity, and its relative success or failure need no longer define the translator in the abstract as, among other things, a traitor. Relative success or failure need not be defined in the abstract, either: it is determined by reader response, by how *people* respond to it. Not, in other words, ideal readers. Not a TL reader-ideal generated by the theorist out of his or her hypostatic interpretations of the SL text, as in Eugene Nida's theory of dynamic equivalence. Real readers, both in the

SL (the original writer, say, who either reads the TL or demands a backtranslation in the SL, or the SL commissioner of the translation) and in the TL (the target group as variously and serially represented by translation commissioners, editors, publishers, advertisers, and "ordinary" target readers). This means that a translation is never "good" or "bad," never a success or failure in essence; it is pronounced good or bad by various people, and their pronouncements may vary in time and space. Translational success or failure is interactional, intersubjective, rather than the ontological property of a text.

My concern in this chapter is one particular translatorial activity: the translator's hermeneutical approach to the SL text, in dialogical interaction (real or imagined) with the SL writer. Here tropes, the open-ended turnings that we make in language when we want it to do something new, can be methodologically useful. A logical bridging requires that the translator be able to stabilize both the SL and the TL long enough to build a stable structure between them. A rhetorical troping requires only that the translator start someplace, start at his or her reading of the SL text, and turn away in the direction of the TL.

I say "the" TL, but in fact subjectively the TL only feels familiar and stable in the abstract, prior to an actual turning; when the translator begins to turn away from the SL, the TL shimmers out of focus and must be interpretively reconstrued through the SL turn. To use the road trope that I mentioned in the Introduction, the translator turning off the well-lit four-lane SL highway into the tropical wilderness is not driving a street vehicle, nor a rally car, nor even a four-wheel drive vehicle, but a bulldozer, progressing slowly and somewhat laboriously to *create* a new road—which *is* the TL text. Turning off the SL highway is not a matter of taking a backroad shortcut to a parallel TL highway. It is, rather, a matter of breaking a new path, blazing a new trail. And, to continue the trope, the new TL road that is thus created may well become a popular new highway, may be kept well lit and maintained— a new Bible translation, perhaps, or a best-selling new translation of a literary classic frequently assigned to college students—but it, too, will eventually fall into disrepair and will be traveled only by archaeologists; and many new roads will be quickly overgrown with trees and vines and other tropical shrubs and will soon become impassable. There are no permanent structures.

The trope of the translation-as-road is a metaphor, obviously, and as such aimed at a rough poetic kind of representational equivalence. By describing translation as a road, I am trying to get you to see it in a new way, but a way that has some significant representational connection with reality, or what I am now in the process of construing as reality. If you trope translation as a bridging, you will see it one way; if you trope it as a turning off a road into the wilderness, you will see it another way. *Metapherein* and *transferre*, the Greek and the Latin roots for metaphor and translation (the latter via the participle form of transferre, *translatum*, "transferred"), are cognates, of course, and it is not surprising that the rough imagistic equivalence (between translation and a road, say) set up by metaphor runs roughly parallel to the rough linguistic equivalence aimed at by most Western translation. I want to argue, in fact, that metaphor is the supertrope driving the Western impulse toward translational equivalence: the attempt to bring two radically different texts, written in two different times and places, in two different languages, by two different people for two different cultures, into a mutually defining relationship.

But note the difference between a *trope* of equivalence, like metaphor, and a *structure* of equivalence as posited by logical theorists of translation. A trope of equivalence is an interpretive tool that encourages us to *think of* two texts (or two images) *in terms of* equivalence. As Kenneth Burke says in his appendix to *A Grammar of Motives,* "Four Master Tropes," the supertrope of equivalence, metaphor, encourages us to "perspectivize" two images:

Metaphor is a device for seeing something *in terms of* something else. It brings out the thisness of a that, or the thatness of a this. If we employ the word "character" as a general term for whatever can be thought of as distinct (any thing, pattern, situation, structure, nature, person, object, act, role, process, event, etc.), then we could say that metaphor tells us something about one character as considered from the point of view of another character. And to consider A from the point of view of B is, of course, to use B as a *perspective* upon A.

It is customary to think that objective reality is dissolved by such relativity of terms as we get through the shifting of perspectives (the perception of one character in terms of many diverse characters). But on the contrary, it is by the approach through a variety of perspectives that we establish a character's reality. If we are in doubt as to what an object is, for instance, we deliberately try to consider it in as many different terms as its nature permits: lifting, smelling, tasting, tapping, holding in different lights, subjecting to different pressures, dividing, matching, contrasting, etc.

Indeed, in keeping with the older theory of realism (what we might call "poetic realism," in contrast with modern "scientific realism") we could say that characters possess *degrees of being* in proportion to the variety of perspectives from which they can with justice be perceived. (503–4)

This offers, I suggest, a powerful new way of coming at translational equivalence. The "metaphorical" translator, rather than subordinating him- or herself to an abstract ideal of structural equivalence (and feeling guilty for not attaining it), can instead use metaphorical equivalence as a poetic tool for bending the SL text into the TL, for generating a TL text that will stand in some significant relation to the SL text. And the translation critic, studying the relationship between two texts, can use metaphorical equivalence, not as a rigid measuring stick for determining translational success, but instead as a perspectivizing device for seeing both texts in a rich and complexly comparative light.

Metonymy, too, is a trope of equivalence—but where metaphor says baldly "this *is* that," metonymy says more cautiously, "this and that are parts of the same thing." Metonymy is etymologically a change (*meta*) of names (*onymia*), which has obvious relevance for translation: a Greek text named the *Odysseia* becomes an English text named the *Odyssey,* but it is still the same story of a return from Troy to Ithaca; it has only changed its name, all its "names" or words. Tropologically, metonymy is usually described as the replacement of one part with another "structurally equivalent" part, equivalence being defined by reference to a stable whole; compare this with sense-for-sense translation, which has traditionally been defined in terms of a single transcendental sense that unites two verbal expressions (the SL and TL words are "parts" of a semantic "whole" called meaning or sense).

But again, the structural "equivalence" thus sought after can only become a binding criterion for translational success if the trope, metonymy, tool for a turning, is reified as a truth, a reliable representation of reality. Kenneth Burke suggests that metonymy is a reductive trope, a way of turning something from greater to less complexity, for reducing something to one of its parts; but that, tropologically, one is not interested in a *substantial* reduction, only a *dramatistic* one:

"Metonymy" is a device of "poetic realism"—but its partner, "reduction," is a device of "scientific realism." Here "poetry" and "behaviorism" meet. For the poet spontaneously knows that "beauty *is* as beauty *does*" (that the "state" must be "embodied" in an actualization). He knows that human relations require actions, which are *dramatizations,* and that the essential medium of drama is the posturing, tonalizing body placed in a material scene. He knows that "shame," for instance, is not merely a "state," but a movement of the eye, a color of the cheek, a certain quality of voice and set of the muscles; he knows this as "behavioristically" as the formal scientific behaviorist who would "reduce" the state itself to these corresponding bodily equivalents.

He also knows, however, that these bodily equivalents are but part of the *idiom of expression* involved in the act. They are "figures." They are hardly other than "symbolizations." Hence, for all his "archaizing" usage here, he is not offering his metonymy as a *substantial* reduction. (506–7)

This would suggest that metonymy is not just sense-for-sense trans-lation; it would also be word-for-word and even letter-for-letter, any kind of translation that proceeds by reducing the SL text to a single "significant" or "typical" component-as-whole and tries to make the TL text stand in the same relation to that whole as the original. Being aware that a metonymical rendering is not a *substantial* reduction—that it does not really reduce the SL text to a single part—means being aware that the "whole" that one is trying to embody in the TL (the writer's intended meaning, or expression, or lettering, or tonalizing, or what-ever) is only a symbolization, a construct, something the translator makes up in order to facilitate a metonymical turning, not a real sub-stance that must be (and, alas, cannot be) rendered perfectly. The writer will understand, this translator knows; the writer knows that "inten-tion" is a tricky business, hard for the writer him- or herself to know exactly and impossible for the translator to perceive in any kind of ob-jectively reliable way, so let's just forget about *true* intention, *true* sub-stance, and translate tropically.

Burke's other two "master tropes" are synecdoche, which he asso-ciates with representation, and irony, which he associates with dialectic. The synecdochic representation that Burke means is not artistic repre-sentation, but philosophical or even political representation: this part, synecdoche says, is so perfectly representative of the whole that it can be substituted for it (just as our political representatives are elected to make decisions *for* us). A synecdochic translation would be one that reduces the SL text to a part that the translator takes as representative—some part that he or she likes best, or agrees with—and expands that part to fill the entire TL text. This is propagandistic translation, for example, in which the translator generates the TL text out of a reduc-tive and partial interpretation of the SL text.

Propagandistic translation already begins to take us beyond the bounds of traditional Western translation theory, obviously—the prop-agandistic translator claims to be striving for equivalence, but most log-ical theorists of translation do not accept the interpretive basis for that claim—and irony takes us farther. The ironic dialectic that Burke seems to be thinking of is Hegel's, in which the movement from SL to TL (to shift immediately to the translational application) would be a movement from thesis to antithesis, which is to say, vis-à-vis more traditional definitions of irony, a denial or negation of equivalence. If the TL text is antithetical to the SL text, it stands in some sort of opposition to it, denying the relationship between them, or else denying some *specific* relationship that might be posited between them.

This is dangerous ground, from a mainstream theoretical perspective. Am I saying that *anything goes?* The very question is authoritarian, of course: the implication is that, if translation is not carefully circumscribed, defined in terms of and confined to the bounds of normative equivalence, chaos will ensue. Apart from all the philosophical and political objections that might be made to that position, I would claim that it is simply not true: in context, in real social situations, anything does not go, because there are so many dialogical and institutional controls on translation. To work, as I said in Chapter 2, a translation has to satisfy people—real people. A propagandistic translation may not satisfy some people (puristic theorists, say, or people who disagree with the translator's position), but it will probably satisfy people in the translator's ideological camp. An ironic translation will not satisfy the naive TL reader who wants to believe that he or she is reading an original text (a "covert" translation, as Juliane House, following Schleiermacher, says), but a more sophisticated, even jaded reader may well be pleased by a self-conscious, "overt" translation that denies its own equivalence.

I claim no comprehensive coverage for my tropes of translation—I welcome you to expand my list at your pleasure—but I do propose to expand them to six, along lines suggested to me by Harold Bloom in *A Map of Misreading*. Bloom adds two tropes to Burke's list, hyperbole and metalepsis, and, while I plan to make Burkean revisions in Bloom's conception of those tropes, I will borrow them directly from Bloom. "Hyperbole heightens," Bloom writes; "metalepsis overcomes temporality by a substitution of earliness for lateness" (*Map* 95). Hyperbolic translations improve on the original; metaleptic translations play on the logical absurdities caused by the passage of time between the writing of the original and the writing of the translation, archaizing or modernizing the SL text in the TL.[4]

These six "master tropes"—metonymy, synecdoche, metaphor, irony, hyperbole, and metalepsis—chart, then, a hermeneutical path through the translator's approach to the SL text and writer. A path— not the only path. They constitute a six-category taxonomy, obviously; but I taxonomize only metaphorically, troping on the study of translation as if it were the study of plants. In other words, while I offer my six tropes as representations of the translator's dialogue with the SL writer/text, I assume that the representations perspectivize real translation, that they offer shifting and I hope interesting but by no means stable or binding perspectives on what translators really do when interpreting an SL text in the TL. Throughout the chapter I will remind you of the tentativeness and contingency of my categories: I know how tempting it is, in an intellectual tradition dominated by logic, to reify calculi as truths.

Metonymy

Metonymy, you will recall, is literally a change of names: a story about a man's return from Troy to Ithaca is first named *Odysseia,* then, by a metonymical switch, comes to be named the *Odyssey.* The English "names" or words are substituted for the Greek words. To be able to perceive two texts as related in this way—same story, different words— we have to be able to reduce the complexity of both texts to a single element that they can be seen to share. Typically, indeed prescriptively, the single element to which texts have been reduced in Western translation norms is meaning, sense, the transcendental "content" or "signified" that is posited as standing above or beyond the actual spoken or written words and unifying them—unifying both the words of a single text ("coherence") and the corresponding words of two texts ("equivalence").

The most rudimentary, and in some sense perhaps the most "natural," sense to reduce a text to is word-sense: the meaning of each word. After all, each word constitutes a coherent whole, is set apart from the other words in a text by blank spaces, and "possesses" a dictionary meaning that can be looked up in isolation from other words, acontextually. So when you see a sentence in a German text like "Johan ist nicht zu Hause," you reduce "Johan" to a single human male referent and find the nearest English equivalent, which may be "Johan" or "John"; you identify "ist" as the third-person form of the verb "sein," whose English equivalent is "to be," yielding "is"; "nicht" becomes "not," "zu" "at," and "Hause" "home." The resulting string looks like this:

> Johan ist nicht zu Hause.
> John is not at home.

In each case, I found my way to the "correct" translation by a two-step process that might be described as transcendentalization-detranscendentalization: I abstracted out of the black marks on the page the transcendental meaning, or "whole," of which each word was a German "part," and then returned from that transcendental level to the equivalent English "part." Schematically, the process would look like this:

meaning	meaning	meaning	meaning	meaning
Johan → John	ist → is	nicht → not	zu → at	Hause → home

The recurring pressure that sense-for-sense theorists of translation seem to feel to rail against this approach to translation is, I think, a good indication of its "naturalness" (natural in the sense of following logically from the standard Western practice of dividing language into discrete words and assigning each one a dictionary definition): despite the overwhelming animus against it in mainstream theory, beginning translators keep doing it and nontranslators keep chastising translators for *not* doing it. And it is, certainly, if naively, perfectly in line with the dominant transcendental and analytical ideology of the West: since the Middle Ages we have all been trained both to reduce all complex entities to the smallest possible meaningful part or unit (analysis, Occam's razor) and to seek truth or reality by abstracting out of sense experience a stable transcendental form (idealization, Platonism). The fact that this approach to translation simply is not practicable, that it does not work (in sentences more complex than the one I carefully designed for the above example), should not overly prejudice us against it either, in a tradition that, again, has always privileged universal principle over untheorized practice.

For whatever reason, however—and the reason had more to do with the authority of Cicero and Horace, I suspect, who attacked word-for-word translation, than with the Christian theology that Augustine and Jerome were applying to translation[5]—mainstream translation theory in the West has always insisted that translators reduce the SL text not to word-sense but to sentence-sense: to the meaning of whole sentences. Intuitively, this seems reasonable enough: a sentence, we assume, expresses an entire "thought," and the transfer of this thought ensures a higher degree of TL coherence than the transfer of word-sense.

But there is a problem with it. The principle has often, as is only to be expected in an intellectual tradition that privileges principle over practice, been overgeneralized. I once overheard a colleague telling his students that the SL writer's full stops are sacred: under no circumstance is the translator to combine two sentences or break a long sentence up into smaller segments. One is not allowed to consider more than one sentence at a time. As recent text-linguists like Juliane House and Robert de Beaugrande have begun to move past the sentential level and discover the cohesive devices that connect and structure sentences into coherent texts, they have been insisting on the importance of translating the sense of *whole texts;* and the broadest type of metonymic sense-for-sense translation would obviously involve the reduction of the SL text to *text*-sense.[6]

Another approach to the sense-coherence of an entire text might be narratological, based not on linguistic devices like back-reference but on narrative structure: the "story" (*fabula,* in Russian formalist theory), a chronological sequence perceived in (or reduced to) a bare bones state of formal abstraction that we associate with structuralist narratology. We recognize not only prose Odysseys but also TV miniseries based on the Odyssey and Odyssey Klassic Komics as metonymic translations of Homer's Greek text. They are TL renderings that "tell the same story" as the original, often in very different styles and media and with frequent truncations or expansions of the SL text to suit the translator's (producer's, publisher's, etc.) conception of metonymic equivalence. We might even be willing to call the "retelling" of a traditional story (for children, say) in the same language a metonymical translation. If the reduction is to story-sense rather than sentence-sense or text-sense, it really makes very little difference (as far as "equivalence" is concerned) whether you use more sentences or fewer, or even whether you use words or pictures—or, in a loose definition, how you conceive the "languages" in SL and TL. It is still the "same" story—much reduced and transformed, but still interpretively recognizable.

(The point here, remember, is not whether the sense *is* the same, ontologically, in some stable transcendental realm; it is whether it can be *construed* as the same, by the translator and/or TL reader. The metonymic reduction that I am exploring is a heuristic tool—not a stable structure of correspondence.)

Word-sense, sentence-sense, text-sense, and story-sense are all relatively traditional reductions of the SL text—all bear the stamp of theological approval, centering as they do around meaning, the semantic equivalent to spirit or soul. A more radical version of metonymy would reduce the SL text to something other than sense and then try to render that in the TL. Sound, for example, or feel—bodily reductions that, in a spiritualizing tradition, feel wrong, are counterintuitive. But suppose we want to render Edgar Allan Poe's poem "The Bells" into another language; we could decide that the poem has very little to do with sense, that the *sound* is the key, or the sound in relation to mood, and write a new poem that reproduced the sounds of merriment, balmy harmony, turbulent terror, and melancholy menace in the TL. Bells would not even be necessary—just TL words that rendered the same sounds and moods.

But that, the traditional objection would go, would not be translation. At most it could be called a "variation" on Poe's "Bells," but probably not even that. This objection derives from the restrictive ideosomatics of Western translation, according to which, as Eugene Nida says in one of his chapter titles in *From One Language to Another,* "Translating Means Translating Meaning." A specifically *metonymic* (tropic) approach to translation keeps reminding us that sense is not the only element to which an SL text can be reduced; it is only the ideologically approved one, the element that Western culture since Plato, Paul, and especially Augustine has isolated as the only important one. A metonymic approach might buy into that ideology tentatively, exploratively, by way of getting started, but would never be bound by it. Metonymy is a tool, not a rule. In fact, metonymy is many tools.

Celia and Louis Zukofsky's Catullus is probably creatively, tropically metonymic in this sense; they say in their preface that "this translation follows the sound, rhythm and syntax of his Latin . . . tries, as is said, to breathe the 'literal' meaning with him" (cited in Kelly 55). "Follows"—that is, metonymically reproduces. A translation like this is metonymic in the sense that Kenneth Burke says "poetic realism" is metonymic when the dramatist reproduces a state of mind through gesture and expression. Sound, rhythm, and syntax are all elements that mainstream translation theorists have insisted we sacrifice to sense; but you do not have to go too far out of the mainstream to find other theorists saying that they are the most important of all. Notice how the Zukofskys find English words that stand in roughly the same relation to sound as the Latin words, words that "carry" or "convey" that sound just as other metonymic translators seek to "carry" or "convey" the sense of SL words (I quote from Kelly again, 55–56):

> Minister vetuli puer Falerni
> inger mi calices amariores,
> ut lex Postumiae iubet magistrae,
> ebrioso acino ebriosioris.
> at vos quolubet hinc abite, lymphae
> vini pernicies, et ad severos
> migrate: hic merus est Thyonianus.

Minister wet to lee, pour the Falernian
and gear me chalices, ah my bitterest,
the law's Postumia, you bet magistral,
eh breezy kin a grape-loving breeziness.
Adieus qualifying between water and
wine are pernicious, let the odd serious
migrate: high! pure the thigh on us's the wine god.

You might protest that this is a *very* rough approximation of the Latin sound—that the aural equivalence leaves much to be desired. But so what? That is a nontropic protest. The metonymic translator picks a trope not as judge and jury but as a tool. The idea is to make the TL text *work*, not to achieve perfect equivalence with the SL.

You might next protest that the Zukofskys' Catullus *doesn't* work: that it makes no sense at all, much less Catullus's sense. The first claim, that it makes no sense at all, comes from the old reification of conventionalized (ideosomatized) speech habits as the only guarantor of sense; any speech that deviates from them makes no sense at all. Read with a willingness to *make sense* of it, as we do with foreigner speech and toddler speech and wartime codes and any number of other problematic utterances, it makes plenty of sense. It would even be possible to read this (on a high enough level of abstraction) as a *coherent* text—to work all the oddities into a single, unifying interpretation. That has been our definition of "sense," that it all fits together in an overriding unity; but I would rather approach this kind of text with an open mind (open somatic response) and let each word, each group of words, make sense as I read, so that the "sense" that I make of the poem keeps shifting ground, like this:

We've got a minister out sailing, and he's just been hit by a wave or something, or maybe it's raining, so to warm him up you pour him a glass of wine, or rather a chalice of wine (since he's a minister, a clergyman, despite the fact that when I first started reading he was a minister of state, an assumption I brought from the "foreignness" of the Latin text, I suppose), and let's see, I guess the wine is bitter, like the wine Jesus was given on the cross, and the law is posthumous (going the Zukofskys one better, here), which I take to mean that the law killed Jesus, the magistrates and high priests and all those other legalistic bastards, but what the hell, forget it, drink up, we're all his breezy kin out here on the sailboat, the wind blowing our hair while we sip our wine, anybody saying goodbye between water and wine qualifies as an asshole, or all right, pernicious, odd serious word, anybody who wants to get *that* serious on us can just get the hell off the boat, migrate, hi there, nice thigh, what luck we thought to bring the wine god along, what a drag this sail would have been without *him*.

And, lo and behold (in answer to the second claim about it not being Catullus's sense), I just checked Kelly's sense-for-sense translation of the Catullus and discovered, after I had "read" the Zukofsky version, that I had not been so very far off. This is in part because the Zukofskys cheated, I suppose: translating "lex" as "law" instead of "licks," say, and "vini" as "wine" instead of "weenie." But again, so what? Metonymy is only a translation tool, or many translation tools; what difference does it make if a radical metonymic translator combines several kinds of reduction in the same rendering?

An entirely different approach to metonymic translation, one that in the twentieth century we associate with Eugene A. Nida, entails equivalence not of texts but of their functions in a language or speech community. It should be obvious that a given text never has a single transparent function in a speech community—"function" is a reification of what individual readers do with a text, and whole speech communities never do single simple things with a text—but as a tropic reduction, as a metonymy, this may well be useful. Nida's concepts of "dynamic" and, in his recent work, "functional" equivalence seem to me specifically metonymic reductions of the text to a dynamic or functional intratextual relationship—a relationship, let us say, in the structuralist terms developed by Wayne Booth and Wolfgang Iser, between the textual structures called the "implied author" and the "implied reader." In Nida's formulation, equivalence is to be sought between the implied author-reader dialogues embedded in two texts: the dialogue between implied SL author and SL reader in the SL text, and between what we might call the implied translator (or TL author) and TL reader in the TL text. Since, tropically speaking, the implied SL author, SL reader, and TL reader are all the translator's hermeneutical projections, intratextual fictions arising out of the translator's interpretive act, there can be no question here of "real" equivalence between these two intratextual dialogues, or even of "real" dialogues. They are all tropes, fictions toward a turning. This does not invalidate the metonymic translation that results; indeed, it is precisely what makes it possible.

Another way of coming at these dialogues would be to say that the metonymic translator seeking "dynamic" or "functional" equivalence proceeds by responding somatically to the SL text, then working to generate a TL text whose effect or function *feels* the same or similar (to the translator him- or herself) as that of the SL text. The translator, in other words, is the model for both SL and TL "effects" (somatic responses). The conscientious metonymic translator may well seek to train his or her somatic response to the SL text by reading up on the period and author, by working up a more complex feel for the time and place it was written, but it is still his or her own somatic response that must form the basis of any "effect" we discuss. A translation critic can carp at a given rendering, saying that the translator responded incorrectly to the SL or generated a misleading effect in the TL; but all this says is that the critic responded differently. In the logicalizing, objectifying tradition of the West, that is not good enough for most people: they feel compelled to elevate their response to the status of objective fact, to reify response as reality; but a tropic (rhetorical, dialogical, dramatistic) approach to translation refuses to buy into that kind of thinking. A response is a response—*my* response, or *your* response. "*This* flesh and *this* voice in the mystery of its onceness," as Buber said. It is my response *to you* (and dialogized by your words), or my anticipation of your response *to me* (and dialogized by my anticipation of your words).

Now, in order to settle for a metonymic stab at equivalence of effect (dialogical equivalence), the translator must accept the image of the SL writer's intention that he or she has gained from that dialogue—must be willing to go with it, to follow it, in the TL. Sometimes this is forced, as in the classic scene of the boss and the translator who must do his bidding. And certainly this writer-translator dialogue has long been idealized in terms of force, of the translator's forced submission to the writer's intention (whether the "force" is imagined as coming from outside, in society, or from inside, in the translator's ideosomatic response). But it need not be that. The translator can imagine his or her dialogue with the SL writer as a friendly one, a dialogue between equals, a cooperative, collaborative relation in which the translator willingly lets the writer lead. Some dialogues are literally collaborative in this sense: the writer and the translator work together at the same table, often as good friends, even husband and wife, but with the translator willingly taking a back seat to the writer. (It is not irrelevant to note that husband-and-wife translator teams tend to be husband-writer and wife-translator teams: in the Platonic-Pauline-Augustinian hierarchy that places writer over translator and husband over wife, these "naturally" [ideosomatically] tend to coincide.)

Again, I stress that there is nothing wrong with this, nothing to be ashamed of, nothing to get angry about—as long as we remember that it is only one way of setting up the writer-translator dialogue. Metonymy only becomes a straitjacket when it is no longer a trope, no longer one creative tool among many, but the only way, the only acceptable way, the only form of "translation."

I want to close this section on metonymy by discussing a metonymic translation of a Jorge Guillén poem, "Desnudo," by Reginald Gibbons, who in his commentary in *Critical Inquiry* links his translation specifically to "functional" equivalence. Here are the two poems:

Desnudo

Blancos, rosas. Azules casi en veta,
　　Retraídos, mentales.
Puntos de luz latente dan señales
　　De una sombra secreta.

Pero el color, infiel a la penumbra,
　　Se consolida en masa.
Yacente en el verano de la casa.
　　Una forma se alumbra.

Claridad aguzada entre perfiles,
　　De tan puros tranquilos,
Que cortan y aniquilan con sus filos
　　Las confusiones viles.

Desnuda está la carne. Su evidencia
　　Se resuelve en reposo.
Monotonía justa, prodigioso
　　Colmo de la presencia.

Plenitud immediata, sin ambiente,
　　Del cuerpo femenino.
Ningún primor: ni voz ni flor. ¿Destino?
　　¡Oh absoluto Presente!

Nude

Whites, pinks. A pale blue swash,
　　Withdrawn, imagined.
Points of light flash a hint
　　Of secret shadow.

But color, unfaithful to the gloom,
　　Consolidates.
Lying in the summer of the room
　　A shape takes light.

And the sharp outline of silhouettes—
　　Out of purity, a hush—

Whose edges can abolish
    The confusion through which they cut.

The flesh is nude, its evidence
    Resolved at rest.
A just monotony, prodigious
    Hoard of presence.

The full sufficiency, immediate and complete,
    Of a woman's body. Not beauty.
Not voice nor bloom, however pleasant,
    Her destiny? Oh absolute present! (661–62)

Guillén's poem is pretty clearly a kind of glorified or transcendental strip-tease, in which a woman is stripped first of her clothes, then of her body, and left with what Platonic-Pauline-Augustinian metonymy conceives as the essence of femininity, "absolute presence." (The poem might well be read as a reenactment of Augustine's path from youthful lust after the bodies of his mistresses, through the rejection of bodily lust in favor of an image of his saintly mother, to a transcendence of his dead mother in the image of the mother church.) In fact, given the traditional association of metonymic translation with the changing of clothes (body as transcendental sense, clothes as the verbal form that can be wrapped around or stripped off the body at will) and then, going deeper, with the resurrection of the body (soul as transcendental sense, body as verbal form that is separated from the soul at death and later, in the New Jerusalem, reattached to the soul in the perfected form of the "spiritual body")—given these obvious link-ups between Guillén's poem and Western (Pauline/Augustinian) Platonism, we might say that the poem dramatizes the antitranslational stance of Western (Pauline/Augustinian) Platonism as well. Thus, we have Guillén's attack on metonymical parts (lines, colors, female bodies) for their "infidelity" to the transcendental (idealized, abstracted, "mentale," which Gibbons renders as "imagined") whole—and that attack neatly translates as an attack on the metonymical parts of an SL text (rhyme, meter, assonance and consonance, alliteration, sound, feel, etc.) that have traditionally been considered unfaithful or unnecessary to the transcendental sense.

It is not surprising, therefore, that Gibbons chooses to render the poem metonymically, specifically in terms of the "function" of rhyme and other verbal forms. His apology for not achieving perfect (metaphorical) identity between SL and TL function *and* form is purely *pro forma,* a kneejerk exorcism of the vestigial guilt that all translators are

programmed to feel and express (until they discover that metonymy
and metaphor are just tropes):

Had the translation been rhymed to match the rhyme pattern of the original
(and taking into account the notable similarities in some of the rhymes em-
ployed, with vowels crossing over in stanza 1 and repeated *l*s in stanza 3, the
overall effect in English could have been musically cloying. A better translator
than I might have managed it—and will, I hope. But the function of the rhyme
in this poem does not appear to be semantic, to *create* meaning. . . . Instead,
the rhyme in "Desnudo" appears to give greater cohesiveness to the stanzas,
and this in turn appears to be necessary for the suggestion, in the poetic progress (rather than in the isolable meanings) of the individual words, of emotional movement as the poem deliberately, slowly, deliciously, reveals a visual
image of the nude by approaching it gradually and then refines or even cancels
the visual image (the effect of phanopoeia) by shifting the poem immediately
to the level of absolute type or abstraction.[7]
    Rather than allowing the nude female figure to suggest itself as its own
meaning (fleshly beauty, mortality, the present moment), the poem explicitly
forces the reader to consider the more philosophical category of the Present,
for which fleshly Beauty stands as an Example. The rhymes suggest an intensifying feeling—they do intensify feeling—so that in this poem, rhyme is su-
premely important as a formal element, but toward an end which does not
necessitate slavish adherence by the translator to the same rhyme *scheme*.
Rather, it demands an understanding of, and an adherence to, the *function* of
the rhyme throughout the poem. Rhyme, rich though it is, seems to be subordinated to the curious mixture of phanopoeic and an almost fastidiously distanced generality of diction. (661)

    It seems fairly certain that Gibbons agrees with Guillén on all this,
the "deliciousness" of the strip-tease, the portrayal of the woman's dehumanization and the reader's forced complicity in that dehumanization in eulogistic terms: "Rather than allowing the nude female figure
to suggest itself [not herself, the woman not as subject but as object]
as its own meaning (fleshly beauty, mortality, the present moment), the
poem explicitly forces the reader to consider the more philosophical
category of the Present, for which fleshly Beauty stands as an Example."
Nor is Gibbons's agreement particularly surprising, since this particular
dehumanization of women is part of our patriarchal conditioning, our
(Guillén's and Gibbons's and my) ideosomatic programming as men in
Western society. Rather than allowing the woman to participate as an
equal in dialogue (to paraphrase Gibbons in a less programmed way),
Guillén and his translator both want to reduce her to a body, her body
to "fleshly beauty, mortality, the present moment," and those things to

"the more philosophical category of the Present," an abstraction that can be controlled by the male viewer.

So, finding himself in agreement with Guillén on this metonymic ideology, Gibbons approaches the poem metonymically, in terms of the "function" of rhyme—although he does not say so, he is clearly talking about the effect of rhyme on the reader, what the rhyme does to the reader somatically. (The reification of response as function is ideosomatically congruent with the other reifications in the poem, woman as body as presence.) And in fact, although Gibbons does not mention his functional equivalents for rhyme by name, I can see several right away. His rendering of Guillén's title, for instance: "Desnudo" in Spanish is literally (or archaically—the modern form would be "desnudado") "denuded," which implies an action, stripping, something someone has done to the woman; and if, as Gibbons argues, the function of rhyme is to intensify the effect of Guillén's "fastidiously generalized" diction, then rendering "Desnudo" as "Nude" has precisely that effect. A "nude," of course, is a static genre, a type of painting or photograph defined by the objectification of an unclothed female body, or it is the female body so objectified.[8] "Desnudo" carries in its morphemic structure the traces of an action, a having-been-performedness, a "doing" in the real world; by shifting to the English "Nude," Gibbons subtly intensifies the objectification and generalization that Guillén seems to intend, by fading out the history of how *a* woman was reduced from living human being to body to two-dimensional image, and from there, finally, to abstraction.

Another functional equivalent of rhyme in Gibbons's translation might be the neutralization of gender, another advantage (from Gibbons's point of view) that English has over Spanish: the masculine-generic "Desnudo" in the title and the feminine-specific "Desnuda" in stanza 4 are both replaced by the gender-unmarked "Nude" in Gibbons's English. The effect is to smooth and flatten the overt sexism of Guillén's masculinization-cum-genericization of the female body in the title and its passing recognition of femininity later in the poem (en route to absolute abstraction) into the "pure" neutered genericism and abstraction of the English "Nude." In fact, note that the ideally despised and eventually discarded female body is associated with a whole barrage of feminine nouns ("carne," "evidencia," "monotonía," "presencia," "plenitud"), all abstractions traditionally associated with femininity, and that it is only in the last throes of abstraction, as the fallen feminine world of matter drops away, that Guillén returns us via the strangely masculine "cuerpo femenino" to the triumphantly masculine "absoluto

Presente." The masculinization of woman that was anticipated in the masculine entitlement of the female body as "Desnudo" is here achieved in the masculine disposal of the female body in "¡Oh absoluto Presente!" But masculinizing a woman gives the game away, doesn't it? It makes it awkwardly clear that the author wants to eliminate otherness, to make the woman not only *his* but *him,* and that desire speaks all too openly of fearful need. Much better the neutered nouns to which Gibbons has access in English: flesh, evidence, monotony, presence, plenitude, feminine body, absolute presence. Here the desire to eliminate female otherness is "ennobled" as a desire to eliminate all gender, masculine and feminine alike, in a "transcendence" of bodies that is only surreptitiously (ideosomatically) associated with male desire: the desire to escape from the body into pure mind. You might say that Gibbons got lucky—or else that he was able to capitalize on the special genius of English for neutering, degendering. Either way, he has succeeded in producing an excellent metonymic rendition of Guillén's poem.

You may have noticed that these reductive or metonymic translation models cover the range of translation as it has been defined in the West: equivalence between two texts based on a convergence of one element (sense at the word or sentence or text level, sound, function) and a divergence of everything else (everything that is made to serve as the disposable vehicle of the "unchanging" tenor). You might call my approach reductive, in fact, in its telescoping of two thousand years of theory and practice into a single trope. And you would be right, of course. But the reduction is another polemical device: it is intended to show how very limited mainstream conceptions of translation have been, how severely circumscribed. For the most part, until the post-World War II period, all translation that has not fit neatly into the categories that I have listed (and some translation that has) has been dismissed as "free" translation, that is, not really translation at all—beyond the pale. So now we move on, beyond that pale, into some of the proscribed variety of "free" (and other) translation.

Synecdoche

What variety? The proscription has had the effect of blinding us or dulling us to the variety that is there. We have to rub the sleep from our eyes.

Gibbons's translation of "Desnudo" (or my not entirely sympathetic response to Gibbons's translation of "Desnudo") may help us move out into that unfamiliar territory. What happens, we can ask, when the translator does not feel quite as comfortable with the writer's views as Gibbons does with Guillén's? What happens when the translator is not inclined to go along with the writer, is not inclined to give the writer the lead? Then the translator does not even touch the SL text, because to distort the SL meaning is to refuse to translate—that is what we have been taught to think. If the translator deliberately distorts the intended meaning, he or she is not a translator, and his or her work is not translation.

But why not? In Chapter 2 we saw Mikhail Bakhtin, coming out of Martin Buber, making a strong case for seeing all communication as translation: we always have to translate what other people say into terms we can understand, whether we operate in one or two or more languages. (George Steiner, coming out of the German romantics, makes much the same case in *After Babel*.) Even if we want to restrict translation to an operation between two languages, the only thing required to produce "translation" in that restricted sense is that two texts, SL and TL, stand in some kind of recognizable relation to each other. Mainstream translation theorists have tried to restrict the kinds of relation between texts that deserve the name "translation," but even they have to admit that their ideal is impossible and that real translation is always one or another form of distortion. The difference between inadvertent distortion and deliberate distortion, in other words, is a difference in degree, not in kind. So why not ease out of all these ever finer and finer criteria for translation, these attempts to reify a difference in degree into a difference in kind, this pretense that a translator who tries for perfect equivalence but fails is somehow better than a translator who deliberately distorts?

Synecdoche is the substitution of a part for a whole, usually a part conceived as a typical quality of the whole, a "representative" part, as Kenneth Burke says. "He's all heart" does not mean that he is a large red blood-pumping muscle, but that I want to portray him in terms of his compassion, his fellow-feeling. I isolate his "heart" (which is in fact a metonymy for feeling, probably based on our somatic response to certain kinds of powerful emotion, the pounding of the heart) as his most representative feature or quality or "part," and I say that he is *all* heart, his heart is the whole him.

A synecdochic translation would be one that isolates a single part of the SL text, treats it as representative of the whole, and renders *that* in the TL. Like the metonymic translator, the synecdochic translator begins by reducing the SL text to a part; unlike the metonymic translator, who wants to make the TL text stand in roughly the same part-whole relation to that reductive element as the SL text, the synecdochic translator wants to treat the part *as* the whole.

But this is too general and abstract. Some examples. Propagandistic translation (or what Louis Kelly calls "signal," chap. 3.3) is typically synecdochic: the translator feels that the SL writer did not quite put things clearly, did not bring the truly important parts of his or her text into proper perspective, and so highlights those aspects in the TL. One part of a text corroborates the translator's views, another contradicts them—so the translator treats the parts that he or she does not like (feels uncomfortable with, disagrees with) as excess, superfluous, as dross that can be sloughed off in the TL, and translates only the parts he or she likes (abridgement), or translates the whole thing *in terms of* the parts he or she likes (assimilation). Naturally, the translator likes to think that the parts he or she favors are representative of the whole— the true core, the heart, the main thing, which the SL writer just failed to stress, through whatever ignorance or ineptitude. So what has happened from the translator's point of view is not a *reduction* of the SL text but its *clarification*.

The synecdochic translator, in other words, sets up a different sort of dialogue with the SL writer: an equally friendly one, perhaps, but the friendliness tends more toward condescension than subservient admiration. The writer and translator collaborate on the TL text, but the writer has to rely on the translator's deeper penetration into the true meaning of the SL text. In my reading of Jorge Guillén's "Desnudo," for example, I assume that Guillén is blind to his complicity in the patriarchal ideology of the West: to him, all this seems quite natural, and in fact complimentary to women. What woman would not like to be thought of as a beautiful nude? What woman would not like to be relieved of her mortal frame and perceived in the light of eternity? I "condescend" to Guillén by assuming that I know the implications of these attitudes better than he. I even assume that I know the reason for his blindness. I assume that it is a kind of programmed masculine fear of otherness, of everything that cannot be assimilated into a controllable object. Deep down, it may be the little boy's fear that his mommy won't come back, a separation anxiety defended against first through anger at the absent mother, then through the idealization of absence as "absolute presence." So, when I turn my hand to translating his poem, I isolate that fear, that anxiety, and base my whole rendition around it, make that "part" (which the poet himself failed to realize was there, but *I know* it is) into my new "whole":

Deluded

Red, white, and a splash of pale blue,
　　But furled, tucked away
In a shadowy realm of forms, where you
　　(Unvoiced) have nothing to say.

I wish. Instead, unfaithful to my gloom,
　　You take on voice and mass:
Hell yes, I can see you there, lying on your ass
　　In the summer of your room.

Listen, why couldn't you be pure for me,
　　A tranquil form, a cut
That *I* make through the otherness I feel?
　　Why couldn't you be mine? Not

You. No: you're distant, blank, aloof,
　　A stranger under my roof.
You make me feel awkward, unsure, incomplete.
　　Your words, your metric feet

Protrude beyond all reasoned rhyme.
　　You hoard your presence.
You stand apart, akimbo, self-sufficient.
　　Damn you! You are not mine.

Now, I am no poet, much less what Harold Bloom would call a "strong poet"—but as a synecdochic rendering of "Desnudo" I think "Deluded" works pretty well. Also as a synecdochic intralingual rendering of Gibbons—"unfaithful to *my* gloom" for "unfaithful to *the* gloom," for instance, and "You hoard your presence" for "Prodigious / Hoard of presence." What I have done is to bring my own idiosomatic resistance to bear on my own (and Gibbons's and Guillén's) ideosomatic programming as a Western white man, resistance that I have bolstered through my experience not only of men and women (and reading in gender studies) but of other poems as well: I detect evidence of other poets here and there in my translation, Wallace Stevens's "Sunday Morning" and "The Emperor of Ice Cream," for example, and Sylvia Plath's "Daddy," and even of the "poem" of flag-waving American patriotism in the first stanza. In my title, "Deluded," I hear not only "Denuded" but Jan Huizinga's title *Homo ludens,* "lude" as play, a playful alternative to the deadly seriousness of "nude," "delusion" therefore as a fearful denial of play, a cutting off of playful dialogue between the man and the woman.[9]

Notice, however (to get back to synecdoche), that in my translation of Guillén's poem I am not actually "deliberately distorting" his mean-ing; I am just not taking his word for it. I am trusting my own feel for the somatic realities that empower an ideological construction (the fears that make him idealize) and thus feeling my way to an SL "mean-ing" that Guillén knew nothing about. It was there, I claim, but it was buried too deep, obscured by too much ideosomatic programming, for him to see. Most people want to be taken at face value, at their word— to be seen as they see themselves, to be equated with their self-image. This seems a reasonable enough expectation, but Freud called it "resist-ance" and identified it as the single most troublesome obstacle to psy-choanalysis. I call it ideosomatic programming and identify it as the single most troublesome obstacle to idiosomatic liberation, but maybe I am just reterming Freud. From my point of view, maybe from Freud's too, the traditional sense-for-sense translator's willingness to "take the writer at his word" is a willingness to take self-image for truth, ideo-somatics for intention. Thus the fundamental conservatism of most translation theory. It says, do not question the way things look; just render what the writer wants to say (*vouloir-dire* as "meaning"). Do not explore what you think the writer might be implying—against his or her will, in contradiction to all he or she holds most sacred. Do not rock the boat. There is nothing beneath the surface. There are no depths. This is all there is.

There is no question here of my being "right" or "wrong" about "Desnudo." Guillén is not my psychoanalytical patient, I am not a psy-choanalyst, and even if he were and I was, psychoanalysis is not an objective science. What I have offered in my translation is an interpre-tation, an imaginative construction of the hidden "part" of Guillén's text that I believe truly represents the whole. My interpretation is grounded in my own ideosomatic self-exploration, but of course that is no guarantee of "accuracy" or "validity." The point is that reading Guill-én more superficially, taking him at face value (or what you take to be face value), is no guarantee of interpretive validity either. You are still interpreting, and still restricting your TL reader's interpretive options, with every TL word and phrase you choose. The only collective guide to interpretive validity we have is ideosomatic response, that gut-level sense about words and phrases that is programmed into all members of a speech community. But even that ideosomatic sense is not monolithic (the ideosomatics of English are different in England and America and India, and in the American upper and middle and working classes, and among whites and blacks and Hispanics, etc.), and there is no reason to assume that a superficial ideosomatic reading (one that hovered timidly around the first seal) would be any more reliable or unreliable in actual language-use situations than one that emerged out of an encounter with the third seal.

I associate synecdochic translation with propaganda, but that is really only one kind of synecdochic rendering. Synecdoche is a substitution of part for whole, a treating of a part *as* the whole, and that means that any kind of radical reduction of the SL text to a representative part might be imagined synecdochically. TV subtitling, for instance—which must reduce the written TL text to a core that can be read at roughly the same speed as it takes the actors to speak the SL text. The rapidities and overlapping complexities of natural speech (in interviews, talk shows, etc.) and even of performed dramatic speech must be reduced to univocal written texts that flash across the screen at a maximum rate of eight syllables per second, which is generally considered to be an average reading speed. This synecdochic reduction at times "possesses" the subtitler's imagination, so that even when the time factor is not present (when nothing particular is being said, for instance), the subtitler may leave the same three or four TL words on the screen while the SL text goes on and on. The redundancy of natural speech is not considered a "representative" part of the SL text—it is not something the TL viewer needs to know—so it gets mercilessly pruned. The synecdochic assumption is that the SL writer/speaker does not know what he or she is trying to say and is just filling up air time with empty blather; the translator knows better, sees through vacant verbiage to the true "content" or core of the SL text, and renders only that.

What complicates this synecdochic representation of the SL text is that the SL text is really much more than the words the actors are saying; it is the whole audiovisual experience, including setting and positioning (two cars careening down a Los Angeles street), noises (police sirens sounding offscreen), props (the truck that pulls in front of the chaser), and paralinguistic signals like tone of voice, expression, gesture, and so on (the clenched fist that belies the friendly words rendered in the subtitles, for example). The TL viewer might be assumed to miss some of this while staring at the bottom of the screen trying to keep up with the subtitles, but cannot miss all of it—so that synecdoche remains a mere translator's tool (how to reduce the SL text to a representative part), not a descriptive device (how to account for what the TL viewer actually receives). The TL viewer receives a lot more than the subtitler provides, in fact more than the SL text alone provides— which is one of the pleasures of watching a subtitled program. But the subtitler still has to do his or her job, and synecdochic reduction is the right tool.

The situation is roughly similar in simultaneous interpretation from speech into sign language, which also entails a radical synecdochic reduction from the lexical richness of speech to the relative simplicity of signs, and from the variety of spoken syntactic structures to a regular subject-verb-object word order. (Parts of "speech" in sign language are determined entirely by syntactic context, so that the sign for "love" may be a noun, verb, or modifier depending on its location in the sentence.) Names are reduced from the fullness of voicing to the metonymical poverty of linear fingering sequences, or even to a single fingered initial.

But lest you think that it is all loss, note also the effect of shifting from phonetics to iconics and deictics (pictures and pointings). The traditional association of speech (via the breath it is carried on) with the "spirit" of sense, meaning, truth, the transcendental signified (in Augustine's term), is replaced with a kinesic image of experience in the world. The signer translating an anecdote about a car accident that the speaker had last week, for instance, is not restricted to pale iconic imitations of spoken words but can restage the whole sequence of events with his or her hands. Emotions are mimed out, laughing and holding the chest for "funny," drawing a line from chest to throat for "fear," and so on. The signs for "look" vary with what is looked at, and how: to "look over a fence" involves making the fence with one hand and peering over it while miming the path one's gaze takes with the other hand. "Travel" is signed by walking down the hand with two fingers. And so on. By contrast with this bodily evocation of lived experience, speech begins to look like mere sound, an illusory representation of a disembodied or absent sense, a nonsensical sense (to the deaf viewer, speech is reduced to the arbitrary movement of the lips). Sign language is a kind of living hieroglyphic that represents no mentalist ideal but human action, a representative "part" of a spoken SL text that we "hearers" often forget all about. Again, the synecdochic signer "penetrates" the dross of speech to the bodily experience buried in it and represents that in the TL, so that what from a "hearer's" point of view is loss (loss of rich spoken nuance) becomes from the deaf TL viewer's point of view real gain.[10]

Other possibilities: what Roman Jakobson calls "intersemiotic" translations, translations from words into images or sounds, say, which reduce a verbal text to a representative feeling and expand that into the TL visual or musical whole. Performative translations like simultaneous interpretation, which interprets an incomplete and potentially incoherent text by performing or presenting it *as* complete, *as* coherent, rendering a representative "core" of the incomplete text (each SL phrase or sentence as it presents itself) as a completed TL whole.[11] These are just suggestions, like all my illustrations in this chapter. Some of them may not work for you; if not, think up your own.

Metaphor

In fact, before I start on metaphor, let me expand those last two lines in "Synecdoche" into a warning, and an encouragement. I am not setting up a rigidly systematic taxonomy of translation here, so don't start complaining about this or that type being missing in my discussion of a specific trope, or this or that illustration not working the way I say it does. Or rather, complain all you like (that is what keeps the dialogue going), but don't reject this chapter because you are unhappy with some of my illustrations. You are welcome to do whatever you like with my tropes and their illustrations: modify them, replace them, supplement them, whatever. In earlier drafts I called TV subtitling and simultaneous signing metaleptic, and here they have become synecdochic. It is all a matter of perspective, of how you look at things. I am suggesting *ways of seeing* translation, ways of construing a translation task, and to flesh out the complexity in a fairly accessible way, I am using six tropes with several different illustrations in each one. But there are hundreds of tropes, each of them probably perfectly applicable to some translation task, if someone would just go to the trouble of making the connection. And my illustrations are just illustrations. I debated whether to place the Zukofskys' Catullus in metonymy, metaphor, or irony; and since in some ways Reginald Gibbons improved on Guillén's original, his translation could have been used to illustrate hyperbole. I realize the temptation you must feel to rigidify my tropes and illustrations into "objective" categories of translation, and if you want to do it badly enough, I cannot stop you. But I do not mean that to happen. I want to liberate translators from objective categories, not create new straitjackets for them. (I can just imagine translation teachers ten years from now saying, "No, that type of metonymy is not appropriate for that type of text.")

Metaphor comes from the Greek verb *metapherein,* to carry over, whose Latin cognate *transferre* gives us translation. And, just as metaphor has been called the "supertrope," the trope that contains or implies all the others, so too is metaphorical translation, the striving for perfect identity between SL and TL, often called the supreme ideal of all translation. Metaphor, at least ideally, equates things: this is that. He is a lion. She is a rose. Metaphorical translation ideally equates texts: the TL is the SL. The two are identical. "Nicht anstatt des andern," as Goethe says of this ideal, "sondern in der Stelle des andern."

It cannot happen, of course: this is an ideal, not reality. Metaphor claims to equate things, but as Kenneth Burke says, it really only perspectivizes them, encourages us to see this in terms of that, that in terms of this. Metaphorical translation, too, claims to equate texts but really only perspectivizes them, encourages us to read English Odysseys in terms of the Greek original and the Greek Odysseia in terms of its English translations. In fact, all tropical translation does this: the part-part substitution of metonymy, the part-whole substitution of synecdoche, the whole-whole substitution of metaphor in its strict sense, all are perspectivizings, ways of juxtaposing two texts, ways of seeing them in interrelation, ways of "turning" in a meaningful way from SL to TL.

It was the romantics who elevated metaphor to primacy among tropes, to supertrope status, and romantic translation theorists from Goethe to Steiner have been the most fervent proponents of metaphorical translation. But because they approach metaphor as a quasireligious *reality*, an impossible ideal that must be possible if life and language are to have any meaning at all, they tend to stress its rarity or even its nonexistence. If we cheerfully admit that it is only a trope, nothing more mystical than that, just a way of seeing, a way of perspectivizing, then it becomes much more ordinary, the sort of translation model that just about anybody could expect to experiment with, and succeed at. (Success, remember, does not mean achieving perfect identity between SL and TL but using that ideal heuristically to create a TL text that works in the overall translation dialogue.) Thanks to the romantics, we tend to associate metaphor with great literature, and metaphoric translation with great literary translation; but, though I do want to take a look at some metaphoric literary translation later, let me demonstrate the ordinariness of metaphoric translation conceived tropically by starting elsewhere.

In the autumn of 1987, Billy Graham was on tour in Finland, and my wife and I went to hear him speak. What interested me when I first decided to go was American fundamentalism, a professional concern of mine; but when we got there I soon found myself more interested in the translation side of things. Graham's consecutive interpreter was a Finnish Lutheran minister named Kalevi Lehtinen—a man in his early fifties who had been living in Germany and working in English for the last ten years. We were at the far end of the stadium and had to watch the two men speak on the video screen (with our naked eyes we could not even tell where the podium was), but that was enough to impress me with the magnificent job Lehtinen did. Not only did he get the "sense" right, in a Finnish evangelical context (he made a few obvious mistakes, not knowing what "syringe" was and guessing at it, rendering it "käsipumppu," or hand-pump, but otherwise he was right on target), he also got the sound or *feel* of Graham's talk exactly right. His consecutive interpretation was no "interlinear version," the romantic ideal since Goethe, but what we might call an "interexpressional version," an identity not of SL/TL sentence and word sense, or of SL/TL function and form, but of SL/TL sense and sound, sense and tone. In theological/philosophical terms, it was an identity of SL/TL mind and body. Lehtinen *sounded* just like Graham. His intonation, timing, pitch, stress, all sounded like Graham. (Like all actual somatic response to language, this is my feeling about equivalence, not something I could prove scientifically.) The TL had (what felt like) the same color and texture as the SL. Lehtinen even gestured like Graham. It was the most astonishing performance I have ever seen. Since we saw it on the video screen, it was almost like a flaw in the PA system, an echo produced by a shadow image—only in Finnish.

Of course, it was not that close a rendition. It was not SL/TL identity. Not only did Graham's voice-echo come out in another language and his afterimage stand shorter and have curly hair; there were cultural differences, or the two renditions provoked culturally different somatic responses in me. Graham had prepared for this audience and was able to hit several Finnish soft spots—the small country's desire to make its mark on the world, combined with the Nordic Social Democratic brand of paternalism, left the Finns ideally vulnerable to Graham's urging that they become missionaries to the world, save the world for Jesus. Here Lehtinen was able to plug into the imperialistic rhetoric that was in the air in Finland just before World War II, and his TL text hit home. But elsewhere Graham's appeals were not always so felicitous: his very American emphasis on the great and mighty with whom he had discussed Jesus over breakfast, for example. Here Lehtinen produced a TL text that, however "metaphoric," felt significantly different from Graham's SL text. I am not quite sure what it was—a constriction of his throat, a clamping down on emotion—that made it feel to me as if Lehtinen knew, or sensed, that this would not go over very well with a Finnish audience. "When I was sitting in the sauna yesterday," yes; "When I was sitting with Prime Minister Adenauer twenty years ago," no. But again, this was no failure on Lehtinen's part; his metaphoric rendition opened up new perspectives on Graham's rhetoric, and in that sense succeeded. I was able to *hear* Graham in Finnish, to respond to his all too familiar SL message (I grew up with it: it is ideosomatic reality for me that anyone who loves Jesus will automatically become a great and mighty person) in an unfamiliar context, and that gave me a new way of thinking (and feeling) about it.

Interestingly, Graham's purpose was the same as Luther's, or Nida's, or any missionary's: to convert his hearers to Christianity. And since the Protestant approach to Bible translation, following Luther, has been seen as strictly metonymic, one might have expected Graham's interpreter to render him metonymically: retiringly, self-effacingly, conveying only Graham's sense and not pretending to *be* a Finnish Graham. But I have heard demagogic speeches and sermons interpreted consecutively in that mode before: first an impassioned SL phrase, then a dispassionate, detached TL rendering. Fire and ice. The idea, I suppose, is for the TL listener to take passion (body) from the SL and meaning (mind) from the TL. Unfortunately, it doesn't work—at least, not for me. I get a dual message—one deeply felt but dumb, the other articulate but inert. It is somewhat like having one child whisper into your ear while another is yanking on your arm—or like reading TV subtitles when you do not understand a word of the SL, except that consecutive interpretation does not have the rich audiovisual context that TV provides. Metonymy seems (to me) to work best for conference interpreters when the SL pretends to be disembodied too—at academic conferences, for example. Then the dispassionate renderer of disembodied meanings fits right in. But when the SL speaker specifically wants to work on the TL listeners' bodies, when the somatic appeal is overt and central to the success of the text, the transfer of a single reductive element of the SL text like "sense" seems inadequate.

To me. I am identifying with the interpreter here, putting myself in an imaginary conference interpretation situation and guessing what I would try to do—not laying down rules for all time. I think that if I agreed with Graham and was asked to interpret for him, I would try to render him metaphorically. Not this part or that, but everything, what he says and how he says it.[12] I would not expect to succeed, in the objective sense, at perfectly rendering everything, making my TL text identical with his SL text, but I would certainly try to give the impression that I was succeeding, as Kalevi Lehtinen did. I am sure that if I had taped the Graham/Lehtinen speech I could go through it pedantically and find all kinds of things to carp at—a cherished task for many translation critics. But tropically speaking, dialogically speaking—in the real world of interaction between real people—the important thing is not objective success but the *feel* of success. A translation that feels successful is successful. Dialogue is all.

As this discussion implies, the dialogue that a metaphoric translator or interpreter will set up (or find him- or herself in) with the SL writer or speaker is very similar to the dialogue that we found in metonymy, only slightly intensified: both the metonymic and the metaphoric translators subordinate their interpretations to what they take to be the SL writer's will, but where the metonymic translator seeks to *follow* the SL writer, the metaphoric translator seeks to *be* the SL writer. After hearing Graham and Lehtinen in Helsinki, I asked around a little (Finland is a small country) and found out that Lehtinen identifies strongly with Graham, and that, according to his wife, he and Graham are similar in many ways. They do not look at all alike (apart from both being white males past middle age), but they respond to similar situations in similar ways. This suggests that for Lehtinen, being asked to interpret for Graham must have been like the actor who has always imagined himself as Hamlet being asked to play Hamlet—to "become" Hamlet, or give the impression that he is Hamlet, at least for the duration of the play. An actor or translator who believed in this, believed that he or she had actually become (or could actually become) a character or the SL writer/speaker, would be on the dirty edge of psychosis: obviously, I am not talking about an objective becoming here, or even about an attempt to achieve objective identity with the SL writer/speaker. Metaphor is a trope, a dialogical image, useful in the turning of SL into TL but nothing more. There is no point, in other words, in accusing the metaphoric translator of being unrealistic. Metaphor is no more unrealistic than acting. It succeeds when you convince your audience that it succeeds, and fails when you fail to convince your audience that it succeeds—not when you achieve or fail to achieve perfect identity with the SL writer/text.

There are other nonliterary examples of metaphoric translation worth mentioning—TV dubbing, say, which seeks to match up SL/TL sense and sound, or various innovative advertising translations—but maybe I should not take my dedication to eclectic illustrations too far and neglect literary translation altogether.[13] Let us look, then, at a translation that I did in 1984 and a variation on my translation by Diana derHovanessian. The SL text is a lyric by the Finnish poet Eino Leino, "Erotessa" (1905):

Erotessa

Muistelen minä sinua:
satakielet soittelevat
yössäni hämärtyvässä.

Muistelet sinä minua:
lepinkäiset lentelevät
pääsi päälle istumahan.

Muistelemme toisiamme:
kaksi kaunista kesällä,
kesälehti kolmantena.

Then, two English versions, mine (A) and Diana derHovanessian's (B):

At Parting (A)

When I remember you
nightingale cries will fill
my deepening night

When you remember me
scudding shrikes will light
on your head

When we remember each other
we'll yet be two, the third
a summer leaf

At Parting (B)

When I think of you
the nightingale song
will fill the night air

When you think of me
a visiting swallow
will brush by your hair

When we remember each other
the summer leaves
will fall through cool air

"Objectively" speaking (idealizing metaphor as equivalence), version A is closer to the original: "lepinkäiset," for example, are literally (ornithologically) "shrikes," not "swallows." But that idealization is based implicitly on a reduction: the dictionary meaning of "lepinkäiset" and "shrikes" is the same. Version A, in other words, comes closer to the original in terms of sense-for-sense and word-for-word equivalence. Version B comes closer to (what is usually taken to be) the original in terms of mood equivalence, "feel" equivalence: the poem as it is traditionally read (and sung) in Finland is a soft, poignant, nostalgic lyric, and B captures that mood nicely. If I were doing traditional translation criticism, I would probably assume that one or the other of these kinds of equivalence was the "correct" or "crucial" or "only important" one and declare either A or B the better translation. Objectively.

But I am not doing that sort of criticism; following Burke, I am looking for perspectives, and what these two renditions offer is precisely a dual perspectivizing of Leino's poem. We can see them diverging, for instance, on the poet's attempt to deal with absence. In B, nostalgia becomes a good enough substitute for the beloved, an artistic presence that more than makes up for the beloved's absence. B is rich with ease, comfort, a calm resting in the sure knowledge of reunion. The poet-as-nightingale metaphor says: the beauty of the poet's song comforts me in my longing; it gives me a new object for my love and therefore takes away the pain. The night is not the absence of light but the medium of sound ("night *air*"), and the nightingale's song seems to point forward to a mystical reunion, a reunion not only as a meeting but as a merging, a mystical marriage in which lover and beloved will become one flesh. (This is, of course, the romantic ideal traditionally projected by metaphor.)

Version A is less sanguine. There the nightingale *cries,* which suggests the Greek myth of Philomela, the woman who was raped by Zeus, had her tongue torn out by a jealous Hera, and was turned into a bird. Is poetry a meaningful singing, a filling of the night air with poetic meaning—or a drowning out of memories with clamor? Here the night is not only *night,* an absence of light, it is *my* night, the darkness inside me, an internal night that deepens as the light fades, deepens like an abyss, an emptiness that longs to be filled not by sounds but by the physical presence of the beloved. (Leino's "yössäni" is literally "in my night"; "hämärtyvässä" is "darkening" or "dusking.") Now, rather than replacing the beloved, the poet's words only make the longing worse.

Stanza 2 shifts from the poet's remembrance of his beloved to the beloved's remembrance of the poet, which he imagines not as an internal singing (a poet's prerogative) but as the arrival of songbirds (synecdoches of himself) to land on her head. Note the effect of B's swallows, though: no songbirds they, but flitting, fleeting migratory birds that *sound* like what you do when you're about to sing (swallow), birds that "brush by your hair," greet you from me (or as me) with a ghostly caress. A's shrikes are predatory songbirds whose song celebrates an impulse toward violence (shrikes impale their victims on twigs), a continuation of the rape image opened in stanza 1. Nostalgia becomes increasingly horrific: longing for the absent beloved is gradually transformed into anger at her absence (why can't you be here with *me?* I *need* you!), which brushes too close to infantile separation anxiety for (adult male) comfort, and the need to defend against regression generates a barely disguised impulse to rape.

In stanza 3, the poem's images shift from the mobility and vocality of birds and the inside/outside considerations of poetry to leaves and number. B's nostalgic mood culminates in the image of the falling leaves whose twoness suggests togetherness, the cool air they fall through a shift from stanza 1's night air to a new dawning, a reunion as resurrection in a paradise of love. Separation is a shared dying that promises new life. Twoness is a sure token of future oneness. A's "third" (and again, it is Leino's too) complicates this by placing twoness in a context where *things* proliferate: first me, then you, next a summer leaf, and soon we have counted a universe of fragments, no two belonging together. Twoness is now a lack of oneness, a being-apart rather than a being-together, and isolation is aggravated by a sense that being apart is no temporary setback, no freak of nature that will be rectified in a future life, but the natural state of things. As the *night* of stanza 1 took us to stanza 2's *light,* no sun but the sinking of bird claws into hair; as the *head* of stanza 2 became the second in a series whose *third* in stanza 3 is a mere thing; so now *leaf* returns us by consonantal inversion to stanza 1's *fill,* suggesting that the only fullness is the ripeness of a summer leaf, which (short-lived, immobile, inarticulate) like King Lear must soon enough die, fall, and decompose.[14]

So the two translations part company, just like the poem's lovers. And like the lovers in the two translations, the translations hurl themselves bodily in opposite directions, B toward radical idealization, A toward radical deidealization. As long as we believe (with scientists and logicians and other people ill at ease with perspectival complexity) that one or the other of these directions must be right, the other therefore wrong, this will disturb us until we determine to our satisfaction what Leino's intention "really" was in the poem and proclaim either version A or version B "correct." (Or neither.) But that just perpetuates the parting that the poem enacts. To paraphrase Robert Frost, the metaphoric (or any tropic) interpreter *can* take both roads and be one traveler. That is the beauty of it. It takes a certain amount of tolerance for somatic complexity (our bodies feeling torn this way and that), but it is not impossible. In fact, it can be quite enjoyable, once one gets the hang of it.

Irony

The ideosomatics of perfectionism, remember, set up a dead-end dialectic between the possibility and the impossibility of translation: we cannot translate, but we must. It is possible to fail (in an infinite variety of ways), impossible to succeed (in the one true way). Augustine called it the overcoming of despair through fortitude, but the continuing need for fortitude speaks of continuing despair and even suggests that fortitude might itself, in its desperate attempts to overcome despair, generate despair.

The tropes that I have looked at so far seek to escape this vicious circle by playing with fortitude, playing with the possibility of translation: not surrendering to idealized aims (you must attain the unattainable) but relaxing them, taking them lightly, using them as tools toward a turning. Metonymy, synecdoche, and metaphor all seek equivalence between the SL and the TL, metonymy by substituting a part for a part, synecdoche by substituting a part for the whole, and metaphor by substituting another whole for the whole; but they seek equivalence, not in the hope or belief that they need to achieve it in order to succeed as translators, but in the hope that striving for it will help them to succeed as all translators and all writers must succeed, by gaining readers, being read, being appreciated.

The ironic translator (or at least one kind) wants to succeed this way too, but not by seeking equivalence—rather, by denying its possibility. If metonymic, synecdochic, and metaphoric translators play with fortitude, the ironic translator plays with despair. Mind you, *plays* with despair—I am not talking about real despair, here. Irony is just a different kind of tool toward a turning. An ironic translation can succeed just as well as any other tropic translation can. It is just a matter of turning translation ideals, or, in this case, anti-ideals, to one's own practical purposes.

There are a number of ironic translation stances. One says, "The SL text is too brilliant, I can't translate this, I'm not a good enough translator, maybe nobody is." A second says, "This isn't the original, this is just a translation, don't start thinking you're reading the real thing, here." A third says, "Look how bad the SL text was, I'm just rendering it faithfully, don't kill the messenger." (There may be others. These are the ones that occur to me.)

To illustrate the first of these, let me translate one of Rilke's *Sonnets to Orpheus* in the self-deprecatory ironic mode. Rilke is perfect for my purposes, because he so insistently sets himself in just this ironic relation to God, the giver of meaning who never gives enough, always withholds something, never gives us access to his full creative power. Just as Rilke says that God's text is too brilliant for him, and for all human poets, I as translator can treat Rilke as God (the traditional stance in postromantic culture worship) and pretend to despise myself for not being good enough to lick his boots, much less translate him. In the process, I can turn out a TL poem that has every chance of succeeding. (If it fails, or rather if you think it fails, it is not because Rilke is inaccessibly brilliant, as my ironic trope claims, but because you dislike my poem. Someone else might like it, and someone else might take my approach and produce a poem that you like a great deal. Success, anyway, is *possible*.) The poem is Rilke's third sonnet to Orpheus:

> Ein Gott vermags. Wie aber, sag mir, soll
> ein Mann ihm folgen durch die schmale Leier?
> Sein Sinn ist Zwiespalt. An der Kreuzung zweier
> Herzwege steht kein Tempel für Apoll.
>
> Gesang, wie du ihn lehrst, ist nicht Begehr,
> nicht Werbung um ein endlich noch Erreichtes;
> Gesang ist Dasein. Für den Gott ein Leichtes.
> Wann aber sind wir? Und wann wendet er
>
> an unser Sein die Erde und die Sterne?
> Dies ists nicht, Jüngling, dass du liebst, wenn auch
> die Stimme dann den Mund dir aufstösst,—lerne
>
> vergessen, dass du aufsangst. Das verrinnt.
> In Wahrheit singen, ist ein andrer Hauch.
> Ein Hauch um nichts. Ein Wehn im Gott. Ein Wind.
>
> Rilke can. But tell me, how do I (his trans-
> lator [read "liar"]) dare call myself his lyre?
> My sense is split. My split is sin. I'm tired
> of being pulled two ways ("this *isn't* that").
>
> Translation, as he taught me, isn't hope,
> desiring something I'll achieve some day.
> Translation's living. Easy for him to say.
> When do we live? When does he turn his poem

or the light of his poetic genius on us?
It's not enough to love, my child, if you
can have your mouth forced open by his voice.

Learn to forget you once broke into song.
That passes. True translation's beyond tune.
A tune for loons. A song not ding nor dong.

You get the idea. There is a risk here, of course: by playing so openly with Western translation ideals ("True translation's beyond tune"), the ironic translator sets him- or herself up to be attacked for failure. The reader may well say, Yes, you're right, you didn't do it, and it can't be done, so why did you try? Yes, translators are liars, and they should not pretend to be lyres (or, metonymically, to follow poets—or gods—through their narrow lyres). But this is a risk that the ironic translator finds worth taking. There are ways of signaling to the reader (to a certain kind of reader, one steeped in modernist aestheticism, say) that you are not serious about all this. My echo of Stevens (again), or even of Gerard Manley Hopkins, in the last line is an attempt to do just this. The idea is that you negate negation ("A song not ding nor dong") in an aesthetically pleasing (maybe faintly goofy) way and thus, in the convoluted aestheticist hope-against-hope, affirm. If, as Stevens says in *Adagia,* "Metaphor creates a new reality from which the original appears to be unreal," irony decreates the new reality that appears to render metaphor real—or, coming at that the other way, decreates the metaphoric reality from which the original appears to be unreal.[15] Either way, irony neither makes the original real nor the metaphor unreal—only suspends everything in an artificial solution. Art may not be possible, but it is not impossible either—it is *there*—and it is enjoyable. Art may not generate meaning, as the romantics believed, but at least it can provide pleasure. Translation may not save the world, perfect identity between SL and TL may not be possible, but the pretense that it is (or even that it is not) can be enjoyable too.

The second ironic approach to translation does not *deny the possibility* of translation but self-consciously *asserts the fact* of translation. This too is aestheticist, and it has its roots in the neo-Kantianism of people like Oscar Wilde and Ernst Cassirer, and close parallels with the "metafiction" of premoderns like Cervantes, Fielding, and Thackeray, moderns like James Joyce, and postmoderns like John Barth. In a novelistic tradition that idealizes novels as "slices of life" and strictly forbids breaking the illusion of reality (the author is supposed to be a mirror or window to reality and not come between the reader and "life"), these writers deidealize their novels by deliberately breaking the illusion, writing little asides to the reader, asking the reader how they should develop the plot or end the novel (John Fowles provides two different endings to *The French Lieutenant's Woman* and tells the reader to make up his or her own mind), introducing characters called The Author, and so on.

Mikhail Bakhtin says that this breaking of the realistic illusion is typical of the novel, going back to Cervantes and beyond; Leslie Fiedler, responding to realistic critics' claim that the novel is dying through self-parody, says that the novel has always been dying. Ever since Cervantes parodied the Cid Hamete Benengali and Fielding parodied Richardson, the novel has played with its own realistic pretensions, inverted them, undermined them through radical self-reference. Shakespeare, too, was self-reflexive in this way: contemporary critics speak of his "metadrama," his inward-turning remarks about the fictiveness of his own plays (Cleopatra knows that she is being played by a boy, Prospero knows that his play is being performed at the Globe, etc.). Modern poets have become metapoetic: William Carlos Williams's "Portrait of a Lady," for example. Since there are "realistic" ideals for scholarly writing, too—ideals of detached, dispassionate truth requiring a depersonalized voice that simply records it—my "openness" with you, my frankness about this or that uncertainty, this or that classification (even leaving some decisions up to you), my direct warnings and encouragements, might all be called "metascholarship" or "metatheory."

And why shouldn't translators do the same? Translators are expected to be heard and not seen. Only bad translators intrude between the reader and the "original." A translator who deliberately, self-consciously intruded, drew attention to him- or herself *as* translator and to the text as a translation, would not only be a bad translator; he or she would be irresponsible, childish, frivolous. But why not? This is an authoritarian, instrumentalist ideal that has to do specifically with illusions, not realities. If the translator did not "intrude" between the TL reader and the SL text, the TL reader could not read it. It would remain in the SL. The instrumentalist taboo on "intrusion" is really a taboo on breaking the receptor's illusion that he or she is reading the original, which tends to be an illusion harbored by the kind of naive reader that Luther wanted all his receptors to be: ideally open to the impression that the German Bible could make on them, uncritical, unresistant, perfectly malleable. The translator's idealized "responsibility" is supposedly to the receptor, who supposedly needs to know what the original is "really" saying, without intrusive "interpretations" by the translator. Deidealize that and you have the translator's enforced submission to the institution that controls the interpretive images of texts to be disseminated to all "naive" readers (and that seeks to keep all readers naive).

The ironic translator who makes it clear to his or her readers that this is just a translation is only "irresponsible" from the viewpoint of the authoritarian institution against which he or she is rebelling. As Stevens says in *Adagia,* "The final belief is to believe in a fiction, which you know to be a fiction, there being nothing else. The exquisite truth is to know that it is a fiction and that you believe in it willingly." [16] It is an aestheticist rebellion, but it seeks to use aestheticism as a critical tool: as Frank Kermode says, fictions only become harmful when they harden into myths, so the aestheticist's task must be to prevent fictions from hardening into myths, by constantly reminding their users of their fictionality. This is ultimately an ethical concern, and I return to it in Chapter 4: the translator wants to invert (subvert, pervert) ideosomatically controlled reader expectations in order to edify the reader, free the reader from enforced naivete. Or the translator wants to divert the reader, provide the critical reader with pleasure in the fictionality of words.

That is why it is done; the next question is how. We might see the translator's note as the most covert form of self-reflexive irony; translator's notes have the function of reminding the reader that this is a translation (and therefore are proscribed by Eugene Nida, for one). But this only works in the Lutheran tradition; in the Augustinian tradition of "critical" translation reading, both translators and their receptors are expected to be scholars, critical thinkers, and a translator's note doesn't affect that kind of reader one way or the other. The ironic translator grows bolder as he or she moves the note from the bottom of the page into the text, first inside brackets, which typographically signal a "nonauthorized" interpolation, then inside parentheses, which could be mistaken for the author's interpolation, then (boldest of all) interrupts the author's voice to remind the reader that it is *not* the author's voice, but the translator's.

These possibilities begin to occur to the ironic translator when the logical absurdities of simultaneously writing in your TL voice and (supposedly) the author's SL voice, or of having the SL author write in the TL, begin to accumulate. In Joseph F. Graham's translation of Jacques Derrida's "Des Tours de Babel," for example, he has Derrida quoting Louis Segond thus: "The first translator, then, Louis Segond, author of the Segond Bible, published in 1910, writes this: 'Those are the sons of Sem, etc.'" (168), as if Louis Segond had actually written his French translation in English. The metonymic translator (which Graham is) ignores these problems: they cannot be solved anyway, so why worry? The ironic translator, especially when translating an ironic writer like Derrida, does worry, or rather pretends to worry in order to complicate the TL text a little, to ruffle its smooth surface, to remind the TL reader (as Derrida is constantly reminding the SL reader) that this is all a fiction.

There are any number of ways the ironic translator might approach the problem that Graham dodges. One might be to start quoting in French, then to interrupt the quote in the voice of the TL reader demanding a translation, and then to protest in the voice of the translator that this is what Segond actually *wrote,* and you wouldn't want me to tell a lie, would you? Another would be to quibble over what Segond actually wrote, and whether he was truly the "author" of the Segond Bible. Didn't God write the Bible (Derrida's concern throughout the piece)? Aren't all writers belated translators of an inaccessible divine script? This means adding to Derrida's text, but so what? It's in the spirit of his text. And even if it isn't, that wouldn't stop the ironic translator, whose concern is not with equivalence anyway, but with the inevitable gaps or abysms between the SL and the TL. A third approach would settle for a simple interpolation on the order of: "The first translator, then, Louis Segond, author of the Segond Bible, published in 1910, didn't write this, he wrote in French, but this is how I've translated what he wrote into English: 'Those are the sons of Sem, etc.'"

The dialogue that the ironic translator sets up (or finds him- or herself in) with the SL writer in these first two types of irony is playful, friendly, even conspiratorial. The mood is, "You and I don't buy this idealized nonsense about you being some kind of inaccessible god or creative genius and me being your humble window, do we, we know better than to believe in all *that*." In the third type, where the translator reveals the weakness in the SL text by striving for a faithful rendering, the dialogue is exactly the opposite: the translator approaches the SL writer with a sense of his or her own infinite superiority over the writer and a disgust or contempt for the writer's failings. The mood is, "I don't want to be seen with you, you slime."

But wait: can irony really be these opposite things? What is the point of including opposites in a single category? Remember that Burke defined irony in terms of dialectic—and that in my first two types of irony the translator succeeded by claiming to fail. That is dialectic. In this third type, the translator deliberately fails (to produce a translation that works) and claims that he or she *must* fail in order to succeed (at metaphorical equivalence). These are not, remember, logical categories. They do not have to be internally consistent, clear, precise, stable, or any of the other things logical categories are supposed to be. They are heuristics—useful, perhaps, but also entirely disposable.

Let me illustrate this kind of irony with a nonliterary example, one I mentioned in passing at the end of Chapter 2. In technical and scholarly translation, the SL writer usually does not think of him- or herself as a writer at all; he or she is a technician or a scholar who has been asked, or is expected for purposes of promotion, to write up his or her work. Such texts are often produced under the pressure of a deadline and often come to the translator in rough draft, with interlineal emendations and the possibility of further textual changes after the translation is completed. They are often riddled with inconsistencies, infelicities, and sheer incomprehensibilities. What is the translator to do with a text like this? Commonsense-for-sense theorists like Peter Newmark say you must improve the text, not translating what the author *says* but what he or she *means*—but, as we will see in the next section (on hyperbole), that assumes the writer *knows* what he or she means, and with problem texts this is often too much to assume.

The ironic translator, or the translator in an ironic mood, sick of rewriting SL texts from scratch, building good arguments out of garbage, doing for the writer what the writer should have done for him- or herself, and then getting no credit for it, not even getting mentioned in the publication, or getting mentioned in a preface along with the writer's spouse and children, and then, on top of all that, having to feel guilty because the translation did not conform to idealized standards of "equivalence"—the translator who is fed up with all of this may just decide to do a "metaphoric" rendering of the text in all its ghastliness. He or she will disambiguate no ambiguous phrasings, silently correct no noun-verb incongruencies, register shifts, or factual errors, prune no repetitiveness or prolixity, mend no style-context conflicts, rearrange no flaccid sequencing. He or she will be faithful to the letter and the spirit of the text—not out of a fanatic adherence to a principle, of course, but out of an extremely gratifying form of malice, indeed a highly creative and artistically demanding form of malice, in which vengeance is exacted against bad writers through an artful search for just the right degree and shade of TL verbal shoddiness. Here faithfulness, the metonymic and metaphoric translator's lofty aim, becomes an insult to the writer; self-effacement becomes a kind of aggression by omission, a passive violence marked by an active *refusal* to do violence to the text. In this way the translator externalizes his or her own TL words, disowns his or her translation, assigns or ascribes it solely to the writer, indeed may even forbid the writer to mention his or her name in connection with the work. In effect, this sort of ironic translator negates his or her own work, negates his or her role in the creation of an inferior text.

There is a deep animus against this sort of translatorial behavior in mainstream translation theory (and practice); but the animus is really directed only against the translator's presumption, the idea that the translator could (or would) ever dare inflict a symbolic wound of this sort on the SL writer. There is a good deal of debate among prescriptive theorists over whether the translator should ever be allowed to improve an SL text, but it is a civilized debate; neither side has ever been branded as irresponsible. What keeps the debate civilized is the shared assumption that, whether the translator improves on a bad text or seeks the closest natural SL equivalent of a bad text, he or she will always remain the docile servant of the SL writer. What will anger or alarm mainstream translation theorists in this third type of ironic translation is precisely my suggestion that the translator might put aside his or her docility and try to "get back at" the SL writer. This, in a tradition that prescribes translatorial introversion (see Chapter 4), is unforgivable.

But all that this last type of ironic translator is really doing is taking to its logical extreme the absurd ideal of instrumentality, in order to demonstrate the absurdity of its blanket application. As long as you agree with the SL writer and feel perfectly comfortable about going along with the illusion of instrumentality, there is no problem. You know that you are not a mere instrument; it takes an immense amount of creative activity even to give the illusion of instrumentality, but never mind: you are willing to do it, you have no qualms, and everybody is happy. But Western translation theory has tried to legislate that willingness, tried to generalize from individual translators' willingness to go along with the illusion of instrumentality in certain cases to a forced submission to that willingness (be willing, or else!) in *all* cases. Anybody who refuses will be denied the name of translator.

The problem, in other words, is not in the illusion; we all have illusions, and as long as they seem to work for us, we do not demand immediate contact with reality. The problem is in the authoritarian generalization of the illusion to all translation, its application to all translators in all circumstances dealing with all texts. It is this idealized universality that the ironic translator seeks to explode—or at least expose.

And whether the irony is playful, cheerful, aestheticist, or angry, malicious, vengeful—whether the ironic translator strives for "accidental," backhanded success or deliberate, instructive failure—the end result in terms of translation ideals is the same: they crumble.

Hyperbole

I mentioned a minute ago that the commonsense-for-sense translation theorist defends improving a bad SL text on the grounds that the translator must translate what the writer *meant,* not what he or she *said.* If the writer's unclear writing reflects unclear thinking (and it always does), and the writer does not therefore even *know* what he or she meant, the translator's task is then to consult the writer, show him or her each problem spot, and present him or her with the alternatives. If one reads this construction to mean *A,* you are claiming *X;* if one reads it to mean *B,* it implies *Y.* That way, you are still acting as the SL writer's humble instrument: helping him or her to bring forth what he or she "means," just as the knife helps the cutter to slice the bread.

But I have done this, and my experience points to different conclusions. You get an unbelievably bad text from a professor of economic history, say, and call him up to discuss the problem areas. At each point you ask him what he means by a certain word or phrase, and he says, "Isn't that clear?"

"No," you say, "it's ambiguous."

"No it's not," he says. "It's perfectly clear."

"Well," you explain, patiently, "it's unclear just what this 'which' is referring to. If it refers to 'statistics,' you're making a methodological claim, but if it refers to 'infant mortality,' you're making a historical claim. Which do you want here?"

"I'm not sure I follow you."

So you explain it, and explain it, until finally, realizing that this poor sod hasn't a clue about what he is trying to say, you make a guess, which you have made already, and really just want to check with him:

"It seems to me that the thrust of your argument is methodological rather than historical—that the historical events are mainly brought in as illustrations of your methodological argument. And in that sense 'which' would probably make the best sense if it referred to 'statistics.'"

"Hm, well," the professor mumbles, not really knowing what you have just said or what possible bearing it has on his article, "maybe you're right."

So you go on through the article, over and over again referring your questions back to that "decision" you and he reached over the methodological thrust of his argument (that's settled, see, he agreed to it, which makes it the one clear thing in his mind about the whole article, and thus a handy reference point). By the end of your phone conversation, you have essentially imposed your reading on his understanding of his own article and have received his permission to cohere your TL rendering around that reading. You have taught him both to write and to think, clarified his understanding of his own field of expertise, his own article, and in an important sense catalyzed the *formulation* of "what he meant to say." This exceeds the metonymic translator's authority, but it is clearly what much technical and scholarly translation entails. In fact, I have stopped going through this charade with scholars and technicians: I just interpret the SL text, assign it an argumentative coherence that seems to work (I have a good feel for these things), and translate my version, not the writer's.

I call this hyperbole (Louis Kelly calls it "symptom," chap. 3.2): the translator's "exaggeration" or improvement of the SL text in the TL, in order to give it its "proper" fullness, a fullness that in (tropic) practice is not actually the writer's but the translator's. "For, after all," John Dryden wrote in his introduction to *Sylvae*, "a translator is to make his author as charming as he possibly can, provided he maintains his character and makes him not unlike himself" (cited in Kelly, 47). But unlike which self—the translator's or the writer's? The ambiguity of Dryden's pronouncement is indicative of the problem at the heart of hyperbolic translation: is he calling on the translator to make the writer not unlike himself the writer, or not unlike himself the translator? This is the crux: whose text *is* the TL? Whose personality does it body forth? It is supposedly the writer's, but when the translator finds the SL text lacking, the contradictions embedded in that supposition begin to surface. As Dryden implies, the translator gives the TL text its "proper" fullness (or charm, as Dryden says) out of a sense of duty to the writer; but all that means is that the translator protects the writer by patronizing him or her, protects the writer from him- or herself, like a parent protecting an immature child. And then, like the proud parent who is too grown-up to demand recognition for doing his or her job, the translator steps back to let the writer take credit for the improved text: the writer's name appears over the translator's words; the translator's name appears, if at all, in the preface or in a note, along with all the other support staff that contributed to the writer's triumph. By the logic of entitlement, the persona of the TL style is summed up in the writer's name, even though it is very largely the translator's invention.

The hyperbolic translator improves a bad text, then, not by submitting to the writer's concealed and then elicited intention, but by bringing his or her own personal vision to an understated text and *creating* the writer's intention. If scholarly and technical translators could recognize that they do this and get others to recognize it too, one important practical consequence might be an improved public (and self-) image. The hyperbolic translator stands to the instrumentalized translator-ideal as the ghost writer stands to the stenographer: as a creator and shaper of ideas and personality through words, as opposed to a mere recorder and transmitter of words. Ghost writers are not only well paid for their work, nowadays they even get their names on the covers of the "autobiographies" they write. As I write this, two books on the *New York Times* nonfiction bestseller list are *Trump: The Art of the Deal*, by Donald Trump with Tony Schwartz, and *Man of the House: The Life and Political Memoirs of Speaker Tip O'Neill*, by Tip O'Neill with William Novak. Book writing is too chancy a business for publishers to leave it to amateurs, so whenever they sign a contract with some famous person for his or her memoirs, they make sure a professional writer does the actual writing—and, in recognition of the importance of this work, they feature the ghost writer's name prominently on dust jackets and all other publicity. Some ghost writers even get a percentage of the royalties—as is only fair, since they do the writing.[17]

I would suggest that FIT, ATA, and the other professional translator organizations bear this parallel with ghost writers in mind when they negotiate for better recognition and remuneration for translators. If translators do a job analogous to ghost writing, they should also receive analogous pay and recognition. Ghost writers are no longer ghosts. They have been brought out into the open, into living flesh and blood, which they always were anyway—it was only a pernicious ideal that kept them ghostly, the illusion that Richard Nixon and Malcolm X were writers like Augustine and Rousseau, that like those great autobiographers they actually set pen to paper and wrote *Six Crises* and *The Autobiography of Malcolm X*. The phenomenal success of *Roots* brought Alex Haley into the limelight, but who wrote *Six Crises*? He is still a ghost. Nowadays we know that Donald Trump and Tip O'Neill and the others do not write their own autobiographies, and we know who does the actual writing. Translators, meanwhile, remain ghosts, their names all too often tucked away in hard-to-find places or not mentioned at all, their pay for writing the TL text roughly equivalent to a copy editor's fee.

Nor is this a sheer oversight on publishers' part. Translators' low status, starvation pay, and poor recognition are conditioned by centuries of idealized equivalence theories that imagine translation in terms of failure. "Too often," George Steiner writes, "the translator feeds on the original for his own increase" (402)—a typical derogation of translators from one of their most eloquent defenders. Why "too often"? What is wrong with feeding on the original for your own increase? I certainly have developed my scholarly style through my translations, and I cannot imagine how anyone could have suffered from it. If anything, my clients have benefited from my increase, since it has meant that their texts have gotten at least the attention they deserve—often more. Hyperbolic translation is one of the most fruitful apprenticeships around for the aspiring poet, one that all the ancients recommended highly under the name of *imitatio*. Harold Bloom, in fact, would claim that "translation" in a broad sense, as misprision from tongue to tongue or from poem to poem within a single tongue, is the strong poet's *inevitable* apprenticeship.

Having lived so long in Finland, I pay particular attention to the hyperbolic crossovers between my native and my adopted countries: the way that the contemporary Finnish novelist Veijo Meri "discovered" the archetypal Finnish male in Hemingway, discovered in essence that Hemingway was the greatest Finnish writer of our century, and donated Hemingway to Finnish literature not by translating him but by making his own novels in the fifties and sixties out of his dialogical engagement with Hemingway's work. Going farther back, Longfellow read the Finnish national epic, the *Kalevala,* in German translation in the early 1850s and, inspired by the shot in the arm that Elias Lönnrot's collection/composition gave Finnish literature, decided to do the same for American literature. The result was *The Song of Hiawatha* in Kalevala meter (trochaic tetrameter), borrowing much of the oral-epic manner of the Germanized Finnish text. It did not quite work, of course: the poem was immensely popular (still is, in some circles), but it did not transform American literature the way that the *Kalevala* did Finnish literature when it appeared in the 1830s and 40s. Longfellow failed to do what he set out to do, partly because *Hiawatha* was not authentic native American oral poetry, as the *Kalevala* was authentic native Finnish oral poetry; partly because nineteenth-century Americans did not identify their "lost origins" with the Indians; and partly because Longfellow did not have the poetic talent of a Whitman, say, who published the truly transformative American epic in the same year as *Hiawatha,* *Leaves of Grass.* Longfellow made the obvious mistake: he thought that Americans needed an illustrious past, a genesis, when what they really needed (as Whitman knew) was an illustrious future, democratic vistas, as Whitman put it, or prospects, as Emerson put it. Neither a new *Beowulf* nor a *Song of Hiawatha* would do: white male Americans had cut themselves off from the European tradition that looked back to *Beowulf,* and they had never assimilated themselves (as the Spaniards had in South America, by interbreeding) to the Native American tradition that might have looked back to a *Song of Hiawatha.* Only the future remained—that, and an expansive present, a geographical breadth whose expansion to date pointed forward to an engulfment of the entire world, of the entire kosmos (to give it Whitman's spelling), ever bigger and bigger hunks until America contained *everything.*

Still, Longfellow had the right idea—just the wrong country. Hyperbolic translation (and the hyperbolizing of "translation" as an ever more inclusive kind of transfer that would embrace *Hiawatha* as well as any more obvious transfer) was perfectly suited to the kind of literary self-engenderment that American writers were attempting in that astonishing decade that has come to be called the American Renaissance. And just as the European Renaissance was born out of the translation of classical texts that had been "discovered" in the Moorish libraries conquered in the south of Spain in the thirteenth century, so too was the American Renaissance born out of hyperbolic translations of foreign literatures near and far. John Irwin has shown the importance of the Egyptian hieroglyphics for the American Renaissance—as Steiner argues, an alien tradition is easier to appropriate than a familiar one, since the cultural clutter of a familiar tradition can shackle the appropriator. Still, Emerson's strong readings of Coleridge and the German Idealists and Poe's strong readings of Shelley and the German romantics were crucial for the American Renaissance. And if Baudelaire's and Mallarmé's strong readings of Poe generated French Symbolism, Eliot's and Stevens's strong readings of the French Symbolists helped shape American modernism.[18] That period was most decisively shaped, perhaps, by Ezra Pound, probably the greatest hyperbolic translator of our time: by creating "modernism" out of Sappho in Greek, Sextus Propertius in Latin, Arnaut Daniel in Provençal, Guido Cavalcanti in Italian, Li Po in Chinese, and on and on—by finding in each writer that spark, that Poundian touch, that Paterian glow of isolated moments, and fanning it into a TL flame—Pound shaped his period into what Hugh Kenner calls the "Pound Era."

You may have noticed how close this trope is to synecdoche, which also rescues from the SL text only that part or quality (that "spark") that fits the translator's needs (or conception of the TL receptor's needs) and sloughs off the rest. Both the synecdochic and the hyperbolic translator condescend to the SL writer, assuming that he or she did not quite know what he or she wanted to say or how to say it, and taking upon themselves the task of preserving what is most representative or lasting in the SL text. We could probably quibble over specific translations, in fact—over whether they were synecdochic or hyperbolic—till the cows came home. But let me remind you once again that the purpose of this chapter is not to set up a stable taxonomy by which the (stable, objective) products of translation can be accurately described; it is to explore the translator's tools, which can be used and abused every which way. (The translator who confuses two of my tropes is like the home-handyman who punches holes with a Phillips screwdriver or adjusts storm windows with a claw hammer or drives nails with a pipewrench: just doing his or her job with the tools at hand. Idealists deplore this sort of sloppiness, but then idealists deplore just about everything—everything that falls short of their ideal, which is to say, everything real.) As Kenneth Burke says, all of the master tropes flow into one another; all troping is perspectivizing. All troping is reducing, representing, dialecticizing. These are just words we use to describe a complex field—not "real" categories into which actual acts of translation must be fit.

But apart from all that, is there any good reason for distinguishing the condescending improvement that the hyperbolic translator makes in the SL from the condescending improvement that the synecdochic translator makes in the SL? The main difference historically is that the hyperbolic translator has typically been a romantic, a believer in creative genius and its transformative effect on all texts, on everything it touches, while the synecdochic translator has typically been a pragmatist, a believer in getting the job done in as effective a way as possible. A good indication of this difference is that when hyperbolic translators delude themselves (or are deluded by their ideosomatic programming) into believing that they are striving for equivalence, they tend to think of equivalence in metaphoric terms (perfect equivalence, the great romantic ideal), while when synecdochic translators delude themselves (or are deluded by *their* ideosomatic programming) into believing that they are striving for equivalence, they tend to think of equivalence in metonymic terms (working equivalence, the great pragmatic ideal).

Still, lest I defend my division too strenuously and make it seem like I am attached to it, believe in it, let me close this section with an open invitation (once again) to do with these tropes what you will, conflate them, splinter them, whatever. I do not always think they work myself.

The only reason I offer them to you is that they seem to work better than anything else I have seen; but they are not perfect, and never will be, and never need to be. They are tools. Use them as you like, or throw them in a drawer and let them collect greasy dust.

Metalepsis

This is Harold Bloom's supertrope for post-romantic poetry, and he gets a lot of mileage out of it in *A Map of Misreading*. I got a lot of mileage out of it, for that matter, in chapter 3 of *American Apocalypses*— and I am still not sure exactly what it is, or rather how it can most usefully be understood. Nor are many other people: it is a confusing trope. Bloom does not really help to clear up the confusion, but he was not the cause of it; it has always been a confusing trope, a hard trope to define with any usefulness, and Bloom just complicates the reigning confusion. The most enlightening definition of it that I have seen is offered by Angus Fletcher in an article on Kenneth Burke, drawing on both classical and Bloomian definitions to characterize Burke's peculiar approach to problems:

To use an athletic metaphor, the transumptive or metaleptic method is set up like a relay race, where each symbolic equation . . . ceases to be a static equation in the mind and becomes the symbolic act by which each symbolic event, each transport of a term, leads to a "handing on." The baton passes; each developed term, each sentence, each figuration of an idea, each paragraph, each section, and finally each summation-scheme becomes only the lap in a relay race. An Elizabethan critic, with the beautiful name of Angel Day, defined metalepsis or transumption thus: "when by a certaine number of degrees we goe beyond that which we intend in troth, and have meaning to speake of, as to say: Accursed soyle that bred my cause of woe." Or, as Blair refined the notion in his eighteenth-century text on rhetoric: "When the Trope is founded on the relation between an antecedent and a consequent, on what goes before, and immediately follows." Quintilian had stated: "It is the nature of *metalepsis* to form a kind of intermediate step between the term transferred and the thing to which it is transferred, having no meaning in itself, but merely providing a transition." Bloom glosses "no meaning in itself" as equivalent to "no presence or time in itself." The definition of the term remains obscure, and examples are rarely given which would help define it. The OED glosses, from Smith, *Mystical Rhetoric* (1657), a possibly useful instance: "Metalepsis, which is when divers Tropes are shut up in one word: as 2 Kings 2.9: I pray thee let me have a double portion of thy spirit," where "portion" encapsulates a variety of apportioning senses through the metaphor of a measured drink. Every sentence in Burke possesses this metaleptic value: it is a crossing (as Bloom would call it) or a bridging (Burke's and Heidegger's term), which draws conscious attention to the *leading* character of the leading question. Each question thus becomes a leading answer to a precedent question and another consequent answer, which in turn becomes a question for what is to follow. Sentences in Burke, paragraphs certainly, are laps in this endlessly overlapping race toward an infinitely receding finish line. (170–71)

The key is time, and specifically a medial location in time, a being (or finding yourself) situated in the middle of time, after the beginning, before the end—or rather, more specifically, after what just came before and before what is about to come after. It is a being torn in two directions, toward the past that defined but deserted you and the future that eludes you as you reach toward it. It is, in Burke's terms, a bridging that never reaches the opposite bank—or, as Fletcher says, a running "toward an infinitely receding finish line."

Translation too, of course, has traditionally been imaged as a bridging. The translator builds a bridge from SL to TL. Unfortunately, in the perfectionist tradition of Western translation theory, nobody ever finishes a bridge. Part of the way across, the translator runs out of funds and leaves the bridge uncompleted. This feeling of being caught in the middle, halfway across with no way of going back and no certainty of being able to going forward either, is (ideosomatically) basic to the translator's sense of his or her task: looking back with nostalgia at the "past," the shore that was left behind, the security of the SL text, which seems completed and whole and perfect but which refuses to shelter the translator on its bank (in fact, the translator begins to feel that the SL bank is withholding the requisite funds—a metaleptic troping on the word "bank"), looking ahead with determination and trepidation at the "future," the shore that lies ahead but seems to recede at the translator's approach, the uncertainty of the TL text that only exists in process, in the doing, in the translating, and even when officially finished will never feel as completed and whole and perfect as the SL text was. Always having left where you were; never having gotten where you are going. Always feeling called back to the place that you left, feeling obliged to your SL host, indebted for the bed and the breakfast and the sandwiches in your bag, feeling that you will never be able to repay what you have been given because you are never going back, you cannot go back into the past, and once you have left it it is gone forever. You cannot be Homer. You cannot be Matthew, Mark, Luke, or John. You cannot be Dante or Racine or Goethe. They have been left behind. You can call up, for a moment, an image of what it must have been like to be them, but only for a moment—and you realize that even that moment is sheer nostalgia, a wishful projection into the past. If you try to express that image, put it into action, put it into practice, put it into words, it vanishes immediately.

The past is not mocked. Always feeling called back—but always feeling called forward, too, lured onward into the future, looking forward with excitement tinged with dread to your meeting with your TL hosts, excitement because of the promise of new possibilities, dread because of the possibility that you will not be up to the meeting, there will be expectations that you cannot meet, they will not like you, you will say something wrong and they will give you the cold shoulder, and you will never even know what you did. And you will never get there. When you get there, you will not be sure that you *are* there, or whether "here" is "there." You will never know whether the people you meet are your hosts, whether they have mistaken you for somebody else, whether you might not be the right person but there the wrong day or for the wrong reason. You may be a TL reader, but you can never be a TL reader of your own text. You can never occupy your own future. You will always remain the *writer* of the TL text, en route to your readership. If you know your TL readers or speak directly to your TL listeners, you have no way of knowing how they are really responding, whether they like or dislike you, approve or disapprove, or like you but disapprove, or approve but dislike you, whether they are even paying attention, whether they have their minds on the rent or the traffic noise or their digestive tracts. If you do not know them, if you never see them, you have no way of knowing whether there even is a response, whether anybody reads you.

In the perfectionist tradition of Western translation theory, all this has been a limitation on perfection, a disagreeable deal that the idealist has had to make with reality. It is the oldest story in the history of translation theory. You can watch just about anybody at it: open the pages at random and you will find some translator lamenting his or her medial position after the SL and before the TL, some translation theorist carefully constructing the argument that will allow for an escape, a retreat back into the SL or safe passage to the TL, but never pulling it off. I would name names (Arnold, for instance), but there is really no point: everybody does it.

Imagining this medial position not as a limitation on perfection, a compromise with translation ideals, but as a *trope,* a guide to a successful turning, may offer a way out. I hope that it will—but of course, from my own position in the middle I have no way of knowing whether it will or not. There is a good chance that when you have finished this chapter you will say that Robinson did not pull it off either. He proved no exception to his own rueful rule.

What would the trope of metalepsis as a translation tool be, then? I will approach it negatively, by asking what it would *not* be. It would not be a bridge: solid, sturdy, built according to all the proper technical specifications, permanently there to carry people safely and unproblematically from the SL to the TL. It wouldn't "exist" like a bridge. It would also not be an ideal image of this sort of solidly existing bridge. Nothing solid or sturdy. Nothing permanent. Rather, a *bridging*—or even a feeling-as-if-one-were-bridging, a feeling-about-being-caught-in-the-middle-in-terms-of-a-bridging. You could use other synecdoches for it too. The great Finnish poet and translator Pentti Saarikoski, who died in 1983, wrote about his own translations of Catullus: "Jos ei saa siltaa rakennetuksi eikä venettä lainaksi, on mentävä uimalla yli"—"If you can't build a bridge or borrow a boat, you have to swim across." But, as I pointed out in a paper I gave on Saarikoski several years ago, "saarikoski" in Finnish means "island rapids," and the swimmer across rapids (Saarikoski, say) may find himself in serious trouble, may never make it, may drown en route, and even if he does make it to the other side, the current will have "turned" him away from his original destination, so that instead of landing on the opposite bank he finds himself on an island. So fared Columbus, for instance, who thought he was sailing to India and discovered America. The point is, if you open yourself up to the trope of metalepsis, you never know what will happen, where you will end up and what will come of it. No solid bridges. No predictability. No perfection. If you lack a solid, sturdy, permanent bridge (the mainstream translation ideal in the West), if all you have is a bridging that cannot guarantee a safe crossing, you have to learn to deal with uncertainty.

To translate metaleptically is to engage the paradoxes of time that are built into the act of translation. Homer should not sound like a contemporary poet; that would be absurd. He was an ancient Greek. But if he was an ancient Greek, he could not speak English, either, which makes the whole idea of reading "Homer" in English—of translating him in the first place—absurd. No matter how you translate him, you will mire yourself in some kind of chronological absurdity. So why not recognize the absurdity, affirm it, play with it, instead of skulking about in the shadows with one or another idealizing "solution" to the problem?

The idealizing translator who sees his or her position in the middle between SL and TL as a limitation on perfection will probably want to sweep the whole problem of time under the mat, by creating a fantasy time and place for the TL, a "time out of time" that is neither (say) ancient Greece nor contemporary America. Nothing wrong with that, of course; plenty of excellent translations have been made that way. But the metaleptic translator will confront the problem head-on: will, for instance, modernize radically, changing everybody's names, changing the plot so as to make it credible in contemporary TL society—will do everything possible to cut off the pull of the SL—or will archaize, TL-archaize, will still change the names and the plot and whatever else has to be changed to make the archaic rendition work, but in an archaic TL form. Either way, the metaleptic translator is attempting to make the TL text "work" for the TL reader; but where the modernizing transla-tor wants it to work for the reader of romances or spy novels or the TV-viewer, the archaizing translator wants it to work for the reader of *Beowulf* (in English), the *Nibelungenlied* (in German), the Eddas (in the Scandinavian languages).

Following Bloom, we might call these two metaleptic approaches "projective" (archaizing) and "introjective" (modernizing). But rather than theorizing those terms for the study of translation, let me simply illustrate what I mean with an example, a passage from the third rune of the *Kalevala,* which I give first in Finnish (in the form in which Lönnrot collected it, not the final edited form) and the metonymic En-glish of Keith Bosley:

> Yks on nuori Joukavainen
> toinen vanha Väinämöinen
> ajoi tiellä vastaksuten:
> rahis puuttu rahkesehen
> vemmel vempelen nenäh.
> Siitä siinä seisottih.
> Vesa kasvo vempelestä
> haavat aisoista yleni
> pajupehko rahkehista.

> Sanoi nuori Joukavainen:
> "Ken on tiiolta pahempi
> sen on tieltä siirtyminen."

> Sano vanha Väinämöinen:
> "Sanos tarkkoja tosia
> valehia muinosia."

Sano nuori Joukahainen:
"Tiiän kuitengin vähäsen
ennemmäiset ymmärtelen:
tiiän linnukse tiasen
kiiskisen veen kalaksi
pajun puita vanhimmaksi,
tiiän kolkot kuokituksi
vuoret luovuksi kokohon
kalahauat kaivetuksi
siverret syvennetyksi."

Sanoi siitä Väinämönen:
"Lapsen on mieli, vaimon tunti,
ei oo partasuun urohon.
Omat on kolkot kuokkimani,
vuoret luomani kokoh,
kalahauat kaivamani.
Olin miekin miessä siellä
urohona kolmantena
seitsemäntenä urossa
kaarta taivon kantaissa
pieltä ilmon pistäissä
taivoista tähittäissä
Otavaa ojentamassa."

First was young Joukavainen
then was old Väinämöinen
driving together head on:
traces were jammed with traces
collar-bow with collar-bow.
          There and then they stopped.
The collar-bow sprang a shoot
and the shafts sprouted aspens
the traces a willow-clump.

The young Joukavainen said:
"He whose knowledge is the worse
must move aside from the road."

The old Väinämöinen said:
"Say some things exactly true
tell some lies of long ago."

The young Joukahainen said:
"And yet I know a little
          I understand more:
I know the tit is a bird

the ruff is a water-fish
the willow is the oldest tree
I know the hollows were scooped
the mountains heaped together
I know the fish-holes were dug
the troughs of the sea deepened."

At that Väinämöinen said:
"A child's mind, a woman's lore
is not a bearded hero's.
The hollows were my scooping
the mountains were my heaping
the fish-holes were my digging:
I was man among men there
        the third hero there
the seventh among heroes
bearing the arch of heaven
pushing up the sky's pillar
spangling the heavens with stars
straightening the Great Bear."

Väinämöinen is not only the hero of the epic cycle; in some sense he might be called the SL author, the singer who sings not only the world but the poem into being. Joukahainen, the youth, the beardless lad, thus makes a good translator, claiming only to *know* what the SL author *did*, forever denied access to the author's temporal priority. Väinämöinen will always have come first. And in this passage Väinämöinen is given (or gives himself) victory over Joukahainen, not only in the narrative (just after this, Väinämöinen sings him into a swamp and will not release him until he gives the old man his sister Aino to wife), but in the poetry as well: the very sound of Joukahainen's belated knowledge in Finnish is childish ("tiiän linnukse tiasen / kiiskisen veen kalaksi"), while Väinämöinen's claims resonate heroically ("kaarta taivon kantaissa / pieltä ilmon pistäissä").

Now, suppose we decide to go along with Väinämöinen in this— suppose we grant him his priority, his originality, his authority over the SL text. Then perhaps we should allow the Finnish to dominate the translation too, as Väinämöinen dominates Joukahainen. Or rather, since that (as we have seen) is impossible, maybe we should allow the principle of earliness (the past) to dominate our translation, by archaizing it. Maybe, in other words, we should cast off our modernity into the once-modern "original" locus of authority and self-consciously pretend to an analogous position of priority or originality. Maybe we should try to *precede* English literary history in the same way that Väinämöinen precedes Finnish literary history—to imagine what poetry in English might be like if something like the *Kalevala* truly had preceded it.

This would mean doing the Longfellow thing, perhaps with Indian myth, Indian names and settings, or else, as I prefer, with the English past, the past of the English language that is, after all, the TL, thus:

> Yowthfull Cyngnus was the fyrste
> auncyent Gulpus was the owther
> drof they toyens on the trayle:
> tweysted tresses into tresses
> swyngilstre with swyngilstre.
> Therbesyde entangeled stodde.
> Spronge an offshoote from the swyngil
> sprowghted aspens from the schaftes
> tred a wyllow from the tresses.
>
> Spak the yowthfulle Cyngnus:
> "Whych of us in witte be werse
> he par force muste turne assyde."
>
> Spak the ayncyent Gulpus:
> "Synge in songe of trewthes tyghte
> schape in saynge auncyent thyngs."
>
> Spak the yowthfulle Cyngnus:
> "Wot I yet a lytel bit
> kenne I yet a lytel more:
> kenne I for a brydde the tytte
> for a fische I kenne the breke
> wot the wylle for the ylste tre
> wot the holks wyth houghs were hollowed
> hills on highe bye houghsfull heped
> fischgraves in the felds were groued
> fynntroughs in the fenns were dregged."
>
> Spak the ayncyent Gulpus:
> "Childers kenning, wiven witting,
> schame for hersute heroes schaping.
> Bye my hough the holks were hollowed
> I bye houghsfull heped the hills
> graves for fisches were my grouing.
> I was there in manly maught
> thrydde amid the hovring heroes
> senfte of the heroes hoast

heving up the arche of heven
pusshing up the aerye posts
strecching up to star the skyne
wynnowing the Cherles Waine."

The first thing that this archaic rendition gives us is two legendary English heroes named Cyngnus and Gulpus: no exotic Finnish heroes uneasily transplanted into English prose but originary mythic predecessors for the history of English poetry.[19] The reliance on Anglo-Saxon roots permits a freewheeling use of alliteration that resembles that of the Finnish (and that is still possible and very viable in contemporary Finnish poetry). It also allows me to revive the useful kenning/witting distinction, which modern Finnish (like most other European languages) retains but which must be approximated awkwardly in modern English by "knowing" and "understanding." It allows us to see in *valehia* ("lies") the etymology of casting or shaping (*valaa*), yielding "schape," whose modern Scandinavian equivalents mean both "to create" and (in the reflexive) "to lie." It permits us to generate English kennings like "fischgraves" and "fynntrowghs"—the first a literal translation from the Finnish, the second an invention inspired by the heady pleasures of alliteration and a desire to "sign" the poem as Finnish, the "fins" of the fish and the "fens" where the troughs are dredged both pointing quietly to Finland. These kennings would strike us as quaint ("interesting") in a semimodern metonymic version like Bosley's but as vividly *necessary* and empowering if we found them in *Beowulf.* Similarly, Ursa Major becomes neither the Big Dipper (modern) nor the Great Bear (quaint) but Cherles Waine or churl's wagon, a now-forgotten Anglo-Saxon designation of the group that seeks to situate our reading in space and time—specifically, as an "early" or originary space and time.

This is, of course, only an illusion. And the illusion may or may not succeed—in being compelling, not in being accurate. For example, I have translated the passage not into Old English but into a more readable Late Middle English—post-Chaucer, post-Langland, thus not originary at all. The main thing for the archaizing metaleptic translator is not the kind of accuracy that a philologist could verify, but casting a spell. If I have failed to cast one, or if you think that I have failed, that does not invalidate the attempt—does not make archaizing translations wrong or worthless or misguided *in theory.* It just means that you disliked it.

Suppose now we decide to take Joukahainen's side in the singing match—suppose we identify with his rebellion against Väinämöinen's and the SL author's temporal priority. Then maybe we should allow the principle of belatedness to dominate our translation, by modernizing it. Maybe, in other words, we should allow the TL (contemporary American English, for me) and the entire modern tradition of contemporary American poetry to dictate the terms of our translation as Joukahainen seeks to dictate to Väinämöinen. This would mean pretending (or pretending to pretend) that the Finnish had never been written; that there is no SL text; that the TL text is an original contemporary American poem, like this:

> Two poets met in a frozen wood, on a trail flanked
> by drifts of mental snow. Neither would give way.
> The one was old, respected, a Name, though
> some said his best work lay behind him.
> The other was young, arrogant, full of a future
> presence hollowed by his present absence. Neither
> would give way.
>   And so they stood: glaring balefully,
> snorting clouds of vapor, while eternity passed.
>
> At last, heavily, the old poet spoke:
> "Read me one of your poems. I'll gladly turn aside
> if I can't trace the words to my own work."
>
> The younger poet shook his head.
> "Dictating terms for my poetry, yes: that you do well.
> Let me hear your work first. Then we'll see."
>
> The old poet sighed.
> "Very well, then. Listen:
> 'IN THE BEGINNING WAS MY WORD AND MY WORD
> WAS WITH GOD AND MY WORD WAS THE ONLY GOD
> THERE WAS I WAS IN THE BEGINNING THE CREATIVE VOICE
> OF GOD AND ALL THINGS HAD THEIR BEGINNING
> THROUGH ME NOTHING WAS MADE BUT BY MY VOICE
> IN MY VOICE WAS LIFE AND THE LIFE WAS THE LIGHT
> OF MEN THE LIGHT SHINES IN THE DARKNESS AND THE DARKNESS
> HAS NOT YET OVERCOME IT.' You come after: your turn."
>
> The younger poet smiled, certain now he would have his day.
> "To precede Creation is not to precede me: attention to
> nature empties claims to have created it: listen:
> 'by transitions the land falls from grassy dunes to creek
> to undercreek: but there are no lines, though

> change in that transition is clear
> as any sharpness: but "sharpness" spread out,
> allowed to occur over a wider range
> than mental lines can keep': move out of my way."

> The old poet nodded, stepped aside, thinking: a poet
> with the brass to read Archie Ammons as his own
> has a future. I stand rewritten.

The traveler's pretense here is, obviously, that he or she owes nothing to the SL host—that he or she never spent the night there, was not fed and provisioned for the journey across to the TL. What SL text? This is not the *Kalevala*—it is contemporary American poetry à la Harold Bloom. The poem's mentors are poets like A. R. Ammons, whose attention to nature (coming out of William Carlos Williams through Charles Olson) does offer a powerful alternative to claims of temporal priority; English translations of the Bible, which long ago "modernized" and "naturalized" a Middle Eastern religion into English culture; and Robert Frost, without whom I found I could not imagine a modern dialogue between poets. The first stanza in particular is Frostian: the winter scene pays homage to his surname (as Frost himself often did), and the first line seems to promise a diverging of paths in a yellow wood, which is certainly apt in a discussion of translation as turning. Of course, there is no inherent reason why I should approach this translation task through Frost—Frost is not required by the text but arises out of my own poetic resources. After all, I am not trying to imagine what an anonymous Finnish poet would have written had he or she spoken contemporary American English. I am trying to imagine what I would have written had I (a white middle-class male American born in 1954) written the original poem. And part of my somatic word-reserve is an acquaintance with Frost.

You noticed the most significant shift brought about by my modernizing approach, besides the modern idiom: the reversal of roles. The old poet is driven to speak first, leaving the younger poet the last word (not counting the older poet's ironic unspoken coda, which of course must be counted). As befits a "belated" translation trope, my rendition elevates belatedness over the original's undisputed claims to priority. Still, aware of the metaleptic translator's sense of being caught in the middle, neither at the beginning nor at the end, and not even after the beginning and before the end but after what came just before and before what is about to come after, I built a double whammy into the two poets' claims to originality. The old poet claims as his own poem a passage from the Bible—but not from Genesis ("In the beginning I created heaven and earth," which is what Väinämöinen claimed) but from John's Gospel, itself a belated text that claims priority over what came before. The death of Jesus awakens the belated revisionism of his disciples, spurring them to establish their Master as originary, the Word that was with God at the beginning.

This passage from John is probably the strongest version in English literature both of the older poet's bogus claim to have been first and of Väinämöinen's pre-Christian cosmogony. The younger poet claims as his own poem a passage from Ammons's "Corson's Inlet," which might stand as a strong contemporary American version of Joukahainen's knowing (he knows all about the fishes and birds and trees, remember). It might—except that he did not write it himself, and the old poet recognizes the source. There is no "original" poetry, the old poet now realizes; there are only tropings on earlier poetry. The younger poet finds his own voice, not by voiding his precursor's words, but by transforming them. Not even the radical hyperbolic translator (like James Macpherson) who "translates" a nonexistent SL text is creating *ex nihilo,* for there simply *is* no verbal void out of which to create. We are always already situated in the middle. We always find ourselves in the midst of already dialogized language. Any claim that we make to originality—if I had given both the old poet and the young poet poems of my own to read, and had thus tried to establish my *own* creative originality at the expense of the SL text, say—is just that, a claim, nothing more. If we get someone to believe it, fine; other people's naivete is their lookout.

The rhetorical use of such a claim, or for that matter the use of a claim to absolute submission to the SL text, or to anything else, is that it helps the translator to make the turn, translate the text. The claim to equivalence: an excellent basis for a metonymic, synecdochic, or metaphoric turning. The claim to nonequivalence, to the impossibility of equivalence: an excellent basis for an ironic turning. The claim to originality: an excellent basis for a hyperbolic or metaleptic turning. In other words, it is not what you claim to do that counts; it is what you do with your claim. If you (seem to) fail to live up to your claims, that does not mean that you have failed at your task; it simply means that your claims have outlived their usefulness. You can stop pretending now. You need not go on insisting that you are original or that you have achieved or failed to achieve equivalence. You can admit frankly that those goals were only means to an end, and that, as far as you can tell, you have attained your end: you have written a damn good TL text.

As far as you can tell: obviously, you are only one of your own critics, only one voice among many pronouncing on the success of your translation. If the translator's best guide to success is his or her dialogue with the SL writer/speaker, the only forum in which success can be judged is his or her dialogue with the TL receptor.

Chapter Four ✦

The Ethics of Translation

Because it is the purpose of infinite players to continue the play, they do not play for themselves. The contradiction of finite play is that the players desire to bring play to an end for themselves. *The paradox of infinite play is that the players desire to* continue the play in others. *The paradox is precisely that they play only when others go on with the game.*

Infinite players play best when they become least necessary to the continuation of play. It is for this reason they play as mortals.

The joyfulness of infinite play, its laughter, lies in learning to start something we cannot finish.

Versions

Translations *are* versions, of course: we speak of an English version of Goethe, a German version of Shakespeare. Just as our word "trope" comes from the Greek word for "to turn," *tropein,* "version" comes from the Latin word for "to turn," *vertere,* which also meant "to interpret, to explain, to translate." (*Tropein* never meant "to translate," although translation's Greek cognate, the tropic *metapherein,* did.) *Convertere,* "to turn with or toward," was also used to mean translation: Cicero, for example, in his famous remarks on translation in *De optimo genere oratorum,* spoke of "converting" something from the Greek:

Converti enim ex Atticis duorum eloquentissimorum nobilissimas orationes inter seque contrarias, Aeschinis et Demosthenis; nec converti ut interpres, sed ut orator, sententiis isdem et earum formis tamquam figuris, verbis ad nostram consuetudinem aptis. (5.14)

That is to say I turned into Latin the most famous orations of the two most eloquent Attic orators, Aeschines and Demosthenes, orations which they delivered against each other. And I "turned" them not as a translator, but rather as an orator, keeping the same ideas and the forms, or as one might say, the "figures" of thought, but in language which conforms to our usage. (Hubbell's translation, slightly modified, 365)[1]

Jerome too, in his letter to Pammachius, uses *vertere* for "to translate" when he means this kind of "oratorical" or loosely interpretive translation, as when Eusebius of Cremona asks him to translate a letter from Pope Epiphanius to John, Bishop of Jerusalem:

Eusebius Cremonensis . . . coepit a me obnixe petere, ut sibi eam in Latinum verterem et propter intellegendi facilitatem apertius explicarem; Graeci enim eloquii penitus ignarus erat. (2.2)

Eusebius of Cremona . . . set to work to beg me to translate it for him into Latin and at the same time to simplify the argument so that he might more readily understand it; for he was himself altogether unacquainted with the Greek language. (Fremantle's translation, 112)[2]

By analogy with the Latin, the modern European languages retained traces of this notion that translation is a turning: just now, for example, I could turn Cicero's *converti* into "I turned into Latin" with only slight awkwardness (and "I converted into Latin" would have been only slightly more awkward), and German "in meiner Wendung" means both "in my opinion" and "as I translate it."[3] The Swedish cognate of German *wenden, vända* ("to turn"), which was also used in Middle and Old Modern Swedish to mean "to translate," apparently served as the model for Finnish *kääntää*, which not only means "to turn" but is the only Finnish word for "to translate."[4]

But these are only traces. Finnish is the only modern European language I know that refers to translation primarily as a turning. Everywhere else, as I noted in Chapter 3, it is a crossing: a carrying over (translatio, translation), a leading over (traduction, traducción), a setting over (Übersetzung, översättning), a metaphor that, as a metaphor, as a perspectivizing or as a metaleptic feeling-caught-between-SL-and-TL-and-wondering-which-way-to-turn, may guide translators to good translations, but that, once idealized as the building of a perfect bridge from SL to TL, only muddies the waters.

Still, as John Hollander points out in "Versions, Interpretations, Performances," our connotations for "versions" are different from those for "translations"—looser, more open-ended, more tolerant. "In 'version,'" he says, "the sense of the 'limited authority' or 'particular point of view' always manages to make itself felt in one way or another, and to qualify the nature of the relationship of the rendering to the original" (221)—

to qualify it specifically in the direction of bias, personal or otherwise (a bias is etymologically an obliqueness, a twist, a turn). "It is usually assumed from the start," Hollander continues, "that, keeping an original text in mind, there is going to be *something* queer about a version of it, whether a French version, or a shortened one, or a version leaning strongly toward the views of Professor von Braun, or a garbled version" (221). "We never seem to speak of the '*right* version,'" he says, "the '*correct* version' any more than we could think of the '*only* version'" (221). Here is Hollander once more:

Now whenever we accept or reject a version of a statement or text, we do so in full recognition of its particular bias or "limited authority," and never make the fact of the existence of such a bias a point of attack against it. One might, of course, ask why such a particular version was needed or desirable in the first place, whether, even though well done, it was worth the effort involved, and so on. The grounds on which we would want to base our praise or blame of a version would involve the success with which a particular version first specified its bias and then proceeded to represent that bias in its rendering. These criteria persist, I think, through other situations in which we use the word: what we would ask of three different "versions" of what had happened in an automobile accident, for example, would be that each one, each witness' recital of "what happened" should adequately represent his particular viewpoint. When, after hearing all of the accounts, we might choose to say that some were closer to what actually happened than others were, we are, after all, choosing among the viewpoints themselves. But this would be a far different matter from rejecting, on the spot, a garbled, or inconsistent, or endless, or hysterical, or insufficient, or stammered account (an implausible one would have to be rejected later, for its viewpoint). In all these cases, the success of the *representation* of the viewpoint would be under the initial scrutiny, and the accounts would be judged as x-biased or y-biased or z-biased versions. Only later would x, y, and z themselves come up for discussion. There is also the sense in which we speak of a version of a joke, or of a folk-song, or of a performance of a musical work (where, in all of these cases, we expect each recital to vary, to be a *version*). Here, too, the success of the recital must be distinguished from the desirability of the bias, even though the latter may operate much more strongly on our feelings than will the former. The version of a folk-song or myth one has learned in childhood, "the way we played it at home" (where some peripheral rule of a game has been varied), like one's own preferred variant of a name ("ketchup," "catsup," "catchup") is always somehow as much fonder as it is more familiar. (222–23)

What Hollander is obviously working toward in this elicitation of the ordinary sense of the word "version" is a personal, pragmatic, real-world, dramatistic approach to translation, an approach based not on idealized correspondences, formal logic, or spatial metaphors of bridging or crossing but on real human interaction. And in fact that very insistence on interaction, on one person saying something to another in a real situation, with all the subjective biases (or, if you like, hermeneutical interpretations, phenomenological intentionalities) that go along with all real human action, begins to move us past even Hollander's formulation.

Traditionally, both tropes and versions are textual matters—intertextual matters, to be precise. A trope is a figure of speech, something on the page, a word or a phrase that can be looked up in the dictionary, classified, and so on. A version, as Hollander too assumes, is a modified text, a midrash, an interpretive variant whose variation from the original can be analyzed by logical tests of correspondence or deviation. But these are "scientist" conceptions, as Kenneth Burke would say. Harold Bloom taught us how to recharge intertextual troping with the emotional power of real dialogues between people, writers/translators and their precursors; and now I want to let Burke teach us to recharge intertextual versions with the emotional and finally the ethical power of real dialogues between people as well, this time between translators and their TL receptors.

Vertical Ethics

Burke is fascinated by what he calls the Latin vert-family: conversion, perversion, inversion, reversion, aversion, and so on. In an article called "Versions, Con-, Per-, and In-," he traces them through Djuna Barnes's novel *Nightwood,* showing how "the idea of Robin as the 'unmoved mover' in connection with Nora's conversion to perversion or inversion does help bring out the sense in which Nora's romantic passion is a secular variant of the religious passion" (243). But as that sentence goes on to remind us, Burke's most productive discussion of the verts comes in *The Rhetoric of Religion,* in his reading of Augustine's *Confessions,* which, he says in the Barnes piece, the "good Bishop of Hippo" probably could never have written "were it not for the many Latin words that grow from this root, meaning 'turn'" (242). This is hyperbole, but Burke convincingly shows how Augustine's rhetoric relies on a turn from *per*version (the stealing of the pears in book 2) to the famous *con*version in the garden in book 8, and how heavily Augustine relies on versions throughout. Here, for example, from the end of book 4, is a passage that Burke draws our attention to (82):

Quoniam firmitas nostra quando tu es, tunc est firmitas, cum autem nostra est, infirmitas est. vivit apud te semper bonum nostrum, et quia inde aversi sumus, perversi sumus. revertamur iam, domine, ut non evertamur, quia vivit apud te sine ullo defectu bonum nostrum, quod tu ipse es: et non timemus, ne non sit quo redeamus, quia nos inde ruimus; nobis autem absentibus non ruit domus nostra, aeternitas tua. (4.16)

When you are our strength, we are strong, but when our strength is our own we are weak. In you our good abides forever, and when we turn away from it we turn to evil. Let us return at last to you, O Lord, for fear that we be over-turned. For in you our good abides and it has no blemish, since it is yourself. Nor do we fear that there is no home to which we can return. We fell from it; but our home is your eternity and it does not fall because we are away. (Pine-Coffin's translation, slightly modified, 89–90)

Burke also draws attention to Augustine's disgust for the "overtur-ners" or *eversores* among his students (3.3, Burke 71), who make teaching a painful chore, and to the "controversia in corde meo non nisi de me ipso adversus me ipsum" (8.11)—the "controversy within my heart, in-volving none other than myself against myself" (translation adapted from Burke, 113), between the vision of Continence and his conversion. After Augustine's conversion, Burke suggests, "The *inner* controversy of chapter xi could be replaced by *outer* controversy, as notably in later struggles with Pelagians and Donatists" (115). One vert that Augustine only implies (and Pine-Coffin makes explicit in translation) in his at-tacks on the theater is "divert": the theater is "diverting" in both En-glish senses of the word, amusing us, moving us to pleasurable sorrow and tears, but in so doing moving us away from God. Augustine uses an unprefixed vert (*vertitur*), but Pine-Coffin rightly hears the English diversion/diversity in it:

lacrimae ergo amantur et dolores. certe omnis homo gaudere vult. an cum mis-erum esse neminem libeat, libet tamen esse misericordem, quod quia non sine dolore est, hac una causa amantur dolores? et hoc de illa vena amicitiae est.
    Sed quo vadit? quo fluit? ut quid decurrit in torrentem picis bullientis, aes-tus inmanes taetrarum libidinum, in quos ipsa mutatur, et vertitur per nutum proprium de caelesti serenitate detorta atque deiecta? (3.2)

This shows that sorrow and tears can be enjoyable. Of course, everyone wants to be happy; but even if no one likes being sad, is there just the one exception that, because we enjoy pitying others, we welcome their misfortunes, without which we could not pity them? If so, it is because friendly feelings well up in us like the waters of a spring. But what course do these waters follow? Where do they flow? Why do they trickle away to join that stream of boiling pitch, the hideous flood of lust? For by their own choice they lose themselves and become absorbed in it. They are diverted from their true course and deprived of their original heavenly calm. (56)

Following and adapting Burke, then, we could schematize the "vertical" argument of the *Confessions* like this:

1. *Diversion*: a turning every which way, which gives pleasure through variety (many mistresses, actors play many parts, enact many feelings in the theater) but that very variety turns every way but toward God.

2. *Aversion*: a turning away from God, the inevitable result of diverse diversions.

3. *Perversion*: a turning upside-down, a confusing or confounding of God's love (the perverse imitation or parody of Christ's sacrifice in the adolescent stealing of the pears, 2.6).

4. *Eversion*: an overturning, the eternal perdition that is God's punishment for those who turn away from him.

5. *Reversion*: a returning to God in response to the fear of eversion.

6. *Controversy*: a two-way turning-against, a dispute or debate or disagreement between those people or forces within people who would turn toward God and those who would turn away.

7. *Conversion*: the turning toward God that brings salvation.

What Augustine can contribute to a discussion of "versions" is an awareness of the dialogical or interpersonal politics of turning: "versions" are not textual modifications but human turnings, what one person does to another (all ultimately, of course, for Augustine, under the great umbrella of what God does to all of us). It should be clear, for example, that translators do things to their TL receptors. Bible translators, however much they talk about "conveying" the content of the SL text in as faithful a way as possible, obviously want to help God and the SL writers convert the TL reader. Secular translators (translators of secular texts), however much they avoid all explicit talk of conversion, by so patently aligning themselves with the SL writer's intentions lean toward conversion too. One is not to fiddle with the neo-Nazi text one has been asked to translate: that would be perverse, which is to say, it would pervert the TL reader's trust in the translator's faithfulness to the SL text. And so one helps the SL writer convert the TL reader.

One implication of Augustine's verts, in other words, might be that there is no textual neutrality, no use of words that is "purely" informational or constative, no innocent "conveying" of meanings from one language to another. All saying, as J. L. Austin said, is doing. If you refuse to pervert, you convert. If you refuse to convert, you pervert. Whether you know it or not. Whether you like it or not.

Of course, it is not that simple. It is not a binary decision between conversion and perversion. That is another thing Augustine can give us: a sense of the complexity of "turning" people, of doing things to them through words. Instead of converting your receptors, you might, say, divert them. Translations can be fun! It is not all the laborious transmission of information as a cover for an attempt to convert. Or you might conceive conversion in a different way, intensify it as reversion, as a returning of the TL reader to something he or she once knew or was, as in romantic theories: the translator as restorer of primeval paradise, where men and women were gods. And so on. This field has been tied up in an idealized straitjacket too long. It is time to look around at the real *diversity* of translation.

And that rhetorical gesture, praise for diversity, for the pleasurable variety that Augustine condemned as evil, suggests yet a third contribution Augustine can make to this chapter: he can stand as progenitive symbol for the mainstream ideology of translation, which reduces all translation to conversion and then mystifies the political act of conversion as an idealized neutral conveyal of information—thus giving me something to *reverse*. Otherwise this business of "versions" might prove a sterile exercise in which I hunt through the dictionary for versions and force translation into the categories I make out of them. Augustine's impulse is totalizing, and thus totalitarian: he wants to convert the world to conversion, to reduce all "doing" to a turning toward God, and a turning toward God specifically in the terms he devises for it. And, thanks to the thousand-year hegemony of the Roman Catholic church in the Middle Ages, and of medieval assumptions in later humanistic thought, translation theory—like most of Western culture, for that matter—has tended, *mutatis mutandis,* to follow in Augustine's footsteps.[5] I want to reverse Augustine, to go the other way, to start from conversion and move toward greater and greater diversity, and end with a version of conversion that I think allows for diversity, "conversation."

This is specifically a modern reversal of Augustine—but it is neither a complete reversal (mirror image or about-face) nor completely modern. It is ideosomatically guided by the liberal revision of Augustinian ethics that privileges diversified growth (becoming a rounded personality) over unified growth (conforming yourself to God's will). To the extent that the ethics of translation I trace remain locked into liberal ideology, they are both modern (historically situated in the period of liberalism, the past three or four centuries) and not modern (heavily grounded ideosomatically in Augustinian Christianity).

But, aware as I am of my own ideological roots in medieval and liberal ethics, I am also aware of a more thoroughgoing revisionism in my approach to the subject. I remain concerned with the translator's progress to self-actualization, a liberal concern that harks back to Christian conversion; but my tracing of that progress through a *regress* from conversion to diversion will take me down emancipatory avenues that seek specifically to subvert, pervert, and avert liberal ideals of common sense, reason, universalized "nature," majority rule, social and psychological stability, and bonhomie. My path proceeds through the dark night occluded by liberal thought; and if it returns in the end to a liberal concern with becoming fully human, that return will be, I hope, dialectically intensified by my exposure to nightmarish distortion.

By the "ethics of translation" I do not, in other words, mean what I assume most people will take that title to mean: the restriction of translation to a set of do's and don'ts. I mean specifically ethical growth *out* of ideosomatically programmed restrictions, *out* of controlled obedience to cultural ideals, out into the world, into a liberating confrontation with and openness to diversity. This will mean working down through the three seals, working through to an awareness of ideosomatic programming and then of the diversity beyond—or, in the schema I developed out of Bloom's primal scene of instruction at the end of Chapter 2, working up out of ideosomatically controlled election-love, through the stages of masking, ideosomatic embodiment, idiosomatic embodiment, and interpretation to a fully aware revisionism.

On a superficial, formal level (the level of my table of contents), this will mean reversing the order of Augustine's verts, beginning with conversion and moving through controversy, reversion, eversion, aversion, and perversion to diversion (and from there to conversation). But, as in my discussion of the tropes, I want to insist throughout that any one of the versions can be a powerful and productive translation tool—that conversion, say, is not inherently a worse intent than diversion or conversation. It is only when conversion is idealized and normatized (and then mystified, repressed, "forgotten") as the only acceptable approach to the TL receptor that it becomes more restrictive, and thus less conducive to ethical growth—especially if (as is typically the case) the translator is not even allowed to realize that he or she is being asked to help the SL writer convert the TL reader. I do not mind admitting, for example, that my own preferences among the translatorial verts are conversion, subversion, and diversion, and, for that matter, that I am trying to convert you to diversity—that I am *acting* on you, trying to persuade you, trying to bring you around to my way of seeing translation. I am enough of a liberal ideologue to despise the liberal embarrassment with conversion, with persuasion, to despise the ludicrous idea that, since everybody is entitled to his or her own opinion (I agree), nobody should ever try to convince anybody of anything (I disagree).[6] Not only is that burying your head in the sand, pretending that you have nothing to do with power politics, when of course everybody always does; it is a way of making your political manipulation more effective because more covert. I intend to risk damaging my effectiveness by acting on you openly.

In fact, my critique of mainstream translation theory is directed not at conversion but at this deviousness, this backhandedness, this idealization of conversion right out of sight: the pretense that the translator does not *do anything,* neither converts nor perverts, but simply conveys. The translator as window between SL writer and TL reader.

Before I get started with Augustine's (reverse) progression from diversion to conversion, therefore, I want to spend some time discussing this idealization in terms of another pair of verts, introversion and extroversion, which I think will help me show how the translator's controlled self-effacement is an ethical "doing" or "turning" as well. (This polemic against traditional or introverted translation theories is my Chapter 4 excursion into Augustinian "controversy.") Kenneth Burke shows how important inwardness is for Augustine: turning inward means turning toward the spark of truth that God planted in each of us in the form of the Holy Spirit, so that introversion becomes an idealization of self-denial. The only alternative, vertically speaking, is extroversion, the controvert of introversion, its polemical opposite, self-aggrandizement at the expense of God, which is always, for Augustine (and for his successors among translation theorists), a perversion: the translator draws the TL receptor's attention to *his* expression, *her* truth, not the expression or truth of the SL text. This is *not* translation. Translation (true translation, translation proper) requires the translator's introversion. Introversion and extroversion thus become the controversial ideal and anti-ideal of mainstream translation theory that I need to dispose of (polemically, controversially) before we can get down to what translators actually do to their receptors.

I will be making a few other adjustments, too, along the way. For example, in contemporary consumer capitalist society, it is worthwhile to complicate a discussion of conversion, which points mainly to Bible translation, with advertising, another vert that converts the reader by getting him or her to buy (and above all believe in) products. It also makes sense to talk about what Augustine calls "eversion" in terms of a vert that is actually used in English, like subversion.[7] These modifications yield the following schema:

1. introversion and extroversion (controversy)
2. conversion and advertising
3. reversion
4. subversion (eversion)
5. perversion
6. aversion
7. diversion
8. conversation

Introversion and Extroversion

The translator conveys the meaning of the SL text to the TL receptor. Period. Nothing else. The translator is a window through which the TL receptor can perceive the SL meaning without distortion or obstruction. The translator is not a *person*, with personal experiences, personal desires, personal preferences. The translator is a *vehicle*. An instrument. A tool used by the SL writer to communicate with receptors whose language he or she does not speak; a tool used by the TL receptor to understand the words of an otherwise inaccessible writer or speaker. A mere tool, like a knife or a screwdriver. A medium, like a window (for sight), like air (for sound). A vehicle, like a wheelbarrow or a truck. Not a person.

Since we are not born tools, the only way for a translator to get from personhood to toolhood is by denying his or her own personality—by systematically suppressing personal experiences, personal desires, personal preferences. We are used to this, of course. Humility is a good Christian virtue, and humility, or its outward appearance, has traditionally been achieved through the systematic suppression of personality. First, parents do it: "It's not nice to brag"; "Others first"; "Mind your manners"; "You have responsibilities"; "You aren't the only person in the world"; "Nice girls always defer to the wishes of others;" "Gentlemen always let ladies go first," and so on. Then, when the lesson has been drummed into the child's head long enough, the child starts to do it to him- or herself. "I'm so selfish; I've got to watch myself." Self-control. Self-monitoring. Self-denial.

If we take Christian ethics at face (idealized) value, there is something fishy about all this. Ideally, humility is something that arises out of love. It is not a product of self-control. The "truly" (ideally) humble person cannot help but be humble. It is an expression of his or her whole being. It is not externally imposed or internally monitored. Conveniently, however, in a "real" world like ours the doctrine of original sin means that we can never love perfectly or completely or selflessly enough to let humility simply flow out of us, so we have to strive toward humility, and that means setting up barricades against pride. This in turn requires rules and regulations. Do this, don't do that. "Conveniently," I say, because *controlled* humility helps to maintain social order by keeping the lower strata of society—the lay public, taxpayers, women, minorities, translators, children—submissive.

Now, please don't get me wrong here. I have nothing against humility. I would even go so far as to say that we should all strive for it. But the only way to strive for true humility is to *stop* striving for it— which is to say, to surrender the ego that strives to achieve greater and greater things, including greater and greater humility (which we can all be proud of), to let it go, let it slip away. What I dislike is controlled humility, which is achieved not by surrendering ego but by battering it down, beating it to a pulp, locking it up, straitjacketing it. How can you surrender something that you have chained to the wall in isolation?

Humility is enforced in the ecclesiastical tradition through introversion, a "turning inward" that blocks all outward expression of personality. For every instrumentalized person there is an acceptable form of behavior—an idealized or ritualized role—and *that* is the only behavior such a person may display. Submissive. Self-effacing. Altruistic. Self-denying. These "personality features" can be expressed—period. If any resentment rises to the surface, suppress it. Turn it inward. Turn it back into your own guts. Deal with it privately, however you can. Never mind if it tears you up. Never mind if the pressure keeps building up, if you feel like you want to explode. Keep the lid on. If the pressure builds, clamp it down tighter. Maintain an absolute barrier between the external role and the introverted person. Never let the introverted person suddenly extrovert, suddenly explode outward in a burst of pent-up rage or ridicule or other personal expression. An angry wife is no wife at all. A rebellious child is no child of mine. A proud black is dangerous. A "free" translator is not doing translation at all, but creative writing. Deviating from the idealized role deprives you of your social status, your safe niche in society. You become an outcast. A pariah. Ultimately, you become invisible, mere air. People look through you. You are not really there.

But then, people always did look through you. You never were there. Idealized roles always make people invisible. The ideology of introversion gives you two choices: invisibility through successful role-conformity, or invisibility through scandalous deviation. Be a good role-robot that does its job perfectly and so never draws attention to itself, or a rebellious human being who does not do his or her job at all and is better ignored, excluded from public view, lest other people get the same idea. Obey the rules, and inhabit the faceless center. Break the rules, and get exiled to the invisible periphery.

Ironically, you often hear the same people complaining both about the low social status and recognition accorded translators (and the work they do is so important!) and about the irresponsibility of some translators who give translation a bad name by "expressing themselves," doing "creative" versions of texts, importing personal meanings into the SL writer's intentions (that isn't translation at all!). This is the crushing double bind imposed by the ideosomatics of instrumentalism. If you do your job right, you are a mere instrument, invisible and ignored. If you do it wrong, you are cast on the dungheap. You cannot win.

One problem is that, where introversion is idealized, the only conceivable alternative to introversion is extroversion. Self-denial—or self-expression. If the translator does not introvert all personal experience, desire, and so on, he or she merely expresses it, in the root sense of that word: presses it out, forces it past the idealized introversional barriers out into the world, hurls it in the faces of the people who enforced his or her humility. For the instrumentalized introvert, extroversion is an act of hostility, a way of saying "Take that!" or "This is *me*, goddammit!" Extroversion thus becomes a fruitless form of controversion in which you do exactly the opposite of what you are supposed to do. If you were supposed to be submissive, you become domineering. If you were supposed to be humble, you become arrogant. If you were supposed to be self-effacing, you become self-centered. Not because this is a deeply felt expression of your whole personality, not because it is "who you are"—but because it is a part of your personality that you were never allowed to express, so when you finally get (or take) the chance to express it, you fling it like mud.

This is the restrictive force of dualism. By idealizing the translator's task and role in dualistic terms—introversion (good) versus extroversion (bad)—we protect ourselves against deviation from the good by making the only alternative seem prohibitively bad. If the translator must choose between passively and submissively conveying the SL writer's intention, on the one hand, and childishly parading his or her own animal fears and drives before the TL receptor, on the other, obviously the self-respecting translator will choose the former. Dualism is a form of ideosomatic insurance: if for some reason the translator begins to grow disillusioned with the positive ideal, fear of falling into the negative ideal will still keep him or her in line.

Of course, this insurance does not always work. All the extroverted translator has to do to escape the idealized introverted role is to invert the traditional dualism, call introversion bad and extroversion good. A good example of this approach might be Goethe's second-stage entrepreneurs, who call on capitalist ideology to make precisely this inversion: if everyone is his own man, and every writer owns his own words, then when I write a translation I as writer own *my* words too, and nobody can make me think otherwise. Capitalism depends just as heavily as feudalism on social hierarchies but differs from feudalism in the value placed on the individual's ability to rise in the hierarchy: I may have been born a worker, but I'm not foreordained to die one. I can quit my job, take out a bank loan, start my own business, hire labor, make my own money, chart my own course. The hierarchy hasn't changed, but I've changed my position in it. Introversion, the extroverted translator can argue, is a virtue only for people on lower rungs of the ladder; if you rise on the ladder, you need to be extroverted, you need to shake off all the old restraining ideals of submission and self-denial and learn to express yourself, assert yourself, demand your rights. You're as good as anybody else, and don't never let nobody tell you different. The extroverted entrepreneurial translator projects the despised instrumentality of traditional introverted translator roles onto another group—secretaries, perhaps—and appropriates the attributes of the writer: translators are verbal virtuosos, master of two or more languages and of various specialized terminologies in each, able to bring coherence to childishly sloppy SL texts, and so forth.

From a comfortable authoritarian position, of course, it is all too easy to look down at the lower orders and tisk your tongue at what they do with power once they have it, their childish indulgence, their defensiveness, their grasping, their persecution of anyone who disagrees with them. It is easy to conclude that the lower orders should avoid making spectacles of themselves by contenting themselves with their "lot"—which is to say, their present state of oppression—or by returning, after the orgy of indulgence, to "normalcy." But that does not solve anything; it just postpones the problem. The impetus for change is already there and cannot be stopped. The dismantling of the Middle Ages over the past six or seven centuries has progressively tapped the repressed personal experience of the so-called lower orders, encouraged its exploration and expression, farther and farther down through the levels of the medieval hierarchy: first the bourgeoisie, then the proletariat, then the unemployed, then the homeless, then the insane and the infirm; first free white landowning men, then free white men, then free men (blacks now included, slaves freed), then women, then children; first God, then the prophets, then the apostles, then monks and priests, then secular writers (artists and intellectuals), then ghost writers and novelizers, now translators—perhaps copy editors and secretaries are next. Each group in turn begins to feel a subtle social pressure toward emancipation, a ground swell of liberatory need seeping down from the newly liberated groups just above them in the old hierarchies, a need to open up, to recover personality, to experience everything that has hitherto been denied them, to glut themselves on it, so that they will no longer be driven by envy for what they cannot have. There is no turning back. The eleventh century, perhaps the last relatively stable century of ecclesiastical hegemony (before the conquest of Moorish Spain and the rediscovery of Aristotle and classical humanism), is gone forever.

Controverting the old dualisms is only the first step toward liberation. But once you have taken that step, there is no going back. Breaking down the idealized barrier between the external role and the introverted person leads first to extroversion, then beyond, ultimately to the dissolution of the entire introversion/extroversion dualism. Beyond extroversion, beyond sheer blind self-expression, forcing the introverted self out past the old barriers, there lies engagement, interaction, dialogue with the people around you. Some will have power over you, some will submit themselves to you, others you will meet as equals; but you will not have to idealize and ritualize your role in terms of just one of these situations. You will not have to force yourself, for example, into a mechanically submissive role. In some translations you may in fact submit. You have nothing against the SL text: it is well written, better articulated than you could have managed yourself, and aimed aptly at the TL readers you would address. So you submit to the SL writer's intention, enlist yourself in the SL writer's cause, help him or her to bring the TL receptor around to his or her way of thinking. This is missionary work, helping a superior convert an audience, which is fine: you go into it with your eyes open, know what you are doing, agree with what is going on.

The important thing is that you are no longer programmed to assume that role in *all* translation tasks. You are flexible, able to psych out a situation and react to it appropriately. Maybe you think that the SL writer does not know how to convert the TL audience most effectively, so you improve on the original, reformulate and redirect it so as to make it work better. Or maybe you feel uncomfortable with the writer's design on the TL receptor, so you soften its appeal, flatten it, neutralize it slightly. A careful choice of words here and there will do it; no major changes needed, no reorganization of sentence structure, no introduction of new text. You just want to take the edge off. Maybe you think the TL receptors would be outraged (and rightly so) with the SL text if it were more explicit, more frank about its covert designs, so you accentuate them a little, expose them to the light of day, make it easier for the TL receptors to connect with their anger.

And so on. From an idealized (ideally dualized) introverted point of view, this is all extroversion, self-expression, self-assertion—but it is not blind self-assertion, the forcing of a denied self on random audiences just because you were told not to. It is a dialogical sensitivity, an awareness of the complexity of specific situations and a flexible response to that complexity. Situational ethics. You read a situation and you respond to it in the most appropriate way you can: this is "responsibility" freed from the steel shackles of universal law.

It is also, you may say, "responsibility" as relativism. I suppose it is. But it is not relativism as randomness, doing any old thing, whatever pops into your head. It is the responsibility of an appropriate response to a specific situation. Try to make up a rule that will apply in every situation: you cannot do it. Philosophers have tried. God tried, when he gave Moses the Ten Commandments, and Jesus promptly went and broke six or seven of them (Blake said he broke all of them). "Ἐπερωτῶ ὑμᾶς, εἰ ἔξεστιν τῷ σαββάτῳ ἀγαθοποιῆσαι ἢ κακοποιῆσαι, ψυχὴν σῶσαι ἢ ἀπολέσαι"—"Let me ask you, is it all right to do good or to do bad on Sunday? To save life or destroy it?" (Luke 6:9, Jordan's translation). "Τίνος ὑμῶν υἱὸς ἢ βοῦς εἰς φρέαρ πεσεῖται, καὶ οὐκ εὐθέως ἀνασπάσει αὐτὸν ἐν ἡμέρᾳ τοῦ σαββάτου"—"Suppose one of you had a child or a cow to fall in a well on a Sunday, wouldn't you try to get it out right away?" (Luke 14:5, Jordan's translation). "Τὸ σάββατον διὰ τὸν ἄνθρωπον ἐγένετο καὶ οὐχ ὁ ἄνθρωπος διὰ τὸ σάββατον"—"Rules are made up to help people structure their lives; people weren't created to force their lives into conformity with the rules" (Mark 2:27, my translation). Situational ethics. Some of the worst persecutions in the history of the Christian church have come out of attempts to universalize Jesus' response to a specific situation to cover all situations.

This situational responsiveness or responsibility is what I mean by an ethical commitment to diversity: not diversity for diversity's sake, not doing any old thing, but responding appropriately to the situational diversity of human life. Vertical ethics. Ethical versions of response: conversion and advertising, reversion, subversion, perversion, aversion, diversion, conversation. The rest of this chapter is an exploration of the diversity of ethical response—of (some of) the complexity of vertical ethics.

Conversion and Advertising

If the Western ideal for translation has been introversion, the introverted translator making him- or herself into a window for the SL meaning to pass through unhindered, the practical aim concealed behind and mystified by the ideal has almost invariably been conversion. Given the hegemony of Christianity in the West, and specifically of a totalitarian institutionalized form of Christianity for a thousand years in the Middle Ages, it is not surprising that the ideal model or exemplum for all translation has been Bible translation; and the purpose of Bible translation is obviously to facilitate the work enjoined by Jesus after his resurrection: "πορευθέντες οὖν μαθητεύσατε πάντα τὰ ἔθνη, βαπτίζοντες αὐτοὺς εἰς τὸ ὄνομα τοῦ πατρὸς καὶ τοῦ υἱοῦ καὶ τοῦ ἁγίου πνεύματος, διδάσκοντες αὐτοὺς τηρεῖν πάντα ὅσα ἐνετειλάμην ὑμῖν· καὶ ἰδοὺ ἐγὼ μεθ' ὑμῶν εἰμι πάσας τὰς ἡμέρας ἕως τῆς συντελείας τοῦ αἰῶνος" (Matt. 28:19–20)—"As you travel, then, make students of all races and initiate them into the family of the Father and of the Son and of the Holy Spirit. Teach them to live by all that I outlined for you. And you know, I am right in there with you—all the time—until the last inning" (Jordan's translation, 97). "Make students of *all races*" (all peoples, all ethnic groups)—you need translators for that. Glossolalia, the mystical version of this commandment, will do for special occasions, but the Apostles seem to have been pragmatic enough to realize that you cannot build a church on mystical moments.[8] To make disciples you must convert the heathen; and to make disciples of *all races* you must translate the Bible.

But wait—that may be true of Bible translation, you say, but not all translation is Bible translation. Interestingly, though, not only is the

ecclesiastical ideal of introverted conversion implicit in all later mainstream theories of translation, it is *only* implicit in ecclesiastical theories
of translation as well. Ever since Augustine and Jerome, translation has
been seen as primarily a technical problem: there are certain obvious
difficulties to be overcome, syntactical divergencies, conceptual and
other semantic mismatches between languages, intention and interpretation, segmentation, and so forth, and one focuses one's attention on
them, on the problems, on *how to do it right*. How to do it best. How
to do it most effectively. One need never even ask what or who determined "rightness" or "bestness" or "most-effectiveness," because that
question has always already been answered. It is implicit in the institutional hegemony of a Christian concept of translation as conversion.
The translator's task is to stay out of the way so that God can do his
work on the TL reader. Stand between God and the TL reader, certainly, but invisibly: as an instrument, an introvert, a window. The purpose behind this is to help God (conceived as the Ultimate SL Writer)
convert the TL reader, but that purpose is so monolithic, so universally
accepted, so hegemonically built into the entire ecclesiastical institution, that the translator need not even be aware of it, let alone be able
to articulate it. It is built into every technical directive ever given the
translator, and hence into every technical question ever asked about the
translator's task: "How do I bring the TL into effective conformity
with the SL?" "Well, the first thing to do is to analyze the SL, make
sure you've got a good solid understanding of the text you're translating." "How do I achieve the same effect on the TL reader as the original
text had on the SL reader?" "Study the SL culture, get a good feel for
the audience the SL writer would have had in mind." The main thing
is: *align* yourself with the SL writer/text. Make his or her purpose your
purpose. You are just a tool, remember, an instrument.

But I overstated my case just now. The hegemonic purpose of all
mainstream translation is not built into *every* technical question ever
asked about translation; only into the ones that can be taken seriously
as questions. "What do I do when the SL writer is an idiot, when his
thinking is patently absurd?" Now the lips tighten; the jaw sets. "That's
none of your affair. Concern yourself with *translating* the text, not interpreting it. Leave to the TL reader the job of figuring out whether it
makes sense." The sensibility of the SL text is a nonquestion for the
translator. It is never allowed to come up.[9]

A more borderline version of this same problem still gives normative
translation theorists gray hairs: "What do I do when I notice that the
SL writer has made all sorts of factual errors, that he contradicts himself

constantly, that he doesn't know what he wants to say?" "Well . . ." The usual answer is that you must divine what the SL writer intended to say and silently bring the TL text into ideal conformity with that. Do not *decide* it; do not just guess at it; divine it. Let it come to you. This means, let the institution guide you to it, ideosomatically. Translate what you *know* the SL writer must be saying, what your body knows he must be saying, what your body has been programmed to know he must be saying. If he seems to be doing science but clearly contradicts himself by bringing politics into it, quietly ease the politics out.[10] Ideosomatically you know that they do not belong there. If he claims to be expounding Christian doctrine but digresses into personal experience that clearly contradicts the doctrine that he is expounding, silently correct his mistake. Ideosomatically you know that he must intend to be consistent; he must want to bring his entire text into perfect conformity with the doctrine that he is expounding. Fix it.

The ideosomatics of translation that I discussed in Chapter 1 lie behind both the implicitness of the translator's missionary (conversion) work in ecclesiastical conceptions of translation and the implicit survival of that conversion work in subsequent secular conceptions of translation. The ideosomatics of a two-thousand-year-old civilization are painfully difficult to change even slightly—and next to impossible to uproot entirely. (The only way to uproot them entirely is to destroy the civilization, to kill all the people and burn or melt down all their cultural artifacts, as God told the Israelites to do in the Old Testament.) God does the converting, in ecclesiastical formulations, not the translator; the translator is just God's instrument. And as the church became more and more "discreet" (read: embarrassed, and therefore deceptive) about the politics of conversion, even that emphasis on *God's* doing the converting shifted to one of God's leaving a door open for the *sinner* to convert. God plants the seed. God provides the necessary information. God makes conversion possible; the sinner converts out of his or her own free will. Ultimately, nobody *does* anything to anybody, because doing something to somebody is overtly political, and religious people have become increasingly embarrassed about exerting political power. So when ecclesiastical norms for translation began to be secularized in the late Middle Ages, translation became determinedly, insistently, the *conveyal of information*. Not converting the reader. Not bludgeoning the reader with a vision that he or she should come to adopt. Just providing the necessary information. "Necessary for what?" Well— just necessary. You need it. "Why do I need it?" You just do. You'll see what I mean. The ideosomatics of conversion remain operative, but they are buried so deep that no one knows that they are there. Language is for saying things, stating things, passing on information, "communication"; and translation is just one form of communication, cross-lingual communication. Nothing more. Passing on information from one language to another. Converting the TL reader? What nonsense.

The great Oxford philosopher J. L. Austin went to some trouble to point out all the ways in which language is used to *do* things, to perform actions—how even saying things, passing on information, always performs some action, does something to someone. He developed the idea most forcefully in a series of lectures that he gave at Harvard in 1955, later published posthumously as *How to Do Things with Words* in 1962. And today, thirty-five years later, you still hear linguists retelling the old story of how language is used primarily for communicating information. The ideosomatics of language die hard. It takes more than one J. L. Austin, no matter how influential, to make a dent in our ideosomatic programming.

But I think that if we relax the programmed reflex that denies the centrality of conversion to mainstream translation, if we relax our fears that someone is going to accuse us of *doing* something to the TL reader, of engaging in the insidious project of propaganda, we might well find that conversion is not nearly as horrible a thing to be doing as we thought. It is not all brainwashing. (All brainwashing is conversion, but the opposite is not true.) Conversion is the aim of language conceived as rhetoric, the art of persuasion. Kenneth Burke would say that all language is dramatic, and drama is always motivated: we always use language for a purpose, we have motives, we want to do something, get something, change something. In the same vein, Austin would say that all language is performative, all language is wrapped up in performance, in the acting out of desires, fears, and hopes, and that every speaker (including the translator) performs actions with language, always. I try to convince you of things. I want you to see things my way. I know that I will probably not succeed, and even if I do, I will probably not succeed entirely: you will fit the new ideas that you learned from me into your own experiences, and that will change them. But it is still worthwhile to me to try to convince you. I speak out of my own conviction, out of the depth of my felt experience. These things matter to me. They feel real. Not to share them with you would feel wrong to me—like denial or negation, like a refusal to let them change our relationship.

And this is all that conversion is. Burke says that "the word 'conversion' itself has a certain ambiguity. Often we think of it as the abandoning of one faith for another (like St. Paul's drastic transformation on the road to Damascus). But there are also converts who merely change to a more exacting attitude towards the faith they had already believed in, as with persons who suddenly feel 'called' to study for the ministry in a religion to which they already subscribed" (*Rhetoric of Religion* 104). And there are converts who have nothing to do with religion at all, who hear something that changes their minds (hearts, bodies) about something. They come to feel differently about something. They undergo a shift in emphasis or priorities. They turn slightly, come to face in a slightly different direction, or look in the old direction with slightly different eyes.

The etymology of conversion implies a turning *with,* meaning that you turn to agree with the person who is working on you, convincing you; you come to share (something like) his or her conviction. But the change need not be spectacular. It can be: "Yes, you're right, I never thought of it like that." Or: "I guess I always knew that, it strikes a chord with everything I believe, but I never quite formulated it that way." You were in the habit of saying certain things that you did not believe, that did not fit your experience; and someone made you realize that they were just empty words, that your feelings were not behind them, your heart was not in them.

All idealized translation partakes in this process: in its ideal state, as we have seen, Western translation is the process of facilitating the SL writer's conversion of the TL reader. In practice, much real translation partakes of it too: whenever the translator works to achieve the ideal, he or she is working first of all to convert the TL reader to his or her reading of the SL text. And whenever the SL writer is trying to convert (convince, persuade) the TL reader, the TL text is doubly aimed at conversion: the TL reader is supposed first to agree (at least tacitly, in the sense of going along with it, taking it seriously) with the translator about the SL text, then to agree with the SL writer about the world.

And I think that we might as well accept this fact, instead of burying our heads in the sand and pretending that we are innocently conveying SL information in the TL. Conversion is nothing to be ashamed of. The only reason that we are ashamed of it at all is that the church fathers built that shame (and its protective theological mystification) into a thousand years of Roman Catholic hegemony, on the understanding that conversion would be more effective if the convert did not know that it was happening—if he or she thought that this was just some information he or she was being presented with. You should *feel* it, feel the impulse toward conversion—feel the pressure, feel the acceptance that you will win if you comply, the rejection that you will bring down upon your head if you resist—but not know it. What is wrong with conversion is not that it acts on people, but that, in its ideosomatic mode, it acts on them deceptively. Conversion as trickery. Conversion as a confidence game. *That* is something to be ashamed of. Convincing people is part of day-to-day life.

There is one kind of translation, in fact, that makes no bones about all this: advertising translation. Advertising is the direct bourgeois descendant of Christian proselytizing anyway, the capitalist version of what in the Middle Ages was done by the Catholic church, so it is not surprising that advertisers *expect* translators to be proselytisers. Here, for example, is John Berger's account of publicity or advertising images from *Ways of Seeing,* an account that does not make the connection between capitalist advertising and Christian conversion explicit but does make it easier to see:

Publicity as a system only makes a single proposal.

It proposes to each of us that we transform ourselves, or our lives, by buying something more.

This more, it proposes, will make us in some way richer—even though we will be poorer by having spent our money.

Publicity persuades us of such a transformation by showing us people who have apparently been transformed and are, as a result, enviable. The state of being envied is what constitutes glamour. And publicity is the process of manufacturing glamour.

It is important here not to confuse publicity with the pleasure or benefits to be enjoyed from the things it advertises. Publicity is effective precisely because it feeds upon the real. Clothes, food, cars, cosmetics, baths, sunshine are the real things to be enjoyed in themselves. Publicity begins by working on a natural appetite for pleasure. But it cannot offer the real object of pleasure in that pleasure's own terms. The more convincingly publicity conveys the pleasure of bathing in a warm, distant sea, the more the spectator-buyer will become aware that he is hundreds of miles away from that sea and the more remote the chance of bathing in it will seem to him. This is why publicity can never really afford to be about the product or opportunity it is proposing to the buyer who is not yet enjoying it. Publicity is never a celebration of a pleasure-in-itself. Publicity is always about the future buyer. It offers him an image of himself made glamorous by the product or opportunity it is trying to sell. The image then makes him envious of himself as he might be. Yet what makes this self-which-he-might-be enviable? The envy of others. Publicity is about social relations, not objects. Its promise is not of pleasure, but of happiness: happiness as judged from the outside by others. The happiness of being envied is glamour. (131–32)

Advertising wants us to transform ourselves—as does the Christian proselytizer. The transformation will make us richer, despite the spending of our money to achieve it—as in Christian conversion, where the inner richness of oneness with God more than makes up for the money you give away to the poor (or to the church), the worldly pleasures you renounce, and so on. Advertising holds up transformed people for our envy, glamorous people—compare the stories of converts in the New Testament, the lives of the saints, charismatic testimonials, and so forth. Advertising sells the product by selling a vision of the buyer's future self—as Christian proselytizers sell a vision not only of future inner peace but of future glory in heaven. That is the "glamour" of the advertising image: the glory of the resurrected believer, living in paradise (compare Samoa, Nassau, even Miami Beach), in a resurrected body, with no aches and pains, no decay, no death (compare antacid and other pharmaceutical advertising, weight-reduction ads, facial cream ads, and all the images of cars, clothes, drinks, exclusive clubs, and so on that make it seem as if the buyer of these products will be invulnerable to decay or death, immortal).

In some sense, then, advertising translation is capitalist Bible translation. At a deep level, the aim of advertising translation is to convert the TL reader or viewer into a buyer of the SL (or, recently, multinational) company's product—or rather, into a *believer* in the company's product, so that he or she will keep buying it. And my guess is that advertisers know this. There is considerably less embarrassment about conversion among advertisers than among other commissioners of translations. When a marketing executive wants an ad translated into three different languages, he or she does not care a whit about equivalence; all that matters is that it *works,* that it has the desired conversional effect on the consumer and thus sells products.[11]

You could say, of course, that a translation that "works" in the sense of selling products has what Eugene Nida nowadays calls functional equivalence: if the function of the SL text is to sell products to the SL audience, the function of the TL text should be equivalent in the sense of selling products to the TL audience. But this is equivalence pared down to its smallest pragmatic core; and in any case, advertisers talk very little of equivalence. "We want a text that's going to appeal to the German consumer." Period. *A* text. Not *this* text, necessarily, however transformed. *A* text. Whatever works.

Whatever works *surreptitiously.* In that sense too, advertising is the direct descendant of Christian conversion. The capitalist idea, like the Christian idea, is that conversion is most likely to succeed if you bypass the sucker's or sinner's critical faculties through a direct appeal to deep-seated ideosomatic needs. Still, I see no point in slinging mud at advertising just because it has typically perpetuated the old Christian thing. Ideosomatically speaking, that is the way Western civilization works. Not only are people ideosomatically programmed to respond to certain kinds of words and images by buying the product advertised, whether that product is a week in the Bahamas or an eternity in the New Jerusalem, people are also ideosomatically programmed to *seek out* certain kinds of words and images when they want to make a powerful appeal to their fellow humans. It is not, in other words, some kind of capitalist conspiracy to swindle the consumer. Advertisers are just as well programmed as buyers. If they were not, they would be ineffective advertisers. They would not have the slightest idea how to appeal to people's deep-seated ideosomatic needs.

More: it is possible to use advertising for other purposes as well, to "translate" advertising images to sell not products but, say, liberation from ideosomatic programming. We have been programmed to think (or feel) paradise when we think of cigarettes: a cool, green paradise with a deep blue lake when we think of Kools, a rugged paradise of rough-hewn men and horses when we think of Marlboros. But what happens when you show an image of a sterile hospital room with a cancer patient hooked up to a lung machine and say only, "Smoke Marlboro"? Antismoking campaigns use advertising imagery to *fight* smokers' deep-seated ideosomatic needs. They use advertising, we might say, to work down through the three seals. Past the first seal, the one that seals off attention to your true somatic response: feel that hot, acrid air going down into your lungs; really *feel* it. Pay attention to what your body is saying to you. Do you still think of paradise? Then the second seal: do you think that you are the only one? Look how many smokers died of lung cancer, respiratory diseases, arterial diseases last year. Look at what they do to you in the hospital when you have lung cancer. Look at these people with no hair. Look at their skin. Then the third seal: do you agree that it is horrible, but that there is nothing you can do about it, because you have tried to quit a million times and you just cannot do it? Listen to these testimonials from people who came to our clinic and quit in just one week. "Quit smoking" clinics are big business these days. We are back to money—somebody is making a profit from antismoking campaigns—but I think that it is possible to agree that there are different kinds of advertising. Not everybody is selling slow death and useless escape.

For the advertising translator, this awareness of the various conversional alternatives can make an immense practical difference. If the translator's task is to be introverted and tacitly to help the SL writer convert the TL reader to anything he or she likes, then it matters little whether you are translating cigarette ads or quit-smoking ads. If you recognize that *you* are using the TL words, *you* are doing the TL converting, *you* are responsible for the TL text, then it does matter. Then if you feel all right about translating ads but do not believe in the ads you typically translate, you will start looking for another job. Or you will look for a way to convert your boss or your clients to your way of seeing things, so that, say, you do not have to convert the TL reader quite so surreptitiously. "Truth in advertising" is a tricky subject, epistemologically speaking, but somatically speaking there are ways of *feeling* relative truth and relative falsity: you can feel yourself leaving something unsaid, for example, for fear that saying it will hurt your case, and you can feel yourself going ahead and saying it anyway. Or, again, if you start working through your feelings about advertising and decide that you really cannot stand playing on people's needs and fears in this backhanded way, and you find that your boss or your clients will not let you be more open (which is likely to be the case), you will get into some other area of translation.

Here is the interesting thing about the ethics of translation: by concerning yourself with the rights and wrongs of what you are doing to other people (the usual meaning of "ethics"), you inevitably bring yourself around to a concern with what doing those things is doing to you, how it is shaping your character (the root meaning of "ethics," a concern for *ethos*, or character). By realizing that you are not a neutral instrument but a human being *acting* in a social context, *doing* things to the TL receptor, you begin to repair the social connections that idealized theory had swept under the ideosomatic rug: what I do to you and how it affects you, how doing that to you affects me. How I want to be affected; how I would want to be affected if I were you. What change I want to bring about in myself (ethical change, psychological change), in the world around me (social change, political change), in the dialogical relations between myself and other people.

Reversion

In Augustine's *Confessions,* reversion was the turning back to God out of a fear of eversion or overturning and, as such, the necessary condition for conversion. I conceive reversion also as closely linked to conversion—so closely that it may be difficult in specific cases to distinguish the two. Etymologically, conversion is the process of bringing someone to believe what you believe (turning *with* you, turning to agree with you), whereas reversion is a process of bringing someone to believe or be what he or she once believed or was (getting him or her to *return* to a previous belief or self). Thus, where the conversional translator says "Become like me," the reversional translator says "Let us become like we all once were." But again, let me say that I am not particularly worried about maintaining the taxonomical purity of these terms: I do not care if you want to say that reversion is really only one form of conversion, or, for that matter, if you want to split conversion and advertising into two different categories. I am not engaging in logic here. I am giving what I take to be a persuasive and above all *usable* form to the diversity of translational ethics. However you want to use it is fine with me. I do not want to quarrel over details.

In any case, the specific sense of reversion that I want to explore here is the romantic one of returning humanity to an original state of unity, one we all once occupied but have since lost—a state that the persuader has not attained him- or herself, obviously, but wants us all to try to return to, or wants the translator as romantic poet-hero to try to teach us to return to. The key text for translation theory in this regard is probably Benjamin's "Task of the Translator," but as André Lefevere points out, Benjamin was really only expanding on ideas that were implicit in the German romantics Herder, Goethe, Schleiermacher—and in fact the central idea remains more or less implicit in Benjamin too, who does not want to press too large a claim for the translator's power to bring about a paradisal reversion.

So I suggest that we look not at translation theorists but at romantics, Ralph Waldo Emerson, say (from *Nature*), and then draw our own conclusions for the practice of translation:

"A man is a god in ruins. When men are innocent, life shall be longer, and shall pass into the immortal, as gently as we awake from dreams. Now, the world would be insane and rabid, if these disorganizations should last for hundreds of years. It is kept in check by death and infancy. Infancy is the perpetual Messiah, which comes into the arms of fallen men, and pleads with them to return to paradise [there's the reversional aim].

"Man is the dwarf of himself. Once he was permeated and dissolved by spirit. He filled nature with his overflowing currents. Out from him sprang the sun and moon; from man, the sun; from woman, the moon. The laws of his mind, the periods of his actions externized themselves into day and night, into the year and the seasons. But, having made for himself this huge shell, his waters retired; he no longer fills the veins and veinlets; he is shrunk to a drop.

He sees, that the structure still fits him, but fits him colossally. Say, rather, once it fitted him, now it corresponds to him from far and on high. He adores timidly his own work. Now is man the follower of the sun, and woman the follower of the moon. Yet sometimes he starts in his slumber, and wonders at himself and his house, and muses strangely at the resemblance betwixt him and it. He perceives that if his law is still paramount, if still he have elemental power, 'if his word is sterling yet in nature,' it is not conscious power, it is not inferior but superior to his will. It is Instinct." Thus my Orphic poet sang. (42)

The idea here, which Emerson puts into the mouth of a fictitious visionary poet, is that the Fall in the Garden of Eden was a fall out of humanity's original divinity into a fallen *perception* of the world. Once upon a time nature was our body, the breath coursing through the body was God's spirit—and we were the whole, a great visionary giant as God. Now we have fallen to a misperception of that paradisal state in which we *think* we are tiny six-foot worms that look up at nature as an object, a thing out there to study or to chop down for firewood and housing subdivisions. It is really our own body, or the shell of our body, a set of clothes that once fit us but now fits us only "colossally." "The problem of restoring to the world original and eternal beauty," Emerson says, "is solved by the redemption of the soul. The ruin or the blank, that we see when we look at nature, is in our own eye. The axis of vision is not coincident with the axis of things, and so they appear not transparent but opake. The reason why the world lacks unity, and lies broken and in heaps, is, because man is disunited with himself" (43). The Fall was a falling out of "coincidence" between the axis of vision and the axis of things; there was a slight shift in vision, which wrenched it out of line with the way things are, so that now we think nature is opaque, for instance, when in fact it is transparent.

What we need is a restoration of paradisal vision. We need to return to our original way of seeing, which we (the sensitized few, the romantics) get passing glimpses of every time we start in our slumber. In order to do that, we must "cleanse the doors of perception," as Blake said. We must shake off the layers of false, fallen perception, and *see* what we already *are,* and become what we always have been: visionary giants living in an original paradisal state. Gods. "But when a faithful thinker, resolute to detach every object from personal relations, and see it in the light of thought, shall, at the same time, kindle science with the fire of the holiest affections, then will God go forth anew into the creation" (Emerson 44).

The romantic reversion might be traced in terms of my three seals: breaking the first seal shows me a somatic "glimpse" or twinge of that original oneness between *my* body and *nature's* body, *my* spirit and *God's* spirit. I feel the oneness: I "muse strangely at the resemblance" between myself and nature. I was not supposed to pay attention to my feelings, my somatic sense of my oneness with nature, but I broke that seal and discovered it, glimpsed it—and the reality passed, but the somatic certainty of the glimpse remained. The second seal tells me that it is just me, nobody else, which means that I am either crazy or the lone Messiah or both—until I break that seal and discover that everyone is the Messiah, everyone must break these seals on their own, and once they do, everyone will be God, everyone will be one with nature. Whitman's "Song of Myself," in its movement from "I" to "you," might be read as a great epical breaking of this second seal:

> I celebrate myself, and sing myself
> And what I assume you shall assume,
> For every atom belonging to me as good belongs to you. (sec. 1)

If I can, so can you. If I am, so are you.

> I speak the password primeval, I give the sign of democracy,
> By God! I will accept nothing which all cannot have their
>   counterpart of on the same terms. (sec. 24)

Well, I'd speak it if I knew it. Maybe I'll hit on it by accident, if I just keep writing long enough—if I exhaust enough words about myself, perhaps I will become the kosmos I (feel I) already am. And if I do, so will you.

The trick for the romantics was breaking the third seal, getting past the block against liberation from fallen perception, getting past the programmed certainty that we are stuck here and actually *breaking out*. To break the third seal in romantic terms would be to smash the final remnants of our fallen worldly programming and explode into the godhead, expand to fill nature with our overflowing currents. It has not happened yet. But if you know that it is possible, if you can feel its possibility in your body, isn't it your responsibility to try to make it happen, to make it possible for yourself and for others?

The romantics do not willingly speak of ethics—that would smack too much of narrow Sunday School rules, or of their Low Church, middle-class parents—but this sense of responsibility to all humanity (if I do it, so will you) is obviously an ethical concern. The romantic reversionary hope is that one person, the poet, the translator, will discover the way, will hit upon the password primeval and speak it; but that person will then teach the password to everybody else, and everyone will speak it in unison, and we will all revert to paradise.

We will all *speak* it: the restorative or reversionary act par excellence for the romantics was a verbal act, a performative word-as-act that re-creates the world as the paradise it always was. As Austin says, "To *say* something is to *do* something" (12). And what the romantic savior seeks to do by "saying something" is to restore humanity to its original paradisal state.

The translator's role in this process has never been made very clear. The obvious reason for bringing the translator into the reversionary myth at all, of course, is the association of fallen perception not only with the Fall in the Garden of Eden but with the scattering of tongues at Babel: our fallen state is marked by a disunity not only of will (Eden) but of language (Babel). This much is clear. What remains unclear is how the translator is to bring about the reversion. Benjamin imagines a kind of cosmic cooperation between language and the translator, a mutually supplementative interaction in which the great slumbering will or intention latent in each language is progressively activated and made manifest by each imperfect act of translation. The translator in Benjamin's conception is no lone visionary poet, transforming the world by the sole power of his or her reversionary word, but a severely limited and rather unlikely savior whose redemptive force lies solely in his or her ability to bring languages into contact with one another. The "intentions" intend a reversion to unity but are powerless to transform intention into action without the linguistic commingling initiated by the translator. The translator, on the other hand, intends only the successful completion of the translation, but in his or her movement toward that goal unwittingly contributes to the great cosmic regress toward (reversion to) revelation. Through the partial mediation of the translator, the great minds or intentions latent in languages come alive, stir and shake, until finally the barriers crumble, the distance between language and language drops away, and the multiplicity of words collapses into a vast Adamic unity.

Well, this is Benjamin, and as I read it his conception is infected with the traditional derogation of the translator's task: the poet creates, and the romantic poet re-creates; the translator neither creates nor re-creates but merely facilitates, acts as the unwitting instrument of the redemptive "intentions" that sleep in language. The translator just sort of bumbles along, and somehow, without his or her even knowing what is happening, regress (reverse progress) is made toward redemption. I suggest that we stop and consider what a fully romantic conception of translational reversion might be.

The reversionary task of the translator (to echo Benjamin) is first of all to break the first two seals, to discover in his or her somatic response the feel of original oneness that Emerson talks of, and the commonality of longing for that oneness among all humans that Whitman celebrates, and to butt up against the third seal: to feel the resistance, to feel the difficulty of achieving the great restorative reversion. The reversionary translator, in other words, begins the translation in this state of readiness, searching for the key that will open the last door, break the last seal.

The question, then, is how to go about breaking it. Since nobody I know has ever done it, this is speculation; but not entirely untrained speculation. As I see it (feel it), the reversionary translator must begin by opening or sensitizing him- or herself to a dialogical conception of the translation: think of yourself in dialogue with the SL writer, especially if you are working on St. John of the Cross or even Carlos Castaneda, but really no matter who you are working on. You are not looking for "content," for something the writer says about reversion or restoration; you are looking for a mystic spark, a dialogized spark that Buber would call the I-You, a somatic moment that commutes the feeling of relation into an expanding, an opening, a swelling into cosmic oneness. Open yourself dialogically to the somatics of linguistic transfer, the felt intermingling of languages in your response to the SL text. There is a way of reducing that swirling somatic confusion to a tidy one-to-one (word-for-word or sense-for-sense) equivalence between SL and TL, but as a reversionary translator you are not looking for equivalence; you are looking for a particle of response that will not fit anywhere, something that sticks out, something that has a certain strikingness to it, an aliveness. Focus on the spark, the shard, the splinter, the ill-fitting piece that feels alive, and gradually incorporate it as dialogue, as the I-You, integrate it into your perception as a dialogized lens or eye (an ocular body), until the somatic transfer, SL to TL, is filtered through it.

Then think of yourself in dialogue with the TL reader, the You that you are addressing, and *say* You in Buber's sense. Say it in your translation. Speak the dialogized password primeval. It is not yours—alone. It is ours. It is a dialogical word that you carry from the dialogue you engaged in with the SL writer to your dialogue with the TL reader; and in your dialogized utterance you and the TL reader revert, together, to paradise. Maybe that reversion will be powerful enough, dialogical enough, to bring the whole world with it, once and for all.

Behind Buber's conception of the I-You explicitly and Bakhtin's conception of internal dialogism implicitly lies the understanding that dialogical connection does contain within in it the seed of mystical union: where two of you are gathered in my name (my spark), I will be present with you. In Buberian/Bakhtinian theory, anyway, true openness to dialogical relation would be an openness to all otherness, the entire universe, all people and all spirits and all rocks and trees and rivers and so on. God lives in the dialogue between two people. God *is* the dialogue between two people.

Theoretically, anybody could bring about the dialogical reversion: you would not need to be a poet or a translator to do it (assuming, for the time being, that it is possible). Anyone able to tap into dialogical relation in a powerful and empowering way could do it, in any dialogue. A barber in dialogue with his or her client. A politician in dialogue with the audience at a political rally. Anyone. A poet would do it in dialogue with the reader(s) of his or her poems. A translator in this sense would not be specially or uniquely qualified to bring about the redemptive reversion; a translator would be special or unique only in his or her ability to bring it about through a translation, in dialogue with a TL reader at least and possibly also with an SL writer. The translator's uniqueness would include his or her ability to work with two languages, which might invoke the spirit of Babel (the power to overcome the disunity of language imposed there)—but that would not necessarily give the translator any unusual power to achieve the reversion.

Well, I am not sure that I believe in any of this. I have personal experience of some of the things I write about here, but not of this. Still, it is one persistent if indifferently articulated conception of the translator's task, and I think worth taking seriously—at least seriously enough to explore its possibilities, its potential for real ethical transformation. Maybe you know better; if so, I hope my text harbors at least a spark of what you want to say, and that it will help you say it so as to make others feel it too.

Subversion

Subversion, you may recall, was my substitution for Augustine's eversion, which has no meaning at all in everyday English. Eversion is overturning, subversion would be underturning; what I take both (or either) to mean in terms of the translator's dialogue with the TL receptor is an undermining or overthrowing of some fundamental assumption or expectation that the receptor brings to the translation, or to translations in general.

What sort of expectations? The expectant mentality that the subversive translator seeks to subvert is most obvious in connection with much-translated texts like Homer and the Bible. Matthew Arnold's famous essay on translating Homer, for example, is an attempt to (get translators to) subvert English assumptions about the archaic nature of Homer's language: Homer's Greek is simple but dignified, and he should be rendered simply and with dignity in English. It is hard for us to appreciate the force of Arnold's argument today, partly because Arnold's own sample translations are so tediously inept, but more importantly because the Victorian view of classical antiquity was so successfully subverted by the moderns—Ezra Pound, especially. Our own expectations about Homer have been built up by modernist translations (mine by Richard Lattimore), so that Arnold's call for subversion can only sound quaint—and not nearly as interesting as the quaintness of Pope. The subversive translator translates—at least in part—to shock TL receptors out of complacent familiarity with the text, and shock has limited historical duration. Old subversions quickly become merely quaint.

An even better example than Homer is the Bible, whose status as sacred text has the ideosomatic effect of elevating complacent familiarity to the level of universal law. The King James Version is not just an outdated translation based on inadequate texts; it is *the* English translation of the Bible. It is the Bible God would have written had he been a Jacobean Englishman. By the time we get to Arnold and what T. E. Hulme called the "spilt religion" of late romantic culture worship, the King James Version is the only possible English translation of the Bible because it is so *poetic*. Every great poet in the English language beginning with Milton has tapped its poetic power. Its language is not archaic at all: it is a vital part of our contemporary vocabulary. If you must do a new version, just modernize the KJV slightly—give us the Revised Standard Version, the KJV in Matthew Arnold's English.

These attitudes remain strong today: there are many churches that will still only use the KJV or the RSV. The field is ripe, therefore, for subversion. One of the best-publicized recent subversions of the KJV/ RSV hegemony was Today's English Version in the mid-sixties—best-publicized because one of its prime movers was the prolific and persuasive Eugene Nida, translation consultant to the United Bible Societies and the foremost theorist of sense-for-sense and response-for-response Bible translation in our day. It may seem strange to call "subversive" a man who upholds the Bible translation principles of Jerome and Luther—but in fact he is as subversive as Jerome and Luther, who similarly burst upon a scene dominated by rigidly fixed expectations and smashed them. It is odd, in fact, that Bible translators like Jerome, Luther, and Nida, who really only keep repeating and applying the same tired old cliches about translating sense for sense rather than word for word—they were tired in Jerome's day, dating back at least to Cicero and probably farther—should over and over again find themselves playing a subversive role. The oddness can only be explained by the extreme conservatism of most Bible readers, for whom the only *correct* Bible translation was the one they read, or were read to out of, in their childhood, that nostalgic locus of all emotional stability and security.

There is, in fact, a kind of bodily reassurance in a translation like the KJV: "The Lord is my shepherd, I shall not want" may sound to Eugene Nida like a lack of desire for God (I shall not want a shepherd— see Nida and de Waard 9), but of course for the Christian who memorized those words in childhood the "normal" somatic response, the response to the words if heard on the street, is massively overridden by the somatics of security. When I say these words, my world feels stable and safe. Nothing can happen to me while I recite Psalm 23. I don't think about those other things, like not wanting *something*. I direct all my thinking to the repression of unsettling somatic responses. When the minister talks about coveting my neighbor's ass, I don't think of rumps, I think of donkeys; and when he talks about the cock crowing, I don't think of penises, I think of roosters. I had a moment of confusion once, perhaps, back when I was small, but someone explained it to me then, and ever since I have carefully maintained ideosomatic control over the giggles that such words might provoke in the irreverent listener. Through that controlled somatic response I keep archaic English alive.

Needless to say, this controlled bodily reassurance also tends to have an anesthetizing effect. The aliveness of a linguistic register maintained by repression typically bears an uncanny resemblance to deadness. Obviously, if the translator wants to *reach* his or her TL reader, to be the instrument not of anesthesis but of conversion, a vehicle not of spiritual death but of reawakening, rebirth, new life, there has to be something striking in the translation, something to catch the reader's attention— which is to say, something subversive. To convert, one must subvert. This is obviously true if one is speaking to nonbelievers; but it is also true if one is speaking to believers who are staid in their ways. Wake up, you Pharisees!

Well, if you are a priest, you cannot afford to say that to your congregation, but that is precisely the subversive subtext of new Bible translations: you have been lulled into a peaceful sleep by dead letter, so you *are* a Pharisee, locked into an atrophied legalistic system perpetuated by a set of words.

What you wake up to, of course, if you read Nida's TEV or the Living Bible or one of the other recent colloquial translations, is the buddy-buddy friendship with Jesus that I described at the end of Chapter 1: Jesus talks just like you and me. He is the boy next door, everybody's pal. Nida's translation principles are not subversive of Christianity, in other words; only of a certain Christian mind-set that is easy to characterize as Pharisaic and therefore un-Christian. It is a subversive move, a subversive gesture, designed to wake people up to a new, easy understanding of the Bible—to give them words that they can respond to normally, so that their whole attention is not directed at repressing improper somatic responses.

As Nida makes clear in all of his books, he directs the Bible Society's subversion (which he does not dare call by that name) at the average Bible reader, the ordinary reader, the fourth-grade reader for whom newspapers are written. Another kind of subversion can be found in the radically literal Bible translations of Buber and Rosenzweig or Chouraqui: here the idea is not to wake up a sleepy, churchgoing audience to easy understanding but to shock an intellectually and artistically sophisticated audience into taking another look at the Bible, a book they had long since "grown out of," given up as childish and boring. The ideal reader of these versions is a person who wants a challenge, a person who would not think it worthwhile if it came too easily. There has to be a higher threshold to understanding. There has to be more alterity, more alienness, there have to be more surprises—otherwise, it is just the same old thing again, ho hum.

As Derrida tells us in his deconstruction of Benjamin, for example, the Hebrew metonymy for language is not tongue but lip, and Chouraqui renders it literally (211/167). This means that every time the French reader happens on "lèvre" in the Chouraqui translation there is a cognitive dissonance, a moment of incomprehension that forces the mind to slow down and start again. At first the text's lip swells, grows enormous in size, protrudes or splits like a boxer's lip; it sticks out so egregiously that the reader does not know what to do with it: it is too powerfully *there,* its image takes up too much space, the lip-chewing reader is stalled by it, puzzled, feels his or her own lip begin to pulse too. Then, fighting to retain control, the intellect takes over, pushes the somatic response aside, says bossily, "Don't you remember, 'lip' means 'tongue,' language." But the imaging process is not so easily switched off: now we have two images, a tongue and a lip, the tongue hanging out over the swollen lip like a lounge lizard pawing his date, and *still* we cannot get to an abstraction like language! What are we talking about here? What could this sentence possibly mean?

Well, for a certain kind of reader (and I must admit that I am one), this is pretty exciting. I would much rather read a really strange, alien translation of the Bible like the Buber-Rosenzweig or the Chouraqui than the KJV/RSV *or* the TEV. Granted, you would not go into New Guinea and translate like that; this is a mode of translation almost exclusively for the jaded and sated intelligentsia, no matter what translators like Buber and Rosenzweig say.[12]

Another subversive approach to the Bible is that taken by Clarence Jordan in his "Cotton Patch" translations of parts of the New Testament.[13] Where the ecclesiastical mainstream of Bible translation seeks to subvert archaically lulled response through the use of modern, easily understood language, and the elitist intellectual tradition of romantic Bible translation seeks to subvert simplistically lulled response through the use of dense literalism, Jordan sought to subvert what we might call "fabulistically" lulled response through the use of modernized *settings*. In most Bible translations, the setting has become a kind of fairy-tale backdrop that allows the reader to distance the NT events in time and space: they all happened two thousand years ago, in Israel, but not in the Israel you can visit today—in a fairy-tale Israel, a place where Pharisees and Sadducees laid down the law, where Samaritans and lepers awakened people's horror, and so on. In that fairy-tale setting it is perfectly natural for somebody to walk on water or drive a legion of demons into some farmer's pigs; it is perfectly natural for people to be cured by touching the hem of someone's robe or to pay taxes with coins found in the bellies of fish. The nice thing about this fairy-tale setting is that it allows good, churchgoing, modern Christians never to be confronted with the discrepancies, say, between their own well-fed, sleek decency and the scruffiness of Jesus and his followers, or with the striking similarities between themselves and the Jews of Jesus' time.[14] There is no need even to recognize, much less worry about, least of all do anything about, your own bigotry, your fear-driven disgust for difference, your closed-mindedness, your unwillingness to change. The New Testament's revolutionary rhetoric can be idealized and distanced as a fairy tale about how nice it is to be a Christian—a fairy tale that becomes the Christian's strongest bulwark against revolution.

And so Jordan modernizes the NT settings, sets the story of Jesus in the American South of the 1960s; makes the Jews good Christians, the Sadducees theologians (Annas and Caiaphas are copresidents of the Southern Baptist Convention), the publicans Yankees (carpetbaggers, probably), the Samaritans (and generally the Gentiles) blacks, and Jesus' followers dirt farmers and hillbillies, the poor white trash that all good Southerners despise.

Clearly, this modernized setting has political designs on the reader. What Jordan calls the "God Movement," for example, a student movement centered around Jesus (it is usually rendered "the kingdom of God"), may have dogmatic roots in the writings of the early church, but it has historical roots in the here and now of Jordan's own writing, in the civil rights movement, in young people of the sixties fighting to bring about change in the South. This polemical linkage of attitudes and actions dogmatically valorized by ecclesiastical tradition with commies, peaceniks, niggers, and nigger-lovers—with "this ragtag and bobtail, who don't understand the Bible, [and who] are going to hell" (John 7:49, 124)—explicitly makes radical kids the good guys and their conservative elders the bad guys. Here, for example, is a briefing of freedom fighters from Matthew 10:

5 Τούτους τοὺς δώδεκα ἀπέστειλεν ὁ Ἰησοῦς παραγγείλας αὐτοῖς λέγων, Εἰς ὁδὸν ἐθνῶν μὴ ἀπέλθητε, καὶ εἰς πόλιν Σαμαριτῶν μὴ εἰσέλθητε· 6 πορεύεσθε δὲ μᾶλλον πρὸς τὰ πρόβατα τὰ ἀπολωλότα οἴκου Ἰσραήλ. 7 πορευόμενοι δὲ κηρύσσετε λέγοντες ὅτι Ἤγγικεν ἡ βασιλεία τῶν οὐρανῶν. 8 ἀσθενοῦντας θεραπεύετε, νεκροὺς ἐγείρετε, λεπροὺς καθαρίζετε, δαιμόνια ἐκβάλλετε· δωρεὰν ἐλάβετε, δωρεὰν δότε. 9 Μὴ κτήσησθε χρυσὸν μηδὲ ἄργυρον μηδὲ χαλκὸν εἰς τὰς ζώνας ὑμῶν, 10 μὴ πήραν εἰς ὁδὸν μηδὲ δύο χιτῶνας μηδὲ ὑποδήματα μηδὲ ῥάβδον· ἄξιος γὰρ ὁ ἐργάτης τῆς τροφῆς αὐτοῦ. 11 εἰς ἣν δ' ἂν πόλιν ἢ κώμην εἰσέλθητε, ἐξετάσατε τίς ἐν αὐτῇ ἄξιός ἐστιν· κἀκεῖ μείνατε ἕως ἂν ἐξέλθητε. 12 εἰσερχόμενοι δὲ εἰς τὴν οἰκίαν ἀσπάσασθε αὐτήν· 13 καὶ ἐὰν μὲν ᾖ ἡ οἰκία ἀξία, ἐλθάτω ἡ εἰρήνη ὑμῶν ἐπ' αὐτήν· ἐὰν δὲ μὴ ᾖ ἀξία, ἡ εἰρήνη ὑμῶν πρὸς ὑμᾶς ἐπιστραφήτω. 14 καὶ ὃς ἂν μὴ δέξηται ὑμᾶς μηδὲ ἀκούσῃ τοὺς λόγους ὑμῶν, ἐξερχόμενοι ἔξω τῆς οἰκίας ἢ τῆς πόλεως ἐκείνης ἐκτινάξατε τὸν κονιορτὸν [ἐκ] τῶν ποδῶν ὑμῶν. 15 ἀμὴν λέγω ὑμῖν, ἀνεκτότερον ἔσται γῇ Σοδόμων καὶ Γομόρρων ἐν ἡμέρᾳ κρίσεως ἢ τῇ πόλει ἐκείνῃ.

16 Ἰδοὺ ἐγὼ ἀποστέλλω ὑμᾶς ὡς πρόβατα ἐν μέσῳ λύκων· γίνεσθε οὖν φρόνιμοι ὡς οἱ ὄφεις καὶ ἀκέραιοι ὡς αἱ περιστεραί. 17 προσέχετε δὲ ἀπὸ τῶν ἀνθρώπων· παραδώσουσιν γὰρ ὑμᾶς εἰς συνέδρια, καὶ ἐν ταῖς

συναγωγαῖς αὐτῶν μαστιγώσουσιν ὑμᾶς· 18 καὶ ἐπὶ ἡγεμόνας δὲ καὶ βασιλεῖς ἀχθήσεσθε ἕνεκεν ἐμοῦ εἰς μαρτύριον αὐτοῖς καὶ τοῖς ἔθνεσιν. 19 ὅταν δὲ παραδῶσιν ὑμᾶς, μὴ μεριμνήσητε πῶς ἢ τί λαλήσητε· δοθήσεται γὰρ ὑμῖν ἐν ἐκείνῃ τῇ ὥρᾳ τί λαλήσητε· 20 οὐ γὰρ ὑμεῖς ἐστε οἱ λαλοῦντες ἀλλὰ τὸ πνεῦμα τοῦ πατρὸς ὑμῶν τὸ λαλοῦν ἐν ὑμῖν.

5. Jesus held a briefing session and sent out the twelve. "Don't go after the people of the world," he said, "and don't enter the black ghetto. Instead go to the deluded racists of the nation. As you travel, preach on the theme, 'THE GOD MOVEMENT IS HERE.' Heal the sick, arouse the sensitive, make the outcasts acceptable, expel devils. Don't bother to take any money or travelers' checks or pocket change, no suitcase, no extra suit, no dress shoes, no toilet kit; for the worker is worth his upkeep. When you go to a city or town, discover who in it is receptive, and stay there till you're ready to leave. Upon entering a house, introduce yourselves. If the home is receptive, let your goodwill and concern rest upon it. If it is not, then hold on to your goodwill and concern. When somebody won't be friendly with you or pay attention to your message, leave that home or city and wash your hands of the whole shebang. I'm telling you a fact, Paris and Berlin will have it easier on the Judgment Day than that city.

16. "Listen, I'm sending you out like sheep surrounded by a pack of wolves. So be as alert as snakes and as pure as doves. Really keep your eyes peeled for people, for they'll trump up charges against you and even attack you in church. You'll be brought before legislative committees and high courts so as to make your witness before them and before the world in general. But when they take you to court, don't get the heebie-jeebies over your defense, because what you shall say will be given to you on the spot. For it won't be you that's talking, but the Spirit of your Father talking through you." (38–39)

Jordan claims in his introduction to Paul's epistles that he has chosen Southern placenames at random, but it cannot be a random choice that renders Bethany, say, as Jonesboro.[15] The Cotton Patch New Testament is liberation theology, politically committed theology, and its political commitment is specifically to liberation in the race-torn South in the 1960s. This is Jordan's rendering of Isaiah from Matthew 12:

18 Ἰδοὺ ὁ παῖς μου ὃν ᾑρέτισα,
   ὁ ἀγαπητός μου εἰς ὃν εὐδόκησεν ἡ ψυχή μου·
θήσω τὸ πνεῦμά μου ἐπ' αὐτόν,
   καὶ κρίσιν τοῖς ἔθνεσιν ἀπαγγελεῖ.
19 οὐκ ἐρίσει οὐδὲ κραυγάσει,
   οὐδὲ ἀκούσει τις ἐν ταῖς πλατείαις τὴν φωνὴν
   αὐτοῦ.

20   κάλαμον συντετριμμένον οὐ κατεάξει
        καὶ λίνον τυφόμενον οὐ σβέσει,
        ἕως ἂν ἐκβάλῃ εἰς νῖκος τὴν κρίσιν.
21   καὶ τῷ ὀνόματι αὐτοῦ ἔθνη ἐλπιοῦσιν.

"See, my man whom I selected,
My loved one of whom I'm so proud.
I will put my breath in him,
And he will shout for justice for the black people.
He won't wrangle and hassle,
Nor make soapbox speeches.
He won't even wring a chicken's neck,
Or cut off a puppy's tail,
Until he has won out in the fight for justice.
His name will inspire hope in the black people." (45)

Unlike Nida's and Chouraqui's translations, which are verbally subversive but politically conservative, Jordan's translation is as politically subversive as the NT writings were at the time of their writing. Jordan takes a political stance and charges his translation with his vision of the world from that stance. This, it seems to me (and I realize that I am revealing my own sixties mentality by saying as much), is ethical translation at its finest.

Needless to say, politically subversive translation is by no means limited to new versions of sacred or classic texts. My colleague at the University of Tampere, Wolfgang Schonert, suggests another possibility: "Imagine that in September 1938 Hitler's blowhard interpreter Schmidt had refused to translate Hitler's bloodthirsty rant; that he had instead (Hitler had no foreign languages) told Chamberlain that . . ." (7, my translation). That Hitler was a madman bent on conquering the world. That Hitler should not be trusted. Suppose Schmidt had subverted Chamberlain's ritualized assumptions about international diplomacy, idealized good faith, trust, and so on—could he have shortened or even prevented World War II? Perhaps not. But it is clear that modern global civilization rests, however partially and uneasily, on the attempts of anonymous translators and interpreters to make sense of what to the monolingual speaker sounds like nonsense; and if an interpreter's "error" (inadvertent turning) may precipitate an international incident, is it not possible that an interpreter's subversive rendering (ethically motivated turning) might prevent one? This is not the sort of thing that you read about in the newspapers—subversive interpreters could be dangerous to vested political interests, and those interests would not want isolated incidents bruited about, for fear that they might spread—but my guess is that it happens more often than we think. Maybe it is time to break the ideosomatic taboos of instrumentalist translation theory and start dealing with difficult ethical issues of this sort.

In some sense, these two groups of examples offer contradictory images of translatorial subversion: where the Bible translators I discussed were concerned to make their SL text come alive in new ways, to bring about a new living piety, to foster an intensity of response (to *enliven* conversion), the political interpreter that Wolfgang Schonert imagined was concerned to deaden the appeal of an SL siren call, to plant suspicion, to foster a critical response (to *prevent* conversion). What both groups have in common is an ethically motivated desire to undermine a rigidified, ritualized SL receptor response that they see as harmful. A Bible reader who protects his or her carefully stabilized image of God's Word against all challenges from competing ideologies or confusing realities is dead not only to God but to life itself; a diplomat who places his or her trust in the SL text perpetrated by a madman is endangering not only his or her country but—especially now, in a nuclear age—the entire world. There is no one "normal" or normative way to subvert an SL response: the subversive translator responds ethically to specific situations (responsibly in specific translator-receptor dialogues).

Once again, this concern with the ethics of subversion leads the thoughtful translator back to a concern with the ethos of the subverter: who am I to force my ethical sense on the dialogue between the SL writer/speaker and the TL reader/listener? Who says my sense of responsibility is truer, more highly developed, than theirs? What *do* I believe, and why? What are the consequences of my beliefs for my own actions, and of my actions for other people? Do I have the personal strength to stand behind a subversive ethical decision that runs counter to the ritualized (and legalized) ethics of all Western translation? Can I withstand censure and blame if my subversive translation backfires, if I am hounded out of the profession, fined, jailed, whipped and scourged? What *is* my character, and what do I want it to be?

Tools are not expected to ask such questions, and they certainly are not allowed to put any answers they might find into practice. They have no character to worry about. Tools do the job they were manufactured to do. They have a prescribed role that defines their ethical responsibilities for them: conform yourself in word and deed to the intentions of the SL writer. Period. It is a simple life: just stay inside the role. People, real people, are more complicated than that.

Perversion

If subversive translation is the undermining of a reader's expectations or assumptions or trust in order to replace them with or redirect them to another and more beneficial set, perverse translation would be the warping of a reader's trust beyond replacement or redirection: a confusion, an unraveling of response, a stymieing of response, a putting the TL reader at sixes and sevens with regard to the SL text. The subversive translator is a revolutionary; the perverse translator is an anarchist or a nihilist.

But why, you ask, would anyone, any *decent* person, want to lend his or her hand to such a project? Wouldn't it be, well, *perverse?*

Obviously. Augustine uses *pervertere* in the *Confessions* to refer to the grotesque parody of Jesus' gratuitous sacrifice on the cross in his boyhood theft of some pears (a pear-verse pear-ody, in Kenneth Burke's telling pun); and perversion is, in normative, ideosomatically correct thinking, precisely parodic, a senseless turning inside-out-and-upside-down-and-every-which-way of all that our culture holds ideosomatically dear. We value meaning? Strive for meaninglessness. (Dada.) We value order? Sow chaos. (Aleatory art.) We value truth? Glory in useless lies. (Oscar Wilde, aestheticism.) We value morality? Cultivate amorality. (The Marquis de Sade.) We value the metaphysics of presence? Deconstruct. (Jacques Derrida.)

But why? The usual perverse answer is, Why not? but there are reasons skulking behind perversions like the famous ones that I just listed—"good" reasons, even, although no self-respecting pervert would willingly call them that. The reasons have a lot to do with the vicious circle or double bind of despair and fortitude that I outlined in Chapter 1 in connection with perfectionism: our culture has programmed us for frustration, programmed us to keep striving for what we can never have and blaming ourselves for not reaching it. Define your happiness in terms of what you can never have. Suppress any base pleasure in what you do have; wrack yourself with guilt over any vestiges of pleasure that survive your suppression. Modernist avant-gardistes tend to associate this kind of repressive thinking with the bourgeoisie (i.e., with their own families, with the normative straitjackets of their own upbringings), but it is much bigger, historically speaking, than the bourgeoisie; it is Western Christianity, Christianity in the Platonic mold cast by Augustine and the medieval church. Ethically motivated perversion seeks to break out of that vicious circle by turning it inside out, turning fortitude against itself in a parodic play with de-

spair: Smash the mold! To hell with repressive perfectionism! To hell
with everything!

Perhaps the most persuasive perverse ethics of translation has been
offered in our time by Jacques Derrida, in passing remarks until very
recently, such as the famous one in *Positions*,[16] but most strikingly since
then in the brilliant deconstruction of Benjamin's "Task of the Translator," "Des Tours de Babel," collected and translated by Joseph Graham
in *Difference in Translation*. Benjamin, as we saw before, tends toward a
mystical poetics of reversion (he denies the ethics of reversion, denies
the TL reader's claim on the translator's loyalty, in a turning away from
or *aversion* toward the reader—see next section) that purports to escape
the cautious bourgeois perfectionism of philological correctness but, as
Derrida shows, only exacerbates it. As elsewhere, Derrida's deconstructive project in "Des Tours de Babel" is to free us from the perfectionist
metaphysics of presence by making us excruciatingly conscious of its
operation in Benjamin's text, by laying bare Benjamin's pathetic attempts to wrap himself in the warm cloak of romantic hope; but, as
Derrida himself ruefully recognizes, even insists, all that he succeeds in
doing is tangling us ever tighter in its folds. (The turns of Babel are
never productive turns, never either tropes or versions, but mere turns
of the screw.) Here, for example, to show how Derrida works to pervert
Benjamin's reversionary poetic, is a passage that Derrida quotes from
Maurice de Gandillac's French version of Benjamin, with Joseph Graham's English version of Gandillac:

Den [vorbestimmten, versagten Versöhnungs- und Erfüllungsbereich der
Sprachen] erreicht es [das Original] nicht mit Stumpf und Stiel, aber in ihm
steht dasjenige, was an einer Übersetzung mehr ist als Mitteilung. Genauer läßt
sich dieser wesenhafte Kern als dasjenige bestimmten, was an ihr selbst nicht
wiederum übersetzbar ist. Mag man nämlich an Mitteilung aus ihr entnehmen,
soviel man kann, und dies übersetzen, so bleibt dennoch dasjenige unberührbar
zurück, worauf die Arbeit des wahren Übersetzers sich richtete. Es ist nicht
übertragbar wie das Dichterwort des Originals, weil das Verhältnis des Gehalts
zur Sprache völlig verschieden ist in Original und Übersetzung. Bilden nämlich
diese im ersten eine gewisse Einheit wie Frucht und Schale, so umgibt die
Sprache der Übersetzung ihren Gehalt wie ein Königsmantel in weiten Falten.
Denn sie bedeutet eine höhere Sprache als sie ist und bleibt dadurch ihrem
eigenen Gehalt gegenüber unangemessen, gewaltig und fremd. (162; my insertions)

Ce royaume il [l'original en traduction] ne l'atteint jamais complètement, mais
c'est là que se trouve ce qui fait que traduire est plus que communiquer. Plus
précisément on peut définir ce noyau essentiel comme ce qui, dans la traduc-

tion, n'est pas à nouveau traduisible. Car, autant qu'on en puisse extraire du communicable pour le traduire, il reste toujours cet intouchable vers quoi s'oriente le travail du vrai traducteur. Il n'est pas transmissible comme l'est la parole créatrice de l'original ["übertragbar wie das Dichterwort des Originals"], car le rapport de la teneur au langage est tout à fait différent dans l'original et dans la traduction. Dans l'original, teneur et langage forment une unité déterminée, comme celle du fruit et de l'enveloppe . . . le langage de la traduction enveloppe sa teneur comme un manteau royal aux larges plis. Car il est le signifiant d'un langage supérieur à lui-même et reste ainsi, par rapport à sa propre teneur, inadéquat, forcé, étranger. (236–37, reconstructed from Derrida's two citations of Gandillac's translation; Derrida's insertions)[17]

The kingdom it [the original] never fully attains, but it is there that is found what makes translating more than communicating. More precisely one can define this essential core as that which, in the translation, is not translatable again. For, as much as one may extract of the communicable in order to translate it, there always remains this untouchable towards which is oriented the work of the true translator. It is not transmissible, as is the creative word of the original ["übertragbar wie das Dichterwort des Originals"], for the relation of this tenor to the language is entirely different in the original and in the translation. In the original, tenor and language form a determinate unity, like that of the fruit and the skin[, while] the language of the translation envelops its tenor like a royal cape with large folds. For it is the signifier of a language superior to itself and so remains, in relation to its own tenor, inadequate, forced, foreign. (193–94, reconstructed from Graham's translation of Derrida's two citations of Gandillac's translation; Graham's insertions)

This is a rich passage, especially when Benjamin's German is flanked by a French translation and an English translation-of-a-translation, which latter Benjamin insists throughout is impossible (the original core can only be translated once, and even then never perfectly, never "tangibly"; no matter how many TL husbands she buries, the original text remains a virgin, retains a pure transcendental spiritual virginity). It would be fruitful (or maybe skinful) to explore the different cores that these three verbal skins generate: the echoes of Frege in Benjamin's *bedeuten*, for example, become echoes of Saussure in Gandillac's *signifiant*, not to mention his *langage/parole* distinction (only *la langue* is missing), and while those are lost in Graham's English, echoes of I. A. Richards spring up in the English "tenor," for which Harry Zohn has merely "content" (75). Each skinny word bears forth a thick (dichterisch) intellectual tradition.[18]

But I must restrain myself, or I will never get to Derrida's perversion of all this. Benjamin makes the standard dualistic move of pushing difference into an excluded category, maintaining the unity of Gehalt and

Sprache in the original by confining disunity to the translation. Derrida perverts the reader's trust in this move (which is, after all, one of the main instituting moves of Western metaphysics) by infecting the privileged category with the excluded difference, playing first with the separability of fruit and skin and the position of the core in relation to that "unity," then busying his tongue around the image of the royal cape, quilting and embroidering it, as he says the translator does as tailor of the cape-as-translation:

Mais on en infère que ce qui compte, c'est ce qui se passe sous le manteau, à savoir le corps du roi, ne dites pas tout de suite le phallus, autour duquel une traduction affaire sa langue, fait des plis, moule des formes, coud des ourlets, pique et brode. Mais toujours amplement flottante à quelque distance de la teneur. (238)

But one infers that what counts is what comes to pass under the cape, to wit, the body of the king, do not immediately say the phallus, around which a translation busies its tongue, makes pleats, molds forms, sews hems, quilts, and embroiders. But always amply floating at some distance from the tenor. (Graham's translation, 194)

Did I say that the translator was the tailor? For Derrida it is the translation itself, of course, the translation that embroiders itself, following Heidegger's principle that language speaks us, but speaks us specifically (in Derrida's perversion of Heidegger's language mysticism) in a falling away from purity that makes the unity of tenor and language that Benjamin and Heidegger both yearn after impossible. The language (the Saussurean *langue* that was missing in Gandillac) that speaks us here becomes a tongue (not to mention lips) in the throes of fellatio: no heterosex, no assault on the SL hymen; translation as royal fellator, not even the translator, translation itself down on its knees amidst the wide folds of the royal cape. Pleasure, sexual pleasure, you would think, but no: "toujours amplement flottante à quelque distance de la teneur," fellatio by mail, by a forcibly inadequate mail, in which the envelope is forever separated from the letter or message or content, tongue from language *and* lip *and* phallus, translation from original *and* meaning *and* translator—you name it.

This is Derrida: drive wedges between all oppositions, or rather find the wedges that the perfectionist metaphysics of presence always leaves lying around but would rather forget about. Find them and put them aggressively, obsessively on display: haul up that wide royal cape and expose the grotesque sucking and slurping that you hear going on down there. Show not the pleasure that is being had but the pathetic distance between mouth and phallus, between the wrinkly royal penis (aging real body) and the stiff scepter (ideal symbol of royal power), between the translation and the original. It goes without saying that that is part of the ideosomatics of perfectionist translation theory, and also between the original itself and "originality," between the source-language text and the text of the source of all language, the gaps not only between the translation and the romantic paradise it is supposedly helping to bring about but between the original and the original paradise to which we are trying to revert, gaps everywhere, connection (let alone unity) nowhere. As Derrida perverts the perfectionist project of mainstream Western translation theory, defined for him first by the Biblical myth of Babel and then intensified for him by Walter Benjamin, not only is translation doomed to failure; its inevitable failure contaminates the original too, finally all signification, all semiosis, all meaning.

Plus ou moins fidèlement j'ai pris quelque liberté avec la teneur de l'original, autant qu'avec sa langue, et encore avec l'original qu'est aussi pour moi, maintenant, la traduction de Maurice de Gandillac. J'ai ajouté un manteau à l'autre, ca flotte encore plus, mais n'est-ce pas la destination de toute traduction? Si du moins une traduction se destinait à arriver. (238)

More or less faithfully I have taken some liberty with the tenor of the original, as much as with its tongue, and again with the original that is also for me, now, the translation by Maurice de Gandillac. I have added another cape, floating even more, but is that not the final destination of all translation? At least if a translation is destined to arrive. (Graham's translation, 195)

Is that the final destination of translation? Derrida coyly makes it a rhetorical question, falling back on the metaphysics of perfectionist presence (perfection as final destination), then undermines that metaphysics by questioning whether translations have their arrival at perfection built into them in the form of "destiny." Deconstruction becomes a mere perverse playing with degree: "Plus ou moins fidèlement," "ca flotte encore plus," "si du moins." Nothing to do but try to eat away at the absolutism of metaphysics, relativize it, differentiate its unity, pull it apart at the seams, peel and core it, squish the fruit and let it rot, and point it out gleefully when the flies converge on the remnants.

All this is Derrida's perverse theoretical project, and while (as he constantly insists) his deconstruction of Benjamin is a translation-as-perverse-reading, a translation that takes liberties with the original, adding other capes that float more freely than Benjamin's, and a translation that, more importantly, fiddles with the fidelity of Benjamin's reader, maybe I should close this section by taking a turn at perverse translation myself, perverse translation per se, perverse translation proper, to invoke two anomalies that Derrida would love to dismantle. Derrida wants to pervert the reader of Benjamin, to spoil once and for all any hope that he or she might have placed in the poetics of reversion; I want to pervert the reader of Derrida, to spoil once and for all any hope that he or she (you) might have placed in the deconstruction of reversion, any reassurance you may have found in the reduction of perfectionism to perversion, in order not to return you to the metaphysics of presence, which Derrida guards as he tears down, but to turn you forward to the next turning, the next translation as turning:

Le roi a bien un corps (et ce n'est pas ici le texte original mais ce qui constitue la teneur du texte traduit) mais ce corps est seulement promis, annoncé et dissimulé par la traduction. L'habit sied mais ne serre pas assez strictement la personne royale. Ce n'est pas une faiblesse, la meilleure traduction ressemble à ce manteau royale. Elle reste séparée du corps auquel cependant elle se conjoint, l'éspousant sans l'éspouser. (237)

The king does have a body, of course, a real one, no body-as-original-text (the metaphor that Benjamin plays with) but that which turns the original toward the translation, that which grounds the translation somatically. This body is not the cape or clothing that Benjamin and Derrida both make so much of, body as separable from soul, clothing as separable from body, words as separable from meaning, signifiers as separable from signifieds, that whole dualistic tradition going back to Augustine and Paul and Aristotle and Plato. Those clothes are only the dissembling promise or announcement of a translation that will never be, the habitual (ideosomatically programmed) promise of perfect new clothes that will never materialize and wouldn't fit even if they did. In perfectionist theories this perfect imperfection is no weakness; it's the resolute denial of weakness, the determined assertion of ideal strength, potency, the king's erection under the wide folds of his cape, ideal fortitude: the perfectionist translation resembles the king's or emperor's new cape, which is visible only to idealists who believe strongly enough in its reality to make it seem real, but none of this is the real body I'm talking about, I'm talking about the body as somatic response.

But wait: am I talking about all this? Wasn't I translating Derrida? Wasn't Derrida speaking there, however perversely? Well, that is one of the ideosomatically controlled fictions of translation that perverse renderings undermine: that the translator is only the vehicle through which the SL writer speaks, the cape through which the SL writer wields his (or her, but in idealized theories always his, only the idealized SL writer has the hidden phallus) power, or alternatively, that the translator *gives* the SL writer TL voice, that the translator speaks *for* the SL writer. One of them has to be the speaker, the owner of the TL words, after all, and if the translator is not introverted enough to let the SL writer speak through him or her, then the TL words become the translator's and cease (we believe) to be a translation. Perverse translation is a way of dismantling these assumptions, exposing the fraudulence of the king's new clothes but leaving the viewer in doubt as to whether the nakedness thus exposed belongs to the king or to the child who cries out, "But he's not wearing anything!"

And this doubt, this radical confusion of speakers and words and sources and targets and generally of everything that mainstream translation theory has tried to keep clear and distinct, is the source of perverse translation's ethical power. It is a techne for not letting the TL reader rest easy in habitual (ideosomatically programmed) assumptions. You *should* be confused, the perverse translator insists. Clarity and certainty are bad faith, signs of a cowardly retreat from the overwhelming complexity of the world, a surrender either to the ideosomatically programmed norms and conventions of your parents and their and your whole culture or to some easy oppositional ideology (dogmatic Marxism in capitalist countries, say, dogmatic Christianity in atheist countries) that answers all the questions for you while allowing you the pleasant feeling of being different, of standing out from the crowd (the big crowd: you still have your own little crowd to confirm your faith, to give you a sense of belonging). The perverse translator wants to smash all that, to smash all easy answers, to learn—and teach his or her TL reader—to live with difficulty.

My bias is probably showing here; I am struggling to make this seem like an ethical concern that is as worthwhile as any of the others that I have considered, and I sense that I am failing. In "absolute" terms (putting aside my own biases, I mean), it may well be worthwhile: perverse translation is an attempt to convert the TL reader to a state of confusion, a muddledness that is the only appropriate response to a hopelessly muddled and meaningless world. If you believe that the world is hopelessly muddled and meaningless, perversion is not perverse; it is the only honest way to live. Since I do not believe that, I tend to think of perverse translation (or Derridean deconstruction, or Dada, or whatever) as more like a first step: confusing a listener or a reader who (you think) is too locked into a rigid, habitual conception of the world is a way of pushing that person out onto the road to understanding, a way of shaking him or her awake, smashing the easy habit of ideosomatic knowing. That the perverse translator has only nightmarish confusions to offer instead of the waking ideosomatic prison that he or she smashes is a drawback, for me: a sign that perversion can only take you up to the second seal, not past it; cannot help you break out of the metaphysics of presence. (I prefer subversion to perversion.)

But for the perverse translator that nightmare *is* life: that is all there is, and teaching the TL reader to live in that world, to get along in it, to face up to it without flinching or simplifying or pretending that it is not there, even to accept and affirm it in all its horror, is (as my echoes of Camus begin to suggest) a profoundly serious ethical concern.

Aversion

Aversion is etymologically a turning away; I take the ethics of translational aversion to be the translator's turning away from the TL reader. This seems at first blush to put me in a difficult spot: I am concerned in this chapter with the translator's various approaches to the TL reader, and here, close to the close of my chapter and my book, I find myself confronted with translators and theorists who want to have nothing to do with the TL reader. It is like stepping onto a rotten stair: you think that it is solid, but it gives way at your touch, and you fall into the blackness below.

Fortunately, things are not quite that desperate. Aversionary translation may be a refusal to have anything to do with the TL reader, but that refusal can be taken as an actual nothing-doing only if we go along with the aversionary translator's or theorist's idealization of this act. I *want* to have nothing to do with the TL reader; I turn away from my readers; therefore I do not act on them, I do nothing to them, they are irrelevant to my concerns. Please have the decency not to mention them. But rhetorically, pragmatically, dramatistically, politically, of course, *not* doing something to somebody is itself a kind of doing; ignoring someone, turning away, does something to that person. As the word "aversion" suggests in contemporary English, turning away from the TL reader (averting your eyes from him or her) is an expression of dislike or disgust or contempt. Everyday synonyms for aversionary translation might be turning a cold shoulder on or snubbing an interlocutor: both are actions in their own right.

In the history of translation theory, in fact, aversion is probably the most conspicuous alternative or opponent to the mainstream theory of introverted conversion: there are traces of it in Boethius, in Dante, in von Humboldt, and in most romantics and postromantics since, whenever translators or theorists despair of the very possibility of translation. Mainstream theorists ensure translatability by reducing meaning to a pale abstraction completely divorced from sensation, sound, and situation, so that what is transferred is not the entire text but a "message," a "content," a Platonic representation, an idea about the way things are, which the translator believes that the TL reader needs. Since the TL reader needs it, every precaution must be taken to ensure that he or she gets it, by translating it into the TL, first of all, because the reader is ignorant of the SL, and by putting it as clearly and as comprehensibly as possible, because the reader is assumed to be linguistically, artistically, and intellectually backward—the fourth-grader that Nida and newspapers address.

Aversionary translators and theorists, on the other hand, tend to be elitists who address a small group of their peers, sophisticated readers who already know the SL text well and do not need the translation for understanding; in fact, they do not need it at all. In any case, if they were to look to the translation for a key to what the original "says" or "means," they would be out of luck, since they understand meaning in a much richer sense than do their reductive mainstream colleagues: meaning is total somatic and situational response, not some pale abstraction that can be transferred from one verbal expression to another without diminishment. If translation is the transfer of meaning from one language to another intact, without change, without diminishment, then translation is impossible; meaning is always bound to sound, sensation, situation. (These are the people who shun metonymical translation and gravitate toward metaphor.) Remember: *if* translation is that, then it is impossible—but translation is only impossible if it is defined as perfect and total transfer. Fortunately, as we have seen, it need not be defined that way. Even if "perfect" translation (ideosomatic translation) is impossible, it is always possible to make a successful turning: to turn from readers and the communication of information to the fleshing out of a private mythology, say, the rendering in the TL of the translator's own personal response to the SL, regardless of whether this sort of intensely private turning is comprehensible to anyone else.[19]

The more traditional and obvious aversionary turning, of course, involves what George Steiner calls trust, in which "the translator does not aim to appropriate and bring home. He seeks to remain 'inside' the source" (310). The translator turns the TL toward the SL, works to bring the TL into literal conformity with the SL text. One thus sheds new light both on the old familiar TL and on a text one thought one knew through and through. Turning the SL text into an SL'd TL complicates one's already highly complex understanding of the original and of both languages. One could easily do without the translation; one does not *need* it. But complexity is a joy in its own right, and one will, occasionally, turn to a radically literal translation with this sort of complication in mind. Buber and Rosenzweig's German Bible, Chouraqui's French. Hölderlin's *Oedipus* and *Antigone*. Browning's *Agamemnon*. Nabokov's *Eugene Onegin*.[20]

I said just above that Benjamin couches his denial of the ethics of reversion in "Aufgabe des Übersetzers" in terms of aversion for, or turning away from, the TL reader; and in fact Benjamin's contempt for the average reader that people like Jerome, Luther, and Nida hold so dear is one of the most articulate statements of translational aversion that I have seen:

Nirgends erweist sich einem Kunstwerk oder einer Kunstform gegenüber die Rücksicht auf den Aufnehmenden für deren Erkenntnis fruchtbar. Nicht genug, daß jede Beziehung auf ein bestimmtes Publikum oder dessen Repräsentanten vom Wege abführt, ist sogar der Begriff eines "idealen" Aufnehmenden in allen kunsttheoretischen Erörterungen vom Übel, weil diese lediglich gehalten sind, Dasein und Wesen des Menschen überhaupt vorauszusetzen. So setzt auch die Kunst selbst dessen leibliches und geistiges Wesen voraus—seine Aufmerksamkeit aber in keinem ihrer Werke. Denn kein Gedicht gilt dem Leser, kein Bild dem Beschauer, keine Symphonie der Hörerschaft.

Gilt eine Übersetzung den Lesern, die das Original nicht verstehen? Das scheint hinreichend den Rangunterschied im Bereiche der Kunst zwischen beiden zu erklären. Überdies scheint es der einzig mögliche Grund, "Dasselbe" wiederholt zu sagen. Was "sagt" denn eine Dichtung? Was teilt sie mit? Sehr wenig dem, der sie versteht. Ihr Wesentliches ist nicht Mitteilung, nicht Aussage. Dennoch könnte diejenige Übersetzung, welche vermitteln will, nichts vermitteln als die Mitteilung—also Unwesentlichen. Das ist denn auch ein Erkennungszeichen der schlechten Übersetzungen. (156)

In the appreciation of a work of art or an art form, consideration of the receptor never proves fruitful. Not only is any reference to a certain public or its representatives misleading, but even the concept of an "ideal" receptor is detrimental in the theoretical consideration of art, since all it posits is the existence and nature of man as such. Art, in the same way, posits man's physical and spiritual existence, but in none of its works is it concerned with his response. No poem is intended for the reader, no picture for the beholder, no symphony for the listener.

Is a translation meant for readers who do not understand the original? This would seem to explain adequately the discrepancy in their respective status in the realm of art. Moreover, it seems to be the only conceivable reason for repeating "the same thing" over and over again. For what does a literary work "say"? What does it communicate? It "tells" very little to those who understand

it. Its essential quality is not communicating—not "constating." Any translation that wants to transmit, therefore, will transmit only communication—i.e., what is inessential. This is the hallmark of bad translations. (Zohn's translation, slightly modified, 69)

Art is never concerned with response—a polemical claim that only makes sense once we have situated Benjamin in the romantic tradition. Art is concerned with redemption (reversion).[21] Writing a poem for readers to talk about at cocktail parties, painting a picture for viewers to look at or hang on their walls, composing a symphony for the bourgeoisie to dress up and listen to at the local symphony hall, doing a translation so someone ignorant of the original will know what the original text "says"—all this is pandering to tastes, to fashion, to habit. What one should be doing instead is directing one's attention upward, onward, toward transcendent truth, led, one surmises, by Goethe's Eternal Feminine. It is retrograde to pay any attention at all to a "public," a readership, other people in any form, and all the more so when one does it for crass utilitarian or mercantile purposes—to be understood, to be appreciated, to make money. Most retrograde of all is to seek understanding, appreciation, and compensation by pandering to one's audience's ignorance—as Benjamin says that the translator does in translating for someone who cannot read the original. That is like a pimp procuring one of his girls for a john who is such a loser that he has to pay for sex (my simile, not Benjamin's). If immersion in the original text is an orgasmic merging in love that transports both lovers to originary paradise, reading a translation just to see what the original says is a dry, mechanical humping in a sleazy hotel room: "repeating 'the same thing' over and over again." Mindless, affectless repetition.[22]

This is Nabokov too, except that where Benjamin the soft-spoken bourgeois tempers his elitist aversion for the hoi polloi with indirection,[23] Nabokov the exiled aristocrat metes out punishments for infractions with the steely, sardonic eye of a prince:

Three grades of evil can be discerned in the queer world of verbal transmigration. The first, and lesser one, comprises obvious errors due to ignorance or misguided knowledge. This is mere human frailty and thus excusable. The next step to Hell is taken by the translator who intentionally skips words or passages that he does not bother to understand or that might seem obscure or obscene to vaguely imagined readers; he accepts the blank look that his dictionary gives him without any qualms; or subjects scholarship to primness: he is as ready to know less than the author as he is to think he knows better. The third, and worst, degree of turpitude is reached when a masterpiece is planished and patted into such a shape, vilely beautified in such a fashion as to conform to the notions and prejudices of a given public. This is a crime, to be punished by the stocks as plagiarists were in the shoebuckle days. ("Art of Translation" 160)

The rhetoric here is God's, SL writer of the Bible and friend to all vigilant watchdogs of SL writers' rights: the first sin is excused as "mere human frailty"; the second takes the translator one more "step to Hell"; the third, punishable (on earth, in this life) by the stocks, seems to be doubly dastardly because it (a) panders to *people*, to a human public, and (b) panders to the "notions and prejudices of a *given* public," people in a specific time and place, historically situated people. Obviously, from the divine viewpoint to which Nabokov (like all authorities in our Augustinian civilization) aspires, a concern for the ephemeralities of mere historical places and moments, passing ticks of the human clock, mere specks of soil on the face of the human earth, is beneath all contempt. God is concerned only with the universal.

There is a price to pay for this radical idealism, of course. By turning his back on historically situated readers, Nabokov also turns his back on himself as a historically situated reader of Pushkin. This is the cost of idealizing translational aversion: your aversion for your reader inexorably expands into aversion for *yourself* as a reader. You always came too late; the author whose masterpiece you read will always have gone before you, lived a life that you were born too late to partake in, had experiences that you will never know, meant more than you will ever understand. The finest scholarship in the world will not close up that gap. Still, as your perfectionist programming bids, you must keep trying, and keep alternating between hating yourself for failing and others for not trying, and whining and wheedling for forgiveness for yourself and others who are just too mortal to live up to such high standards:

On Translating Eugene Onegin

I

What is translation? On a platter
A poet's pale and glaring head,
A parrot's screech, a monkey's chatter,
And profanation of the dead.
The parasites you were so hard on
Are pardoned if I have your pardon,
O, Pushkin, for my stratagem:
I traveled down your secret stem,
And reached the root, and fed upon it;

Then, in a language newly learned,
I grew another stalk and turned
Your stanza, patterned on a sonnet,
Into my honest roadside prose—
All thorn, but cousin to your rose.

2

Reflected words can only shiver
Like elongated lights that twist
In the black mirror of a river
Between the city and the mist.
Elusive Pushkin! Persevering,
I still pick up Tatiana's earring,
Still travel with your sullen rake.
I find another man's mistake,
I analyze alliterations
That grace your feasts and haunt the great
Fourth stanza of your Canto Eight.
This is my task—a poet's patience
And scholiastic passion blent:
Dove-droppings on your monument.

Pushkin the monument, the dead stone of worshipped statuary; Nabokov the reverent dove that can only defecate on what he venerates. This is all that the self-respecting translator can do: "My *EO* falls short of the ideal crib. It is still not close enough and ugly enough. In future editions I plan to defowlerize it still more drastically. I think I shall turn it entirely into utilitarian prose, with a still bumpier brand of English, rebarbative barricades of square brackets and tattered banners of reprobate words, in order to eliminate the last vestiges of bourgeois poesy and concession to rhythm" ("Reply" 301–2). Shitting on the statue is the highest form of worship, for Nabokov; the "canned music of rhymed versions" ("Reply" 301) is aimed at a debased reader, not at Pushkin, and is thus no worship at all. "Promoters and producers of what Anthony Burgess calls 'arty translations,' carefully rhymed, pleasantly modulated versions containing, say, eighteen per cent of sense plus thirty-two of nonsense and fifty of neutral padding, are I think more prudent than they realize" ("Reply" 301)—prudent, because they pander to the average reader as democratic god, *boobus Americanus,* Mencken called him, that fearful peasant who don't know nothing about art but knows what he likes and won't put up with being made to feel stupid by elitists. "Only suspicion and bloodhounds await the gaunt, graceless literalist groping around in despair for the obscure word that would satisfy impassioned fidelity" ("Reply" 301), which is the translator's only true god. And a most exacting and vengeful god he is, too—a god who turns the translator's humblest, most reverent libations into birdshit before they even hit the monumental page.

In its idealized form, aversionary translation inherits and intensifies the medieval hierarchy of loathing according to which readers of translations are more loathsome than translators, translators-as-readers more loathsome than original writers. (Theoretically, at least, at the highest level original writers are more loathsome than God—but like the apostles and later the church fathers, they are so elevated by their reverent successors as to be virtually or emotionally coterminous with God.) The direction of idealization runs away from readers, toward writers; away from receivers, toward givers. This is, of course, an idealization of what Harold Bloom calls election-love, the love of the passive, empty receiver for the all-active, all-containing giver, and as such it stands at the very core of our ideosomatic programming, our enforced humility, our ritualized toolhood. Idealized to its extreme, in other words, aversion becomes introversion.

Unlike mainstream introversionists, however, who require conformity to the SL writer's communicative (conversionary) design on the TL reader, idealizing aversionists require conformity to the SL text as holy writ. As we saw a moment ago, this traditionally means loyalty to the "letter" of the SL text, the word order and word feel of the original, rather than to an abstract "sense"; and it also means a loyalty to the SL (the vehicle of the immortal author) rather than to the TL (vehicle of the lowly reader). In his *Agamemnon*, George Steiner tells us, Browning "set out to be 'literal at every cost save that of absolute violence to our language.' Browning purposed 'the very turn of each phrase' to be 'in as Greek a fashion as English will bear'" (312): make English suffer (to extremity, but not past it—don't do absolute violence, don't let English die) in order that ancient Greek might still live in comfort. The aversionary translator turns away from both the TL reader and the TL itself, in a radical loyalty to the SL.

In some sense, of course, as I suggested in the "Metonymy" section of Chapter 3, this is the most natural of all responses to a text, much more natural than the mainstream injunction to help the SL writer communicate to the TL reader.[24] You do not actually *turn away* from TL readers; you just never turn toward them. After all, you *are* a reader; why should you bend your response to make room for another reader, someone you have never even met? As you read the SL text, you are filled with its glory; you are made over in the image of its verbal splendor. It seems to you as if none of this could ever be said better; there is a calm rightness to it all that makes the thought of changing anything, even the word order, seem like sacrilege, like painting a mustache on the Mona Lisa.[25] The naturalness of this loyalty to the SL text to the exclusion of the TL reader and at the expense of the TL itself is evident in translation classes, where the communicative principles enjoined upon translators by mainstream theories must be *learned,* drilled, practiced. Translation students fall inadvertently and very naturally into word-for-word translation—which is why sense-for-sense theorists feel that they have to keep warning against it, why, despite the paucity and historical insignificance of aversionist theory, they feel that word-for-word translation is always a potent threat.[26] All that aversionist theorists have had to do, then, is to tap into that natural tendency and escalate it to elitist principle: *refuse* to communicate! Keep your back to the reader, your full attention on the text!

This is the second stage of translation as Goethe first imagined it, the alienation of the familiar. In Benjamin, however, who advocates aversion, not (like Nabokov) out of sheer blind elitist culture worship, but in the service of ultimate romantic reversion, things are more complicated: the familiar that is alienated is at once the TL, which is radically distorted by literal assimilation to a foreign model, and the SL, once familiar to the translator and his or her elitist cronies but now transformed through the literal TL rendering into something both less and more:

Es ist daher, vor allem im Zeitalter ihrer Entstehung, das höchste Lob einer Übersetzung nicht, sich wie ein Original ihrer Sprache zu lesen. Vielmehr ist eben das die Bedeutung der Treue, welche durch Wörtlichkeit verbürgt wird, daß die große Sehnsucht nach Sprachergänzung aus dem Werke spreche. Die wahre Übersetzung ist durchscheinend, sie verdeckt nicht das Original, steht ihm nicht im Licht, sondern läßt die reine Sprache, wie verstärkt durch ihr eigenes Medium, nur um so voller aufs Original fallen. Das vermag vor allem Wörtlichkeit in der Übertragung der Syntax, und gerade sie erweist das Wort, nicht den Satz als das Urelement des Übersetzers. Denn der Satz ist die Mauer vor der Sprache des Originals, Wörtlichkeit die Arkade. (166)

Therefore it is not the highest praise of a translation, particularly in the age of its origin, to say that it reads as if it had originally been written in that language. Rather, the significance of fidelity as ensured by literalness is that the work reflects the great longing for linguistic complementation. A real translation is transparent; it does not cover the original, does not block its light, but allows the pure language, as though reinforced by its own medium, to shine upon the original all the more fully. This may be achieved, above all, by a literal rendering of the syntax which proves words rather than sentences to be the primary element of the translator. For if the sentence is the wall before the language of the original, literalness is the arcade. (Zohn's translation, 79)

But let me turn this discussion away from the instrumentalizing idealizations that aversionists (like most translation theorists) prefer, back to the ethical, pragmatic, dramatistic terms that have been my guides throughout. (While summarizing aversionist theories on their own terms, I cannot keep the polemics out of my tone; I have to caricature, satirize, ridicule. Turning back to dramatistic ethics allows me to find some good even in translatorial aversion.) As I said at the beginning of this section, aversion too does something to the reader. It says, "If you are to be taken seriously you must be like me: put by your lamentable ignorance, read the original, not bad translations, stop looking for some facile *message* to take home with you, immerse yourself in the original, bathe in its light, and then, only then, if you want to look at (or, more difficult, create) a brilliant literal translation of it, treat the translation as a kind of weird glow cast on the original, a distorting but somehow also enhancing glow, a commingling of SL phrasing with TL materials that pushes language toward revelation." Readers are not excluded from this club; only run-of-the-mill readers. The aversionist subtext is: you are welcome to join if you can meet our standards. But good luck; not even we can meet them.

In a democratic age—at least an age that idealizes democracy in principle and enforces it in outward behavior—this kind of elitist hazing meets immediate resistance. Who do you think you are, calling me a hick for wanting English translations of the classics? Where do you get off telling me what art is or isn't, what it does or doesn't do? What makes you think you know all about it? Good questions—ones that I am enough of a peasant to want to ask Benjamin and Nabokov and Browning and the others myself. I suppose I am no more inclined toward aversionist translation theory than I am toward Derrida's perversionism. Still: the translation theory that I call aversion is not frivolous and is not to be dismissed lightly. It too is motivated by serious ethical concerns—specifically, a concern to avert cultural facility, cultural superficiality, cultural aridity, the kind of Big-Mac-medium-Coke-small-fries culture that I personally feel comfortable with but that does, certainly, have a powerful, flattening effect on our civilization. Apart from their concern with saving the world, elitist romantics like Benjamin truly believe that we would all live richer lives if we let the classics of world literature guide us, *in* their original language, to undying truths.

And however at home I feel with the fast-food and fast-translation culture that these theorists attack—however inclined I am to call fancy theories and terminologies bullshit and to cultivate a slangy critical fast-talk (which I have, here and there, throughout this book)—I am also drawn to the elitists and their vision of striving toward union with truth, as witness my obvious preference throughout this book for the romantics and their successors. My argument with romantic aversion-ists is not, I suppose, with their scorn for certain superficial readers, but with their blind rebellion against ideosomatic programming, their iconoclastic stance that makes them idealize a laudable ethical desire to *educate* the reader (complicate and deepen his or her response) as a haughty elitist refusal to *pander* to the reader. The ideosomatics of in-strumentalism teach us the superiority of the SL writer to the TL reader; and where Augustinians and Lutherans (to invoke my first two Chapter 2 paradigms in the history of translation theory) require the translator to identify with the SL writer in order to help the institution control the reader, the romantics simply require the translator to iden-tify with the SL writer in order to help the artistic genius strive toward truth. They do not want to participate in the institution's "education" of the reader to ideal submission, so they will have nothing at all to do with the reader. It is much better, I think, to educate the reader to awareness, to inculcate in the reader the translator's (and writer's?) own aversion for ideosomatic control, and bring the reader step by step into a dedication to truth.

Here, then, would be my own aversionist program, were I inclined to set one up: through an ostensible expression of aversion for the "reader," the translator pragmatically teaches the real reader aversion for an ideosomatically programmed reader *role*, a submissive role that en-courages interpretation along institutionally approved lines. "Critical" reading as it is taught in the schools is suspicion toward anything that does not conform to an ideosomatically controlled "inner sense" of rightness. We have been taught to feel comfortable with safe transla-tions, communicative translations, informative translations, transla-tions with some easily grasped "message" that is, in fact, easy to grasp precisely because it is perfectly aligned with our ideosomatic program-ming. We have been taught to feel ill at ease with "difficult" transla-tions, or with any text that challenges the safe and solid assumptions with which we have been programmed. We have been robotized, pro-grammed in the ideal submissive image of the "good citizen." And yes, as long as we remain content with that robot role, we are going to fit in, be one of the crowd, and that will yield a certain emotional security;

but it will also deaden us to life, flatten experience, routinize it. If we want to learn to live, we must learn to hate the role that we have been trained to perform. We must learn to see that it is not us, that it is an addition to us, a kind of emotional brain implant, and that we can fight it; we can be rid of it.

Once this aversion for the ideosomatically controlled reader role has been conveyed, then the diverse range of radical turnings that I have been exploring takes on an enormous transformative power—the power to defamiliarize the familiar landscape of ideosomatic world views, to articulate the buried inarticulate glimmerings of another reality (an unprogrammed experience, an unpredestined truth), and to move the reader toward accessing that reality. Ethically conceived, every one of the vertical turnings that I am exploring here—conversion, advertising, reversion, subversion, perversion, aversion, and diversion— is a way of teaching the reader to avert introversion. Each is a way of encouraging the reader to fight the ideosomatics of repression (turn everything inward, don't let it out). It teaches the reader to fight repressive introversion, not through a sheer iconoclastic extroversion or blind expression of what was repressed, but rather through a careful, considered progress down through the three seals: discovering the significance of somatic response (*this* is what I feel! *this* is how I experience reality), discovering the commonality of somatic response (other people feel this way too! I'm not alone!), and discovering the malleability of somatic response (I'm not trapped in that prison, there is an escape!). Translation as liberation.

Diversion

And then, diversion: not only Big-Mac-medium-Coke-small-fries, but movies and television, pop music, video games, and Monday Night Football. Is this how I want to end this book? Have I come all this way, from the lofty seriousness of Protestant/capitalist conversion and romantic reversion, through the increasingly more sinister seriousness of subversion, perversion, and aversion, translation as liberation, translation as revolution—to the empty fun of *diversion?* Is this it? Is this all there is left?

Or shall we speak of diversion in the other sense, sheer mindless diversity, liberal pluralism, sure, do your own thing, I'm a tolerant sort of guy, I don't mind how you translate, I don't care what you do to me, heck, do whatever you like! Is that the culmination of this book's argument?

Let me start back at the ideosomatic sense of diversity that I assume most of my readers come to this book with, the idealized "diversity" of mainstream translation theory. (I want to teach you aversion for that restricted diversity in order to liberate you to the true diversity of the field.) When I claimed, in the last chapter, in my section on metonymy, that the whole range of translation models considered possible and even marginally admissible ("discussable") by mainstream theorists was contained in that one section, I was exaggerating—but not much. There is an ideosomatically controlled tendency among many translation theorists first to cordon off a tight little garden and ignore everything else, *fiercely* ignore it, banish it to the darkest realm of forgottenness, throw it in a ditch, stamp TABOO all over it and mail it to the Dead Letter Office; and then to lavish immense love and care on the "diversity" of the cozy little garden left inside the perimeter, the many different kinds of sense-for-sense translation, technical translation, scholarly translation, literary translation, conference interpretation, and so on, and all of them sense-for-sense, all of them conceived as attempts to convey in the TL a sense equivalent to that of the SL, to convey the SL information to the TL reader in such a way that he or she does not notice that it is a translation, since it reads (or sounds) just like an original text! Analyze in ever greater detail the techniques by which equivalence can (and must) be achieved—sense-for-sense equivalence, of course; that goes without saying. For what else is there? What else is worth talking about? Read all of Eugene Nida's books; contemplate the diversity that he finds in the tiny garden that he tends. Read Wilss, Jumpelt, Reiss, House, de Beaugrande, Newmark, Catford, and Vinay and Darbelnet, and marvel at the diversity that they find in the same garden—or rather, the many gardens they claim to cultivate on that same ground. Not only does everyone have his or her own terms for word-for-word and sense-for-sense translation (formal and dynamic equivalence, semantic and communicative translation, overt and covert translation, and so on, which *they* will tell you are all significantly different from the terms devised by their predecessors), but there are whole *schools* planting diverse-looking plants on that ground, Saussureans and Firthians, comparative linguists and text-linguists, logicians and pedagogues, terminologists and cyberneticists, et cetera, et cetera. And I only spend a lousy ten pages discussing all that? I only mention most of those names and those schools now, in the eleventh hour of my book? What kind of pervert am I?

I think, in fact, that it was no coincidence that the present interest in translation sprang up roughly concurrently with the development of high-speed computers—and, for that matter, that the "science" of language on which most contemporary translation theory more or less uneasily rests was developed at the turn of the century, roughly concurrently with the shift from early craft capitalism to late mass-production capitalism. In his brilliant book on the political economy of music, *Noise,* Jacques Attali calls these two phases "representation," the era of once-off production, and "repetition," the era of the infinitely repeatable mold:

Ces moules sont partout: programmes d'ordinateurs, plans de voitures, formules de médicaments, dessins d'appartements, etc. Cette mutation change également l'usage des choses. Le travail représentatif avait un usage qui disparaît dans la série. L'objet le remplace mais perd son sens personnalisé, différencié. Paradoxe: l'objet échange son utilité contre son accessibilité. Un travail important doit alors être consacré à lui donner un sens, à produire une demande pour cette répétition.

La répétition se met en place par le dépassement, dans la production en série, de toutes les productions marchandes encore aujourd'hui inscrites dans le réseau de la représentation. Forme ultime, elle signifie la répétition de toute la consommation individuelle ou collective, le remplacement du restaurant par les repas cuisinés, de la couture par le prêt-à-porter, de la maison individuelle établie sur des plans personnels par des productions en série sur des plans types, de l'homme politique par le bureaucrate anonyme, du travail spécialisé par la tâche standardisée, du spectacle par son enregistrement.

Dans ce réseau, la production n'est plus le lieu essentiel de la création ni de la compétition. Celle-ci a lieu en amont lors de la création des moules, ou en aval dans la production de demande. Car l'existence de séries ne suppose pas nécessairement leur uniformité ni le grand nombre d'exemplaires. Comme dans la musique, la répétition exige au contraire de tenter de maintenir la diversité, et de produire un sens à une demande. (255–56)

Molds of this kind [in our day] are everywhere: computer programs, car designs, medicine formulas, apartment floor plans, etc. The same mutation also transforms the usage of things. The usage to which representative labor was put disappears with mass production. The object replaces it, but loses its personalized, differentiated meaning. A paradox: the object's utility is exchanged for accessibility. Considerable labor must then be expended to give it a meaning, to produce a demand for its repetition.

Repetition is established through the supplanting, by mass production, of every present-day mode of commodity production still inscribed within the network of representation. This is in fact the central project now under way in translation theory, the construction of a reliable machine-translation program to replace the unreliable "representative" human translator. Mass production, a final form, signifies the repetition of all consumption, individual or collective, the replacement of the restaurant by precooked meals, of custom-made clothes by ready-wear, of the individual house built from personal designs by tract houses based on stereotyped designs, of the politician by the anonymous bureaucrat, of skilled labor by standardized tasks (roles and robots), of the spectacle by recordings of it, of the translator by the computer program.

In this network, production is no longer the essential site of creation or competition. Competition takes place earlier, in the creation of the molds—who will develop the first reliable MT program?—or later, in the production of demand—who will sell their idea to the mass audience, who will have the advertisers on their side? For the existence of molded objects does not necessarily imply their uniformity or a great number of copies. On the contrary, as in music, repetition requires an attempt to maintain diversity, to produce a meaning for demands. (Massumi's translation, slightly modified, 128–29)

To *maintain* diversity, despite the increased pressure to "repeat 'the same thing' over and over again," as Benjamin put it. You cannot sell your brand of aspirin if it is exactly like everybody else's, and aspirin is pretty much the same everywhere, so you have to package yours differently, maintain diversity through the manipulation of signs. As this process becomes more and more sophisticated, Attali says that

La marchandise aussi peut disparaître: comme la monnaie est devenue substitut comptable du dialogue, la marchandise peut être remplacée par le signe pur, forme commode du stockage: pochette de disques, ticket de voyage, de restaurant, de vêtement, de vie, de mort, passeport, billet d'amour. (258)

The commodity could also disappear: just as money has become the accountable substitute for dialogue, the commodity could be replaced by the pure sign, a convenient way to stockpile—record jackets; tickets for travel, restaurants, clothes, life, death; passports; love certificates; translation theories. (Massumi's translation, slightly modified, 130)

Already translators feel alienated from proliferating theory, which seems to have so little to do with what they actually do—it seems mainly to be about distinguishing one theory from another, not about the actual work of translation. And what about the future? What if machine translation becomes as successful and popular a repetitive mode as, say, pop music? Then it may be enough to own the MT program or that polyglot tourist toy, The Voice—you would not even have to use it.[27] You would have bought it, paid for it, contributed to the flow of money in a repetitive economy; that would be enough. Or maybe you could buy a blank diskette with the title of a popular MT program emblazoned on it in bright colors—if you weren't going to use it, wouldn't that be enough too? Wouldn't that still provide for diversity in a repetitive society?

Obviously, we are not that far yet, and may never get that far: translations are harder to mold than cars or houses. Machine translation at present is more like Muzak than tract houses: a denatured version of some human translator's or group of translators' specific response(s) to a specific text or text type (the computerization of weather report translations, for example)—not an infinitely proliferable pattern. The formulation of a reliably repeatable pattern remains the ultimate goal of mainstream translation theory (the repetitive culmination of Augustine's authoritarian prescriptivism), but from where I sit, anyway, it does not appear likely that that goal will ever be reached.[28]

For the time being, therefore, translatorial diversion remains more representative than repetitive: once-off humorous translations, translations just for fun, translations of amusing or diverting texts that have no real information content and do not really need to be translated at all, but that provide enjoyment for the translator and the TL reader alike. C. H. Carruther's Latin rendition of "Jabberwocky," say (or any of the other diverting translations that Theodore Savory discusses in his sixteenth chapter):

'Twas brillig, and the slithy toves
    Did gyre and gimble in the wabe.
All mimsy were the borogoves,
    And the mome raths outgrabe.

Est brilgum: tovi slimici
    In vabo tererotitant;
Brogovi sunt macresculi,
    Momi rasti strugitant. (in Savory, 177)

Translation *can* be fun. Diversion takes on a new note of ethical seriousness when it becomes tinged with subversion, with fun at the expense of some text or expectation regarding a text, or when it drifts into diversity as divergency, errancy, the kind of wandering past accepted boundaries that breaks new paths. Parodic translations are diversionary in this sense, translations that begin by playing with the SL reader's ritualized expectations about a canonic (much-translated) text for fun, for the sheer hell of it, and end by shaping a distinctive translatorial voice. Translation as caricature: the secret glee that the business translator feels when he or she diverts the boss's "Yours sincerely" into "Yours earnestly," perhaps, or "Yours in Christ" is *empowering*. It charges the translator's private vision of the boss's earnestness (say) with the power of textual confirmation, and thus may have the effect of propelling him or her into psychopolitical (ethical) growth. I am *not* confined by ideosomatic introversion! I *can* grow beyond the inner bounds set for my being! Jacques Attali finds a prophetic message of change in this direction in contemporary rock music:

Déjà, dans la répétition même, certains détournements annoncent sa remise en cause radicale: la circulation proliférante d'enregistrements pirates, la multiplication des stations de radio interdites, le détournement des signes monétaires en mode de communication de messages politiques interdits, annoncent l'invention d'une subversion radicale, un mode nouveau de structuration sociale, une communication non réservée à une élite de parole. (261–62)

Already, from within repetition, certain deviations announce a radical challenge to it: the proliferating circulation of pirated recordings, the multiplication of illegal radio stations, the diverted usage of monetary signs as a mode of communicating forbidden political messages—all of these things herald the invention of a radical subversion, a new mode of social structuring, communication that is not restricted to the elite of discourse. (Massumi's translation, 131–32)

And this growth begins to open up a field of diversion as truly liberating and ultimately liberated cosmic play, diversion as a pathway to and enactment of escape from the three seals, a discovering of one's own voice, a tapping of experiential resources that have been blocked off by uniformative ideology. This involves the discovery of what is *really* fun, not just what is touted as fun on Coke commercials. This Attali calls "composition," the phase that he prophesies will follow repetition:

Les codes détruit, même celui de l'échange dans la répétition, aucune communication n'est plus possible entre les hommes. Alors nous sommes tous condamnés au silence, sauf à créer avec soi-même son propre rapport au monde et à tenter d'associer d'autres hommes au sens ainsi créé. Composer, c'est cela. C'est faire sans autre finalité que l'acte de faire, sans tenter de recréer artificiellement les codes anciens pour y réinsérer la communication. C'est inventer des codes nouveaux, le message en même temps que la langue. C'est jouer pour jouir soi-même, ce qui seul peut créer les conditions d'une communication nouvelle. Un tel concept vient naturellement à l'esprit à propos de la musique. Mais il va bien au-delà, et renvoie à cette émergence de l'acte libre, dépassement de soi, jouissance de l'être au lieu de l'avoir. (267–68)

There is no communication possible between people any longer, now that the codes have been destroyed, including even the code of exchange in repetition. We are all condemned to silence—unless we create our own relation with the world and try to tie other people into the meaning we thus create. That is what composing is. Doing solely for the sake of doing, without trying artificially to re-create the old codes in order to reinsert communication into them. Playing (or translating, or playing at translating) for one's own pleasure, which alone can create the conditions for new communication. A concept such as this seems natural in the context of music, less natural in the context of translation. But it reaches far beyond the ideosomatics of "naturalness"; it relates to the emergence of the free act, self-transcendence, pleasure in being instead of having. (Massumi's translation, slightly modified, 134)

Turning from the SL toward the TL, not knowing what lies ahead, not plotting the turn in advance, not coding it, not pinning it down. Not molding and then building a bridge and refusing to take a step until the bridge is safety-tested. Setting out more or less blind, turning toward a TL that does not exist until you turn to it, on a road that your feet form under them with every step you take. Being willing to backtrack, start again, set off in a new direction—and to return to the first path if the second one does not turn out to your liking. Being willing to risk getting lost, to risk incoherence, to risk failure. Being willing to please yourself, without being sure that your reader will be pleased. Being willing to please yourself *and* your reader, even though you know the critics will probably hate it and the normative theorists condemn it. *Doing* it—for fun. For fun as self-therapy, as a growing up into the playfulness of childhood, a growing out of rigidly solemnized adulthood, self-protective maturity.

Produire dans la composition c'est d'abord jouir de la production de différences. Ce concept nouveau est bien pressenti par les musiciens. Ainsi, improviser se dit dans la langue du jass *"to freak* (dévier) *freely."* *Freak,* c'est aussi le monstre, le marginal. Improviser, composer, renvoie donc à l'idée de différences assumées, de corps retrouvé et épanoui. "Quelque chose qui me laisse trouver entre les mesures mon propre rythme" (Stokhausen). Elle relie la musique avec le geste; dont elle est le support naturel; elle branche la musique sur les bruits de la vie et du corps à qui elle donne une énergie pour son mouvement. Elle est alors risquée, inquiète, remise en cause instable, fête anarchique et menaçante, comme un Carnaval dont la fin serait incertaine. (284)

In composition, to produce is first of all to take pleasure in the production of differences. Musicians foresaw this new concept. For example, in the language of jazz, to improvise is "to freak freely." A freak is also a monster, a marginal. To improvise, to compose, is thus related to the idea of the assumption of differences, of the rediscovery and blossoming of the body. "Something that lets me find my own rhythm between the measures" (Stockhausen). Composition ties music to gesture, whose natural support it is; it plugs music into the noises of life and the body, whose movement it fuels. It is thus laden with risk, disquieting, an unstable challenging, an anarchic and ominous festival, like a Carnival with an unpredictable outcome. (Massumi's translation, 142)

Conversation

La composition n'interdit pas la communication. Elle en change les règles. Elle en fait une création collective et non plus l'échange de messages codés. Se parler, c'est créer un code ou se brancher sur un code en cours d'élaboration par l'autre.

Travail sur des sons, sans grammaire, sans pensée directrice, prétexte à la fête, à la rencontre des pensées, la composition cesse d'être un faisceau central, inévitable monologue, pour devenir potentialité réelle de relation. Elle énonce que les rythmes et les sons sont le mode suprême de relation entre les corps, une fois rompus les écrans du symbolique, de l'usage et de l'échange. La composition dégage ainsi la musique comme rapport au corps et transcendance.

. . . Traversée directement par les désirs et les pulsions, la musique n'a même jamais eu d'autre sujet que le corps, à qui elle offre un trajet complet dans le plaisir, avec un début et une fin. Une grande oeuvre musicale est toujours un modèle de rapports amoureux, un modèle de relation avec l'autre, d'exaltation et d'apaisement éternellement recommençable, une figure exceptionnelle de relation sexuelle représentée ou répétée. . . .

Mais il ne s'agit plus, dans la composition, de marquer le corps comme dans la représentation, ou de le produire comme dans la répétition, mais de jouir par lui. C'est à cela que tend la relation. Echange entre les corps par leur oeuvre et non par des objets. Là est la subversion la plus fondamentale ici esquissée: ne plus stocker des richesses, les dépasser, jouer pour l'autre et par l'autre, échanger les bruits des corps, entendre les bruits des autres en échange des siens et créer, en commun, le code où s'exprimera la communication. (285–86)

Composition does not prohibit communication. It changes the rules. It makes it a collective creation, rather than an exchange of coded messages. To express oneself is to create a code, or to plug into a code in the process of being created by the other.

Composition—a labor on sounds, without a grammar, without a directing thought, a pretext for festival, in search of thoughts—is no longer a central network, an unavoidable monologue, becoming instead a real potential for relationship. It gives voice to the fact that rhythms and sounds are the supreme mode of relation between bodies once the screens of the symbolic, usage and exchange, are shattered. In composition, therefore, translation emerges as a relation to the body and as transcendence.

. . . Translation, directly transected by desires and drives, has always had but one subtext—the body, which it offers a complete journey through pleasure, with a beginning and an end. A great translation is always a model of amorous relations, a model of relations with the other, of eternally recommenceable exaltation and appeasement, an exceptional figure of represented or repeated sexual relations. . . .

But in composition, it is no longer, as in representation, a question of marking the body; nor is it a question of producing it, as in repetition. It is a question of taking pleasure in it. That is what relationship tends toward. An exchange between bodies—through work, not through objects. This constitutes the most fundamental subversion we have outlined: to stockpile wealth no longer, to transcend it, to play for the other and by the other, to exchange the noises of bodies, to hear the noises of others in exchange for one's own, to create, in common—Attali and Massumi and I all working together on this one—the code within which communication will take place. (Massumi's translation, slightly modified, 143)

Translation is conversation, of course, and always has been. Dialogue. Relationship. And, in more subtle ways than music, it has always been embodied conversation, somatic relating: as I read, then type and alter, Massumi's translation of Attali, I feel Attali's and Massumi's collective presence, their participation in the dialogue I am having first with them, now with you. When I edit Massumi's translation, when I do to it what I always do to my own writing before I am satisfied with it, improve it, make it say what I want to say better, by substituting "translation" for "music," say, or inserting my own comments, it feels right to me, because I am typing the words, and when I type a word my fingers cannot tell whether it is mine or somebody else's. (My mind has been taught to make that distinction, and my mind is just a specially trained part of my body.) They are my words—and Massumi's—and Attali's. They belong to all of us; and why not? They are dialogized words, as Bakhtin says all words are dialogized. They are in the public domain—or should be, and perhaps some day, as a result of compositions like this one, will be.

The paradigm shift that I call for in this book is more, then, than a new theory of translation. It is a new way of understanding the use of words in human society, the use of words to bring people together, to make them feel good or bad or frightened or empowered, the use of words to bring about change in bodies, bodies politic and psychologic, ideo- and idiosomatic. Translation as conversation, as embodied dialogue, as a taking of conversational turns in two or more languages, is not only immeasurably more richly diverse than we have thought, it is also more somatically powerful, more able to bring about real change. Conversation as conversion—but conversion not to an institutionally controlled doctrine, not to a way of seeing that excludes and includes, not to a set of taboos, but to an open-ended compositional relatedness, a nomadic sensitivity to idiosomatic needs inside and out, in your own body and the body of the person you are conversing with, in me and in you, a playful awareness of who we are that is potentially redemptive.

Translation is already, and can be more and more, as we free ourselves from the reptile claws of idealized mainstream theory, a humanizing process. Through its insistence that we immerse ourselves in cross-cultural conversation, in the *felt* connections between people who speak different languages, translation can restore us to ourselves—to our full humanity. It is the translator's turn not only to be alive, be a real person with deeply felt experiences, but to become more alive, feel experience more deeply, and to channel feeling and experiencing through translating, into both better translations and richer, more playful living.

Conclusion

The argument of this book could be reduced to a few fairly simple and truistic propositions:

1. Translators choose the TL words and phrases that *feel* right.
2. Translators feel their way to the "right" TL words and phrases in a complex two-way dialogue with the writer of the SL text and the reader of the TL text.
3. Translators turn from the SL text toward a TL rephrasing in a wide variety of ways.
4. Translators act upon their TL readers and can direct their influence over the TL reader in a wide variety of ways.

Put like this, these claims seem so commonsensical and obvious, so inevitable, even, that it would be difficult to quarrel with them—difficult, indeed, to imagine what possible position I could be arguing against. And certainly, if my case were that these propositions should simply be added to the current propositional content of mainstream translation theory—that mainstream theory be supplemented with them, expanded to contain them—I doubt that many readers would protest.

In fact, of course, my theoretical revisionism is much more radical. The negative burden of my argument would include at least the following as well:

5. Equivalence between texts is not the final goal of all translation. Equivalence is an interpretive fiction that helps the translator work toward the true goal of translation, a working TL text—and is only one of many such fictions.
6. The striving for sense-for-sense equivalence is based on a reductive and ideologically contingent interpretation of the SL text and is really only fruitful with certain relatively uninteresting texts: unprepossessing technical and scholarly texts, for example. Most SL texts are more demanding and will require more innovative turnings.

7. Normative rules intended to govern the translator's choice of TL words and phrases are not only irrelevant to the practice of translation, they are, insofar as they alienate translators from their best intuitions about texts, actively pernicious.

8. Translators are never, and should never be forced to be (or to think of themselves as), neutral, impersonal transferring devices. Translators' personal experiences—emotions, motivations, attitudes, associations—are not only allowable in the formation of a working TL text, they are indispensable.

This second group of propositions underlines the oppositional thrust of my argument. I want to incorporate from mainstream theories certain practical approaches to the act of translation—attempting to render in the TL the sense of individual words, sentences, or whole texts (metonymy), for example, and attempting to persuade the TL reader to the SL writer's position (conversion)—but only as specific methods of limited scope in a broad and complex field; and I want to displace the *entire* rhetoric and ideology of mainstream translation theory, which, as I claim, is medieval and ecclesiastical in origin, authoritarian in intent, and denaturing and mystificatory in effect.

The specific taxonomic formulations that I offer are expendable. The six tropes (metonymy, synecdoche, metaphor, irony, hyperbole, and metalepsis) and the seven versions (conversion, reversion, subversion, perversion, aversion, diversion, and conversation), my specific conceptions of those tropes and versions, and even my conception of translation in tropological and ethical terms—these are more illustrations of the paradigm shift that I want to effect than its substance, which is, I suppose, best summed up in the eight propositions listed above. I certainly do not expect my tropes and versions to be adopted wholesale, and I would be horrified if they were adopted wholesale in an authoritarian, normative manner, imposed on translators as "correct" or "acceptable" approaches to translation. They are, I repeat, entirely expendable, and it is my sincere hope that they *will* be expended in translatological debate: literally used up, subsumed into future (and finer) formulations of the translator's hermeneutical tools and stances.

Notes

Introduction

1. For fairly typical recent applications of this procedural translation theory to the problems of machine translation, see the essays collected by Veronica Lawson in *Practical Experience of Machine Translation,* especially W. John Hutchins's article "The Evolution of Machine Translation Systems."

2. I must admit that, having grown up in Los Angeles, I image "turning" as something you do mainly in a car. A car is a machine, of course, and since the Enlightenment the logical, analytical, rational, cognitive theories of translation as abstract equivalencing that I am trying to displace here have often been imaged mechanistically (the Newtonian universe). But a Californian doesn't think of a car as a machine, a static system that operates in certain predictable ways; a car is an extension of your body and of your personality, your embodied self. It is a way of getting from one place to another that also interacts with you, making you over in the image of someone who drives this particular car (the car makes the man) and being made over in the image of a car owned and driven by you. In this sense, the whole point of translation as turning is not to build a stable bridge but to *get* somewhere in an interactive way, to let the act of translation change you as you change the TL reader, to shape and be shaped by the SL text. I even considered letting this conception of turning show in the Table of Contents—calling this Introduction "Onramp" and the Conclusion "Offramp," say, and naming my chapters after LA freeways (Pomona, Santa Monica, San Diego, Santa Ana—a roundabout route from our house to Disneyland). I did not do it (I decided it would be like dotting my *i*'s with little hearts), but the idea that you turn onto a freeway, change freeways, change again, the whole time supposedly driving "freely" but in fact usually (in LA) creeping along bumper to bumper, then finally turn off the freeway, and you have gotten someplace, more slowly than you had hoped, and with more turns and detours than you had planned—that idea still appeals to me. I only wish I could liven up the bumper-to-bumper traffic you will experience reading this book by turning on the car stereo.

Chapter One: The Somatics of Translation

1. When I call Augustine's position linguistic doctrine, I do not mean that Augustinian doctrine (which, of course, after the Reformation was almost

never called that) has gone entirely unchallenged; I will be examining some persuasive challenges in a moment. I only mean that no challenge to Augustinian doctrine has been so successful as to supersede it. The strongest challenge to Augustine before our century was probably the romantic linguistics of Wilhelm von Humboldt; for a good discussion, see part 2 of V. N. Voloshinov's *Marxism and the Philosophy of Language.*

2. Saussure does not actually write, I should note, about the meaning of words—about semantics. He does not even write about the structure of sentences, syntax, although structuralist syntax is probably what Saussure's linguistics is best known for. He writes about oppositions between phonemes, a concern of his since his dissertation on the phonemic structure of Indo-European languages. In the classic example, neither /p/ nor /b/ has any significance of its own, but each takes on significatory power only in a differential system that opposes the two, in words like "pan" and "ban." Only in that differential system is it meaningful to distinguish, say, the voicelessness of /p/ and the voicing of /b/.

Structuralist semantics, which I read back into Saussure for the sake of argumentative symmetry, was developed later out of Saussure's work by linguists like Louis Hjelmslev and Roman Jakobson, and then further, in the heyday of Chomskyan TG-grammar, by Chomsky himself and followers of his like Jerrold Katz, under the rubric of componential analysis. The idea in componential analysis is that words like "man," "woman," "boy," "girl," "buck," "doe," "fawn," and so on, can be broken up into differential oppositions like ±HUMAN, ±MALE and ±ADULT, so that "man" would be +HUMAN +MALE +ADULT, while "girl" would be +HUMAN −MALE −ADULT. Presumably, since the positive term in each opposition invariably describes the researcher and the negative term his ideological other, a structuralist semanticist would have to notate "black working-class man," for example, as +HUMAN +MALE +ADULT −WHITE −BOURGEOIS, and "black middle-class woman" as +HUMAN −MALE +ADULT −WHITE +BOURGEOIS. The strategy is clear: reify ruling-class ideology as the transcendental (ideally stable, universal) system, and identify ideologically-controlled hierarchies with the mathematical signs of + and −. For uncritical discussions of semantic components, see, for example, Geoffrey Leech, *Semantics,* p. 96ff., and John Lyons, *Introduction to Theoretical Linguistics,* chapter 10, especially 10.5.

3. See Chomsky's *Syntactic Structures* and *Aspects of the Theory of Syntax.* Chomsky's notion of the transcendental "deep structures" that underlie the divergent "surface structures" of actual languages, and of the carefully defined operations or "transformations" by which we can move freely between the two, is unmistakably Augustinian, as is his preference for aprioristic reasoning about language over empirical observation of actual language use. For spirited attacks on Chomskyan linguistics along similar lines, see the books by Geoffrey Sampson and Ian Robinson listed in the Works Cited.

4. See, for example, Lacan's famous pronouncement that the unconscious is

structured like a language—specifically, like *la langue,* Saussure's differential system underlying speech. For a good discussion of Lacan's extensive reliance on Saussurean linguistics in his deconstructions of Freud, see Anthony Wilden's commentary on his translation of Lacan's *Speech and Language in Psychoanalysis,* 204–49.

5. For the classical observations, examples, and theoretical formulations of schizophrenogenesis, and the therapeutic treatment of schizophrenia, see Gregory Bateson's essays on schizophrenia in part 3 of *Steps to an Ecology of Mind.*

6. Talking with a brother of mine who never liked to read when he was younger, I discovered that he did not have this ability to "feel" the writer talking his or her words; the words were just words for him, abstract things, and therefore dead. When words are ungrounded in somatic response, reading is a tedious and meaningless task. Recent studies show that children—and adults, for that matter—with reading difficulties usually have trouble visualizing, and that visualization exercises help them to get over their reading problems. Considering the difficulty some people have in "reading" visual images, however, I would guess that the real difficulty that problem readers have is not the inability to visualize but the inability to *feel,* the inability to ground words in somatic response. Most likely, visualization is a shortcut to the body, to somatic response, which makes the words come alive. Images and words alike "make sense," "feel real," only when they reach down to the body.

7. This reading seems to me something of a parody of James's position, an unintentional one that may in fact be based on translation—or at least on the bringing to bear of a German feeling about "ein" to a reading of the English "a." Whether Wittgenstein read James in German *translation* or in German *somatics,* his stressing of *ein* in "Bist du sicher, daß es *ein* Wenn-Gefühl gibt; nicht vielleicht mehrere?" seems a little off-base, even as a response to James's famous sentence taken out of context—"We ought to say a feeling of *and,* a feeling of *if,* a feeling of *but,* and a feeling of *by,* quite as readily as we say a feeling of *blue* or a feeling of *cold*"—and seriously off-base as a response to James's entire chapter. The German *ein* does translate both "a" and "one," but somatically it leans toward "one," in the sense of "a single," and Anscombe reflects that in her translation of the above line as "Are you sure that there is a single if-feeling, and not perhaps several?" In the context of James's whole chapter, however— let alone the whole book, as well as his pragmatist philosophy—it seems clear that he himself would have leaned somatically toward a more indefinite and pluralistic "a," in the sense of "one of an infinite number of possibilities." The chapter is, after all, titled "The Stream of Thought," and James is at some pains to establish the radical mutability of that stream:

For an identical sensation to recur it would have to occur the second time *in an unmodified brain*. But as this, strictly speaking, is a physiological impossibility, so is an unmodified feeling an impossibility; for to every brain-modification, however small, must correspond a change of equal amount in the feeling which the brain subserves.

All this would be true if even sensations came to us pure and single and not combined into "things." Even then we should have to confess that, however we might in ordinary conversation speak of getting the same sensation again, we never in strict theoretic accuracy could do so; and that whatever was true of the river of life, of the river of elementary feeling, it would certainly be true to say, like Heraclitus, that we never descend twice into the same stream. (1: 232–33)

And, obviously, if each individual never has the same feeling twice, no two individuals are going to have exactly the same feeling even once: this is as radical a pluralism as Wittgenstein could desire.

On the other hand, James still does not make it clear how we ever communicate with each other. If each of us walks around with a radically different and mutable stream of subjectivity flowing through our heads, it seems unlikely that there could ever be sufficient commonality to make understanding possible. This is a criticism that Wittgenstein, himself steeped in the same liberal ideology as James, never raises.

8. For comprehensive discussions of Wittgenstein's critique of James's feeling-theory, see especially Garth Hallett's *Wittgenstein's Definition of Meaning as Use* (48–75) and the relevant passages in his *Companion to Wittgenstein's "Philosophical Investigations"* (e.g., 631–37). Hallett is clearly on Wittgenstein's "side" in the debate, and, while admitting that Wittgenstein does not reject the notion of word-feelings out of hand, gives the impression that the definition of meaning as use is "right" and somehow replaces or supersedes the definition of meaning as feeling—as, indeed, Wittgenstein himself seems to do, particularly in the passage I quoted above from p. 181. Elsewhere, however, Wittgenstein is quite open to an affective or somatic theory of language; see, for example, his discussion (§169–70) of the way feelings "guide" our reading of strings of letters that we "understand" (i.e., construct as meaningful language), as opposed to strings of unfamiliar symbols, which generate no feelings in us and therefore remain meaningless.

9. Here Wittgenstein's speech-act theory, sketchy as it is, is more advanced than Austin's, who insists on retaining a hierarchy between primary or ordinary or "serious" speech acts, which mean what they say, and secondary or literary or "parasitical" speech acts, which only pretend to mean what they say (104). Paul Grice offers a way out of this retrograde analytical strategy in "Logic and Conversation," but as I argue in "Metapragmatics and Its Discontents" (esp. 660–67), Grice too limits himself to constative or locutionary implicature, implied statements, ignoring the ways in which we pretend to *do* things with words. Parasitical speech acts are one of the focal issues in the famous Searle-Derrida debate as well: see Derrida, *Limited Inc,* and Searle, "Reiterating."

10. Note also, in this connection, the work done by philosophers of language like John Searle and Jerrold Katz to assimilate the radical contextualism of J. L. Austin's theory of speech acts back to (respectively) Saussurean and Chomskyan idealizations. "It might seem," Searle writes cautiously in *Speech Acts,* his 1969 transcendentalization of Austin's 1955 lectures and 1962 book, *How to Do Things with Words,* "that my approach is simply, in Saussurian terms, a

study of 'parole' rather than 'langue.' I am arguing, however, that an adequate study of speech acts is a study of *langue*" (17). In *Propositional Structure and Illocutionary Force*, Katz takes issue with Austin's rejection of the constative/performative distinction:

Austin mistakenly thought that cases like [these] were counterexamples simply because he restricted himself to talking about utterances and actions, to performance. . . . The competence-performance distinction provides us with the benefits of idealization. Like the use of idealization in the theory of gases and mechanics, we do not have to state laws in terms of real objects and events—in our cases, utterances and the speech acts they perform. Instead, we can state them in terms of their idealized objects and events such as sentence types, their meaning in the language, that is, their meaning in the null context, and context types. (184–85)

For an excellent discussion of Austin and his idealizing followers, see Shoshana Felman, *The Literary Speech Act*.

11. For another attempt to assimilate Wittgenstein's theory of meaning as use to Saussurean linguistics, this time undertaken by a Wittgensteinian philosopher, see Charles S. Hardwick, *Language Learning in Wittgenstein's Later Philosophy*, especially chapter 3.

12. In addition to Burke, my work with the Indian-born psychologist Akhter Ahsen has shaped my understanding of the somatics of language: Ahsen has shown how mental images are stored somatically, how somatic response is our surest sign of the meanings we have imposed on or derived from our images, and how imagery exercises can help us to reshape our somatic response and thus bring about real inward change—a cure, for example. See Ahsen's *Psycheye, Rhea Complex,* or *Trojan Horse*.

13. The infamous late sixties-early seventies feminist attacks on all men for their de facto participation in the ten-thousand-year history of patriarchy were motivated and guided, we could say, by the ideosomatic anxiety feminists felt when they said the word "daddy" or "father." The anxiety we men felt when women did that to us arose out of our ideosomatic responses to the word "mommy" or "mother."

14. As Eugene Nida has reminded me in private correspondence, my model fails to take into consideration the biological coding involved in this programming. I plead guilty as charged and ask the jury only to bear in mind these mitigating circumstances: (a) I am not a biologist, I am a language theorist, and so "naturally" tend to thematize speech in terms of my own competence; (b) as far as I know, biologists (neurologists, etc.) are still pretty much in the dark about how speech is biologically coded; and (c) also as far as I know, there has been a move recently away from deterministic (Newtonian) paradigms in biological research toward a more open-ended understanding of the dialectical relations between biological and social programming. This open-endedness leaves an opening, not only for ideological critics who want to see human behavior primarily in terms of social programming, but also for ideological critics like me, who want to leave human beings some tiny, vestigial power to modify

or even break free of their social programming. Charles Osgood's work on meaning is relevant here.

15. Here is Pound himself, from "Notes on Elizabethan Classicists": "It is much better that a man should use a crib, and know the content of his authors than that he should be able to recite all the rules in Allen and Greenough's *Grammar*. Even the teaching by rules is largely a hoax. The Latin had certain *case feelings*. For the genitive he felt source, for the dative indirect action upon, for the accusative direct action upon, for the ablative all other peripheric sensation, i.e. it is less definitively or directly the source than the genitive, it is contributory circumstance, lump the locative with it, and one might call it the 'circumstantial'" (239). He does not come right out and say it here, but his juxtaposition of the "content" gotten through a crib and the "case feelings" of Latin suggests that for Pound content was something felt, a somatic response.

16. Not only in "good" translation, either. When I took Latin in college, I was fascinated by the etymological link-ups with English but bored with the grammar and never really did go to much trouble to learn it; but I did well on the final, a straight translation exam, because I had a good intuitive feel for what the Latin *had* to mean. You make silly mistakes this way—in the exam text there was a description of a statue made *ex aere,* and not knowing that *aere* could also mean bronze, I generated a powerful image of a statue made of air, something like the Emperor's new clothes. But the mistakes you make that way, irritating as they are to pedants, are always less devastating to the life of the translation than are somatic failures to project. Better a living text with a few solecisms than a letter-perfect text that no one will ever want to read. Well—I should say *almost* always less devastating. There are SL texts and TL receptors, I have to keep reminding myself, that would prefer lifeless letter-perfection to a living approximation: certain technical texts and readers, for instance. But rather than being the rule, as many translation theorists have taken them to be, these are a rather insignificant exception. They shouldn't be forgotten (and I won't forget them, once I get to the "workshop" chapters of the book, 3 and 4); but neither should they be generalized to cover all translation.

17. It is no coincidence, as Barbara Johnson points out in "Taking Fidelity Philosophically," that we evaluate translations in terms of sexual loyalty or fidelity and worry as much about normative fidelity in the translational field as we do in the marital field. The Western ideosomatics of fidelity in both fields are directed at making it feel right to subordinate the variability of physical response to the transcendental norms of stasis and nondeviation.

18. Once again, I have Ezra Pound in mind. Here is Pound again, from "Early Translators of Homer": "I do not know that strict logic will cover all of the matter, or that I can formulate anything beyond a belief that we test a translation by the feel, and particularly by the feel of being in contact with the force of a great original" (271).

Happily, there are, of course, others as well. For a delightful deviation from the usual uneasy talk about "this-is-how-I-did-it-and-you-might-want-to-do-it-the-same-way-though-maybe-not" that untheoretically-minded translators typically produce when asked to speak at conferences, see Richard Howard, "A Professional Translator's Trade Alphabet," in the "context" section of Arrowsmith and Shattuck, *The Craft and Context of Translation*:

> X Y Z: Can a translation be better than the original? This is a hypocritical question I put here because I cannot think up any more letters. Since, as John Hollander says, no translation can ever be correct in quite the same way as an answer to a question like *Is it Tuesday?* the first answer, if *better* means what Mr. Nabokov asks of a translation—lucid accuracy in the literal rendering of the author's words—is no. On the other hand, questions like *How do you feel?* have answers which seem to be correct in a very different sense, and it is to this class of questions that my XYZ question belongs, and therefore gets the answer: yes. The point is, whether better or not, it can only be better English than the original French, which is the same thing as asking whether Molière wrote better plays than Milton wrote poems. (171)

Although Howard is not interested in developing a theoretical argument to support his position, he is stating clearly, in the face of all normative theories of equivalence that coach professional translators to guilty subservience, that questions about equivalence in terms of objectively demonstrable correspondences between texts must be superseded by ones about felt equivalence. There is a healthy self-confidence in Howard's dismissals of normative theories as "hypocritical" and tantamount to comparing plays and poems: there is simply no way that anyone can measure equivalence (or "betterness" or any kind of textual comparison), and the mainstream insistence on talking about translation as if we could measure or otherwise objectively control it is—well, not hypocrisy, perhaps, but certainly mystification of the worst sort.

19. Of course, it is also possible that I am allowing my somatic dissatisfaction with Steiner's magisterial pronouncements on the success and failure of the translations he deals with to slip into a factual claim too: I feel that he objectifies his response as the translation's features, and I treat my feeling as fact. The temptation to reify feeling as fact is great in an intellectual tradition that has not encouraged recognition and affirmation of local somatic insight.

20. This is a simplification, especially in light of recent developments in translation theory, but one that reflects the ideosomatically inscribed dualisms of Western thought: for "linguistics" and "hermeneutics" read mind and body, reason and emotion, science and art, classicism and romanticism, etc. This entire book is conceived as an attack on, and as an attempt to supersede, precisely these dualisms; but I am aware that I lean heavily throughout on the latter pole of each of these dualisms (body, emotion, art, romanticism). My argument is post- or transromantic, but that very move *through* romanticism leaves romantic traces everywhere.

The most vital impulse in current translation theory that is excluded by these dualisms is a social one—a concern with what translators (and translation theorists) *do,* in a social context, who they interact with, how social (historical, economic, intersubjective) factors condition their professional activities, and so on. The work of Hans Vermeer and Justa Holz-Mänttäri is of particular interest here, and in future work on translation the concerns they raise will have to play a more central role than they do here; for an earlier and culturally and theoretically narrower approach to the politics of translation, see Ginsburg's discussion of the ways in which the Soviet Union has commissioned and used translation(s) as political propaganda.

21. In this context, let me mention a Finnish television weather report I once saw, which cut to a photo of a snail before putting the weather maps on the screen. I was completely puzzled by this picture, but to my wife it was immediately obvious: it was an oblique metaphorical allusion to a Finnish children's rhyme, "Etana, etana, näytä sarves, tuleeko huomenna poutaa"—"Snail, snail, show us your tentacles, will it be sunny tomorrow?" There was no pressing reason for this, except that someone—some *human*—on the weather report team felt it might be different, might bring some variety into what is a rather repetitive news item. There is no way to program a computer to anticipate "messages" like this; even a human translator would be hard-pressed to come up with a good English equivalent (a groundhog? a bunion?). Even weather reports, in other words, can be literature—when handled by human beings.

22. Need I add that texts which both require and nourish feeling are only "deviant" in an ideological tradition that normatizes dehumanized cognitive system? This is the Western legacy of anticarnal medieval theology, with its roots in Plato both directly, through Ambrose's and Augustine's and the other church fathers' reading in Plato, and indirectly, through the Hellenization of Judaism that preceded and molded the New Testament.

23. "Ideology" as I use it has been associated with Marxist thought, beginning with Marx and Engels's *German Ideology.* It has been sharpened and tightened up by later Marxists, especially by the French political philosopher Louis Althusser. "Hegemony" is the Italian Marxist Antonio Gramsci's term for roughly the same "programming" phenomenon, by which the ruling class of a society engraves its values in each citizen's head. My use of the term is heavily influenced by Frank Lentricchia's book *Criticism and Social Change,* which is centered (like this book) around the work of Kenneth Burke. Since I agree (for the most part) with Marxist analyses of capitalist ideology but disagree both with Marxists' Platonist belief in superstructures and economic bases and with their Providential-Christian-Hegelian belief in "History"'s progress from feudalism through capitalism to a socialism that is always just around the corner, I do not think of my approach to ideology as "Marxist." It is borrowed from there—the word, some of the ideas, some specific analyses, the stress on the internal collectivization of the individual; but the same idea can be found in Nietzsche (the "internalization of mastery," in the *Genealogy of Morals*) or Freud (the internalization of the Ideal-I or image of the father in the Oedipus complex), or contemporary ethnologists and anthropologists (enculturation). I am a liberal ideologue who finds Marxist analyses of liberalism persuasive and useful in the process of transforming liberal ideology ethically, from the inside.

24. This is a considerably more complex ideosomatic phenomenon than I am able to deal with here. It seems contradictory, for example, to suggest that we are ideosomatically programmed both to be liberals and avoid typecasting and to be bigots and construct (or maintain) racial stereotypes even where they don't exist in reality. But ideology is somatically highly stratified. The liberal ideology of tolerance for the uniqueness of others is a very recent phenomenon in Western thought, tied ultimately to the rise of the bourgeoisie in the thirteenth century and really only taking firm hold in educational systems and childrearing programs in the nineteenth century. In the geological metaphor I broached above, we could say that liberalism forms a thin ideosomatic topsoil on the many layers of solid rock beneath, and that the rock contains plenty of suspicious xenophobia, territorial protectiveness, racial and sexual prejudice, and so on, all of which are considered somehow bestial and subhuman in the liberal order. The liberal strata of our ideosomatic makeup is like a lid on a volcano: it teaches us to control (suppress, lock up) the lower strata, but never quite succeeds.

Also, of course, each group and subgroup in society continues to receive tailor-made ideosomatic programming, so that, for example, ethnic and gender programming continues to make cultural differences between ethnic groups, or between the sexes, look like biological ("natural") differences. Different groups do act differently; they have been trained to. This has the effect of reinforcing programmed bigotry.

25. This difficulty is reflected in the terms themselves, which sound identical when spoken (they are homophones) and look almost identical when written (they are distinguishable only by a single orthographical mark). On the page, at a glance, they can easily be confused; in speech one has to resort to awkward measures like "idiosomatic-with-an-i" and "ideosomatic-with-an-e." But this difficulty is, I think, appropriate in light of the ease with which these blend together in our bodies.

26. I suppose I have been implying an ideal model in which, by a certain somatic economy, breaking through the three seals in one area brings about a liberation from ideosomatic programming in all others as well—thus, all you have to deal with once you have broken through the third seal is other people's seals. The practical reality that corresponds to this ideal model might be various kinds of miraculous conversion, faith healing, and rebirth experiences (secular and religious): a single word or image triggers a process that changes the person completely, once and for all. More common, certainly, is an ongoing process by which the seeker works through the three seals in a series of areas, dealing with each area and then moving on to the next—various mystical disciplines, say. In that case, the process will not be tidily linear, but complexly layered, so that perhaps the seeker may have broken through the third seal in his or her need to compete but still be struggling with the second seal in his or her need to suppress guilt.

27. In 8.1, when he says that he was a weaker man than Paul, I am inclined

to believe him. This is not just the rhetoric of Christian humility, and it is not sheer precursor worship, either. Augustine felt the pull of sexual desire as a real threat to be defended against with all the strength he had.

28. See John Berger on nakedness/nudity and publicity, in *Ways of Seeing*.

29. Except where otherwise noted—for example, I use Pine-Coffin's translation of the *Confessions* throughout, even where I do not so state—only those translations unmarked by translator's name and page number are mine. Wherever appropriate, I mark location of what I cite in the original text by section (in this case, by book and chapter), and the translation by page.

30. "cui rei ego suspirabam," he tells us in 8.5, "ligatus non ferro alieno, sed mea ferrea voluntate. velle meum tenebat inimicus; et inde mihi catenam fecerat et constrinxerat me"—"I longed to do the same, but I was held fast, not in fetters clamped upon me by another, but by my own will, which had the strength of iron chains. The enemy held my will in his power and from it he had made a chain and shackled me" (164). I would agree wholeheartedly, only identifying the inimical force that has shackled his (and our) will not as Satan but as ideology, that political belief system that conditioned our parents, teachers, advertisers, etc. to program us the way they did.

31. Or perhaps, to use John Rowan's term from *The Horned God*, "unconsciousness-raising" (33), a transformation of that complex of ideosomatic responses that was programmed into us so early that we find it almost impossible to bring into consciousness, and so name the "unconscious."

32. My discussion of pornography as anti-sex is indebted to Susan Griffin's book *Pornography and Silence*.

33. Noam Chomsky's transformational-generative approach to language was seen as revolutionary when he first started arguing it in the fifties; but of course he too only perpetuated the Saussurean (and ultimately Platonic, Pauline, Augustinian) mind-body split by insisting that we ignore "performance," the muddled, confused, error-ridden ways in which real people use language in real situations, and concentrate on "competence":

Linguistic theory is concerned primarily with an ideal speaker-listener in a completely homogeneous speech community, who knows its language perfectly and is unaffected by such grammatically irrelevant conditions as memory limitations, distractions, shifts of attention and interest and errors (random or characteristic) in applying his knowledge of the language in actual performance. (*Aspects*, 3)

That Chomsky could seriously suggest such a "garden of Eden" approach, as Dell Hymes (a former student of Kenneth Burke's) has called it; that his approach could be widely accepted as "linguistics," the study of language (even a revolutionary new approach to language); and that even when Chomsky's specific formulations are criticized and superseded, as they have been in the last ten or fifteen years, the search for idealized structures "behind" actual language use should continue—for all this, we have Augustine to thank. Or, if that is too simplistic for your tastes, we have the ideosomatics of Platonic/Christian/scientific mind-body dualism to thank.

34. Reason and faith, incidentally, are not analogous to the other dualisms; they are rhetorical tags variously attached to positions in the debate over ideosomatic programming. In the transition from the Middle Ages to Renaissance humanism, "faith" came to mean an uncritical acceptance of Catholic ideology *as* catholic, i.e., as universal, while "reason" came to mean a skeptical intellectual questioning of that ideology. As that questioning was increasingly institutionalized as "science," however, reason supplanted the Holy Spirit in the Christian explanation of the universe, and science became the new faith, the new ideosomatic program that I (among many others in our century) am now trying to question and supplant. Murray (26off.) points out that the etymological roots of the words "heresy" and "intellect" point to *choice,* and choice is, I suggest, the real issue here: whether to accept whatever ideosomatic program is already functioning inside you or to make your own choice. My emphasis on the body is, strictly speaking, heretical in the intellectualized faith of modern science; but it is also, insofar as I urge a bringing to consciousness of somatic response, "intellectual"—the body will not rise up against its own programming unless it is encouraged and taught to do so by what we like to think of as "mind."

35. Note that the ascension that began with a "conversion" or turning toward a fear of (divine) criticism now ends with perfect invulnerability to "adversity." I return to these two verts in Chapter 4.

36. It is significant that Augustine's ideal model of translation, wherein the Holy Spirit guides seventy translators independently of one another to the same translation of the Old Testament, should be based on a language that is not Augustine's native tongue, but that, owing to its immense cultural authority, he has learned well enough to read fluently: Greek. Hebrew is too far removed for him to speak it, and he admonishes Jerome to use the Septuagint rather than the Hebrew original as his SL text; and Latin, later to be the "alien authoritative language" of Western Europe, is too close, too familiar, to carry the authority Augustine finds in the Greek.

In *Marxism and the Philosophy of Language,* V. N. Voloshinov (Mikhail Bakhtin's student and possibly also, in this case, pseudonym) aligns the Augustinian/ Saussurean linguistic tradition specifically with the alienating authority of the foreign language word, along lines that are highly suggestive for my discussion of perfectionism:

Первыми филологами и первыми лингвистами всегда и всюду были *жрецы.* История не знает ни одного исторического народа, священное писание которого или предание не было бы в той или иной степени иноязычным и непонятным профану. Разгадывать тайну священных слов и было задачей жрецов-филологов.

На этой почве родилась и древнейшая философия языка: ведийское учение о слове, учение о Логосе древнейших греческих мыслителей и библейская философия слова.

Для того, чтобы понять эти философемы, нельзя ни на один миг забывать, что это—*философемы чужого слова.* Если бы какой-нибудь народ знал только свой родной язык, если бы слово для него совпадало с родным словом его жизни, если бы в его кругозор не входило загадочное чужое слово, слово чужого языка, то такой народ не создал бы подобных философем.

Свое слово совсем иначе ощущается, точнее, оно обычно вовсе не ощущается как слово, чреватое всеми теми категориями, какие оно порождает в лингвистическом мышлении и какие оно порождало в философско-религиозном мышлении древних. Родное слово—"свой брат", оно ощущается, как своя привычная одежда или, ещё лучше, как та привычная атмосфера, в которой мы живём и дышим. В нём нет тайн; тайной оно могло бы стать в чужих устах, притом иерархически-чужих, в устах вождя, в устах жреца, но там оно становится уже другим словом, изменяется внешне или изъемлется из жизненных отношений (табу для житейского обихода или архаизация речи), если только оно уже с самого начала не было в устах вождя-завоевателя иноязычным словом. Только здесь рождается "Слово", только здесь—incipit philosophia incipit philologia. (75–76)

The first philologists and the first linguists were always and everywhere *priests*. History knows no nation whose sacred writings or oral tradition were not to some degree in a language foreign and incomprehensible to the profane. To decipher the mystery of sacred words was the task meant to be carried out by the priest-philologists.

It was on these grounds that ancient philosophy of language was engendered; the Vedic teaching about the word, the Logos of the ancient Greek thinkers, and the biblical philosophy of the word.

To understand these philosophemes properly, one must not forget for one instant that they were *philosophemes of the alien word*. If some nation had known only its own native tongue; if, for that nation, word had always coincided with native word of that nation's life; if no mysterious, alien word, no word from a foreign tongue, had ever entered its purview, then such a nation would never have created anything resembling these philosophemes. . . .

One is sensible of one's native word in a completely different way or, to be more precise, one is ordinarily not sensible of one's native word as a word crammed with all those categories that it has generated in linguistic thought and that it generated in the philosophical-religious thought of the ancients. Native word is one's "kith and kin"; we feel about it as we feel about our habitual attire or, even better, about the atmosphere in which we habitually live and breathe. It contains no mystery; it can become a mystery only in the mouth of others, provided they are hierarchically alien to us—in the mouth of the chief, in the mouth of the priests. But in that case, it has already become a word of a different kind, externally changed and removed from the routine of life (taboo for usage in ordinary life, or an archaism of speech); that is, if it had not already been from the start a foreign word in the mouth of a conqueror-chief. Only at this point is the "Word" born, and only at this point—*incipit philosophia, incipit philologia.* (Matejka and Titunik's translation, 74–75)

The Greek word (the Logos) that alienates Augustine from real translation comes to him through the mouth of Alexander the Great, of course, conqueror of the known world and student of the totalizing, universalizing philosopher Aristotle; the Latin word that will alienate medieval theology from real language comes to Augustine through the mouth of Julius Caesar, Alexander's Roman successor as conqueror of the world, and to the Middle Ages through the mouths of Augustine and Jerome, theologian-conqueror and translator-conqueror of medieval Europe. Aristotle will reinvade Europe with the conquest of Moorish Spain in the twelfth century, with the result that the late Middle Ages and then the Renaissance (and the intellectual heirs of those epochs) will increasingly translate the divine Logos as Logic, the mathematical alien word that alienates contemporary linguists and philosophers from real or "natural" language, conceived precisely as priest-philologists have always conceived the ordinary speech of the profane, as a "fallen" or "messy" or "carnal" copy of the perfected purity of the alien (Greek, Latin, mathematical) word.

As Augustine's perfectionism makes clear, the alien word alienates specifically by idealizing language out of human reach, or out of the reach of ordinary speakers, and mystifying the idealizing process whereby the alien importation becomes the true, authoritative reality and the familiar word it displaces becomes its poor cousin, its fallen copy—what Chomsky calls the imperfect "execution" or "performance" by ordinary speakers of their perfect transcendental linguistic "competence."

37. Note that the Latin *traditor* is literally a "hander-over," someone who passes on the words of a writer to a reader who would not otherwise have access to them. In this etymological sense, the Italian aphorism *traduttore traditore* is not a cynical or bitter attack but a simple statement of the facts. The split history of the word since Rome is revealing: the *traditor* who handed words over to a reader conceived as an enemy became a traitor, while the *traditor* who handed words over to a reader conceived as a son generated tradition. Whether it is treason or tradition to hand over words thus becomes situational—or, rather, begins as situational and then is transformed politically into a rigidly polarized "reality." Many significant revolutions have devolved on the shifting of these terms, "enemy" and "son": in the Old Testament story of Jacob and Esau, for example, "son" (Esau) becomes "enemy," or Gentile, while in the New Testament story of Jesus "enemy" (the Gentiles) becomes "son" (God's children). Jacob's theft of his older brother's birthright should, according to patriarchal law, have been condemned as "treason"; the political success of Jacob as "Israel" valorizes it as "tradition." Jesus' extension of God's salvation to the Gentiles was condemned by the high priests of his day as treason; again, the political success of Christianity has valorized it as tradition.

From my point of view, the question of whether we condemn translation as treason (the handing over of an SL text to a TL enemy) or valorize it as tradition (the handing over of an SL text to a TL son) is really secondary: whether we drive a wedge between the SL writer and the TL reader or arrange them genealogically, in either case we are trapped in a patriarchal ideology that dualizes by splitting or dualizes by hierarchizing. In that sense, both conceptions constitute a binding tradition that forces the translator to be a traitor to him- or herself.

38. Burke quotes a theological account of the Tower of Babel myth from *The Interpreter's Bible*, according to which "man's 'arrogance' was also 'revealed

in the attempt to build a tower which should reach to heaven. . . . This attempt has the fragmentation of society as its 'sole result'" (231), and then reformulates it in logological terms: "The image of the Tower but reveals the problems implicit in the idea of hierarchical order with which the account of the Creation begins. . . . The fragmentation that is said to *result* from the building of the Tower is but a restatement of the hierarchical principle which the Tower itself (as a kind of Babylonian *ziggurat*) exemplifies" (231).

Chapter Two: The Dialogics of Translation

1. It might be argued, against this rather monopolizing claim that I make for somatics, that paradigm shifts can be brought about in the humanities intellectually as well: the revolutionary thinker reasons his or her way through the old paradigm's failures of logic or realism (failures of internal coherence or external representation) to a new theoretical construct. This is certainly true, as far as it goes. The problem is that, if an intellectual argument is not felt, not backed up by somatic experience, its hollowness or emptiness will be felt by the revolutionary thinker's peers—it will be clear to everyone, for example, that this is theory for theory's sake, or theory for fame's sake. This is a person who wants to develop a new theory in order to make a name for him- or herself, not because he or she has a new vision rising out of personal experience. In a truly successful paradigm shift, somatic experience may motivate the erection of an intellectual structure for the effective propagation of the new vision: certainly I am not saying that paradigm shifts in the humanities are all inarticulate cries of anguish or writhing moans of ecstasy. The felt need for a change does lead to an intellectualization process, invariably. But the hot air in any humanistic field—the useless theories that nobody pays attention to—can usually be traced to a felt need not for a paradigm shift, but for status, stardom, recognition.

2. I am painfully aware, in making a sweeping claim of this sort, of its pathetic blindness to the vast complexity of the field it proposes to describe. I think, for example, of the immense sensitivity to the many tugs and pulls in various directions traced by Louis Kelly in *The True Interpreter* and feel a little silly talking about two major paradigm shifts—three major paradigms in all. All I can say in my own defense is that, first of all, I am working on a higher level of generality than Kelly, so that it becomes possible to see, for example, the continuity of "scientific" theories of translation through the Renaissance and Enlightenment, right on into contemporary linguistic and cybernetic theories, with the medieval theories of Augustine and Aquinas (and, for that matter, the continuity of Augustine's Platonism and Aquinas's Aristotelianism); and, second, that my postromantic insistence not on static periods or positions but on the paradigm shifts brought about by pioneering theorists is appropriate to the paradigm I am arguing for. In the paradigm established by Augustine, representative accuracy is a primary virtue; in those terms, my "history" of trans-

lation theory is an oversimplification. In the new (Buberian, Bakhtinian, Bloom-ian, Burkean) paradigm I want to propose for translation theory, accuracy of representation is less important than what Burke calls "equipment for living": it is not how right you are about the past, it is what you do with it. In that sense, I am not really interested in the history of translation theory or in making truth claims about that history—but rather in fleshing out a sense of where we might possibly be headed and how we might try to get there.

3. For a concise formulation of Augustine's "scientific" principles, see paragraphs 48–59 of book 2 of *On Christian Doctrine,* where Augustine embeds in the heart of the medieval dogmatic system a Platonic rationalism according to which God instituted the "science of numbers" in the "reasonable order of things" (2.31.48, 2.32.50). True, he distinguishes this science from institutions pertaining to the "corporal senses" (2.31.48), which gives the bourgeois scientists of the seventeenth and eighteenth centuries the edge they need to swerve from Augustine; but the Augustinian principle that mathematical logic (the "science of numbers") is the language of nature, the Logos of God's creation, remains fundamental to empiricism as well. And since the empiricists were and are most interested in piercing the chaotic veil of observed sense-data and discovering the stable forms or natural laws that underlie them—a rationalist project directly derived from Augustine (and Aquinas) and only thinly disguised as empiricism—the scientific swerve was never very great.

4. "Now Luther did begin the modern mood of depending on things not merely intellectual. It is not a question of praise or blame; it matters little whether we say that he was a strong personality, or that he was a bit of a big bully. When he quoted [no: translated] a Scripture text, inserting a word that is not in Scripture, he was content to shout back at all hecklers: 'Tell them that Dr. Martin Luther will have it so!' That is what we now call Personality. A little later it was called Psychology. After that it was called Advertisement or Salesmanship. But we are not arguing about advantages or disadvantages. It is due to this great Augustinian pessimist [Chesterton defends Aquinas by lining Augustine and Luther up on one side and Aquinas on the other] to say, not only that he did triumph at last over the Angel of the Schools, but that he did in a very real sense make the modern world. He destroyed Reason, and substituted Suggestion" (195).

5. Luther later gloats, "Wie könnt ich mich besser rächen"—"How could I have better been revenged"—and as Nietzsche points out in *Thus Spake Zarathustra* (pt. 2, chap. 5), in German "gerecht/justified" and "gerächt/revenged" are homophones. Given Luther's defensive attack on the institutional power of the Roman Catholic church, which he associates with the Law, his German rendering of Paul could certainly be read: "Wir halten, daß der Mensch sich gerächt werde ohne des Gesetzes Werke allein durch den Glauben," or even "*an* des Gesetzes Werke": "We hold that man is revenged on the Law alone through believing."

6. This gradual movement from insight to action might be schematized in

terms of the three seals: Luther breaks the first seal blocking access to somatic response (pay no attention to your body; your immortal soul is the key to salvation) and discovers the spark that he calls Glauben, believing. This brings him up against the second seal, which enforces his aloneness: you are all alone; it is just you; nobody else feels the same way as you; there is no support for the way you feel; everybody else here at the monastery (like all right-thinking people everywhere) is normal—we have no such spark. Breaking the second seal and realizing that others have that spark, too, but have been prevented from contacting it by that very seal, Luther must face the third seal, which brands the spark sin, human infirmity, the fallen impulse of the body to pull us back to earth, away from heaven, away from spirit, away from God—and yes, it is probably there; unfortunately, we will not be rid of it until the resurrection of the body in the New Jerusalem. In order for Luther to expand that spark, that "aloneness of believing," into a movement (Lutheranism), he must break that third seal too and rework the *sinful* spark into a *faithful* spark, the bodily impulse of sin into the true source of faith. Breaking that last seal propels him out of the monastery and into the world, where his insight becomes a political breakthrough, a ground for action on a broad popular scale.

7. If it sounds too simplistic to say that Augustine is the father and Luther the mother of Western civilization, maybe I should say that until Luther we had a collective papa (Plato, Aristotle, Paul, Plotinus, Augustine, Aquinas), and in Luther we got our first influential (if still symbolic) mama. Actual female mamas did not start to exert real influence over Western civilization until the late eighteenth to mid-nineteenth centuries, which saw the rise of female evangelists, essayists, educators, novelists, and so on, to positions of cultural prominence (see, for example, Ann Douglas's book *The Feminization of American Culture*). But in a larger sense the whole bourgeois era has been the era of women, of emerging feminism and women's liberation on the positive side and, as my reading of Luther suggests, of the increasing use by men in positions of power of the backhanded, manipulative emotional appeals of traditional mothers on the negative side—in advertising, for example. In the bourgeois era, producers of ideological commodities (both material and rhetorical, consumer goods and political propaganda) began to discover that the surest path into the consumer's belief structure is not through an autocratic paternal rhetoric but through an indirect maternal rhetoric—and Luther was one of the first to make this discovery.

8. For André Lefevere's tamer version of this, see p. 9.

9. George Steiner expresses some surprise at this association with Luther: "Can he really have meant to say that Luther's immensely conscious, often magisterially violent reading is an instance of humble style, imperceptibly insinuating a foreign spirit and body of knowledge into German?" (258) Such, at any rate, was Luther's intention, as we have seen; and from where I sit, neither Luther's conscious manipulation of the TL reader nor his magisterial violence to the SL text suggests that that intention might have failed. Violence to the

SL text (*as* an SL text, as a culture-bound document) is precisely what this kind of translation requires; and the translator's consciousness of what he or she is trying to do to the TL reader only endangers the success of this particular operation if the reader becomes conscious of it too.

10. A Marxist translation theory could be constructed along much the same lines: the translator would be the proletarian alienated from the means of production, denied access both to capital and to "credit" for his or her own work, in both the financial and the reputational sense of that word. The author signs the translator's words, appropriates the fruits of the translator's work. Especially in light of the thinly disguised ecclesiastical hierarchy that underlies traditional translation theories, one could imagine Marxist translation theorists pressing consistently for liberation of translators from capital. Apart from some extremely timid work along these lines being done in Eastern Europe, however—and passing hints in the work of Mikhail Bakhtin—I know of none such. Medieval instrumentalist thinking is politically useful even in countries that have no truck with theology. Soviet translation theory, for example, is ideologically very close to Augustine and to the bourgeois translation theory of the capitalist West: linguistic and semiotic.

11. For one admirable attempt to theorize the impulse that led to the Zukofskys' Catullus, see George Steiner's discussion of the translation in terms of appropriation, the second move or epoch in his (expanded from Goethe's) hermeneutical movement (352). Steiner, like Goethe, is less interested in stable dualistic description than in a progressive dialectical approximation to truth. Also like Goethe, however, Steiner remains blind to the survival in his dialectic of rigid systematizing and idealizing thought. A good example of this is his expansion of Goethe's first epoch into "aggression" and "incorporation":

> After trust comes aggression. The second move of the translator is incursive and extractive. The relevant analysis is that of Heidegger when he focuses our attention on understanding as an act, on the access, inherently appropriative and therefore violent, of *Erkenntnis* to *Dasein,* the "thing there," "the thing that is because it is there," only comes into authentic being when it is comprehended, i.e. translated. The postulate that all cognition is aggressive, that every proposition is an inroad on the world, is, of course, Hegelian. It is Heidegger's contribution to have shown that understanding, recognition, interpretation are a compacted, unavoidable mode of attack. (297)

> The third movement is incorporative, in the strong sense of the word. . . . No language, no traditional symbolic set or cultural ensemble imports without risk of being transformed. Here two families of metaphor, probably related, offer themselves, that of sacramental intake or incarnation and that of infection. The incremental values of communion pivot on the moral, spiritual state of the recipient. Though all decipherment is aggressive and, at one level, destructive, there are differences in the motive of appropriation and in the context of "the bringing back." (298–99)

This division of "appropriative" ("aneignete") translation into two distinct (although related) epochs is probably useful; Steiner certainly gets a lot of good mileage out of it. Because his movement is not historically dialectical, however—because it does not situate itself progressively and hermeneutically in the dialogical engagements of specific translation theorists, but rather claims to be a kind of ideal model of "the" act of translation—strange things happen in it. Luther's Bible and Nabokov's *Eugene Onegin* both get classified under incorporation, for example, both being "shadings of assimilation and placement of the newly-acquired" (298). Steiner's second move, "aggression," appears to be nothing more than the translator's construction of the SL text, imagined in aggressive terms; his third move, "incorporation," then becomes the translator's approach to the TL reader, imagined in terms of old wine in new skins. Implicitly, therefore, in Steiner's conception, all translation must be aggressive; some translations just illustrate it better than others. All translation must likewise be incorporative: it incorporates the fruit of its aggressive act, its appropriation, in the TL. Again, some translations serve as better illustrations of this event than others, but any text can serve. The hermeneutical movement has its idealized existence in a realm far beyond all actual translations, which only function in Steiner's chapter as illustrative executions or expressions of the ideal model.

This sounds like Augustine, or like the kind of stable descriptive idealization that I have been associating with him. To his credit, as it turns out, Steiner waffles on his own descriptive stability, wavers between Augustine and the historical dialectic of Goethe, and in the course of his long fifth chapter over and over elicits the historical complexity of translators coming to grips with translation ideals, mastering them and being mastered by them, molding and transmuting them. But he waffles as Goethe waffles: out of a confusion of ideosomatic programming (there must be a stable model for translation!) and genuine idiosomatic insight.

12. Note that the desire to excrete the ideosomatic programming that undermines (even while it affirms) our belief in self-possession constitutes the excremental values of liberalism that correspond to and complicate what Steiner calls the "incremental values of communion." What is taken into the body only corrupts or infects if it cannot be excreted whole. We would like to believe—we have been taught to want to believe—that we can incorporate collective values without being infected by them; that they go straight through, leaving our individual autonomy untouched. Needless to say, the infection is all the more effective if we go on believing that it never happened and never can happen.

13. A bilingual English/Spanish book that I read to my children, *The King, the Mice, and the Cheese/El rey, los ratones, y el queso,* by Eric and Nancy Gurney and translated by Carlos Rivera, seems typical; on the back of the title page there is a note that reads: "Some English phrases do not translate word-for-word into Spanish. In these cases the English idea has been translated into Spanish idiom."

14. I have the same reservations about James Carse's rigidly dualized conception of finite and infinite games, which I have been quoting in my epigraphs

throughout. Carse lacks a sense of the ways in which finite games are ideosomatically programmed into us, and therefore of the enormous difficulties we have in trying to put aside finite for infinite games. For the same reason, he lacks all sense of how we might move from the finite games that we are programmed to play into the infinite games that give us life.

15. See Caryl Emerson's remarks on Bakhtin's implicit attitudes toward translation in her editor's preface to her translation of Bakhtin's *Problems of Dostoevsky's Poetics:*

> It must be said at the outset that nowhere does Bakhtin offer us a theory of translation. Theory, in the quantitative sense of a "technology," is not to be found in his work. But what can be said with certainty is that for Bakhtin, to translate was never to betray; on the contrary, translation, broadly conceived, was for him the essence of all human communication. Crossing language boundaries was perhaps the most fundamental of human acts. Bakhtin's writing is permeated by awe at the multiplicity of language he hears. These are not just the bluntly distinct national languages—Russian, English, French—that exist as the normative material of dictionaries and grammars, but also the scores of different "languages" that exist simultaneously within a single culture and a single speaking community. In fact, Bakhtin viewed the boundaries between national languages as only one extreme on a continuum; at the other extreme, translation processes were required for one social group to understand another in the same city, for children to understand parents in the same family, for one day to understand the next. These stratifications of language, Bakhtin argued, do not exclude one another; they intersect and overlap, pulling words into various gravitational fields and casting specific light and shadow. Living discourse, unlike a dictionary, is always in flux and in rebellion against its own rules. Bakhtin delighted in the fact that procedures for conveying meaning were forever multiplying— and that the nonreducible individual had such a unique "speech energy." "It might even seem that the very word 'language' loses all meaning in this process," he writes, "for apparently there is no single plane on which all these 'languages' might be juxtaposed to one another" [*Discourse in the Novel* 291]. Each language embodies its own specific worldview, its own system of values. And this means that every speaking subject speaks something of a foreign language to everyone else. It also means that every speaking subject has more than one native language at his disposal. To understand another person at any given moment, therefore, is to come to terms with meaning on the boundary between one's own and another's language: to translate.
>
> What happens in translation, therefore, is not an exception to our everyday practice of communication through direct and indirect discourse; it could even be seen as a dramatic illustration of these processes. This celebration of difference in language is a bit awkward for a translator—who inevitably must, at some level, be concerned with equivalence. That very concept is somehow incompatible with Bakhtin's insights into language. (xxxi–xxxii)

The traditional conception of translation as "inevitably . . . concerned with equivalence" is incompatible with Bakhtin's language theories—and yet Emerson clings to that conception when translating Bakhtin. This, gentle reader, is the force of ideosomatic programming. "One of Bakhtin's major premises, in fact," Emerson continues, "might be called the vitality of nonequivalence. Multilingual environments, he argued, liberate man by opening up a gap between things and their labels; analogously, the novel is more free than the epic because novelistic heroes are never equivalent to their plot. Nonequivalence is not a matter for despair but is rather the impulse to life. In fact, the interaction of two different, discrete systems is the only way a true *event* ever comes to pass" (xxxii). And yet, "translation always involves creating a hierarchy of fidelities" (xxxiii). Sigh. Must it always be like this?

16. For further discussion of this point, see my article "Intentions, Signs, and Interpretations."

17. For an introduction to men's studies, see the essay collections edited by Kaufman and Brod and the book by John Rowan listed in the bibliography.

18. This caricature sounds perhaps overly focused, as if only those translation theorists like Peter Newmark whose avuncular prescriptivism made them resemble Matthew Arnold were perpetuating the Augustinian tradition. Actually, I am thinking of just about everybody, including those theorists who do the normative (authoritarian, prescriptive) thing in "scientific" guise, whether they lean toward Renaissance humanism or Enlightenment common sense, romantic messianism or Victorian moralism, structural linguistics or transformational grammar, philosophical or cybernetic logic. Take Robert de Beaugrande, for instance, who tentatively drops his anchor in the phenomenological sediment of Roman Ingarden and Wolfgang Iser, a philosophical tradition that potentially, at least, takes us into the area of the interpreter's motivated or intentional subjectivity—but finds in Ingarden and Iser precisely those elements that permit him to insist on the translator-interpreter's subjection to the SL writer's intentional subjectivity. Having turned his back on the rich complexity of literary theory (he thematizes that complexity as "chaos"), de Beaugrande insists that all "descriptive" translation theory must be implicitly prescriptive, and behind all the fancy phenomenology and text-linguistics he sets about the old project, determining the norms of fidelity to which the translator must bind him- or herself. (I have shown how Iser himself modifies phenomenology back in the direction of analytical rationalism in "Reader's Power, Writer's Power.")

19. See Mitchell, *Against Theory.* I have discussed the position of one of the participants in this debate, Stanley Fish, in my "Trivial and Esoteric Pursuits," pp. 219–21.

20. This makes the definition of success circular, of course, since satisfaction was first taken to be the criterion of success and now is defined by a feeling of success. But circular reasoning is only against the rules in the idealized world of formal logic; in real, pragmatic situations, the consequences of interpretations in action invariably solve the problems that logic is set up to crack.

Chapter Three: The Tropics of Translation

1. Here is one focal formulation of Holz-Mänttäri's method:

Im Rahmengefüge translatorischen Handelns werden mit den Segmentierfragen alle Handlungsrollen erfragt und erfaßt: Wer bestellt den Text? Wer erstellt den Ausgangstext? Wer rezipiert den Zieltext? Wann, wo, unter welchen Umständen und zu welchem Zweck wird der Zieltext vorgetragen? usw. Auf dieselbe Weise werden die Sachverhalte in Texten (Translationsbeitrags-, Ausgangs-, Ziel-, Recherchiertexte) erfragt und erfaßt: Die Fragen WER (TUT) WAS?, WEM (GESCHIEHT) WAS?, WAS (EREIGNET SICH)?, WAS (IST)? usw. ergeben die Grundaussage des Textes, WOZU WIE usw. ergeben die Ergänzungen dazu, also z.B. die Strategien. Wesentlich ist, darauf wurde bereits bei der Vorstellung der Methode als translatologisches Instrument hingewiesen, daß über die Position des Steuer-Elements präzise nach dem gefragt wird, was der Analysator wißen will. (99)

Analytically segmented in the framework of translatorial activity, all actantial roles will be posed and grasped through these questions: Who commissions the text? Who prepares the SL text? Who receives the TL text? When, where, under what circumstances, and to what purpose is the TL text executed? etc. In each text (not only SL and TL texts but the text in which the translation is commissioned and the texts the translator uses to research his or her project as well) the facts will be posed and grasped in the same way. The questions WHO (DOES) WHAT?, TO WHOM (HAPPENS) WHAT?, WHAT (COMES TO PASS)?, WHAT (EXISTS)?, etc., yield the text's basic predication, while WHAT FOR, HOW etc. yield its supplementation, e.g., its strategies. The main point is that in the very conception of the method as translatological instrument, attention is so drawn to these questions as to enable the analyst to discover what he or she wants to know by interrogating the position of the (parenthesized) steering-element.

In other words, the translator and the translation theorist proceed in much the same way, by asking 5 *W*-type questions of the various texts, placing them in a complex dramatic situation, and exploring the placement of the predicative or "steering" elements (Burke would call them ratios) that join any two *W*'s. Holz-Mänttäri's concern to integrate the methods of the translator and the theorist seems to me salutary—apart from the fact that the integrating method is analytical, i.e., owes fealty to the ideosomatics of theory, and thus "joins" practice and theory by assimilating the former to the latter.

"The text in which the translation is commissioned" (the "order text," "commission text," the letter that says, "Could you please translate *X*") is an authorized translation for Beitragstext (facilitating or support text), which Justa tells me should have been Austragstext. Here the SL author's authority poses interesting difficulties: she claims that it was a typo, but if it was, it was a typo that survived who knows how many editings and proofreadings. With her authorial authority, Justa is asking me as translator to "forget" the actual word printed in the SL text, to dissolve it mentally into the "real" word printed there, the Platonic form of the Beitragstext, which is only a bad copy or imprint (*tupos*) of Austragstext. If I submit to her authority as SL author, I will idealize her declared retrospective intention as the "true meaning" of the text and translate accordingly—as, in fact, I did. But in the dramatics of real-life translating, her authorization of my translation does not establish her account of the way things are as the ideal Platonic reality behind her text; it is only one more Beitragstext facilitating my translation.

See also Hans Vermeer's discussion of Holz-Mänttäri's theory (which she ascribes partly to his pioneering work in the mid-seventies) in *Voraus-setzungen für eine translationstheorie*.

2. Significantly, when Paul wants to distinguish the shadowy letter of Old Testament law from the divine substance incarnated in Christ, he refers specifically to the *body* of Christ: "these things are only a shadow of what is to come; but the substance [*soma*] belongs to Christ" (Col. 2:17). My somatic modification of Burke is not much of a deductive leap, in fact. He is at some pains all through his later work to establish the significance of the body to drama: in the development of the negative, as we saw in Chapter 1 (from "A Dramatistic View of the Origins of Language"); in his essays "Mind, Body, and the Unconscious" and "The Thinking of the Body," also collected in *Language as Symbolic Action;* in his tracing of Augustine's conception of eternity to the infantile sensation of clinging to the mother's breast in *The Rhetoric of Religion,* and so on. What I bring to Burke's scattered discussions of the "thinking of the body" is not only an extended exploration and highlighting of the issue but the idio/ideosomatic distinction and the *techne* of the three seals: Burke offers no way out, no escape route, only brilliant mappings of the dungeon. My way out may *be* no way out, only a map that will take us to another floor of the dungeon; but it is a start.

3. I say "ways of focusing an inquiry," but as anyone who has read Burke knows, Burke tends to proceed by generating what he calls "perspectives by incongruity," and that usually means something different from what we normally understand focusing to mean. Burke expands and complicates things by reaching outside a focus into its denied or repressed periphery, and jumping from there to the periphery of a related focus, and from there to another periphery still, so that the reader is often left guessing what focus he is trying to explain. The focus, of course, is the obvious part, the superficially evident part, and therefore, from Burke's point of view, the easy and uninteresting part. One example, from his discussion of ratios:

One discerns the workings of the act-agent ratio in the statement of a former cabinet member to the effect that "you can safely lodge responsibility with the President of the United States," owing to "the tremendously sobering influence of the Presidency on any man, especially in foreign affairs." Here, the sheer nature of an office, or position, is said to produce important modifications in a man's character. Even a purely symbolic act, such as the donning of priestly vestments, is often credited with such a result. And I have elsewhere quoted a remark by a political commentator: "There seems to be something about the judicial robes that not only hypnotizes the beholder but transforms the wearer."

Ordinarily, the scene-act and scene-agent ratios can be extended to cover such cases. Thus, the office of the Presidency may be treated as a "situation" affecting the agent who occupies it. And the donning of vestments brings about a symbolic situation that can likewise be treated in terms of the scene-agent ratio. But there are cases where a finer discrimination is needed. For instance, the resistance of the Russian armies to the Nazi invasion could be explained "scenically" in terms of the Soviet political and economic structure; or one could use the act-agent ratio, attributing the power and tenacity to "Russian" traits of character. However, in deriving the act from the scene, one would have to credit socialism as a major scenic force, whereas a derivation of the act from the agents would allow for a much more felicitous explanation from the standpoint of capitalist apologetics. (16–17)

I would add that, if we think of the presidency or vestments or socialism as "producing" or "causing" a certain act or quality in a human agent, then those things are scenes or acts as *agents,* and the human agents become their agencies. And that, if we want to understand the Soviet repulsion of the Nazi invasion as resulting from socialism or the Russian character in order to bolster our own ideological inclinations (purpose), then each explanation as drama is an agency that we wield as agents—except that insofar as we feel "driven" to support socialism or capitalism or whatever, we are the agencies of our ideosomatic programming as agents. "Perspective by incongruity" means a constant shifting of perspective with no attempt to unify the incongruous observations thus produced into a single "truth."

Note that Burke's ratio as a "principle of selectivity" by which the theorist or translator focuses his or her inquiry is very close also to what Holz-Mänttäri called Steuer-Element.

4. Bloom's tropology is far too complex to summarize competently here; I will be returning to it periodically throughout this chapter. I do, however, want to record the interpretive shift that I make in Bloom's conception of the tropes, which (Bloom's) is explicitly Kabbalistic and organized around three dialectics moving from reduction through substitution to representation:

Burke associates irony with dialectic, metonymy with reduction, metaphor with perspective, and synecdoche with representation. Hyperbole and metalepsis I add as progressively more blinded or broken representation, where "blinding" or "breaking" is meant to suggest the Lurianic breaking-of-the-vessels or scattering-of-the-light which I have carried over into the poetic realm as substitution. As tropes of contraction or limitation, irony withdraws meaning through a dialectical interplay of presence and absence; metonymy reduces meaning through an emptying-out that is a kind of reification; metaphor curtails meaning through the endless perspectivizing of dualism, or inside-outside dichotomies. As tropes of restitution or representation, synecdoche enlarges from part to whole; hyperbole heightens; metalepsis overcomes temporality by a substitution of earliness for lateness. (*Map* 94–95)

In Bloom's map of misreading, he claims that the post-romantic crisis-lyric invariably follows the same tropic/imagistic pattern: the first stanza (or first group of stanzas or lines) moves from the reductive trope of irony (images of absence and presence) to the restitutive trope of synecdoche (images of part and whole); the second stanza moves from the reductive trope of metonymy (images of fullness and absence) to the restitutive trope of metaphor (images of inside and outside); and the third stanza moves from the reductive trope of hyperbole (images of high and low) to the restitutive trope of metalepsis (images of earliness and lateness). In my first application of this map to translation, a still-unpublished manuscript written face-en-face in English and Finnish titled "The Tropics of Translation/Kääntämisen kääntöpiirit," I shifted the tropes a little: chapter 2 traced a movement from the reductive equivalence of metonymy (sense-for-sense translation) to the selective equivalence of synecdoche (propagandistic translation); chapter 3 moved from the desperate romantic striving for (and ironic denial of) perfect metaphoric equivalence to the postromantic generation of hyperbolic meaning in excess of equivalence; and chapter 4 set up an internal dialectic between what Bloom calls metaleptic introjection and metaleptic projection.

Metalepsis was to be my "preferred" trope, my overall model for rich, complex translation, but the field was too complex to fit into a single trope like metalepsis; I realized that, by following Bloom and seeing some tropes as "restricting" creation, others as "restituting" it, I built a polemic into my tropics that split my discussion right down the middle. On the one hand, I wanted to say that there was nothing wrong with translating metonymically, for instance, as long as you realized that you were successfully *troping*, not failing to achieve sense-for-sense equivalence. As long as logical (static, analytical) equivalence is held up as the ideal for all translation, and translation theorists quarrel over the best kind of equivalence to strive for, I said, those strivings will never amount to anything, since equivalence ideals have their own failure built in; but strivings toward equivalence might produce good, successful translations if the translator were aware that the ideal was just a trope to facilitate a turning, not an inaccessible goal to measure relative failure by.

On the other hand, I wanted to attack the mainstream ideology of translation, which had sedimented around what I was calling the tropes of metonymy (the Augustinian/Lutheran mainstream) and metaphor/irony (the romantic alternative), so I ended up painting those two tropes in rather black shades. And then synecdoche and hyperbole, too, became mainly crowbars for opening up the locked closets of these two idealizing tropes, tools to be used and discarded on my way to my supertrope, metalepsis. I praised synecdochic or propagandistic translations, cautiously, making it clear that praise for propaganda was praise for the devil: heuristically useful in a God-dominated tradition, but ultimately a dead end. I praised hyperbole more enthusiastically but was careful there too to show its limits, its failure to live up to its own promise. I wanted to clear the field for metalepsis.

But that will no longer do. One trope cannot bear the entire burden of dialogical translation. They all have to be understood dialogically, in terms of a productive interaction with the SL writer (metalepsis was the only trope that I tied to the SL writer in that earlier book), and they all have to be understood as useful tools for approaching the SL writer and text.

5. This question is beyond the scope of my argument here; suffice it to say that, intuitively, word-for-word translation would seem to fit Augustine's dogmatic system better than sense-for-sense translation. There is no obvious reason to isolate the sentence as the minimum linguistic unit and render its sense in the TL; the individual word, besides being a more "natural" unit to isolate, is the obvious human correlate to the single divine Logos. Augustine, it seems to me, not being a translator himself, would have been perfectly capable of insisting on the dogmatic purity of word-for-word translation, were it not for the

authority of Cicero and Horace and, perhaps, of his brilliant but quirky contemporary, Jerome.

6. I am beating around the bush that Louis Kelly, following Sydney Lamb, identifies as "segmentation" (chap. 4.3): "The act of translation," Kelly says, "begins from assumptions about the unit of translation" (120). I would qualify that to read: the act of *metonymic* translation begins from assumptions about the unit of translation. It is only when translation is definitionally restricted to idealized metonymy that segmentation comes to be seen as the source of all (initial) translation decisions.

7. I have taken the liberty of touching up Gibbons's punctuation here—of "translating" the sentence hyperbolically, if you like.

8. See John Berger's *Ways of Seeing*, chapter 3, for an excellent discussion of the ideosomatic differences between "nude" and "naked."

9. As it happens, the "lude" I hear in "Deluded" is there etymologically, which means that you could have looked the word up in a dictionary and discovered what I just explained, that delusion is historically a denial of play. But I did not first look it up in a dictionary. I responded to it. It felt right. As I started wondering why it felt right, I remembered Huizinga's book, and a book by Rosalie Colie called *Paradoxia Epidemica,* which used Huizinga to coin the adjective "ludic" for playful—verbal associations. It was only then that I checked the dictionary and found I had been what logicians and historians like to call "right": there was "objective" (ideosomatic) evidence for what I felt. That means, looking back on my somatic response, that you might have responded in more or less the same way I did, and "discovered" my intentions in rendering "Desnudo" as "Deluded," even if I had not gone ahead and explained the joke. Maybe I insulted your "intelligence" (actually, it wouldn't have been your intelligence, but your sensitivity to somatic response) in explaining it. The thing is, once you give up the ideosomatic illusion of objectivity, you can never be sure just how you will be understood. To trope is to take a step in the dark, or onto rotten stairs. Because tropic translators believe that rotten—or at least rottable, *real*—stairs are all we have, they are not eager to delude themselves into believing that refusing to climb them is a climbing of ideally solid stairs.

10. I am indebted for much of this discussion to Lauri Aaltonen, minister for the deaf in Lapua, Finland. See also Hans Furth's *Thinking without Language,* Harry Bornstein et al.'s *The Signed English Dictionary,* and Oliver Sacks's *Seeing Voices.* The similarity between simultaneous signing and TV subtitling is that for the lip-reading deaf and the listener who reads signs, as for the TV viewer who understands both the SL and the TL, the SL and the TL are simultaneously present, available for comparison and fuller understanding.

11. For a more detailed discussion of conference interpretation along these lines, see my remarks in Chapter 1, pp. 28–29.

12. I can imagine someone like Eugene Nida protesting here that he agrees with me completely: that "dynamic" or "functional" equivalence in practice should mean precisely that the translator conveys the SL message to the TL

receptor just as the SL writer/speaker gives it, and that all he is arguing against is naive literalism. Thus, what I call metaphor should be seen as just an intensified form of metonymy, or what I called sentential metonymy should be understood broadly enough to include my examples of metaphor. Either way is fine with me; as I say, I am not interested in establishing a stable classification system and arguing over what goes where. All I would say is that conference interpretation highlights the inadequacies of traditional cognitive, or mentalist, approaches to language by underscoring the role played by somatic response. The translator does not "analyze" the SL text and then restructure what he or she has generated analytically in the TL; the translator responds receptively in the SL and productively in the TL. In fact, all of my tropes (and versions, in chapter 4) finally collapse into the overarching multiplicity of somatic response: tropes and versions are just ways of talking about that multiplicity.

13. A Finnish example of an advertising text that seems to contain its own ingenious metaphoric translation (for export, to render translation into English unnecessary) might be a recent television commercial made by the candy manufacturer Fazer for a confection of theirs called "Kiss-Kiss": two cats are shown romping and then kissing on screen, while the voice-over says, "Kiss-Kiss pusspussissa." If we take this as both SL and TL text, as a reflexive text that contains its own translation, the lexical elements crisscross: you call cats in Finnish by saying "kiss-kiss" and in English by saying "puss-puss," and the English touching of lips in "kiss-kiss" in Finnish becomes "puss-puss." (Finnish *kissa* is cat; for purposes of calling, that is shortened to the first syllable. And one Finnish word for kiss is *pusu,* which again in the kind of cutesy talk the commercial employs is shortened to the first syllable.)

The element in the Finnish text that doesn't translate is *pussissa,* in a/the bag (the package the candy comes in): one literal translation of the commercial might be "Kiss-Kiss in the bag-bag" (*pussi* "bag" + *-ssa* "in"). The only "automatic" or reflexively "implicit" translation of this that the English speaker might derive would be an invitation to oral sex ("Kissy-kissy in my pussy") that would not sound particularly appropriate in the sentimental context of the commercial as a whole.

14. My interpretation of Leino's poem was dialogically conditioned or directed by Jaakko Pakkasvirta's interpretation of "Erotessa" in his 1978 film version of Leino's life, *Runoilija ja muusa* (The Poet and the Muse). Pakkasvirta has Leino write the poem on his wedding night (and it was in fact written the year Leino got married) instead of taking his new bride, the wealthy but unpleasantly bourgeois Freya Schoultz, to bed. "What are you writing?" she asks, sitting on the bed in her wedding gown. "A poem," Leino says, "about us." "Is it in Finnish?" (Freya spoke no Finnish; they communicated in Swedish and German.) "Yes." "Translate it for me." "It can't be translated." "What's it called?" "'At Parting.'" As the camera flits from the determinedly isolated Leino, huddled in a shadow on the floor (in his deepening night) with the poem and a bottle of wine, to the puzzled Freya on the bed, her puzzlement

slowly changing to a terrible foreboding as the import of the scene sinks in (like bird claws), the strains of "At Parting" set to music by Otto Donner sound out a lovely nostalgia that in Pakkasvirta's context rings most ironically hollow.

15. I take the term "decreation" (a tropical or reconstructive alternative to deconstruction) from an article on John Ashbery by Charles Altieri called "Motives in Metaphor" (661):

Decreation I take to be a deliberate poetic act intending to disclose possible forms of relatedness, and consequently other possible grounds for identity and value, sharply different from the host forms, the dramatic lyrics, which the decreation parasitically restructures. Decreation, in essence, is a means for working within the seams and expectations of discourse by disclosing fresh ways of making sense. It blends the parodic and the transcendental because it continues to seek qualities of perception and forms of poetic knowledge by at once cleansing and transforming outmoded expressive or descriptive vehicles. Decreation alters the economy of consciousness by exploring new modes of exchange among its used and various coins. Deconstruction, on the other hand, invokes the spirit of sceptual lucidity without a lyric counterpressure. Deconstruction is primarily a critical act devoted to displaying the irreducible interchange of sense and nonsense in the overlapping codes on which any discourse is ultimately dependent. Deconstruction shows contradictions in intentions while decreation intentionally posits contradictions to suggest new integrations.

16. This is one of Stevens's central premises; see his treatment of it in poems like "Asides on the Oboe" and "A High-Toned Old Christian Woman." In my discussion of Stevens's and Kermode's aestheticism, I draw on Frank Lentricchia's discussion in chapter 1 of *After the New Criticism*.

17. This is the case with William Novak, according to a recent *Newsweek* article ("The King of the Ghosts," by Mark Stark). Stark quotes Stuart Appelbaum of Bantam Books on Novak's achievement: "He has helped change the profession from that of literary sharecropper to one that is at the very least respectable—and perhaps even glamorous" (54). For his best-selling ghosting of Lee Iacocca, Novak got a flat fee of "only" $45,000 (when did a translator ever get paid so well?); but after the smash success of that book, he has been paid a fee in six figures (more than that *Newsweek* could not worm out of the industry) and a royalty cut. Stark cites unnamed "publishing sources" who estimate that the O'Neill memoirs will earn Novak a quarter of a million dollars.

18. For a good discussion of the transatlantic Poe in terms of Harold Bloom and creative translation, see Jefferson Humphries' *Metamorphoses of the Raven*. I also deal with Emerson's borrowings from his European contemporaries in *American Apocalypses*, chap. 4.

19. Finnish *jouka* is related to *joutsen*, "swan," which, archaized and Latinized, yields Cyngnus; Finnish *väinä* is a wide river, Estonian *väin* a gulf, as in the Gulf of Finland, whence the archaic and Latinized Gulpus.

Chapter Four: The Ethics of Translation

1. I have modified this translation by playing with the English words for translation, in order to highlight Cicero's distinction: *converti* becomes "I turned into Latin," rather than Hubbell's "I translated," and *ut interpres* becomes "as a translator," rather than Hubbell's "as an interpreter." Cicero specifically means the translator here, the translator conceived as humble TL amanuensis of the SL text, the *fides interpres* or faithful translator. Render *interpres* as "interpreter" (expounder, explainer) here, and you get a person who does more or less exactly what Cicero said he did when he translated as an orator: someone who makes the idea behind the SL text clear to the TL reader. The explicit burden of Cicero's distinction would seem to be that *convertere ut interpres* is word-for-word translation and *convertere ut orator* (keeping the same ideas but putting them in terms of our own usage) is sense-for-sense translation, especially since he goes on to rule *verbum pro verbo* translation unnecessary. Implicit in his choice of the orator (subject of the whole treatise where this remark appears) as an alternative to the translator, however, is another distinction that is not made explicit in translation theory until Luther: that between abstract logical correspondence between texts (what Eugene Nida will call formal equivalence) and rhetorical correspondence between SL and TL writerly appeals to the reader, or between SL and TL reader responses to the text (what Nida will call dynamic equivalence). The orator is a rhetor, clearly, a persuader, an actor in a human drama; in my terms, *convertere ut orator* would be to translate ethically, in purposeful dialogue with a TL receptor.

2. Cf. 4.6, 12.1, where Jerome also uses *vertere* in reference to that papal letter. He once uses *vertere* (8.4) in reference to the work of the Seventy when they add a phrase ("look down on me") to the opening words of the Twenty-third Psalm (*Eli, eli, lama sabachthani*, Jesus' words on the cross); his usual words for translation, even when (as is his case throughout) he shows the Seventy translating "freely," loosely, inserting and deleting, doing "versions" rather than "strict" word-for-word translations, are *translatio/transfero/translator* and *interpretatio/interpres*.

3. I am indebted for this German example to George Steiner in personal correspondence.

4. I take this etymological development from *vertere* through *wenden* and *vända* to *kääntää* from Lauri Hakulinen, *Suomen sanaston käännöslainoja* (Translation loans in Finnish vocabulary).

5. I have not done justice to this claim that I make for Augustine's centrality in Western civilization, and I do not have room to do it here. The bare bones of the historical argument would look something like this: Augustine happened to live at a crucial turning point in Western civilization. Born in A.D. 354, forty years after the conversion of the Roman Empire to Christianity (A.D. 313), he witnessed the disintegration of that empire into barbaric chaos (he was fifty-six years old in 410 when Rome was sacked, and he watched the destruction

spread the last twenty years of his life—his city, Hippo, in what is now Algeria, was sacked the year of his death, 430). The conversion of Rome to Christianity required a reinterpretation of the Book of Revelation and generally of Christian political doctrine, which had conceived of Rome as the enemy and the Christians as revolutionaries: Augustine's *City of God* filled that bill, formulating an authoritarian Christianity for the newly converted empire. And the fall of Rome cemented the church's dependence on Augustine's ideal images of cultural and political (theocratic) order. His rhetorical brilliance was unsurpassed in his day, of course, which gave his writings all the persuasive power that sheer textuality can yield; and that power was solidified by his political brilliance, his astonishing success in the political consolidation of African Catholicism and the eradication of various "heretical" (read "competing") sects over the last four decades of his life. Augustine became the key transitional figure between imperial Rome and medieval Rome, the rhetorical and political founder of an institution cohesive enough to dominate the West for a thousand years. See Peter Brown's *Augustine of Hippo* and Bernard McGinn's *Visions of the End* for further discussion.

6. This "liberal" embarrassment is, of course, derived from the medieval embarrassment with conversion and persuasion; where the medieval church mystified conversion as submission to the universal voice of God, early liberal ideologues mystified it as submission to the universal voice of reason.

7. I was also tempted to pair "inversion" with either subversion or perversion, especially given the great love shown by the "perverse" Jacques Derrida and his deconstructive disciples for the rhetorical trope of inversion. Somehow it did not happen.

8. The Pentecostal church is not built on mystical moments either; they have their church bylaws and their Bible translations just like any other denomination. Even among the Pentecostals and other charismatic groups, glossolalia has never to my knowledge been used pragmatically, to render translation unnecessary; its function is more ornamental, to display faith rather than to spread it.

9. In some sense this question is buried pragmatically, through the institutional canonization of certain texts that are considered worth translating precisely *because* they conform to institutional norms of ideological acceptability. A text that the translator might legitimately be expected to reject on ideological grounds would probably never even get published, let alone translated—it would languish in manuscript, yet another forgotten text by a misunderstood genius (the writer's view), or (the institutional view) yet another piece of textual insanity by a crank. If a text has been published and so thoroughly accepted by ideology-enforcing institutions that it is offered up for translation, there *can be* nothing wrong with it, and the translator that questions it is therefore out of line.

Social transition tends to bring erstwhile "heretical" and therefore suppressed texts out of the woodwork, of course: as the Protestant middle class rose to power in the sixteenth and seventeenth centuries there was a gradual relaxing of censorship over heretical texts; the academic validation of Black Studies and Women's Studies since the 1960s has facilitated the emergence of hundreds of "lost" diaries and other suppressed texts by women and blacks. But this only poses problems for the instrumentalized translator in the early stages of the transition (the Renaissance, for example); once the previously excluded groups have established a position of institutional power in the changed social fabric, the norms of ideological acceptability shift, and once again everything that is published can and must be translated uncritically.

10. See, for example, Susan McClary's discussion of Heinrich Schenker's musicological treatise of 1935, *Der freie Satz,* which she says "is expressly meta-physical in intent—the work of an Austrian Jew between the world wars who sought evidence of transcendental certainty and meaning in this music" (151). "Ironically," she says,

> while his treatise provides the key to much of the implicit ideology of the standard Ger-man repertory, Schenker conceals his observations in formalisms. As a further irony, Schenker's work has been accepted as one of the principal modes of academic analysis in the United States, but only after it was stripped of its ideological trappings: in the recent translation (trans. Ernst Oster [New York: Longman, 1979]) the sections involved with mysticism and German supremacy have been moved to an appendix. The book now reads like a cut-and-dried method and is meant to be used as one. If Schenker silenced the cries of uncertainty and anguish apparent in the discontinuities of so much nineteenth-century music by showing that it all is—in the final analysis—normative and consistent with the laws of God, American Schenkerians have in turn silenced his metaphysical quest. (151–52)

But in one sense Ernst Oster was simply bringing Schenker's text into conform-ity with his own implicit intention, an intention that Oster does not put there (he thinks), but ideosomatically *knows* is there. Formalism is obviously more central to his project than the ideology of German supremacy; the formalism is what makes his book the important methodological treatise it so clearly is. Whatever detracts from that must be extraneous, peripheral, unfocused, unin-tended, and can therefore be safely excised. This interpretation feels convincing because the backgrounding of ideology and the foregrounding of form, struc-ture, techne have been at the center of Western institutional practice at least since Augustine.

McClary's musicological remarks also have interesting translatological ap-plications, since the musician has traditionally stood in almost exactly the same relation to the composer as the translator to the SL writer: "The performers on whom we rely to flesh our notated scores into sound are trained *not* to interpret (understood as the imposition of the unwanted self on what is fanta-sized to be a direct transmission of the composer's subjective intention to the listener), but rather to strive for a perfect, standard sound, for an unbroken, polished surface" (152). It would be an interesting project to trace the parallels between the social and political contexts in which music and translations are made: composer/conductor/musician/agent/recording technician/record company/record manufacturer/record distributor/music store/musicologist/music teacher/concert performance/home play, etc., and the equivalents in translatorial practice.

11. This is something of a sweeping generalization, and not strictly true. Those of my students who have worked for or done research on (multilingual) advertising agencies or translation bureaus that specialize in advertising translations make it clear that there are clients who insist not only on equivalence but on word-for-word equivalence—and may even require a back-translation to verify that their instructions have been carried out to the letter. But these tend to be exceptions. Not only will a substantial number of clients explicitly instruct translators to do whatever will work best in the TL (and commission market studies to help determine that), the ideosomatics of advertising translation (the gut-level norms shared by advertisers and translators alike) privilege "what works" over equivalence—so that clients who require word-for-word equivalence in advertising translations occasion a good deal of scorn in the business.

12. Or their advocates, like Walter Kaufmann:

Nor did anything he [Martin Buber] ever published seem as absurd to his readers in Germany as did his translation of the Bible. What was familiar seemed to have become incomprehensible.

In the beginning all this was due at least as much to Rosenzweig's uncompromising nature as to Buber, but Buber persisted even after Rosenzweig's death, and neither ridicule nor criticism ever moved him to relent. When he left Germany in 1938, the vast undertaking that had required so much effort looked like an almost total loss.

After the war, Buber was delighted when two German publishers asked him to resume his enterprise. He did, and brought it to completion shortly before his death. Gershom Scholem, a great scholar whose view of Hasidism differs from Buber's, toasted the achievement, adding: But who will read it?

What had seemed outrageous in the twenties and thirties was merely ahead of its time. A new generation that no longer expects all prose and poetry to be so easily accessible finds no extraordinary difficulty with the Buber Bible. It is widely read in German. (Prologue to *I and Thou* 40)

What Kaufmann neglects to add is that his "new generation that no longer expects all prose and poetry to be so easily accessible" is also the increasingly large college-educated part of that generation who reads Rilke and Musil and the others—not just anybody. "Widely read" by intellectuals. See also Rosenzweig's important essay on translation anthologized by Störig, and Buber's preface to the completed Bible translation from which I quoted and translated in Chapter 2 (also anthologized by Störig).

13. Jordan was a Southern preacher and New Testament Greek scholar (Th.M. and Ph.D. from Southern Baptist Theological Seminary) who had translated most of the NT (Mark, some of John, and Revelation remained untranslated) at his death in 1969. He founded Koinonia Farm in Americus, Geor-

gia, an interracial farming commune based on the economic principles of the early church—which of course is a nice way of saying communistic principles.

14. In his introduction to his rendition of Paul's epistles, Jordan writes:

> It may be said that the language of the "cotton patch" version is not elegant, dignified or even nice. Such expressions as "hell, no" and "the damned bastard" might offend those who think of the New Testament characters as dainty saints rather than sweaty men with deep feelings and sensitivities. But Paul may have been exaggerating only slightly when he called himself "the chief of the sinners" (I Tim. 1:15). So I have tried to let him be himself, without artificially clothing him with the image of immaculate sainthood. I feel sure that our beloved brother would prefer his "thorn in the flesh," given to him "lest I should be exalted above measure" (II Cor. 12:7), to the fake halo which his would-be admirers insist that he wear. (10)

He continues with a disclaimer of subversive intent:

> By the use of these uncouth expressions there has not been the slightest intent to shock, offend or startle—or to please—anyone. But at the same time, no effort has been made to shield the reader from the blunt, vigorous language of these letters. (11)

But of course, in an ecclesiastical tradition that daintifies the "blunt, vigorous language of these letters," a translator's willingness *not* to daintify must necessarily be intended to shock, offend, and startle. Jordan protests his innocence of subversive intent for good rhetorical reasons: he wants to convince good, churchgoing Christians that this is what the Bible *really* sounds like, so as to shame them into reading his rendition.

15. In Matthew 21 Jesus goes into "First Church," throws the "whole finance committee" out on its ear, tears up "the investment and endowment records," and scraps "the long-range expansion plans" (70–71)—and then retires to Jonesboro for the night.

16. This is the oft-quoted interview remark from *Positions:*

> That this opposition or difference [between signifier and signified] cannot be radical or absolute does not prevent it from functioning, and even from being indispensable within certain limits—very wide limits. For example, no translation would be possible without it. In effect, the theme of a transcendental signified took shape within the horizon of an absolutely pure, transparent, and unequivocal translatability. In the limits to which it is possible, or at least *appears* possible, translation practices the difference between signified and signifier. But if this difference is never pure, no more so is translation, and for the notion of translation we would have to substitute a notion of *transformation*: a regulated transformation of one language by another, of one text by another. (20)

17. Note how Benjamin's *Bereich,* or realm of pure language, is infected in Gandillac's imagination by the *Königsmantel* and becomes *ce royaume,* and how Graham, faithful to Derrida's fidelity to Gandillac's royalizing version of Benjamin, will go on to give us "the kingdom."

18. To invoke Heidegger's famous play on the root sense of *Dichtung,* or poetry, as a "thickening" of language. I hear an echo of Heidegger's *Zwiefalt,* or twofold, in the *weiten Falte* of the king's cape, too, probably because Derrida has coached me on the polysemy of the *plis* that Maurice de Gandillac replaces

those folds with in French. Here is Derrida in "D'un ton apocalyptique adopté naguère en philosophie" ("Of an Apocalyptic Tone Recently Adopted in Philosophy"):

Dans ce cas, si l'apocalypse révèle, elle est d'abord révélation de l'apocalypse, autoprésentation de la structure apocalyptique du langage, de l'écriture, de l'expérience de la présence, soit du texte ou de la marque en général: c'est-à-dire de l'envoi divisible pour lequel il n'y a pas d'auto-présentation ni de destination assurée. Mais laissons, il y a là un pli apocalyptique. Non seulement un pli comme envoi, un pli induisant un changement tonal et une immédiate duplicité tonale en toute voix apocalyptique. (471)

In that case, if the apocalypse reveals, it is first the revelation of the apocalyptic structure of writing, of the experience of presence, either of the text or of the mark in general: that is, of the divisible dispatch [*envoi*] for which there is no self-presentation nor assured destination. But let us not worry, there is an apocalyptic *pli* [fold, envelope, letter, habit, message] there. Not only a *pli* as dispatch, a *pli* inducing a tonal change and an immediate tonal duplicity in every apocalyptic voice. (Leavey's translation, 87–88)

19. This example, and the short shrift that I give it, reminds me that I really ought to have a chapter in this book on the "mystics" or "mysticism" or "mystique" of translation, moving from the brief hints that I have dropped in that direction (in my discussion of reversion, especially) into the whole realm of translation and taboos on translation in the mystery religions. The entire Kabbalistic/romantic tradition of translation theory most powerfully represented in our century by Walter Benjamin and George Steiner would be relevant here, but not only that; any time a translator discovered the significance of his or her work in a move from technical transfer not to ethical growth but to mystical insight, we would have a mysticism of translation. The ethics of translation as I understand them stand somewhere between the private, personal, intensely emotional experience of the mystics of translation (idiosomatic insight as its own reward) and the public, collective, intensely action-oriented experience of the politics of translation (idiosomatic insight subordinated to ideosomatic shift)—another area that I have not properly explored here. In my exclusion of extremely privatized and extremely collectivized translation (mystics and politics), in my preference for the partly private, partly collective ethics of translation, I suppose that I have remained more or less liberal and bourgeois: you break through the three seals in order to become a better person, and you become a better person in order to treat others better, and you treat others better by way of making society better. This is, of course, the liberal bourgeois dream.

20. For a useful discussion of Browning, Nabokov, Hölderlin, and other radically literal translators, see Steiner, 310–33.

21. Another important consideration in translational aversion is social class: the scorn for the bourgeois reader's needs that we find in writers like Walter Benjamin and Vladimir Nabokov reflects an aristocratic haughtiness that Nabokov inherits and Benjamin, like most of the postromantic intelligentsia, affects. The upper middle class since the late eighteenth century has been increas-

ingly concerned to distinguish itself from the lower rungs of the bourgeoisie (and to align itself with the nobility) by disavowing the importance of money and in general all pragmatic concerns, like what *good* is it, and turning increasingly to pursuits like art and religion whose "uselessness" in worldly terms proclaims this cultural elite's spiritual nobility—and the intelligentsia has assiduously followed the haute bourgeoisie's lead.

22. The analogy of the pimp suggests a somewhat different deconstruction of Benjamin's text from Derrida's: when Benjamin says that the "intentions" dwelling in all languages want to commingle with other languages until that commingling produces the harmony of pure language, but that they need the translator's help to bring it about, to bring them into contact, all that he is doing, really, is idealizing the pimp: the translator should pimp for whole languages in the interests of redemption, not for individual people (writers and readers) in the interests of communication. If you take Benjamin's images seriously, they flesh out an awesome scene of great visionary giants humping madly in a cosmic hotel room, individual languages driven by their intentions to keep demanding more sex, more body contact, and the poor translator is caught in between, in constant danger of being crushed by the forces he has helped set in motion, and yet constantly required to keep them in motion, to keep procuring new hookers, new johns, more sex, more build-up, until at long last they achieve it, do it, the Big Bang, the greatest orgasm of them all, the long-awaited apocalypse.

23. "Das scheint hinreichend den Rangunterschied im Bereiche der Kunst zwischen beiden zu erklären," for instance: only scheint? Only seems? Aren't you more solidly convinced than that? And what Rangunterschied? Just what is that discrepancy in status? Is it that translation is regarded much more highly than original art? Benjamin's essay is rhetorically extremely restrained, even decorous; I suppose that Derrida's talk of the translation busying its tongue about the king's penis and my talk of pimping for losers would have shocked him.

24. My guess is that this is why George Steiner reverses the order of Goethe's epochs: his first movement of trust corresponds to Goethe's second epoch or maxim (in his first formulation, in *Zum brüderlichen Andenken Wielands*), in which the translator subordinates the TL to the SL; and his second and third movements of aggression and incorporation together correspond to Goethe's first epoch, in which the translator takes from the SL what he or she needs or considers valuable or feels comfortable with and brings it home. In the psychohistory of the translator's approach to a text, trust or literalism does come first; the aggressive and incorporative movements by which Steiner demystifies sense-for-sense translation come later. (He comes at this demystification by understanding "sense" not ideally but ideologically and politically—not as a stable, abstract universal but as the only recognizably valuable SL property that the imperialist or colonializing translator can discern, the raw materials required by the TL cultural industry, for which the translator plun-

ders the SL. "Sense" is the translator's aggressive reduction of the SL text to a commodity framable in TL terms.)

To be sure, Steiner waffles on all this. His unwillingness to take a stand on the theoretical status of his movements (whether they are psychohistorical phases in every translator's approach to a text, sociohistorical phases in a culture's approach to foreign texts—as they were for Goethe—or static logical categories into which specific translations can be classified) leaves it unclear why trust, say, comes first. The hermeneutic motion does seem to resemble a single (idealized) act of translation, with the translator first trusting the SL text, then invading and plundering it, then bringing home the spoils, then making restitution of some sort (the vaguest, most idealizing movement of the four)—and this would suggest that trust comes first because it is most natural. But Steiner does not want to leave literalism in its debased status as the sloppy product of amateurs, which would seem to follow from this "psychohistorical" model of the motion, and so lets Benjamin guide him to the romantic conception of literalism as the ultimate act of translation:

> Far from being the most obvious, rudimentary mode of translation, "literalism" or as Dryden called it, *metaphrase,* is in fact the least attainable. The true interlinear is the final, unrealizable goal of the hermeneutic act. Historically, practically, the interlinear and *mot-à-mot* may indeed be a crude device. But rigorously conceived, it embodies that totality of understanding and reproduction, that utter transparency between languages which is empirically unattainable and whose attainment would signal a return to Adamic unison of human speech. (308)

And he goes on to quote the end of Benjamin's piece. But if "the true interlinear is the final, unrealizable goal of the hermeneutic act," then trust should be the fourth movement, not the first. Does Steiner agree with Benjamin or not? Here it seems he does. In fact, his conception of his fourth movement as restitution owes a lot to the romantic reversionary imagination on which Benjamin bases his own claims for literalism. (The two are differently conceived, Steiner's leaning more toward Goethe's third epoch as synthesis between going away and coming back, but both are insistently redemptive.) Steiner wants to have his cake and eat it too: wants to let literalism be the translator's first *approach* to the SL text, thus be historically and pragmatically a "crude device"; and also to elevate it to an eminently respectable kind of translation, perhaps the most respectable of all. This might have worked better dialectically: the "crude" amateur literalist (thesis) learns to translate sense for sense (antithesis), but discovering what an impoverishing violence this does to the SL text, comes back to literalism with new appreciation, literalism raised to a higher power, literalism as perfect word-for-word *and* sense-for-sense equivalence between two texts, the ultimate unattainable ideal of Western translation (synthesis). The vagueness of Steiner's fourth movement surely has something to do with his desire to retain something of this synthetic resolution (and its redemptive potential) while not falling into the trap of unattainability. My own conception of translation as an embodied dialogical turning is another attempt to solve the same problem on a higher level: I seek to synthesize Steiner's restitutive ideal with the category excluded by all equivalence theories, "free" translation.

25. The word-for-word vs. sense-for-sense debate reduces to something like the issues that Benjamin and I are raising: those who favor word-for-word translation tend to stress the fullness of meaning, its participation in both somatic and semantic response, and, while therefore denying the possibility of translation in general (the fullness of meaning so defined has no equivalents in any other language), they also insist that the translator turn away from the TL and the reader who speaks it toward the SL and its writer. Those who favor sense-for-sense translation tend to stress the reduction of meaning to a stable transferrable abstraction (a Platonic idea or form) and the separability and disposability of the verbal body or vehicle of this meaning; in order to facilitate the smooth communication of the abstracted meaning, they insist that the translator turn away from the SL toward the TL reader (in an introverted way that permits the SL writer to do his or her proselytizing work).

26. It is instructive, for example, to watch Eugene Nida describe his approach to translation as "new," as in "A New Concept of Translating" (Nida and Taber, chap. 1): "The older focus in translating was the form of the message, and translators took particular delight in being able to reproduce stylistic specialties, *e.g.,* rhythms, rhymes, plays on words, chiasmus, parallelism, and unusual grammatical structures. The new focus, however, has shifted from the form of the message to the response of the receptor" (1). It is as new as Jerome and Luther, and is at least implied in Cicero's preference for an "oratorical" or rhetorically equivalent translation—but it is new to each beginning translator who has yet to be indoctrinated into the rhetorical tradition, and who therefore still clings too closely to the letter of the SL text.

27. The Voice is a one-way translating machine that will translate two thousand spoken phrases in English, German, French, or Spanish into their spoken equivalents in one of the other languages. "One-way" translating means that it will not translate the local's reply to your question—it cannot process natural language, which makes it next to useless. But it *is* an expensive toy for the man who has everything, which is certainly something.

28. At least until all language is as rigidly ritualized as weather reports. And that, of course, is certainly a possibility, what with the progress that biologists and cyberneticists have been making lately with gene splicing and brain implants. You never know. Maybe MT will be a reality at popular prices by the year 2000.

Works Cited

Ahsen, Akhter. *Psycheye*. New York: Brandon House, 1977.

———. *Rhea Complex: A Detour around Oedipus Complex*. New York: Brandon House, 1984.

———. *Trojan Horse*. New York: Brandon House, 1984.

Aland, Kurt, et al., eds. *The Greek New Testament*. 1966. Reprint. New York: American Bible Society, 1975.

Althusser, Louis. "Idéologies et appareils idéologique d'Etat." *La pensée* 151 (1970): 3–38. Translated by Ben Brewster, "Ideology and Ideological State Apparatuses (Notes toward an Investigation)." In *Lenin and Philosophy and Other Essays*, 121–73. 1969. Reprint. London: New Left Books.

Altieri, Charles. "Motives for Metaphor: John Ashbery and the Modernist Long Poem." *Genre* 11 (Winter 1978): 653–87.

Ammons, A. R. "Corson's Inlet." In *Corson's Inlet: A Book of Poems*, 5–8. Ithaca: Cornell University Press, 1965.

Aquinas, Thomas. "Contra errores Graecorum." Vol. 1 of *Divi Thomas Aquinatis doctoris angelici opuscula omnia*. Antwerp, 1612.

Arnold, Matthew. *Culture and Anarchy*. 1869. Reprint. Cambridge: Cambridge University Press, 1971.

———. "On Translating Homer." In *On the Classical Tradition*, edited by R. H. Super, 97–216. Vol. 1 of *The Complete Prose Works of Matthew Arnold*. Ann Arbor: University of Michigan Press, 1961.

Arrowsmith, William, and Roger Shattuck, eds. *The Craft and Context of Translation*. Austin: University of Texas Press, 1961.

Attali, Jacques. *Bruits: Essai sur l'économie politique de la musique*. Paris: Presses Universitaires de France, 1977. Translated by Brian Massumi, *Noise: A Political Economy of Music*. Minneapolis: University of Minnesota Press, 1985.

Augustine, Aurelius. *Confessiones*. 2 vols. 1912. Reprint. London: Heinemann, 1970. Translated by R. S. Pine-Coffin, *Confessions*. 1961. Reprint. Harmondsworth: Penguin Books, 1975.

———. *De doctrina Christiana*. Vol. 32 of *Corpus Christianorum, Series Latina*. Turnholti, Belgium: Typographi Brepols, 1962. Translated by D. W. Robertson, Jr., *On Christian Doctrine*. 1958. Reprint. Indianapolis: Bobbs-Merrill, 1979.

Austin, J. L. *How to Do Things with Words.* Edited by J. O. Urmson and Marina Sbisa. 1962. Reprint. London: Oxford University Press, 1980.

Bacon, Roger. *Opus Maius.* Edited by J. H. Bridges. 3 vols. 1266(?); London: Clarendon Press at Oxford University Press, 1900. Translated by Robert Belle Burke, *Opus Majus.* New York: Russell & Russell, 1962.

Bakhtin, Mikhail. *Slovo v Romane.* In *Voprosy literatury i estetiki.* Moscow, 1975. Translated by Caryl Emerson and Michael Holquist, *Discourse in the Novel.* In *The Dialogic Imagination: Four Essays,* edited by Holquist, 259–422. Austin: University of Texas Press, 1981.

Bally, Charles. *Linguistique générale et linguistique francaise.* 1932. Reprint. Berne: Franke Verlag, 1965.

Bassnett-McGuire, Susan. *Translation Studies.* London: Methuen, 1980.

Bateson, Gregory. *Steps to an Ecology of Mind.* 1972. Reprint. New York: Ballantine Books, 1985.

Benjamin, Walter. "Die Aufgabe des Übersetzers." In *Das Problem des Übersetsens,* 182–95. *See* Störig 1963. Translated by Harry Zohn, "The Task of the Translator." In *Illuminations,* edited by Hannah Arendt, 69–82. 1955. Reprint. Glasgow: Fontana/Collins, 1982.

Berger, John. *Ways of Seeing.* 1972. Reprint. Harmondsworth: Penguin Books, 1974.

Bergström, Matti. "Communication and Translation from the Point of View of Brain Function." In *Translationstheorie—Grundlagen und Standorte,* edited by Justa Holz-Mänttäri, 23–36. Studia translatologica, ser. A, vol. 1. University of Tampere, 1989.

Blake, William. *The Marriage of Heaven and Hell.* In *The Complete Poetry and Prose of William Blake,* rev. ed., edited by David V. Erdman, 33–45. 1965. Garden City, N.Y.: Doubleday, 1982.

Bloom, Harold. *A Map of Misreading.* 1975. Reprint. New York: Oxford University Press, 1980.

Boethius. *In isagogen Porphyrii.* Edited by S. Brant. Vol. 48 of *Corpus scriptorum ecclesiasticorum latinorum.* Vienna and Leipzig, 1906.

Bornstein, Harry, ed. *The Comprehensive Signed English Dictionary.* Washington, D.C.: Gallaudet College Press, 1983.

Brod, Harry, ed. *The Making of Masculinities: The New Men's Studies.* Boston: Allen & Unwin, 1987.

Brower, R. A. *On Translation.* New York: Oxford University Press, 1966.

Buber, Martin. *Ich und Du.* Berlin: Schocken Verlag, 1936. Translated by Walter Kaufmann, *I and Thou.* New York: Scribner, 1970.

———. "Zu einer neuen Verdeutschung der Schrift." In *Das Problem des Übersetsens,* 322–62. *See* Störig, 1963.

Burke, Kenneth. "A Dramatistic View of the Origins of Language." In *Language as Symbolic Action,* 419–79.

———. *A Grammar of Motives.* 1945. Reprint. Berkeley: University of California Press, 1962.

———. *Language as Symbolic Action: Essays on Life, Literature, and Method.* Berkeley: University of California Press, 1966.

———. "Mind, Body, and the Unconscious." In *Language as Symbolic Action,* 63–80.

———. *The Rhetoric of Religion.* 1961. Reprint. Berkeley: University of California Press, 1970.

———. "Terministic Screens." In *Language as Symbolic Action,* 44–62.

———. "The Thinking of the Body (Comments on the Imagery of Catharsis in Literature)." In *Language as Symbolic Action,* 308–43.

———. "Versions, Con-, Per-, and In- (Thoughts on Djuna Barnes' Novel *Nightwood*)." In *Language as Symbolic Action,* 240–53.

Campbell, George. *The Philosophy of Rhetoric.* 1776. Reprint. New York, 1850.

Carse, James M. *Finite and Infinite Games: A Vision of Life as Play and Possibility.* New York: Free Press, 1986.

Catford, J. C. *A Linguistic Theory of Translation.* London: Longmans, 1965.

Chesterton, G. K. *Saint Thomas Aquinas.* 1933. Reprint. Garden City, N.Y.: Doubleday, 1956.

Chomsky, Noam. *Aspects of the Theory of Syntax.* Cambridge: MIT Press, 1965.

———. *Syntactic Structures.* The Hague: Mouton, 1957.

Cicero, Marcus Tullius. *De optimo genere oratorum.* Translated by H. M. Hubbell, *On the Best Kind of Orator,* 347–73. Vol. 2 of *Cicero in Twenty-Eight Volumes.* 1949. Reprint. London: Heinemann, 1968.

Colie, Rosalie. *Paradoxia Epidemica: The Renaissance Tradition of Paradox.* Princeton: Princeton University Press, 1966.

Dante Alighieri. *Il convito.* Edited by M. Simonelli. Bologna, 1966. Translated by Katharine Hillard, *The Banquet.* London: Kegan Paul, Trench, 1889.

de Beaugrande, Robert. *Factors in a Theory of Poetic Translating.* Assen/Amsterdam: Van Gorcum, 1978.

Deleuze, Gilles, and Félix Guattari. *L'Anti-Oedipe.* Paris: Minuit, 1972. Translated by Robert Hurley, Mark Seem, and Helen R. Lane, *Anti-Oedipus.* Minneapolis: University of Minnesota Press, 1983.

Derrida, Jacques. "Des Tours de Babel." In *Difference in Translation,* edited by Joseph F. Graham, 209–48. Ithaca: Cornell University Press, 1985. Translated by Joseph F. Graham, "Des Tours de Babel." In Graham, 165–207.

———. *De la grammatologie.* Paris: Minuit, 1967. Translated by Gayatri Chakravorty Spivak, *Of Grammatology.* 1976. Reprint. Baltimore: Johns Hopkins University Press, 1982.

———. "D'un ton apocalyptique adopté naguère en philosophie." In *Le fin de l'homme,* 445–79. Paris: Editions Galilée, 1981. Translated by John P. Leavey, Jr., "Of an Apocalyptic Tone Recently Adopted in Philosophy." *Semeia* 23 (1982): 63–97.

———. *Limited Inc.* Edited by Gerald Graff. Translated by Samuel Weber and Jeffrey Mehlmann. Evanston, Ill.: Northwestern University Press, 1988.

————. *Positions.* Paris: Editions de Minuit, 1972. Translated by Alan Bass. 1981. Reprint. Chicago: University of Chicago Press, 1982.

Douglas, Ann. *The Feminization of American Culture.* New York: Knopf, 1977.

Dryden, John. "Preface to Ovid's Epistles" and "Dedication of the Aeneis." Excerpted in *English Translation Theory,* 68–74. *See* T. R. Steiner 1975.

Du Bellay, Joachim. *La deffence et illústration de la langue français.* Edited by E. Person. 1549. Reprint. Paris, 1878. Translated by James Harry Smith and Edd Winfield Parks, "The Defense and Illustration of the French Language." In *The Great Critics: An Anthology of Literary Criticism,* edited by Smith and Parks. 1932. Reprint. New York: Norton, 1967.

Emerson, Caryl. "Editor's Preface." In Mikhail Bakhtin, *Problems of Dostoevsky's Poetics,* xxix–xliii, edited and translated by Caryl Emerson. Minneapolis: University of Minnesota Press, 1984.

Emerson, Ralph Waldo. *Nature.* In *Nature, Addresses, and Lectures,* 7–45. 1836. Reprint. Cambridge: Harvard University Press, Belknap Press, 1979.

Erasmus. *Novum Instrumentum.* Translated by William Tindale. Basel: Froben, 1516.

Erikson, Erik H. *Young Man Luther: A Study in Psychoanalysis and History.* 1958. Reprint. New York: Norton, 1962.

Felman, Shoshana. *Le scandale du corps parlant.* Paris: Seuil, 1980. Translated by Catherine Porter, *The Literary Speech Act: Don Juan with J. L. Austin, or Seduction in Two Languages.* Ithaca: Cornell University Press, 1983.

Fetterley, Judith. *The Resisting Reader: A Feminist Approach to American Fiction.* Bloomington: Indiana University Press, 1978.

Fletcher, Angus. "Volume and Body in Burke's Criticism, or Stalled in the Right Place." In *Representing Kenneth Burke,* edited by Hayden White and Margaret Rose, 150–75. Baltimore: Johns Hopkins University Press, 1982.

Fowles, John. *The French Lieutenant's Woman.* Boston: Little, Brown, 1969.

Furth, Hans. *Thinking without Language: Psychological Complications of Deafness.* New York: Free Press, 1966.

Gerver, David. "Empirical Studies of Simultaneous Interpretation: A Review and a Model." In *Translation: Applications and Research,* edited by Richard W. Brislin, 166–207. New York: Gardner Press, 1976.

Gibbons, Reginald. "Poetic Form and the Translator." *Critical Inquiry* 11 (June 1985): 654–71.

Ginsburg, Mirra. "Translation in Russia: The Politics of Translation." In *The World of Translation,* 351–60. New York: PEN American Center, 1971.

Goethe, Johann Wolfgang von. *Aus Meinem Leben: Dichtung und Wahrheit.* Excerpted in *Das Problem des Übersetsens,* 34–35. *See* Störig 1963. Excerpted and translated as "The Pedagogical Value of Prose Translations" in *Translating Literature,* 37–38. *See* Lefevere 1977.

————. *Faust.* Edited by Max Beckmann. 2 vols. Wiesbaden: Drei Lilien Verlag, 1953. Translated by Charles E. Passage. Indianapolis: Bobbs-Merrill, 1965.

————. *West-Östlicher Divan*. Edited by Ernst Beutler. Bremen: Carl Schöne-mann Verlag, 1956. Excerpted in *Das Problem des Übersetsens*, 35–37. *See* Störig 1963. Excerpted and translated as "The Three Epochs of Translation" in *Translating Literature*, 35–37. *See* Lefevere 1977.

————. *Zum brüderlichen Andenken Wielands*. Excerpted in *Das Problem des Übersetsens*, 35. *See* Störig 1963. Excerpted and translated as "Author, Reader, Translator: The Two Maxims" in *Translating Literature*, 39. *See* Lefevere 1977.

Gramsci, Antonio. *Lettere dal carcere*. Vol. 1 of *Opere*. 7 vols. Turin: Binaudi, 1947–67. Translated and edited by Quintin Hoare and Geoffrey Nowell Smith, *Selections From the Prison Notebooks*. New York: International Publishers, 1971.

Grice, H. Paul. "Logic and Conversation." In *Speech Acts*, edited by Peter Cole and Jerry L. Morgan, 41–58. Vol. 3 of *Syntax and Semantics*. New York: Academic Press, 1975.

Griffin, Susan. *Pornography and Silence: Culture's Revenge against Nature*. New York: Harper & Row, 1981.

Gurney, Eric, and Nancy Gurney. *The King, the Mice and the Cheese/El rey, los ratones, y el queso*. Translated by Carlos Rivera. New York: Beginner Books/Random House, 1967.

Hakulinen, Lauri. *Suomen sanaston käännöslainoja*. Publications of the Finnish Literature Society, vol. 293. Forssa: Forssan Kirjapaino, 1969.

Hallett, Garth, S.J. *A Companion to Wittgenstein's "Philosophical Investigations."* Ithaca: Cornell University Press, 1977.

————. *Wittgenstein's Definition of Meaning as Use*. New York: Fordham University Press, 1967.

Hardwick, Charles S. *Language Learning in Wittgenstein's Later Philosophy*. The Hague: Mouton, 1971.

Heidegger, Martin. *Der Satz vom Grund*. Excerpted in *Das Problem des Übersetsens*, 395–409. *See* Störig 1963. Translated by Michael Heim. Bloomington: Indiana University Press, 1984.

————. ". . . dichterisch Wohnet der Mensch . . ." *Aksente, Zeitschrift für Dichtung* 1 (1954): 57–74. Translated by Albert Hofstadter, ". . . Poetically Man Dwells . . ." In *Poetry, Language, Thought*, edited by Hofstadter, 211–29. 1971. Reprint. New York: Harper & Row, 1975.

Herder, Johann Gottfried. *Fragmente*. In *Sämtliche Werke*, vol. 1, edited by B. Suphan. Berlin: Weidmannsche Buchhandlung, 1877. Excerpted and translated in *Translating Literature*, 30–34. *See* Lefevere 1977.

Hölderlin, Friedrich. *Übersetzungen*. Vol. 5 of *Sämtliche Werke*, edited by Friedrich Beissner. Stuttgart: W. Kohlhammer Verlag, 1952. Translated and edited by Thomas Pfau, *Essays on Letters and Theory*. Albany: State University of New York Press, 1988.

Hollander, John. "Versions, Interpretations, Performances." In *On Translation*, 205–31. *See* Brower 1966.

Holz-Mänttäri, Justa. *Translatorisches Handeln*. Helsinki: Finnish Academy of Science, 1984.

House, Juliane. *A Model for Translation Quality Assessment*. North Amsterdam: Benjamins, 1977.

Huizinga, Jan. *Homo Ludens: Versuch einer Bestimmtung des Spielelements der Kultur*. Basel, 1944. Translated by Huizinga, *Homo Ludens: A Study of the Play Element in Culture*. Boston: Beacon Press, 1950.

Humphries, Jefferson. *Metamorphoses of the Raven*. Baton Rouge: Louisiana State University Press, 1985.

Hymes, Dell. "On Communicative Competence." In *Sociolinguistics: Selected Readings,* edited by J. B. Pride and Janet Holmes, 269–93. Harmondsworth: Penguin Books, 1972.

Ingarden, Roman. *Das literarische Kunstwerk: Eine Untersuchung aus dem Grenzgebiet der Ontologie, Logik, und Literaturwissenschaft*. Halle: Niemeyer, 1931. Translated by George G. Grabowicz, *The Literary Work of Art*. Evanston: Northwestern University Press, 1974.

Iser, Wolfgang. *Der Akt des Lesens*. Stuttgart: Uni-Taschenbucher, 1976. Translated by Iser, *The Act of Reading: A Theory of Aesthetic Response*. Baltimore: Johns Hopkins University Press, 1978.

Jakobson, Roman. "On Linguistic Aspects of Translation." In *On Translation,* 232–39. *See* Brower 1966.

James, William. *The Principles of Psychology*. 2 vols. 1890. Reprint. New York: Henry Holt, 1908.

Jerome. "Liber de optimo genere interpretandi (epistula 57)." Edited by G. J. M. Bartchuk. Leiden: Brill, 1980. Translated by W. H. Fremantle, "Letter LVII to Pammachius on the Best Method of Translating." In *The Principal Works of Jerome,* vol. 6 of *A Select Library of Nicene and Post-Nicene Fathers of the Christian Church (Second Series),* edited by Philip Schaff and Henry Wace. New York: Christian Literature Company, 1893.

Johnson, Barbara. "Taking Fidelity Philosophically." In *Difference in Translation,* edited by Joseph F. Graham, 142–48. Ithaca: Cornell University Press, 1985.

Jordan, Clarence, trans. *The Cotton Patch Version of Hebrews and the General Epistles*. 1963, 1964, 1969. Reprint. Piscataway, N.J.: New Century, 1973.

———. *The Cotton Patch Version of Luke and Acts*. Piscataway, N.J.: New Century, 1969.

———. *The Cotton Patch Version of Matthew and John*. Piscataway, N.J.: New Century, 1970.

———. *The Cotton Patch Version of Paul's Epistles*. Piscataway, N.J.: New Century, 1968.

Jumpelt, R. W. *Die Übersetzung naturwissenschaftlicher und technischer literatur*. Berlin: Schöneberg, 1958.

Katz, Jerrold. *Propositional Structure and Illocutionary Force*. New York: Crowell, 1977.

Kaufman, Michael, ed. *Beyond Patriarchy: Essays by Men on Pleasure, Power, and Change*. New York: Oxford University Press, 1987.

Kaufmann, Walter. "I and You: A Prologue" to translation of Buber's *I and Thou*, 7–50.

Kelly, Louis. *The True Interpreter: A History of Translation Theory and Practice in the West*. Oxford: Basil Blackwell, 1979.

Kenner, Hugh. *The Pound Era*. Berkeley: University of California Press, 1971.

Kermode, Frank. *The Sense of an Ending*. New York: Oxford University Press, 1967.

Kuhn, Thomas S. *The Structure of Scientific Revolutions*. 1962. Reprint. Chicago: University of Chicago Press, 1970.

Kuusi, Matti, Keith Bosley, and Michael Branch, eds. and trans. *Finnish Folk Poetry: Epic; An Anthology in Finnish and English*. Helsinki: Suomalaisen Kirjallisuuden Seura, 1977.

Lacan, Jacques. *Speech and Language in Psychoanalysis*. Translated by Anthony Wilden. 1968. Reprint. Baltimore: Johns Hopkins University Press, 1981.

Lattimore, Richard, trans. Homer, *The Odyssey*. 1965. Reprint. New York: Harper & Row, 1975.

Lawson, Veronica, ed. *Practical Experience of Machine Translation*. Amsterdam: North-Holland, 1982.

Leech, Geoffrey. *Semantics*. Harmondsworth: Penguin Books, 1974.

Lefevere, André. *Translating Literature: The German Tradition from Luther to Rosenzweig*. Assen/Amsterdam: Van Gorcum, 1977.

Leino, Eino. *Runot*. Edited by Aarre M. Peltonen. 4 vols. Helsinki: Otava, 1961.

Lentricchia, Frank. *After the New Criticism*. Chicago: University of Chicago Press, 1980.

———. *Criticism and Social Change*. 1983. Reprint. Chicago: University of Chicago Press, 1985.

Levý, Jiri. *Die literarische Übersetzung: Theorie einer Kunstgattung*. Translated (from Czech into German) by Walter Schamnschula. Frankfurt am Main: Athenäums Verlag, 1967.

Longfellow, Henry Wadsworth. *The Song of Hiawatha*. In *Poetical Works*. New York: Oxford University Press, 1904.

Lönnrot, Elias, ed. *Kalevala*. 1835–1844. Reprint. Helsinki: Otava, 1983. Trans. e.g. W. F. Kirby, *Kalevala: Land of the Heroes*. 2 vols. 1907. Reprint. London: Dent/Everyman Library, 1974.

Luther, Martin. "Sendbrief vom Dolmetchen." In *Das Problem des Übersetsens*, 14–32. *See* Störig 1963. Trans. e.g. W. H. Carruth, "Luther on Translation." *Open Court* 21 (1907): 465–71.

Lyons, John. *Introduction to Theoretical Linguistics*. 1968. Reprint. Cambridge: Cambridge University Press, 1975.

McClary, Susan. "Afterword" to Massumi's translation of Attali's *Noise*, 149–58.

Marx, Karl, and Friedrich Engels. *Das deutsche Ideologie.* 1845–46. Reprint. Moscow: Marx-Engels-Lenin-Institut, 1932. Translated by W. Lough, *The German Ideology.* Edited by C. J. Arthur. New York: International Publishers, 1970.

Mencken, H. L. "On Being an American." In *Prejudices: A Selection,* edited by James T. Farrell, 89–125. New York: Random House/Vintage, 1958.

Mitchell, W. J. T., ed. *Against Theory.* Chicago: University of Chicago Press, 1986.

Murray, Alexander. *Reason and Society in the Middle Ages.* London: Clarendon Press at Oxford University Press, 1978.

Nabokov, Vladimir. "The Art of Translation." *New Republic* 105 (1941): 160–62.

———. *The Portable Nabokov.* Edited by Page Stegner. 1968. Reprint. Harmondsworth: Penguin Books, 1978.

———. "Reply to My Critics." In *The Portable Nabokov,* 300–324.

———. "On Translating *Eugene Onegin.*" In *The Portable Nabokov,* 531–32.

Newmark, Peter. *Approaches to Translation.* Oxford: Pergamon Press, 1981.

Nida, Eugene A., and Charles Taber. *The Theory and Practice of Translation.* Leiden: Brill, 1969.

Nida, Eugene A., and Jan de Waard. *From One Language to Another: Functional Equivalence in Bible Translating.* Nashville: Thomas Nelson, 1986.

Nietzsche, Friedrich. *Also Sprach Zarathustra.* Vol. 13 of *Nietzsches Gesammelte Werke, Musarionausgabe.* 23 vols. 1883–92. Munich: Musarion Verlag, 1920–29. Translated by Walter Kaufmann, *Thus Spoke Zarathustra.* New York: Viking, 1966.

———. *Zur Genealogie der Moral.* Vol. 15 of *Nietzsches Gesammelte Werke, Musarionausgabe.* 23 vols. 1883–92. Munich: Musarion Verlag, 1920–29. Translated by Walter Kaufmann, *The Genealogy of Morals.* Printed with *Ecce Homo.* New York: Vintage, 1968.

Novalis. *Blüthenstaub.* Excerpted in *Das Problem des Übersetsens,* 33. See Störig 1963. Excerpted and translated as "Three Kinds of Translation" in *Translating Literature,* 64. See Lefevere 1977.

O'Neill, Tip, with William Novak. *Man of the House: The Life and Political Memoirs of Speaker Tip O'Neill.* New York: Random House, 1987.

Osgood, Charles E., George J. Suci, and Percy H. Tannenbaum. *The Measurement of Meaning.* Urbana: University of Illinois Press, 1957.

Pope, Alexander. "Preface to the Iliad." Excerpted in *English Translation Theory,* 90–95. See T. R. Steiner 1975.

Pound, Ezra. *Cathay.* In *Translations.* New York: New Directions, 1953.

———. *Literary Essays of Ezra Pound.* Edited by T. S. Eliot. New York: New Directions, 1954.

———. "Notes on Elizabethan Classicists." In *Literary Essays,* 227–48.

———. "Translators of Greek: Early Translators of Homer." In *Literary Essays,* 249–75.

Reiss, Katharina. *Texttyp und Übersetzungsmethode*. Kronberg: Scriptor Verlag, 1976.

Rilke, Rainer Maria. *Die Sonette an Orpheus/Sonnets to Orpheus*. In *Selected Poems of Rainer Maria Rilke* (bilingual), translated by Robert Bly, 194–213. New York: Harper & Row, 1981.

Robinson, Douglas. *American Apocalypses: The Image of the End of the World in American Literature*. Baltimore: Johns Hopkins University Press, 1985.

———. "Intentions, Signs, and Interpretations: C. S. Peirce and the Dialogic of Pragmatism." *Kodikas/Code/Ars Semeiotica* 8, nos. 3/4 (1985): 179–93.

———. "Koskenko yli saareen? Pentti Saarikoski kääntäjänä ja käännösteoreetikkona." In *Käänntäjät kulttuurivaikuttajina: Kääntäjäseminaari Jyväskylässä, 3.–5.7.1986*, edited by Arja Ollikainen and Martti Pulakka, 143–65. Publications of the University of Jyväskylä Literature Department, vol. 35. Jyväskylä, 1987.

———. "Metapragmatics and Its Discontents." *Journal of Pragmatics* 10 (1986): 651–71.

———. "Reader's Power, Writer's Power: Barth, Bergonzi, Iser, and the Modern-Postmodern Period Debate." *Criticism* 28, no. 3 (1986): 307–22.

———. "Trivial and Esoteric Pursuits: The Power Politics of Interpretive Communities." *Southwest Review* 72 (Spring 1987): 202–23.

Robinson, Ian. *The New Grammarians' Funeral: A Critique of Noam Chomsky's Linguistics*. Cambridge: Cambridge University Press, 1975.

Rowan, John. *The Horned God: Feminism and Men as Wounding and Healing*. London: Routledge & Kegan Paul, 1987.

Rosenzweig, Franz. "Die Schrift und Luther." In *Das Problem des Übersetsens*, 220–48. *See* Störig 1963. Excerpted and translated as "The Impossibility and Necessity of Translation" in *Translating Literature*, 110–11. *See* Lefevere 1977.

Saarikoski, Pentti. *Asiaa tai ei*. Helsinki: Otava, 1980.

Sacks, Oliver. *Seeing Voices: A Journey into the World of the Deaf*. Berkeley: University of California Press, 1989.

Sampson, Geoffrey. *Forms of Language*. Oxford: Oxford University Press, 1975.

———. *Liberty and Language*. Oxford: Oxford University Press, 1979.

———. *Making Sense*. Oxford: Oxford University Press, 1980.

Saussure, Ferdinand de. *Cours de linguistique générale* [1916]. Rev. ed., edited by Julliode Mauro. Paris: Editions Payot, 1983. Translated by Roy Harris, *Course in General Linguistics*. London: Duckworth, 1983.

Savory, Theodore. *The Art of Translation*. London: Jonathan Cape, 1968.

Schleiermacher, Friedrich. "Über die verschiedenen Methoden des Übersetzungs." In *Das Problem des Übersetsens*, 38–70. *See* Störig 1963. Translated as "On the Different Methods of Translating" in *Translating Literature*, 67–89. *See* Lefevere 1977.

Schonert, Wolfgang. "Erokirje Lutherille." Translated (from German into Finnish) by Eero Mattila. *Tampereen yliopistouutiset* 23 (August 7, 1984): 6–7.

Searle, John. "Reiterating the Differences." *Glyph One,* 198–211. Baltimore: Johns Hopkins University Press, 1977.

———. *Speech Acts: An Essay in the Philosophy of Language.* Cambridge: Cambridge University Press, 1969.

Stark, Mark. "The King of the Ghosts: Have Pen, Will Travel." *Newsweek* (February 8, 1988): 54.

Steiner, George. *After Babel: Aspects of Language and Translation.* New York: Oxford University Press, 1975.

Steiner, T. R., ed. *English Translation Theory, 1650–1800.* Assen/Amsterdam: Van Gorcum, 1975.

Stevens, Wallace. *Adagia.* In *Opus Posthumous,* edited by Holly Stevens. New York: Knopf, 1957.

———. *The Collected Poems of Wallace Stevens.* 1954. Reprint. New York; Random House/Vintage, 1982.

Störig, Hans Joachim, ed. *Das Problem des Übersetsens.* Darmstadt: Wissenschaftliche Buchgesellschaft, 1963.

Thouin, Benoît. "The Meteo System." In *Practical Experience of Machine Translation,* 39–44. *See* Lawson 1982.

Trump, Donald, with Tony Schwartz. *Trump: The Art of the Deal.* New York: Random House, 1987.

Tytler, Alexander Fraser. *Essay on the Principles of Translation.* 1791. Facsimile reprint. Amsterdam: John Benjamins, 1978.

Vermeer, Hans. *Voraus-setzungen für eine translationstheorie—einige kapitel kultur- und sprachtheorie.* Heidelberg, 1986.

Vinay, Jean-Paul, and Jean Darbelnet. *Stylistique comparée du français et de l'anglais.* Paris, 1958.

Voloshinov, V. N. *Marksizm i Filosofija Jazyka.* 1930. Reprint. New York: Seminar Press, 1975. Translated by Ladislav Matejka and I. R. Titunik, *Marxism and the Philosophy of Language.* New York: Seminar Press, 1973.

von Humboldt, Wilhelm. "Einleitung zur Agamemnon-Übersetzung." In *Das Problem des Übersetsens,* 71–96. *See* Störig 1963. Excerpted and translated as "A Theory of Translation" in *Translating Literature,* 40–45. *See* Lefevere 1977.

Vonnegut, Kurt. "Harrison Bergeron." In *Welcome to the Monkey-House,* 7–13. New York: Dell, 1970.

Whitman, Walt. *Leaves of Grass.* In *Complete Poetry and Selected Prose,* edited by James E. Miller, Jr. Boston: Houghton Mifflin, 1959.

Williams, William Carlos. "Portrait of a Lady." In *The Collected Earlier Poems of William Carlos Williams,* 40. New York: New Directions, 1951.

Wilss, Wolfram. *Übersetzungswissenschaft: Probleme und Methoden.* Stuttgart: Klett, 1977. Translated by Wilss, *The Science of Translation.* Tübingen: Gunter Narr Verlag, 1982.

Wimsatt, W. K. *The Verbal Icon: Studies in the Meaning of Poetry.* Louisville: University of Kentucky Press, 1954.

Wimsatt, W. K., and Monroe C. Beardsley. "The Affective Fallacy." In Wimsatt, *The Verbal Icon,* 3–18.
———. "The Imitative Fallacy." In Wimsatt, *The Verbal Icon,* 21–39.
Wittgenstein, Ludwig. *The Blue and Brown Books.* 1958. Reprint. New York: Harper & Row, 1965.
———. *Philosophische Untersuchungen/Philosophical Investigations.* Translated by G. E. M. Anscombe. New York: Macmillan, 1953.
Wright, George T. *The Poet in the Poem: The Personae of Eliot, Yeats, and Pound.* Berkeley: University of California Press, 1962.
Wycliffe, John. *De veritate sacrae scripturae.* Edited by R. Buddenseig. 3 vols. 1377–78. Reprint. London, 1905–7.

Index